The Real-World Network Troubleshooting Manual:

Tools, Techniques, and Scenarios

Printed and bound in India

Edition: 2010, *Edition* : 2026

ISBN : 978-81-3180-014-0

FRE-2870-699-REAL-WORLD NET TROU MAN-SUG

Price: ₹ 699.00

Branches

©	Bengaluru	080-26 75 69 30
©	Chennai	044-24 34 47 26
©	Guwahati	0361-254 36 69
©	Hyderabad	040-27 55 53 83
©	Kochi	0484-405 13 03
©	Kolkata	033-40 04 77 79
©	Lucknow	0522-430 36 13
©	Ranchi	0651-224 24 64

PUBLISHED IN INDIA BY

FIREWALL MEDIA
(An Imprint of Laxmi Publications Pvt. Ltd.)

An ISO 9001:2015 Company
113, GOLDEN HOUSE, GURUDWARA ROAD, DARYAGANJ,
NEW DELHI - 110002, INDIA

Corporate Office : B-33, Sector-5, Noida,
Gautambuddha Nagar (U.P.) -201 301, INDIA
Telephone : +91-120-44 46 900
www.laxmipublications.com
info@laxmipublications.com

This book is dedicated to my darling wife and best friend, Suzanne,
and my mother who is suffering from Alzheimer's disease.
Ten percent of the royalties of this book will go
to Alzheimer's research.

Acknowledgments

Some of the Troubleshooting Scenarios in this book first appeared in *Windows & .NET Magazine* (Soon to be *Windows IT Pro*). A special thank you goes to Penton Publications, Inc. and Penton Media, Inc. and their staff for allowing me to use some of the scenarios in this book.

When I was first approached to write this book, I knew it would be a lot of work, but I had no idea! A special thank you to my wife Suzanne, for putting up with my crazy work schedule while writing this book and juggling clients. Dan Balter, I am grateful for your insight and suggestions, your ideas have made this a better book. Thank you to all of my staff at ADS Consulting Group, Inc. for their support and encouragement—especially Amy Ota for quick turnaround on correcting all of my typos! A final thank you goes out to God for making all things possible!

Contents

Dedication v
Acknowledgments vii
Preface xix

1 An Introduction to Troubleshooting 1

Chapter Preview 1
Basic Troubleshooting Tips 2
Problem Isolation 2
Cut the Problem in Half—A Binary Search Example 3
General Troubleshooting Rules 10
Don't Make a Bad Situation Worse 10
Be Conservative 11
Be Mindful of Downtime Costs 12
Isolate the Problem 12
Try the Latest Drivers 12
Update the Firmware 12
Don't Upgrade over an Existing Operating System 13
Ask, "What's Changed?" 13
When You Become Stuck, Retrace Your Steps 14
Verify the Obvious 14
Don't Become Discouraged 14
Be Persistent 14
Try Something Else 15
Try One Solution at a Time 15
Always Work Toward Building Critical Mass 15
Don't Panic 16
Walk Away from the Problem for a While 16
The More Painful the Experience, the Less Likely You Will Forget the Solution 17
Realize that Troubleshooting Can Be Very Scary 17
Take Good Notes 17

Know When You're In Over Your Head 18
Know What to Do When You Don't Know What to Do 18
Sometimes You Have to Punt, but Only as a Last Resort 18
Practice Your Troubleshooting Skills Regularly 19
Document the Solution 20
Use Good Hardware 20
Contacting Technical Support 20
Chapter Summary 21
Review Questions 23

2 Network Printing 25

Chapter Preview 25
Printer Sizing 26
Dedicated Print Servers 28
Queue Configuration 28
Installation of Additional Printer Drivers 29
Web-Based Printing 30
Garbled Printing 32
Troubleshooting Scenarios 34
Scenario 1: A Network Printer Cannot Be Added on Windows XP 35
Scenario 2: Users Are Unable to Print to a Network Printer 36
Scenario 3: Users Cannot Print to Network Printers 38
Scenario 4: Users Receive a "Printer Installation Failed" Error Message When Attempting to Install a Printer from Their Web Browsers 40
Chapter Summary 41
Review Questions 42

3 Workstation Troubleshooting 45

Chapter Preview 45
Troubleshooting Categories 46
Troubleshooting the Windows Operating System 47
Basic Workstation Network Troubleshooting Tools 48
`Ping/Pathping` 48
`Ipconfig`(NT, 2000, XP)`/WinIPCfg`(Win 9X) 52
`IPConfig /flushdns` and `IPConfig /registerdns` 53
Troubleshooting Scenarios 54
Scenario 1: Workstation Cannot Connect to Windows Server 54

Scenario 2: Workstation Cannot Connect to Windows Server 58
Scenario 3: Workstations Drop Off the Network 61
Scenario 4: Workstation Cannot Use Resources on Windows 2000 Server 66
Scenario 5: Workstation Cannot Connect to the Network Server 71
Scenario 6: Workstation Cannot Connect to the Network Server 73
Scenario 7: Workstation Takes a Long Time to Log in to the Server 77
Scenario 8: Workstation Is Unable to Surf the Internet 81
Scenario 9: Workstation Is Generally Unstable 82
Scenario 10: Unable to Add a Networked HP2000C Printer to a Windows XP Workstation 84
Scenario 11: In Outlook 2002, Typing a Partial Name in the To: Field Defaults to the Wrong User 86
Scenario 12: User Is Unable to Install NAV Corporate Edition on a Workstation 88
Chapter Summary 89
Review Questions 90

4 Windows Server Troubleshooting 93

Chapter Preview 93
Server Hardware 94
Disk Configuration 95
Memory 98
Processor 98
Uninterruptible Power Supply (UPS) 99
Server Software 100
Operating System 100
Disk Partitions 100
i386 Setup Files and Service Pack Integration 100
Terminal Server in Remote Administration Mode 101
Domain Controllers 102
DNS Configuration 102
IP Addresses and DHCP Servers 105
Virus Protection 106
Server Backup 106
Server Problem Categories 108
Server Troubleshooting Tools 109
Server Event Viewer 109

Task Manager 109
Performance Monitor 110
Server Recovery Tools When the Server Doesn't Start 122
Windows Server Startup Disk 122
Safe Mode 123
Last Know Good Configuration 124
Recovery Console 124
Restoring a Windows Server 133
Troubleshooting Scenarios 134
Scenario 1: Data Faction Server Does Not Boot 134
Scenario 2: Unable to Access Files from a Windows 2003 Server 136
Scenario 3: Inaccessible Boot Device Error Stop 0000007B 142
Scenario 4: After a Complete System Restore, `net view`, `net use`, and Browsing My Network Places Do Not Work (Continuation from Scenario 3) 146
Scenario 5: Server Disappears and Reappears in My Network Places 149
Scenario 6: Users Cannot Connect to the Server 151
Scenario 7: Users Complain of Slow Server Performance 154
Scenario 8: SCSI Bus Timeout Errors on HP DLT 70 Tape Drive 155
Chapter Summary 157
Review Questions 158

5 SQL Server 2000 Troubleshooting 159

Chapter Preview 159
SQL Server Basics 160
SQL Server Versions 161
Hardware Selection 161
SQL Server Structure 162
Physical File Location for Databases 163
Connecting to SQL Server 164
Backup/Maintenance of SQL Server 166
Backup Types 166
Backup Strategy 167
Differential versus Transaction Log Backups 167
Database Maintenance Plans 168
Best Practices Analyzer 169
SQL Server Security 169
Database Administrators 171

Troubleshooting Scenarios 171
Scenario 1: Users Cannot Access the SQL Server 171
Scenario 2: Poor Performance on the SQL Server 176
Scenario 3: SQL Server Runs Especially Slow When Restarted, and Has Poor Overall Performance 177
Scenario 4: Access Application Cannot Update Records on SQL Server 2000 179
Chapter Summary 181
Review Questions 182

6 Exchange Server Troubleshooting 183

Chapter Preview 183
Exchange Databases 184
EDB Files 184
STM Files 184
Log Files 184
16-GB Database Limitation for the Standard Version of Exchange 185
Exchange 2000/2003 Enterprise Edition: Distribute the Mail Store Across Several Physical Databases 186
Exchange Server Performance 186
Monitor Disk Space 186
Proper Exchange Server Placement 187
Exchange Server Placement on a WAN 187
Exchange Clustering 187
Back It Up! 188
Virus Protection 188
Exchange Server and Internet Mail 189
Register Your Domain 189
Mail Exchange (MX) Records 189
Internet Mail Connector in Exchange 5.5 190
Firewall Configuration 190
Telnet to Exchange Server on Port 25 for Testing 190
Setup Authoritative Name Servers 190
Spam 191
Anti-Spam Filtering 191
Is Your Exchange Server an Open Relay? 192
What If My Server Is Marked as an Open Relay? 192
Outlook Web Access 193

Install Secure Sockets Layer Certificate on OWA 194
OWA Architecture 194
Firewall Configuration 196
OWA with an SSL Proxy 196
Make Sure Your Firewall Supports WebDAV for Exchange 2000/2003 198
Troubleshooting Scenarios 199
Scenario 1: Exchange Server Is Running Very Slow 199
Scenario 2: Exchange 2000 Server Unable to Deliver Mail to Specific Domains 204
Scenario 3: Windows 2003 Server Event Viewer Displays Event 9582 208
Scenario 4: Exchange Is Unable to Receive Internet Mail 210
Scenario 5: Users Are Unable to Open Their Messages on Exchange 2003 212
Scenario 6: Users Cannot Send Scheduling Information to Each Other 216
Scenario 7: Outlook Web Access Inbox Is Empty 218
Scenario 8: Exchange Server Is Unavailable 219
Scenario 9: Public Folders Do Not Fully Replicate On Exchange 2000 Server 221
Chapter Summary 222
Review Questions 223

7 Wide Area Networks and IP Routing 225

Chapter Preview 225
TCP/IP Basics 226
Address Format 226
Reserved Addresses 226
Subnet Mask 227
Default Gateway 227
DNS Servers 228
Selecting a WAN Topology and Carrier 228
Types of WAN Connections 228
WAN Considerations 230
Active Directory 231
Global Catalog Servers 231
Active Directory Sites and Services and Site Replication 231
Increase Remote Application Performance with Terminal Server 238
IP Routing 240
Static versus Dynamic Routing 240
Static Route Example 241

Troubleshooting Routes Using Windows Computers 242
Using Windows Server as a Router 245
Cisco Routers 246
Connecting to the Router 246
Setting Passwords 247
Recover a Lost Password 247
Basic Commands 247
Document the Router Configuration 247
Making Remote Changes 248
Cisco 2600 Frame Relay Router Configuration 248
Troubleshooting Cisco Routers with the Show Command 253
WAN Documentation 253
Troubleshooting Scenarios 254
Scenario 1: Users In Los Angeles Have Difficulty Accessing Servers In Chicago and New York 254
Scenario 2: New User Is Unable to Access Exchange Mailbox 257
Scenario 3: Users Are Unable to Access Remote Servers 259
Scenario 4: Users Are Unable to Access Company Web Site 260
Chapter Summary 263
Review Questions 263

8 Wireless Networking 265

Chapter Preview 265
Wireless Standards 266
Wireless Authentication Methods 267
No Authentication 267
Media Access Control Address 267
Wired Equivalent Privacy (WEP) Key Authentication 267
Remote Authentication Dial-In User Service (RADIUS) Authentication 267
RADIUS Authentication with Certificates or Smart Cards 268
Wireless Encryption 268
No Encryption 268
WEP 268
Wireless Vitual Private Network 269
Cisco's Lightweight Extensible Authentication Protocol (LEAP) or Extensible Authentication Protocol-Transport Layer Security (EAP-TLS) 269
Wi-Fi Protected Access 269

Purchasing AP Equipment 269
Preparing the Wireless Network Infrastructure 270
Perform a Site Survey 270
Plan Your Public Key Infrastructure 270
Decide on the Authentication Method for Your Wireless Clients 270
WLAN Diagram 271
Set Up the Certificate Server 272
Issue Computer Certificates 278
Install User Certificates 281
Install and Configure IAS (RADIUS) 287
Configure Wireless Access with Group Policy 293
Configure APs to Work with IAS Server 296
Client-Side Setup 297
Wireless Clients and Windows Firewall 298
Wireless Client Configuration on Windows XP 298
Upgrading the Firmware on a Cisco AP1200 298
Troubleshooting Steps for Wireless Clients 306
Setting Up WPA for Home Users 308
Configure the Cisco AP1200 308
Configure the Windows XP Workstation 311
Wireless Tools 313
NetStumbler 313
WEPCracking Tools 313
Troubleshooting Scenarios 313
Scenario 1: Internet Connection Running Very Slow 313
Scenario 2: Hacker Attacks Web Site 315
Scenario 3: Wireless Users Cannot Connect to the Network 317
Scenario 4: Unable to Flash the Cisco AP1200 Using HTTP 319
Scenario 5: Unable to Authenticate to Cisco AP1200 Using WPA With Pre-shared Key (PSK) 320
Chapter Summary 322
Review Questions 322

9 Firewall Troubleshooting 325

Chapter Preview 325
Are Firewalls Necessary? 326
Firewall Topology 327
Selecting the Proper Firewall 328

Packet Filtering versus Stateful Inspection Firewalls 328
Packet Filtering versus Stateful Inspection—An Analogy 329
Number of Ports 329
Number of Users 330
Traffic Load 330
Virtual Private Network (VPN) Traffic 330
Fault Tolerance 330
Proper Configuration 331
Dangerous Ports for Windows 331
Firewall Maintenance 333
Stay Current with Patches/Firmware 333
Review the Logs on a Regular Basis 333
Firewall Backup 334
Run Port Scans on a Regular Basis 334
Have a Hacking Recovery Plan In Place 334
Basic Firewall Troubleshooting Tools 337
Firewall Log Files 337
Syslog Servers 338
Troubleshooting Scenarios 338
Scenario 1: Unable to Access Online Banking Site 338
Scenario 2: Unable to Access the Internet 341
Scenario 3: Users Are Unable to Connect to the Internet 343
Scenario 4: Problems with a SonicWALL Pro 4060 346
Scenario 5: PIX Firewall Scrambles Rules 350
Chapter Summary 354
Review Questions 354

10 Virtual Private Network Troubleshooting 357

Chapter Preview 357
What Is a VPN? 358
VPN Limitations 359
Video Conferencing and Voice over IP (VoIP) 360
Implementing a VPN 361
What's Required for a VPN? 361
Expected Throughput 361
Fully Meshed Network 361
VPN Topology for Remote Users 362
Ordering Internet Services—Get Static IP Addresses 363

- ISP Blocking VPNs? 363
- Cross-Vendor Firewall VPNs? 363
- Fixed versus Dynamic IP Addresses 364
- Mobile Client Software 364

Defining the VPN Connection on the Firewall 365
Setting up a VPN with a Dynamic IP Address on One Side 367
VPN Troubleshooting Tools 368

- Firewall Log 368

Troubleshooting Scenarios 368
Scenario 1: VPN Going Up and Down 369
Scenario 2: VPN Tunnel Goes Down 370
Scenario 3: Two Mobile Clients on Same Laptop 372
Scenario 4: Cannot Establish a VPN With a Dynamic IP Address 374
Scenario 5: Unable to Communicate Across a VPN 378
Scenario 6: Unable to Communicate Across a VPN 376
Chapter Summary 382
Review Questions 382

Appendix A: Answers to Review Questions 385

Appendix B: About the CD-ROM 387

Index 389

Preface

Welcome to the wonderful world of troubleshooting! This is the book I wish existed when I was first learning how to troubleshoot computer problems. It is intended to bridge the gap between the theoretical and real world. When I first started working as a consultant at Coopers & Lybrand (now PriceWaterhouseCoopers), I quickly learned that there was a tremendous difference between what I had learned in college and what I faced in the working world. The first thing I learned as a consultant is that I didn't know anything. I felt like such an idiot. One of my first assignments while working at Coopers was to prepare some database files for a client's IRS audit. I should have known I was in trouble when everyone looked at me and said, "Hey, let's give this to the new guy!" I was asked how long it would take to complete the work, and I answered (naively) that it would take 8 hours—40 hours later, I was feeling a little less confident. The problem was that I didn't even know to ask the basic questions: How many records? What system generated the records? What format is the file in? In what format does the IRS want the file? It was a very humbling experience.

Looking back, it probably was a blessing in disguise, because often I was the only person around who was expected to fix technical problems. It was either sink or swim. Because I didn't have a mentor to guide me, I often had to learn things the hard way. The first part of each chapter contains items that I have learned from the school of hard knocks—read them carefully, and learn from my pain. Troubleshooting can be incredibly frustrating; don't get discouraged if you feel the same way. When troubleshooting, always try to understand the *concepts* behind the item you're troubleshooting, rather than memorizing the details—which will get you in big trouble. You can install the same thing 10 times, but you might have to install it 10 different ways because of subtle differences in hardware and networking environments.

This book is written for the IT professional who has at least one to two years of experience with computers and networking, although seasoned veterans might learn a few tips as well. To fully understand the last three chapters of the book, you might need five or more years of experience to grasp some of the advanced concepts. This book was written to complement your troubleshooting skills with increasingly difficult problems as your skills progress. It is written with the assumption that you have a basic understanding of computers and networking. The first three chapters deal with the basic components of a network. These are the items you will most likely be exposed to first when attempting to fix problems. The next three chapters address problems you will most likely encounter as your troubleshooting skills progress. The remaining chapters in this book deal with advanced topics that require a good fundamental understanding of security, networking, and TCP/IP. A constant theme in this book is to concentrate on the troubleshooting *process*. For the purposes of this book, the process is more important than the outcome, because it is the process of troubleshooting that will allow you to fix problems in the future. Once you progress to the point where you can figure out problems that other people are unable to solve, the market value of your skills will rise tremendously. If you can obtain this level of troubleshooting skill, you are almost guaranteed success in this profession.

Because the world of IT changes so quickly, always strive to learn new things. Not a day goes by when I don't learn something new. You should always feel a little uncomfortable and always strive to push the limits of your knowledge and understanding of IT. The moment you feel comfortable is the moment you're in trouble—it means you've stopped learning. In this industry, you can lock yourself in a closet for two years, and come out worthless—things change that quickly. If you're a person who doesn't like new things and constant change, this industry is probably not for you. However, if you're the type of person who likes to tinker with things and find out how they work, and gets bored with the "same old thing," you will do well in this field.

After reading this book, you should come away with an understanding of how to troubleshoot and how to approach any problem. You might not know how to fix the problem, but you should at least be able to narrow it down. Quickly solving problems will help you become the troubleshooting "superstar" in your company. Good luck on your troubleshooting adventures!

1 An Introduction to Troubleshooting

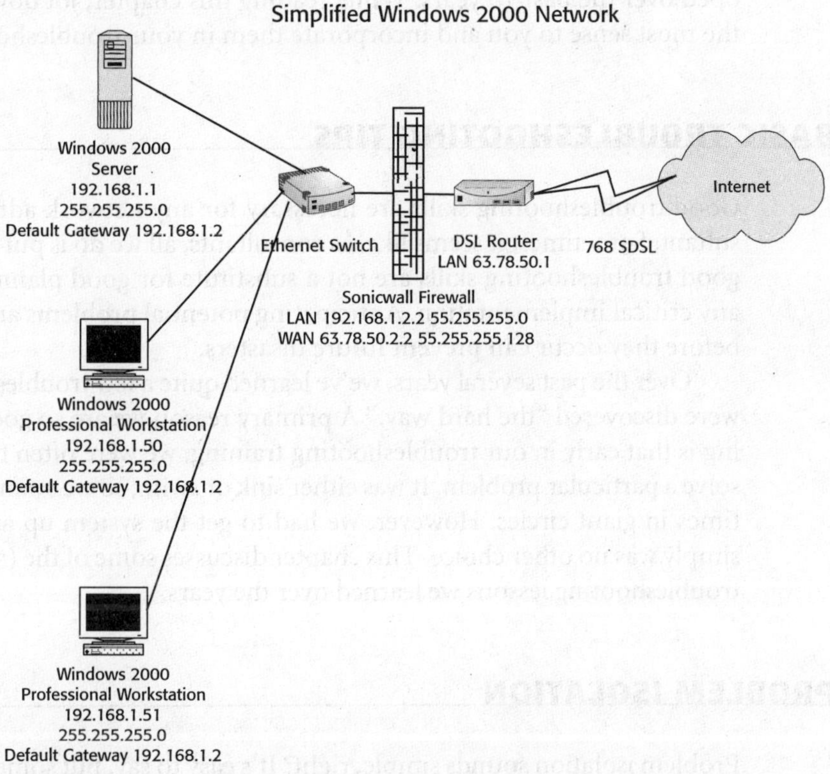

CHAPTER PREVIEW

Welcome to the world of troubleshooting! All of the items mentioned in this chapter are the tips and tricks that we have learned in our troubleshooting adventures. In this chapter, we cover basic troubleshooting tips, problem isolation, and general troubleshooting rules. We suggest reviewing this chapter before attempting any troubleshooting scenario. At least one of the rules in this chapter will pertain to any troubleshooting problem you will encounter. When you are stuck on a particularly difficult problem, review this chapter to refresh your memory for possible solutions or techniques to resolve the problem. Remember, good troubleshooters "know what to do when they don't know what to do."

Good troubleshooting skills will ensure you great success in the IT profession. The ability to solve a problem that no one else can is an incredibly valuable skill. Of course, everyone approaches problem solving slightly differently. The tips and tricks listed in this chapter comprise a troubleshooting method that we've developed over the past 15 years. While reading this chapter, jot down items that make the most sense to you and incorporate them in your troubleshooting bag of tricks.

BASIC TROUBLESHOOTING TIPS

Good troubleshooting skills are necessary for any network administrator or consultant. Sometimes, it seems like, as consultants, all we do is put out fires. However, good troubleshooting skills are not a substitute for good planning and testing for any critical implementation. Anticipating potential problems and addressing them before they occur can prevent future disasters.

Over the past several years, we've learned quite a few troubleshooting tips. Many were discovered "the hard way." A primary reason we are so good at troubleshooting is that early in our troubleshooting training, we were often the only resource to solve a particular problem. It was either sink or swim, so we swam like crazy—sometimes in giant circles. However, we had to get the system up and running—there simply was no other choice. This chapter discusses some of the (sometimes-painful) troubleshooting lessons we learned over the years.

PROBLEM ISOLATION

Problem isolation sounds simple, right? It's easy to say, but sometimes very difficult to do. Sometimes we see end users and even network engineers try to troubleshoot a problem, but have no idea how to do so. To solve the problem, you must know where the problem is located. What sounds better? "It's still not working," or "I've narrowed the problem down to an issue with the Ethernet switch."

Even if you cannot solve the problem, try to narrow it down. The process of problem isolation will save the technical support person or consultant a tremendous amount of time. To isolate the problem, you must search for and find it. Consider a troubleshooting scenario in which a user cannot get out to the Internet. The problem could center on one or more of the following:

- Firewall
- Internet connection

- Ethernet switch/hub
- Network interface card (NIC) in the workstation
- Cabling
- Corrupted Winsock (possibly the TCP/IP protocol stack on the workstation is damaged)
- Incorrect TCP/IP settings, including incorrect default gateway, IP address, and/or Domain Name Service (DNS) settings

Where do we begin? The example illustrates how critical it is to quickly isolate the problem. Later in this chapter, we examine some quick tests that you can run to locate the problem area.

Cut the Problem in Half—A Binary Search Example

To solve the problem, you must first find it. Often, finding where the problem lies is more than half of the battle of solving it. The better you are at locating the problem, the better your troubleshooting skills will be. While we were in college, a professor (thanks, Dr. Glen Grey, professor of Business Administration at California State University, Northridge) told us an amusing story about a person (let's call him Dave) in Las Vegas who made a lot of money at one of the casino bars. Dave bet that he could guess a number between 1 and 128 in only seven or fewer guesses. Sounds impossible, right? Would you take the bet? Interested persons were told to pick a number between 1 and 128, write it down on a piece of paper, and hide the paper. Assume that the person placing the bet picked 27 as his number. Dave would then ask the bettor whether the number selected was the following.

Q: Higher or lower than 64? A: Lower (Guess one)

Q: Higher or lower than 32? A: Lower (Guess two)

Q: Higher or lower than 16? A: Higher (Guess three)

Q: Higher or lower than 24? A: Higher (Guess four)

Q: Higher or lower than 28? A: Lower (Guess five)

Q: Higher or lower than 26? A: Higher (Guess six)

The number is 27. (Guess seven) You lose!

Many people took the bet and lost. How is this possible? If you're familiar with how a computer typically performs a search, you might know that the method that Dave used is a *binary search*. In the worst-case scenario, you can find any number in a range based on the power of 2. For example, 2^8 = 256, so you can find any number between 1 and 256 in eight or fewer guesses. You simply ask "higher or lower" repetitively and then divide the search increments by 2 for the next range. In the example, you would start at 64 because 128/2 is 64. For the next increment, you would use 32. If the number the person picked was 108, he would answer "higher," and you would then add 32 to 64. Your next question would be "higher or lower than 96?" You would continue to divide your search increments by 2, adding or subtracting from the current number depending on the bettor's answer to "higher or lower." Therefore, the sequence is 64, 32, 16, 8, 4, 2, 1.

How is this story relevant to troubleshooting? You must divide the problem in half to quickly isolate the problem. Remember the binary search algorithm when trying to isolate a problem; that is, keep dividing the problem in half until you find the answer. Figure 1.1 shows a simplified flowchart of the binary search algorithm.

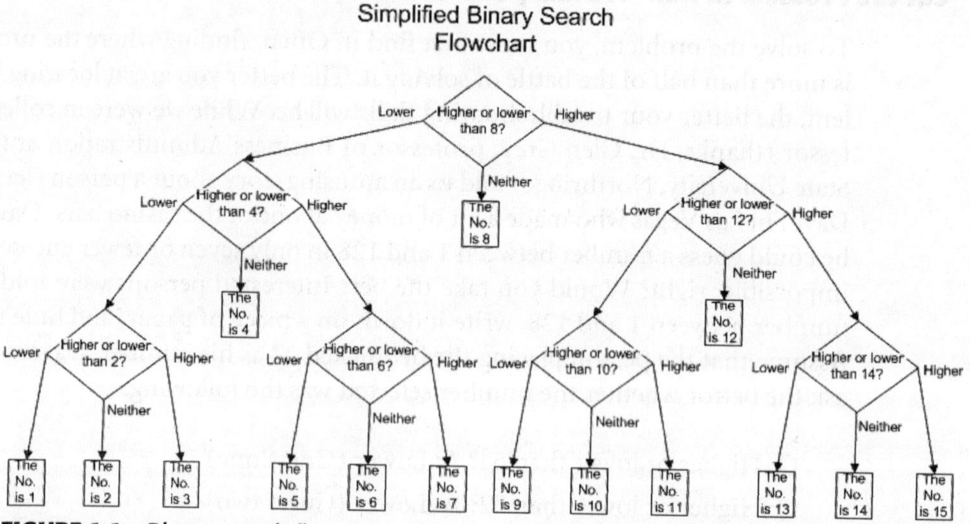

FIGURE 1.1 Binary search flowchart.

Consider a user who cannot connect to the Internet. Some simple tests can determine what path to take to find the correct answer. Assume that we have a magic troubleshooting crystal ball and know ahead of time that an Internet connection problem is due to a downed wide area network (WAN) connection. So, how do you locate the source of the problem? Assume that the workstation having the problem is running Windows 2000 Professional and is installed on a network that has one Windows 2000 server. A SonicWALL firewall protects the network from Internet hackers, and the network is connected to a digital subscriber line (DSL) for Internet access. A diagram of the network is shown in Figure 1.2.

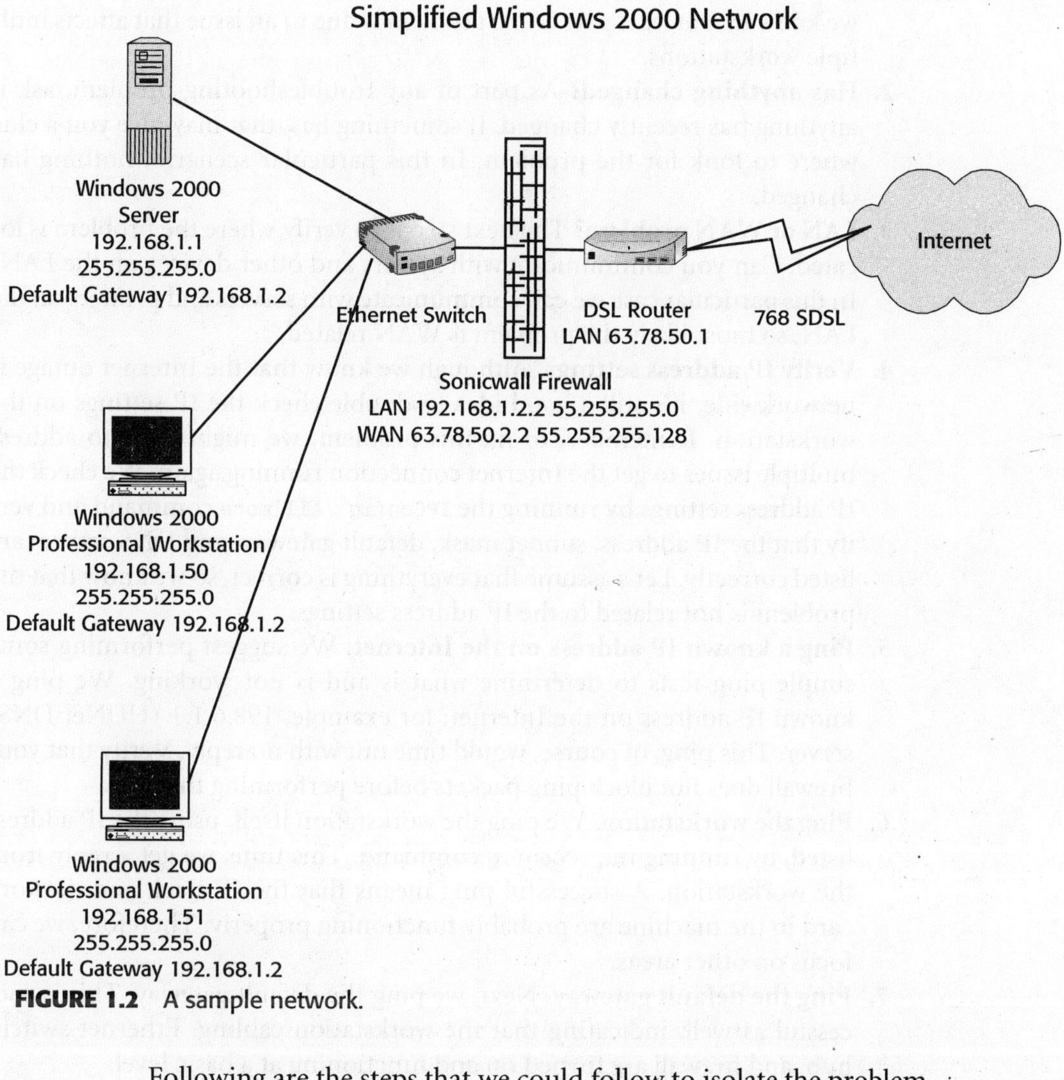

FIGURE 1.2 A sample network.

Following are the steps that we could follow to isolate the problem.

1. **Verify that the problem exists.** We try to surf the Internet to verify that the problem still exists and is not caused by the user. Is there a link light on the NIC? Is everything plugged in? Remember, verify the obvious. So, we load Internet Explorer (IE) and try to surf the Internet. Of course, IE times out and we receive an error message that the page could not be displayed. We also try to get out to the Internet from another workstation to verify that the problem is networkwide and not workstation specific. From this test,

we know that at least part of the problem is due to an issue that affects multiple workstations.

2. **Has anything changed?** As part of any troubleshooting problem, ask if anything has recently changed. If something has, that may give you a clue where to look for the problem. In this particular scenario, nothing has changed.
3. **LAN or WAN problem?** The next step is to verify where the problem is located. Can you communicate with servers and other devices on the LAN? In this particular case we can communicate with servers and printers on the LAN, so most likely the problem is WAN related.
4. **Verify IP address settings.** Although we know that the Internet outage is networkwide, it's still a good idea to double check the IP settings on the workstation. Remember, to fix this problem, we might have to address multiple issues to get the Internet connection running again. We check the IP address settings by running the `IPConfig /All|more` command and verify that the IP address, subnet mask, default gateway, and DNS servers are listed correctly. Let's assume that everything is correct, so we know that the problem is not related to the IP address settings.
5. **Ping a known IP address on the Internet.** We suggest performing some simple ping tests to determine what is and is not working. We ping a known IP address on the Internet; for example, 198.6.1.1 (UUNet DNS) server. This ping, of course, would time out with no reply. Verify that your firewall does not block ping packets before performing this test.
6. **Ping the workstation.** We ping the workstation itself, using the IP address listed, by running the `IPConfig` command. This time, we get a reply from the workstation. A successful ping means that the IP stack and network card in the machine are probably functioning properly. Therefore, we can focus on other areas.
7. **Ping the default gateway.** Next, we ping the default gateway. This is successful as well, indicating that the workstation cabling, Ethernet switch/hub, and firewall are turned on and functioning at a basic level.
8. **Verify that DNS is working.** We ping an internal server on the network by its fully qualified domain name (FQDN), such as *server.mydomain.com.* The FQDN resolves to an IP address because we are using internal DNS Windows 2000 servers on our network. This tells us that DNS is working at least for internal hosts and that the workstation is probably using the correct DNS server.
9. **Examine the firewall.** SonicWALL firewalls are managed via a browser, so we load IE and type in the IP address of the default gateway. After logging in with a username and password, we verify the IP settings on the firewall (WAN address, WAN subnet mask, WAN default gateway, local area

network (LAN) address, and LAN subnet mask). We verify that a rule was created to allow HTTP traffic out to the Internet.

10. **Perform ping tests from the firewall.** The SonicWALL firewall includes some basic diagnostic tools. From the firewall, we ping the workstation on which we are working. This is successful, so most likely the firewall is working properly. Next, we ping the WAN default gateway listed in the SonicWALL configuration, which times out. At this point, we suspect a problem with the DSL router or with the line.
11. **Visually inspect the DSL router.** A visual inspection of the DSL router indicates an alarm situation on the router. Before calling our Internet service provider (ISP), we attempt to reset the router by powering it off and then on to see if the line comes back up. Unfortunately, in this case, the line does not come back up.
12. **Call the ISP.** After verifying that everything looks okay on our side, we are fairly sure that the problem resides with the ISP. We call our ISP and report a problem with the line, explaining that we reset the router already and that didn't fix the problem. We most likely will be issued a trouble ticket, and we ask for an estimated time when the DSL service will be restored.

By performing the preceding steps, we can quickly zero in on the source of the problem. For an exercise, run through the following scenarios and try to think of the symptoms that would occur with each.

1. **Incorrect IP address settings.** If the IP address is manually assigned, a symptom of an incorrect IP address is the ability to ping the workstation itself but not the default gateway or any other IP address. If the default gateway was incorrect, you might still be able to ping the default gateway IP address, but it might not be the correct firewall or Internet router. In this example, you could load IE with the default gateway IP address and see if the SonicWALL login screen appears. If it does, you at least know that you have the correct IP address. If the login screen does not appear, either the firewall is down or you do not have the correct default gateway IP address.
2. **Incorrect DNS settings.** Incorrect DNS settings allow you to ping a host by IP address (e.g., 192.168.1.2), but not by the host's FQDN (e.g., *server.mydomain.com*). A simple test for DNS settings is to ping a host first by its IP address and then by its FQDN. Make sure that your firewall is not blocking ping packets if you try to resolve a host located on the Internet. Even if ping packets are blocked by your firewall, when you attempt a ping by a host's FQDN, you should still see the ping utility resolve the host to an IP address before the ping is attempted. Incorrect settings in the hosts or lmhosts files can also cause incorrect name resolution problems.

3. **Inability to obtain an IP address automatically.** If the Dynamic Host Configuration protocol (DHCP) server is down or not working properly, you usually get an Automatic Private IP Address (APIPA) (169.254.*xxx.xxx* if you're running a Windows 9*x*/2000/XP workstation). If this happens, verify that the DHCP server is running correctly. See if you can obtain an IP address on another workstation by issuing the `IPConfig /renew` command. If you are unable to obtain an IP address from a second workstation, the problem is usually the DHCP server. If you can get an IP address on the second workstation, look for a problem that is workstation specific, such as a cabling, NIC, or Ethernet switch port problem.
4. **Cabling problem.** If a workstation drops off the network, has intermittent problems, or seems to run slowly at first and then speeds up, consider a closer inspection of the cabling. The best way to diagnose a cabling problem is to test the cable with a Time Domain Reflectometer (TDR) tester. We like the testers from Hewlett Packard (HP) and Microtest. If you don't have a TDR tester, the quickest way to test the cable is to swap out the workstation with a working second workstation on the problem cable and see if the problem persists. If it does, the problem is probably with a cable and/or hub/switch port. If the second workstation works fine with that cable, the problem is most likely located in the workstation.
5. **Bad NIC in the workstation.** If a workstation has a bad NIC, you usually cannot ping the workstation itself or any other device on the network. If you have a managed switch or hub, check the switch/hub port for fragmented packets, transmit errors, and receive errors. Excessive traffic on the port is a sign of a beaconing NIC. A beaconing NIC will transmit a lot of malformed packets and garbage onto the network that will interfere with normal LAN traffic. To determine this, look at the number of packets sent/received on a workstation that has a similar traffic load. A quick way to test for a bad NIC is to swap out the suspect NIC with a good NIC. If you are replacing the bad NIC with a different model NIC, then before you physically remove/disable the suspect NIC, uninstall the NIC with the Windows Device Manager by right-clicking the NIC and selecting Uninstall from the menu. If you do not uninstall the old NIC before you install the second NIC, Windows 2000/XP will not allow you to uninstall the old NIC without the NIC physically present in the machine. If you forget to uninstall the NIC before you remove it, you must reinstall the old NIC, uninstall it using the Device Manager, and then physically remove the NIC. If the workstation has an embedded NIC on the motherboard, make sure to disable the NIC before installing the other NIC and use the latest drivers for the new NIC.

6. **Corrupted firmware or settings on the SonicWALL.** If the firmware or settings are corrupted on the firewall, no one will be able to access the Internet and there will be a global Internet outage on the network. This type of problem doesn't happen too often, but when it does, it can be difficult to diagnose. Hackers can change the firewall settings or corrupt the firmware if they have access to the firewall. We suggest logging in to the firewall and double-checking the firewall configuration and settings. Double check the LAN and WAN IP addresses of the firewall, and verify that all of the rules are in place. We strongly recommend documenting the firewall configuration (as well as any other critical network device) so that you can compare the current firewall settings to the documentation. In the worst case, you can rebuild the firewall's settings from the documentation. Alternatively, you can export the firewall configuration to a file and use this file to restore the firewall settings. However, we have run into situations in which we were unable to import the settings from the configuration file and we then had to rebuild the configuration from scratch. This usually happens when you save the firewall configuration with one version of the firmware and try to restore the firewall configuration when the firewall has a later version of the firmware. For this reason, it's a good idea to have a manual backup (screen shots, printouts, or other method) of your firewall configuration, especially if you have a complex configuration that would be difficult to rebuild. If you suspect a corrupted firmware, try reflashing the firmware with a current version. A quick way to check the firewall is to plug a workstation directly into the DSL router and set the workstation's IP address to the same settings as the WAN settings on the firewall. If the workstation can get out to the Internet, the problem is most likely the firewall. If you can't get out to the Internet, the problem is probably with the DSL router or DSL line.
7. **Corrupted DSL router settings.** If the DSL router settings are corrupted, no one will be able to get out to the Internet. Often, corrupted DSL router settings appear like a failed DSL line. Typically, DSL routers are configured though a Telnet or Internet browser. However, if the router settings are corrupted, the router will be unreachable. Some ISP will not allow you to change the configuration on the DSL router. If your ISP does allow changes to the DSL router, try to connect to the router directly with a serial cable from a workstation, or perform a hard reset to return the router to its default factory settings. If you have to perform a hard reset, refer to the router documentation on the state the router will be in after you perform the reset. This problem doesn't happen very often, so it should be one of the last items to check. One common cause of a DSL router corruption is a power surge, either on the router power line or on the DSL line. Therefore,

it's a good idea to have the DSL router and firewall connected to an uninterruptible power supply (UPS).

Most problems can be diagnosed with two tools: `ping` and `ipconfig`. Just because the tool is simple to use doesn't mean it can't be an effective diagnostic tool for fixing workstation connectivity problems. In this book, we focus on the *process* of troubleshooting rather than the outcome, because the process is significantly more important than the outcome. Knowing the process will enable you to grow and prosper in this field. If you have the *process* mastered, you can always find the answer.

GENERAL TROUBLESHOOTING RULES

Some general troubleshooting rules apply to solving any problem. Of course, some rules are made to be broken, so apply each rule to the specific situation. Do not blindly follow each rule, possibly with the exception of rules one and two discussed in the following subsections. Not every rule will apply in every situation, so use common sense when troubleshooting a problem.

Don't Make a Bad Situation Worse

Just as physicians swear to "do no harm," make sure that your troubleshooting techniques don't make a bad situation worse. Make sure you have a very recent incremental backup (with a full backup readily available) before you try anything, especially when working on a server. If you are troubleshooting a workstation, consider backing up files that you want to change by either renaming them or copying them to a different folder. Always make sure that you can at least restore the computer to the state it was in before you started working on it. For example, you might attempt to update a disk driver because an Event Log error reported a potential disk performance issue on a Windows 2003 server. After you update the driver, the server will not reboot. If you assume that the new driver prevented the server from booting, you can't quickly recover from this situation if you don't have a good backup of the old driver. Instead, rather than just an annoying error message in the Event Viewer, you now have a server that is completely down—and some very unhappy users. Not having a good backup of the system before you start working on the computer is almost a guaranteed way of losing your job or at least getting into serious trouble. Never paint yourself into a corner; always make sure you have an escape route.

Be Conservative

When faced with two or more possible solutions to a problem, try the most conservative one(s) first. In the previous example, assume that you updated the disk drivers on your server and now it refuses to reboot. Also, assume that you made a backup of the drivers before you installed the new drivers. You might consider the following as possible solutions:

a. Attempt to boot the server in safe mode, and reinstall the old driver.
b. Attempt to load the Last Known Good Configuration (LKGC) from the Startup menu.
c. Reinstall the operating system (OS), and restore from the backup.

Which of these solutions would you pick first, and why? You should also consider which alternative will bring the server back up the quickest and has the least potential to damage existing data. In this example, we suggest trying (a), (b), and (c), in that order, for the following reasons:

a. You can start Windows Server 2003 in safe mode by pressing F8 when the OS first starts to load and then selecting Safe Mode in the Startup menu. Starting a server in safe mode should have very little impact on the server. Once in safe mode, you should be able to load the original driver and then restart the server to verify that it loads properly. This solution has a very low probability of causing damage to the server and will get the server up and running very fast.
b. Attempting to load the LKGC can potentially cause other problems. Selecting the LKGC restores the information from the registry subkey HKEY_LOCAL_MACHINE\SYSTEM\CurrentControlSet. The biggest problem with the LKGC is that it is sometimes difficult or impossible to tell in what state the LKGC will leave the server. Often, if a user has not successfully logged in to the server in quite some time, the LKGC will restore the server to a much earlier state than anticipated. Using the LKGC can force you to reinstall tape drivers or other hardware devices, which can lead to more headaches. Because booting in safe mode does not update the LKGC registry key, we suggest trying safe mode first, because you still have the option of LKGC if safe mode fails.
c. The last option, to reload the OS and restore from backup, should be performed only as a last resort. Even if you verify your backups, you still have a great deal of exposure if something goes wrong, not to mention a very long day (and night). To reload the OS and restore from backup is very risky and probably will take at least 8 to 12 hours depending on the amount

of data that must be restored. You should probably call someone in to assist you before you try this last and most radical option. It amazes us how many times technical support will suggest reloading the OS as a catchall solution to a problem. It's usually better to try to find the problem and fix it rather than attempt the "shotgun" approach and hope that a reload of the OS will fix the problem. Even worse, if the problem is fixed, it will be virtually impossible to find the cause of the problem if it happens again.

Be Mindful of Downtime Costs

Any potential solution must be weighed against the cost of downtime. It would be nice to have an unlimited budget to fix every problem, but time and budget constraints might force you to attempt a more radical approach earlier on. We leave these types of decisions up to the client. We inform them of the options, give them an estimate for each option, our suggestions, and let them decide.

Isolate the Problem

As mentioned earlier in this chapter, to fix the problem, you must first locate it. Remember, try to cut the problem in half and isolate it quickly. Problem isolation is at least half of the fix. Even the most complex problem is but a collection of smaller, easier-managed problems.

Try the Latest Drivers

In some instances, when you've identified a problem with a specific hardware device, updating the drivers can solve the problem. This applies especially when you are first installing a workstation or server and it's unstable. This solution can also solve a problem if the server or workstation is under a heavy load. Many driver updates address performance or stability issues when a device is heavily stressed. Be aware that sometimes driver updates can cause further problems if the new version has not been fully tested. For this reason, make sure to have a good backup of your system before you attempt any driver updates.

Update the Firmware

Updating firmware is often performed in concert with updating a driver. Generally, if you update the firmware for a device, make sure also to install the latest driver for the device at the same time. The reverse is usually not as critical, although it might be a good idea. We've seen more devices fail because the firmware was updated without the latest driver installed than vice versa. More significantly, we've seen servers that didn't boot after firmware was upgraded because the drivers weren't updated at the same time. Updating firmware can be tricky. If the firmware is bad, it can prevent the device from booting. When possible test the firmware in a non-production environment before releasing it into production.

Don't Upgrade over an Existing Operating System

As a general rule, if you are changing the OS on a workstation, or especially on a server, do not upgrade! Instead, do a clean install. This is especially important if you are upgrading to Windows 2000 or XP from an earlier version of Windows. If you perform an upgrade and not a clean install, Windows 2000/XP will, for compatibility reasons, place items in different locations than it will as part of a clean install. You might get the workstation to work properly initially, but other issues can arise if you attempt another OS upgrade on the same workstation or if you try to install software that interacts very closely with the OS. The conservative solution is to obtain a complete backup of the workstation, make sure you have access to the applications and they are supported on the new OS, format the drive, and then reinstall the applications and user data. Even though this sounds like a lot of work, you will save time in the long run by preventing future stability/performance issues.

An exception to this rule is an in-place upgrade on a Windows NT to a 2000 or 2003 server. If you are introducing a Windows 2000/2003 server into an NT network, you must first upgrade the primary domain controller (PDC) to Windows Server 2000/2003. We suggest introducing the first Windows Server 2000/2003 to an NT network by performing an in-place upgrade on the PDC. To perform an in-place upgrade, install Windows NT on the new server first as a backup domain controller (BDC), and then promote the new server to a PDC. (Make sure that you run this promotion when no one is logged in to the network because users will be disconnected from the server during the promotion process.) After the PDC is in place, you can perform an in-place upgrade to Windows 2000/2003. Do not install any other applications until the server has Windows 2000/2003 installed on it. We always perform an in-place upgrade and have never had any problem with this method. Another alternative is to use the Active Directory Migration Tool (ADMT) to perform the migration.

Ask, "What's Changed?"

When faced with any troubleshooting situation, ask yourself, or the user: "What has changed?" Often, a recent event (however innocent) is the culprit. Other related questions include, "When did this problem start?" "Has this happened before?" "When does this problem occur?" "Is the problem reproducible?" and "What were you doing when this problem happened?"

When You Become Stuck, Retrace Your Steps

For particularly difficult problems, retrace your steps and verify that each step was performed correctly. This is especially important when following a tech note or knowledge-based article where you are required to perform multiple steps to resolve the problem. Retracing and verifying can prevent a potentially embarrassing call to technical support, when you discover that you typed something incorrectly or missed a step. Retrace your steps when the solution is complex, requires you to perform multiple registry hacks, or requires multiple command-line entries to solve the problem.

Verify the Obvious

Occam's Razor states that "plurality should not be posited without necessity." One interpretation of this philosophy is that when multiple solutions are available, the simplest one tends to be the correct one. Sometimes, we see administrators hit their heads against a wall in frustration and yet a very simple solution fixed the problem. "Is the computer turned on?" "Is the printer turned on?"

"Is the patch cord plugged all the way in?" These are simple questions, but sometimes their answers fix the problem.

Sometimes, a simple reboot will make the problem go away. If you try the reboot solution, however, be sure to tell the user to call back if it does not work—you do not want to be known as the "reboot king" when it comes to solving problems. Often, users will feel like they're being dismissed if you tell them to reboot every time they have a problem. We suggest training your users to try a reboot first before they call IT support. This should eliminate some calls to technical support and reduce the amount of time it takes to solve problems.

Don't Become Discouraged

If you try a solution and it doesn't work, at least you know it wasn't the right solution. In many circumstances, it's just as important to know what doesn't work as to know what does. By attempting a solution, even though it doesn't solve the immediate problem, you're one step closer to solving that problem. Remember, problem isolation! If you do attempt a possible solution and it doesn't work, we suggest returning the computer to its original state before trying another solution.

Be Persistent

Persistence can and will pay off. Don't give up on a problem. We take particularly difficult problems personally and go on a crusade to resolve the issue. When you can solve problems that other people can't, you can tremendously raise your value to the company. Some of the problems we explore in this book took us weeks, sometimes months, to resolve. Sometimes, it's you versus the computer. Who will win? Don't admit defeat. If you have to go down, go down swinging.

Try Something Else

According to Benjamin Franklin, "The definition of insanity is doing the same thing over and over and expecting different results." In the world of computers, this reads like "I've tried reloading the OS four times and that still hasn't solved the problem!" Guess what? That's not the correct solution! Don't waste time trying the same solution repeatedly and magically expect it to work. This is not to say that trying the same solution twice or possibly three times won't sometimes solve the problem. Because the environment might be slightly different on a server reboot during a second or third attempt, the solution might work. If it doesn't work on the third try, it's probably time to move on and try something else.

Try One Solution at a Time

When dealing with any problem, try one solution at a time. If a solution does not work, back out the change and try something else. Resist the temptation (however great) to make wholesale changes on the computer. Even if this "shotgun" approach fixes the problem, it will be very difficult to tell which of the many changes fixed the problem. This will make it difficult to solve the problem if (when) it occurs in the future.

Always Work Toward Building Critical Mass

Always strive to gain more knowledge about the current system and any new technologies that arise. If you are new to troubleshooting, always work toward understanding concepts rather than memorizing facts. You must understand at least conceptually how something works before you can start to troubleshoot it. When we first started troubleshooting, we often lacked a basic knowledge about the item we were troubleshooting—that was very frustrating! Be patient, critical mass will come, but not without hard work. Strive to learn at least one new item a day, and take good notes. Make sure to review your notes weekly to ingrain them in your memory. Even we learn something new every day. If you stop learning, you should be worried. You never want to feel comfortable in this field—you should always feel a little uncomfortable. That means you are continuously learning something new. Always work on concepts, not on memorizing the facts. Memorizing in this field will set you up for failure. If you don't understand how something works and just memorize the steps, one small variance in the solution can spell disaster. While tutors in college, we heard students often say, "I read the chapter four times, memorized it, and still failed!" What the students didn't realize is that memorization is not the answer. They could read the chapter a million times, memorize each word, and probably still fail. Just memorizing the facts and recalling them is not enough in this field. You must understand how items work and the concepts behind them if you want to be a good troubleshooter. If you understand the concepts behind how something works, you can always find the details. If you memorize the steps to fix a problem and don't bother to understand the problem, you're in big trouble! This will become painfully obvious the next time you try to fix the same problem, the solution doesn't work, and you have no clue how to fix it. When trying to grasp new concepts or products, we find it helpful to draw analogies between items we are already familiar with to get up to speed. You can remember and understand new items quickly if you can relate it to familiar concepts.

Don't Panic

At least, don't panic in front of the head of the company or the end user. Don't announce that, to fix the problem, you'll probably have to reformat the drive and employees will lose all of their data. When the expert panics, that *really* makes everyone nervous. Keep cool and collected. We don't mean to downplay any serious problem. However, we often find that a problem can be fixed with a little work, although at a critical moment it might seem disastrous. Make sure to exhaust all of your troubleshooting resources before communicating the worse-case scenario. Premature panicking on your part will usually make users worry, often for no good reason. Working well under pressure and keeping your cool is something they don't teach you in school. Staying calm is a vital skill if you want to survive in this industry. Resist the urge to run out of the room screaming "fire! fire!" even though that's exactly what you want to do.

Walk Away from the Problem for a While

Sometimes, it helps to take a break from the problem, especially when you're stuck. Go for a walk, use the restroom, get some sleep, get something to eat (we always think better on a full stomach)—just get away from the environment for a while. Often, in the heat of trying to solve the problem, you almost get manic in your attempt to solve it. By leaving the problem, you get a chance to clear your head and think of other possible solutions. We cannot count the times when we were stuck on a problem that we took a break and then returned, armed with the resolution. If the problem wasn't fixed, we at least had some pretty good ideas on how to solve it. This technique can be helpful when identifying obvious problems. You can leave a problem and then come back to it, and the answer will be abundantly clear.

The More Painful the Experience, the Less Likely You Will Forget the Solution

In this case, pain is good, and the more pain the better. If an experience is particularly painful, you'll never forget it. The next time the problem appears, you will be able to fix it quickly. Remember that the greater the level of pain in the present will benefit you in the future, so just bear down and take the abuse.

Realize that Troubleshooting Can Be Very Scary

Troubleshooting can be a very scary experience. Being well prepared mentally, conceptually understanding how something works, and having the necessary tools and correct attitude will help you solve the problem. We often walk into situations in which we have absolutely no idea how to fix the immediate problem. However, isolating the problem quickly reveals the solution. We've seen people with a great deal of potential decide that troubleshooting was not their field simply because of one or two bad experiences. Of course, if all of your troubleshooting experiences are bad, this probably is not the field for you. Most of the troubleshooting scenarios in this book are based on actual events or combinations of events that happened to us in our consulting adventures. Don't let a bad experience discourage you from continuing to improve your troubleshooting skills. You have to get past the "I know enough to be dangerous" point in order to improve. Everyone has to go through the "I can break it (really well), but I don't know how to fix it" phase in order to get good at troubleshooting.

During any major implementation, we plan for the worst but hope for the best. Expect things to go wrong. That way, you'll not be caught off guard when they do go wrong and will be pleasantly surprised when things go smoothly. Be prepared for everything to go wrong. Believe us, it will happen, it's just a question of when. Remember the rule of "not making a bad situation worse" to protect yourself when things go really wrong. If you have a good backup of the system, at least you can restore it to the way it was before you attempted to fix it. This can often make the difference between recovering somewhat gracefully from a difficult situation to the worst-case scenario of an extended system outage with the potential of losing all of a company's data.

Take Good Notes

During any complex troubleshooting problem, take good notes about the situation. Reflect on everything you've tried and the results of each attempt. Even if you can't solve the problem yourself and have to call technical support or an outside consultant, your notes will be very helpful by ensuring that the outside person doesn't "reinvent the wheel" when attempting to find the solution. After the problem is resolved, your notes can be an excellent teaching tool and the basis for an internal knowledge base that your company will find invaluable.

Know When You're In Over Your Head

It's important to know when to stop before disaster strikes. Often, you know this only after you've crossed that critical line before. Listen to your instincts and know when it's time to call for outside help. If you are considering a solution that is irreversible and has the potential for data loss, it's probably time to call for some outside assistance. Know your personal limitations. If it's 3:00 A.M. and you've been up for 20 hours, you're probably doing more damage than good. Consider the ramifications of your actions before you try that next critical step. This reminds us of some amusing hourly rates that were posted at a carpenter's shop: $50/hour if you watch, $100/hour if you help, $200/hour if you worked on it before.

Another good measure of knowing if you're in over your head is the potential for recovery. You don't want to hear these words from an outside source, "If you only had called us sooner. . . ." Know your limitations. The greater exposure you have trying to solve the problem, the more inclined you should be to call for outside help.

Know What to Do When You Don't Know What to Do

We often say, "Good troubleshooters know what to do when they don't know what to do." By this, we mean that when good troubleshooters get stuck, they still know how to solve the problem. This might mean calling a coworker to look at the problem, developing other solutions to the problem, calling an outside consultant to look at the problem, opening up a case with technical support, looking for the solution in a knowledge base, submitting the problem to a newsgroup, or any other possible solution. Good troubleshooters know that it takes work to get the job done, and they are willing to go the extra mile to get it solved. They might not know how to solve the problem themselves, but they know how to contact a person or resource that can. This will make the difference between someone who can occasionally solve a problem and someone who becomes a lifesaver for someone in a real bind. Good troubleshooters never run out of ideas. They know the solution is out there—they just have to find it.

Sometimes You Have to Punt, but Only as a Last Resort

Unfortunately, in some situations you have to try the most radical approach; for example, format a drive, reload the OS, restore from backup, blow away a router configuration and start over, or rebuild a system from scratch. Of course, these should be last-resort solutions when problem solving. Make sure you've considered all other alternatives before using these. It's a good idea to run your ideas by another person just to make sure you haven't forgotten to try something. Before you take any radical step, make sure you have a good backup, and double-check the backup log for any skipped critical files.

Practice Your Troubleshooting Skills Regularly

The quickest way to get better at troubleshooting is to practice it. You might be amazed at how quickly someone with a lot of experience can solve a problem. How did they get so good (and I get to be so bad)? you ask. Practice, practice, practice! There really is no substitute for experience. The more you troubleshoot, the better you get at it. We feel it takes people a couple of years of practice before they become proficient at troubleshooting. If you feel like you're not improving, possibly consider a career change. Not everyone has the ability to solve problems quickly. Even those who get good at troubleshooting have to practice on a regular basis. After a while, you should be able to "smell" the problem; that is, to have that sixth sense about where the problem lies. We know when people on our staff have good troubleshooting skills: We ask them a few questions about a problem, and they indicate that they've tried all known solutions, and maybe even a few more. For example, consider a problem whereby a company does not receive incoming Internet mail. The company's e-mail, which was working fine, suddenly stopped working. They're running Exchange 2003 with a SonicWALL firewall connected to a DSL line. We might ask the following questions:

Q: Is the server running? A: Yes.

Q: Are the Exchange server services started? A: Yes.

Q: Can users connect to the Exchange server and open Outlook? A: Yes

Q: Are there any errors in the Event Viewer? A: Yes, but nothing appears to be related to this problem.

Q: Can you get out to the Internet? A: Yes.

Q: Have you performed a mail exchange lookup (MX) for the company's domain? A: Yes, and it's pointing to the correct IP address.

Q: Can the users send internal mail? A: Yes.

Q: Can the users send outgoing Internet mail? A: Yes.

It looks like we have a real problem here! One of these questions should have provided at least a clue to a possible solution to the problem, yet all of them check out okay while incoming Internet mail is still broken! What else can the problem be? Refer to Chapter 6, which deals with Exchange, for the answer. And remember, practice.

One word of caution: Don't practice on production systems. You don't want to play around and risk taking down a system just so you can improve your troubleshooting skills. Start with a low-profile workstation, and work your way up. If you're experimenting, consider using a package such as Virtual PC or VMWare that allows you to load different virtual machines on a host machine, play around with the system, and then blow it away with no damage to the host computer. It's great for testing and trying out new configurations before they go into production.

We suggest using the mentor approach for any new hire. During the troubleshooting process, we supply the new hire with the different techniques and traps related to each situation. After a while, we quiz the new person to check for understanding, asking, "What would you do in this situation?" or "What's the next step?" This gives us a good idea of whether the new hire is grasping the ideas and how soon he can be on his own.

Document the Solution

After a problem is solved, document both the problem and its solution. Be as specific as possible. If you're like us, you can't remember what you did last week, let alone what you did last month. Don't reinvent the wheel. Work smart and take good notes. Although it might seem like a waste of time, this effort will pay off in the future. Make sure your documentation is written up on a timely basis. The faster you document the problem and solution, the more accurate it will be. Try to write up the problem on the same day or the day after. If you wait until the end of the week, you'll probably forget most of the important details.

Use Good Hardware

Although this isn't necessarily a troubleshooting rule, using good hardware can prevent network outages and keep your network running smoothly. We suggest using name-brand computers for workstations and especially servers. Usually, the driver and technical support are better with larger companies. If a problem turns out to be hardware related, there is a good chance that someone else has experienced the same problem. Generally, the larger the company, the better, because their hardware is already out in a variety of different environments and configurations.

CONTACTING TECHNICAL SUPPORT

At some point, everyone must contact technical support. When you've run out of ideas, or have narrowed the problem to a specific area with hardware or software that you're unable to resolve on your own, contacting technical support is the next logical step. Here are a few suggestions to follow when dealing with technical support:

- **Get authorization.** Many vendors charge for technical support. Make sure you have authorization to contact technical support or have a support contract in place before making the call.
- **Use phone versus e-mail support.** Some vendors offer e-mail support at a reduced rate. We suggest either using phone support, or if the problem is not urgent, posting your problem on a newsgroup/message board. E-mail support, no matter how good, is usually slower than phone support. Remember to factor in the cost of downtime when accessing your support options. It's difficult enough to solve complex problems using phone support, and almost impossible to solve difficult problems via e-mail.
- **Update drivers/firmware.** When you contact a hardware vendor for support, one of the first questions they will ask is if you have the latest drivers and firmware. Save yourself and technical support's time by installing these items before you make the call.
- **Service packs.** If you're contacting a software vendor, make sure you have the latest version of the software with any service packs and hotfixes.
- **Serial numbers.** Have any serial numbers handy for hardware and software.
- **Don't be afraid to escalate the case.** If you feel like you're not making progress or you feel that the tech support person is fishing for the answer, ask him or her to the escalate the case, or request a different person to handle your case.
- **Be cooperative, but hold your ground.** Obviously, both of you want the problem fixed. Be polite and perform any reasonable request. However, if you feel the support person is too aggressive, or the suggested step could cause more damage, don't be afraid to suggest a different course of action.

If you post a message in a newsgroup, be as specific as possible with your problem. Be sure to include the operating system version, service pack level, conditions when the problem occurs, and troubleshooting steps you have already performed. The more information you can provide about the problem, the better.

CHAPTER SUMMARY

The chapter summarizes all of the tips and tricks we've learned over the years. Remember, the first step to fix a problem is to isolate it. If you can't find the problem, you can't fix it! The next time you're stuck on a problem, ask yourself, "Am I looking in the right place? Have I eliminated all the possible areas where this problem might occur?" After you have located the problem, selectively apply the tips found in the *General Troubleshooting Rules* section.

Remember, practice makes perfect. The more troubleshooting you do, the better you'll get at it. Good troubleshooting skills will help you to identify potential problems and address them before they cause major outages and data loss. Remember to apply your skills when implementing any new project. For any major project we implement, we try to anticipate all of the things that could go wrong, and plan accordingly. We always plan for the worst and hope for the best. The hardware and software seems to know when you're on a tight schedule and will make your life difficult on purpose. Make sure you give yourself enough time to get the job done, and budget time for things to go wrong, because they inevitably do.

One of the most frustrating things we've encountered in some troubleshooting books is too much theory and not enough practical application. If you are new to this field, you'll quickly find that nothing ever goes like it does in class, and variables always seem to crop up. Nothing ever seems to be easy! One of the first implementations we experienced was a NetWare server that had to be installed over a weekend. After attending a NetWare implementation class, we were confident that we could get the job done. By 3:00 A.M. on Sunday, we were feeling a little less confident. The problem was that the particular drive we were installing in the server required a different disk driver than the one we were using. Unfortunately, the computer never came back and said, "Hey dummy, you're using the wrong disk driver!" The system would only abend (crash) every time we tried to start the server. Of course, it took us only more than 10 failed installation attempts to solve the problem. Unfortunately, this is usually the case with any troubleshooting problem. The error messages are often vague, and sometimes misleading. Careful interpretation of error messages can reveal clues to the final solution, but don't take them at face value.

The rest of this book addresses the lack of practical applications of troubleshooting scenarios. (We've done a fair amount of programming, and we've found that the easiest way to understand how a new feature works is with examples.) In that way, you can see how and where the new feature fits into the scheme of things. For every troubleshooting tool, we give at least one real-world example of how and where it is used. This should make it easier for you to incorporate these tools and troubleshooting tips in your bag of tricks. Each chapter is dedicated to a specific area of troubleshooting. In the first part of each chapter, we examine concepts, best practices, tools, and techniques that you should be familiar with in order to solve problems listed later in the chapter. After we discuss the tools, we list real-world troubleshooting examples that we've encountered in our daily troubleshooting. Some of the resolutions tend to be a little obscure—in our opinion, the more obscure the better. Remember, the emphasis will always be on the process and not on the outcome. The goal of this book is to teach you the skills to fix, or a least narrow down the solution to, any problem. Because we obviously can't anticipate every problem that you might encounter, we try to do the next best thing: to give you the skills you need to keep out of trouble and to fix any problem that you might encounter in our profession.

REVIEW QUESTIONS

1. What are the three most important general rules of troubleshooting?
   a. Practice makes perfect.
   b. Do no harm.
   c. Isolate the problem.
   d. Be conservative.
   e. Don't panic.
2. What is the symptom of a failed firewall? Assume that the network only has one firewall and one Internet connection. (Choose one.)
   a. Not all users will be able to get out to the Internet.
   b. Some workstations will be able to get out to the Internet and others will not.
   c. Internet performance will be slow.
   d. You will not be able to ping workstations on the LAN.
   e. You will not be able to renew an IP address on the workstation with the command ipconfig /renew.
3. What can you do to improve your troubleshooting skills? (Choose all that apply.)
   a. Practice your troubleshooting skills daily.
   b. Take good notes.
   c. Document your solutions.
   d. Conceptualize, don't memorize.
   e. Always work toward obtaining critical mass.
4. What does it mean in troubleshooting to "know what to do when they don't know what to do?" (Choose one.)
   a. Try a reload of the OS.
   b. When you're stuck, you're stuck.
   c. Call someone for help.
   d. Open a call with technical support.
   e. A good troubleshooter never runs out of ideas, and doesn't give up on the problem until it's solved.
5. Memorizing the details of a solution is good because (choose one):
   a. The solutions to computer problems never change.
   b. Memorizing the details allows you to gain a conceptual understanding of the problem.
   c. The more memorization you do, the closer you are to critical mass.
   d. When something changes, memorizing the details of a previous solution will help you determine why the solution is not working.
   e. None of the above.

2 Network Printing

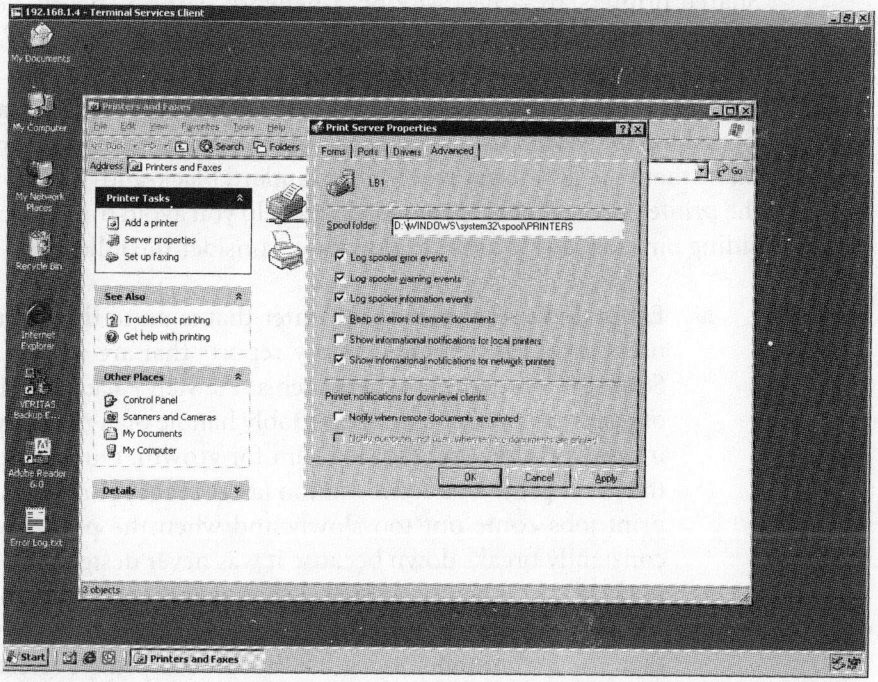

CHAPTER PREVIEW

Printing is always an issue on a network. In this chapter, we look at printer sizing, dedicated print servers, queue configuration, printing from the Web, and printer troubleshooting steps. If the printer is shared on the network, we strongly suggest using a dedicated print server to share the printer. If you attempt to share a printer from a workstation, you are asking for trouble. Remember that you'll need a network drop in order to use a print server with the printer. The second half of the chapter examines printing troubleshooting scenarios that we've encountered on our clients' networks and some review questions to test your understanding of the printing concepts discussed here.

PRINTER SIZING

Shared printers are a necessity on a network. For a network, you can buy a few shared printers instead of purchasing a local printer for each user. By consolidating print resources, you can save money by investing in higher-end printers that perform better, have more features, and have higher duty ratings than do printers designed for individual use. Even color laser printers have fallen in price enough to make them viable alternatives to the standard black-and-white printers. Matching the printer size and anticipated load will help you avoid future problems. When deciding on a network printer to purchase, consider the following:

- **Estimated use.** Purchase a printer that is up to the printing tasks of your users. Don't forget any lengthy reports that are run on a monthly basis. Some printer manufacturers such as Hewlett Packard (HP) list the number of pages the printer can comfortably handle on a monthly basis. When sizing any printer, leave some room for growth. Our clients never complain that their print jobs come out too fast, but they sure let us know when their print jobs come out too slowly and when the poor overworked printer constantly breaks down because it was never designed to handle the printing load that is placed upon it. When sizing a printer for an application, we usually estimate the number of pages per month, double that number, and then use that number as a guideline for our printer selection.
- **Speed.** In general, the faster the printer, the higher the duty cycle, and the more expensive the printer is. When considering the speed of the printer, always plan for peak periods and size the printer accordingly. For example, if your client is an accounting firm, make sure to size the printer for income tax season, when printing loads are typically very high, because the printer must print year-end reports and tax returns. If you're considering a color printer, also consider speed as one of your printing requirements, because color printing speed is usually significantly slower than that of black-and-white printing.

- **Features.** Duplexing (printing on both sides of the paper), color, paper tray capacity, scanning, faxing, copying, networking, and paper handling capability are factors you should consider when sizing a printer.
- **Location.** Obvious, right? Well, perhaps too obvious. For a shared printer that will see heavy use, consider placing the printer in an area central to all users. We try to avoid placing a shared printer in any one person's office because other users must go into that office and interrupt the office's occupant. For shared printers, geographically neutral locations are usually the best for heavily used networked printers. Remember that the printer requires a power source. A network drop is required if a dedicated print server will be used to connect the printer to the network.
- **Need for multiple printers.** Except for the smallest network, consider configuring at least two shared network printers, even though one might only be used as a backup. If one of the printers goes down for repairs, you have a backup shared printer that users can use until the other printer is repaired.
- **Cost of consumables.** Consumables are a hidden cost of a printer. When selecting a printer, check the prices for toner/ink cartridges, fusers (laser printers only), and other parts that must be replaced as part of normal use. Often, less popular printer manufacturers might appear to have a better price on a printer, until you purchase your first toner cartridge and find out that it's double the price of a cartridge for the other printer you were considering. Over the life of the printer, you must take into account the cost of consumables because they will often add up to more than the original cost of the printer. Be aware that color laser printers usually have four toner cartridges that are necessary for color printing.
- **Outsourcing possibilities.** If your company has specific high-volume printing requirements, consider outsourcing your high-end printing needs. One of our clients is an architectural firm that routinely prints large blueprints. In the past, these print jobs were sent off-site to a printer. Later, they brought a company in-house (OCB Reprograhics) to provide their high-end printing needs. Not only are they able to turn around the print jobs much faster, but the company tracks and charges their clients for these printouts. This has turned a cost center into a revenue center that pays for this service and generates revenue for the firm.

By considering these factors, you avoid most of the printer sizing problems on the network. If your requirements place you right in the middle of two printer models, we always suggest purchasing the bigger model.

DEDICATED PRINT SERVERS

Regardless of whether a print server is internally installed in the printer or externally connected to the printer via universal serial bus (USB) or parallel cable, we strongly suggest purchasing a dedicated print server for all of your shared printers. An internal print server installs directly into a slot in the printer and has an Ethernet port that is plugged directly into the network. External print servers have a parallel/USB port and an Ethernet port. The parallel/USB port connects to the printer, and the Ethernet port connects to the network. Such a print server is assigned an IP address, usually through a Web-based management interface, and computers use this IP address as their printing port to use the printer.

We manually assign an IP address to the printer and do not use DHCP. We label each printer, using a label maker, with the fixed IP address so that it's easier to identify the printer in the future. In that way, the printer IP address is constant and does not change if the server is rebooted. If you want stable network printing, use dedicated print servers with fixed IP addresses. Dedicated print servers are more stable, faster, and more reliable than are shared local printers at a workstation. If the workstation is not turned on or freezes during a print job because of an application error, often the active print jobs in the queue will be lost. (Of course, the print job that is lost is a critical month-end report from an accounting application and cannot be reproduced.)

QUEUE CONFIGURATION

When we configure network printing, we create queues on the server and create a port with the corresponding IP address of the dedicated print server. Then, we configure the workstations to access the shared printers through the Windows server instead of printing directly to the dedicated print server.

We suggest developing a naming convention for your print queues. This convention might be based on location and printer model. Use the location and comments fields to help users determine the model, location, and capacity of the printer. Printing through the server might be more a question of style, but there are some distinct advantages to configuring the print queues in this manner:

- **Enables central printer management.** By having the workstation print through the server, you can have a central point of control for all print jobs. Print jobs can be started, stopped, and redirected from a central location. You can control access to server print queues by user or group. Make sure that you have enough room on the server's hard drive to spool print jobs. By default, print jobs are stored in C:\winnt\system32\spool printers, but you can change this location by clicking Start, then Settings, and then Printers. Then, right-click the white space in the Printers folder, select Server Properties, and then select the Advanced tab, where you can redirect the location of the spool folder to a different drive on the server.
- **Allows the addition of more printer drivers.** When you create a shared printer on a Windows server, you can install additional printer drivers on the server so that the workstation will receive the correct printer drivers when the printer is created on the workstation. This prevents the workstation from having to search or download the correct printer driver for the printer.
- **Enables jobs to be shifted to a different printer.** If you must redirect a queue to a different printer, because the originally selected printer is down for repairs, all you have to do is change the IP address of the printer on the server. If the workstations print directly to the printer, you must write a script to change the printer to the new IP address or manually visit each workstation and change the IP address of the printer.
- **Enables Web printing.** By making the printer sharable on an Internet Information Server (IIS), you can make this printer accessible to Web users.

The biggest disadvantage of routing print jobs through the server is that when the server goes down, no one can print. In addition, there is an increased load on the server because print jobs must be spooled from the server to the printer; however, this is usually minimal.

Installation of Additional Printer Drivers

When you create a shared printer, make sure to install all of the printer drivers for the different types of workstations you have on your network. In that way, when users install the shared printer on their workstations, they will not be prompted for the printer drivers during the installation process. To install additional printer drivers on the server, click on Start, Settings, Printers, right-click a printer, click Properties, and then click the Sharing tab. Figure 2.1 illustrates this process.

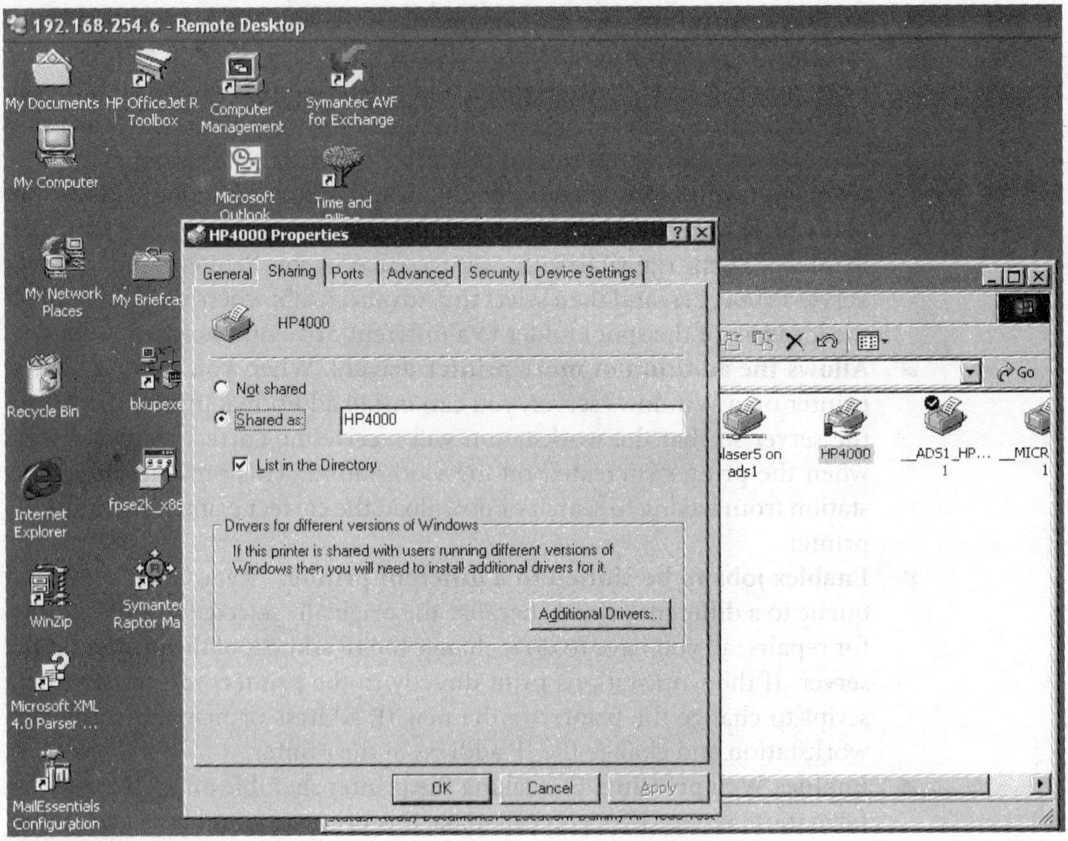

FIGURE 2.1 Installing additional printer drivers for workstations.

Click the Additional Drivers button, and the window depicted in Figure 2.2 will appear.

When you click the OK button, you will be prompted for the location of these drivers.

Web-Based Printing

Web-based printing is a new printing feature beginning with Windows 2000/2003. It allows you to install a shared printer and manage the printer on a server that has IIS installed on it. To access the printer, open Internet Explorer (IE) and go to *http://<server_name>/printers*. This will bring up a screen that has all of the shared printers installed on the server (see Figure 2.3).

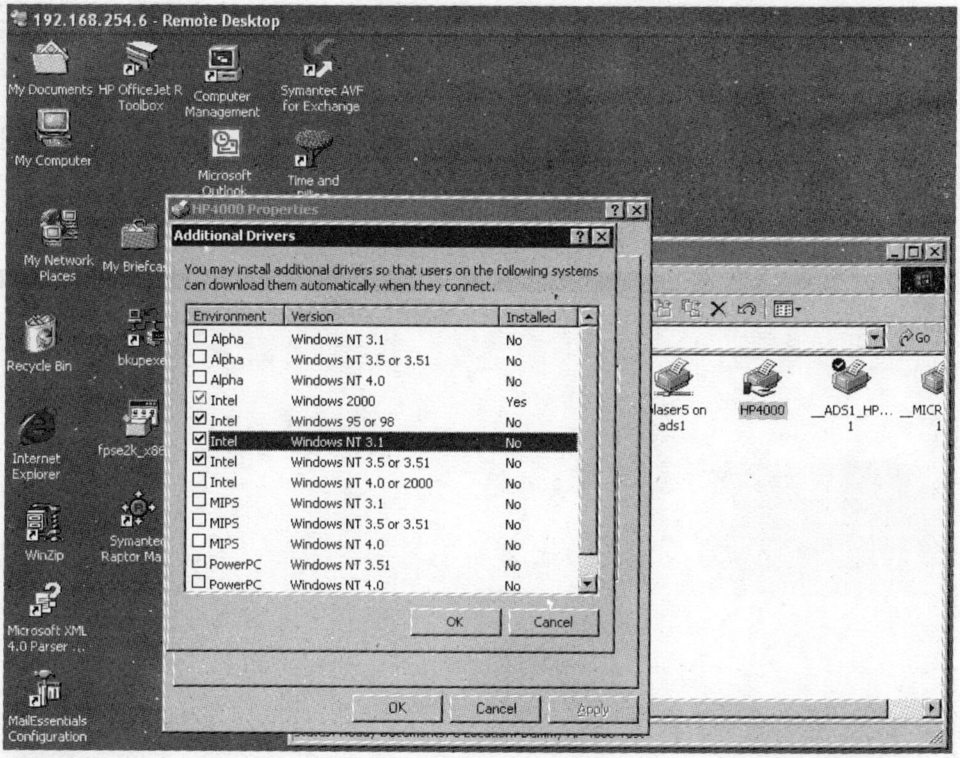

FIGURE 2.2 Installing printer drivers for other workstation OSs: Windows 95/98/NT 3.51/NT4.0.

By clicking the printer and then clicking Connect, you can automatically install the printer onto the workstation (see Figure 2.4).

Make sure to install the appropriate printer drivers for the workstations on your network. This is a very convenient way to add new printers to workstations because the users can install the printers by themselves. For more information on setting up a Web-based printer, refer to *http://support.microsoft.com/default.aspx?scid=kb;en-us;313058&Product=win2000.*

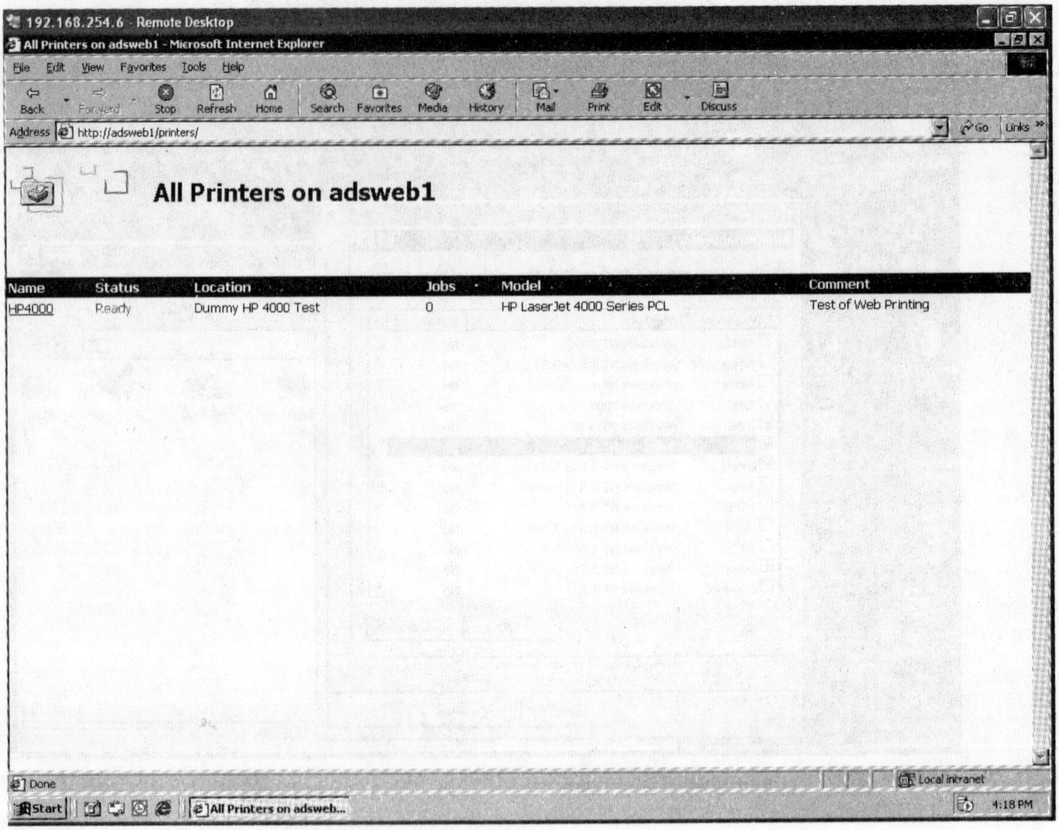

FIGURE 2.3 Web-based printing on Windows 2000 server.

GARBLED PRINTING

A fairly common printing problem is garbled printing. When you send a print job to the printer, the print job is unreadable or the printer ejects a bunch of blank pages, sometimes with one or two characters on each page. When this happens, complete the following checklist to solve the problem:

1. **Check for problems on the workstation or server.** Determine the location of the problem. Does this problem happen on just one workstation or on any workstation that uses the printer? If the problem happens on a specific workstation, focus on the printer driver for that workstation. If the prob-

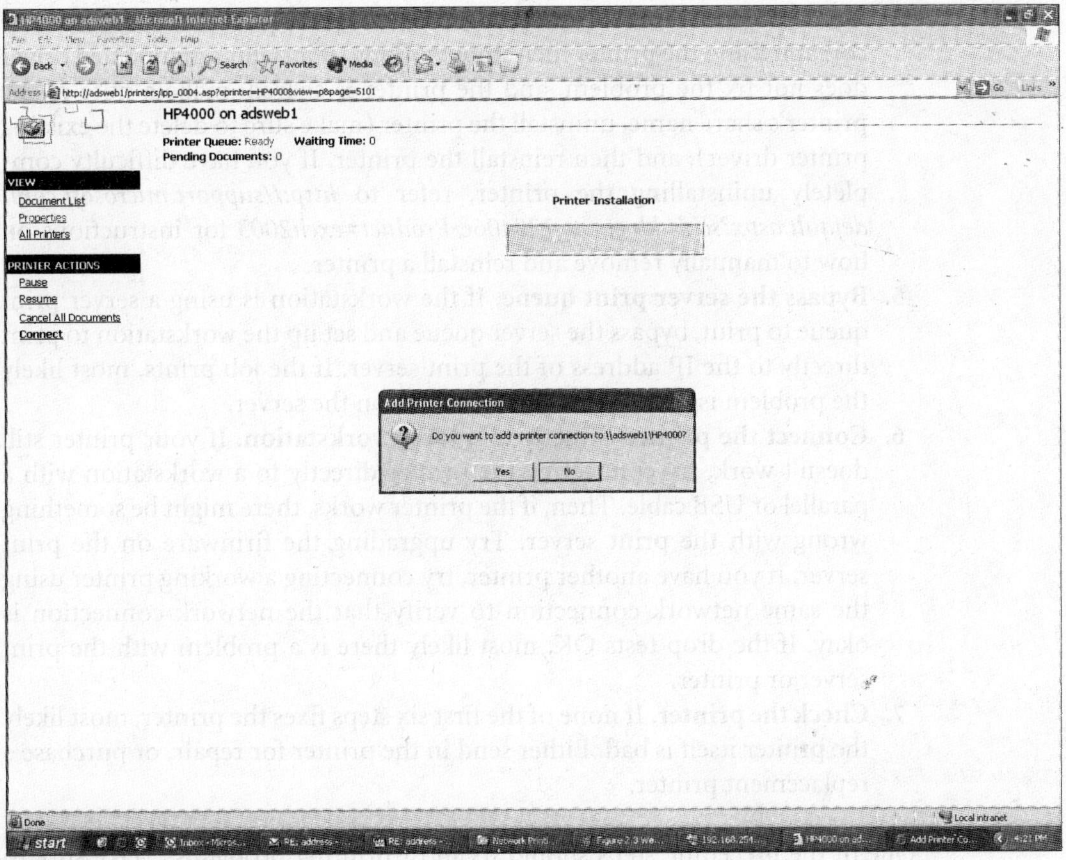

FIGURE 2.4 Installing a new printer using Web-based printing support.

lem happens when anyone prints to the printer, look at the drivers on the server, or the printer itself.

2. **Verify the printer driver.** Make sure the workstation/server has the correct version of the printer driver. Make sure the printer can handle the features of the printer driver. For example, if you install a PostScript™ driver for an HP4000 and the printer does not support PostScript, you will have a problem.
3. **Check for an updated printer driver.** Check the printer manufacturer's Web site to determine whether it offers an updated printer driver for the printer. If an updated driver exists, download and install it on the workstation/server.

4. **Uninstall and reinstall the printer.** Sometimes, printer drivers become corrupted and the printer then stops working. If installing an updated driver does not fix the problem, and the printer is shared, make a note of the printer's share name, uninstall the printer (make sure to delete the existing printer driver), and then reinstall the printer. If you have difficulty completely uninstalling the printer, refer to *http://support.microsoft.com/default.aspx?scid=kb;en-us;135406&Product=exch2003* for instructions on how to manually remove and reinstall a printer.
5. **Bypass the server print queue.** If the workstation is using a server print queue to print, bypass the server queue and set up the workstation to print directly to the IP address of the print server. If the job prints, most likely the problem is related to a printer driver on the server.
6. **Connect the printer directly to a local workstation.** If your printer still doesn't work, try connecting the printer directly to a workstation with a parallel or USB cable. Then, if the printer works, there might be something wrong with the print server. Try upgrading the firmware on the print server. If you have another printer, try connecting a working printer using the same network connection to verify that the network connection is okay. If the drop tests OK, most likely there is a problem with the print server or printer.
7. **Check the printer.** If none of the first six steps fixes the printer, most likely the printer itself is bad. Either send in the printer for repair, or purchase a replacement printer.

One of the preceding steps should fix most printing problems. Make sure to have at least a surge protector on each printer to protect it from power outages. Avoid connecting laser printers to an uninterruptible power source (UPS) that is smaller than 3000 Kilo Volt Amps (KVA), because most laser printers draw a significant amount of wattage (600 to 700 watts) when they print.

TROUBLESHOOTING SCENARIOS

Many printing problems can be avoided if you follow the suggestions set out earlier in this chapter. Using dedicated print servers should help you avoid most network printing problems.

Following are some scenarios for you to consider as practice for troubleshooting printing problems.

Scenario 1 A NETWORK PRINTER CANNOT BE ADDED ON WINDOWS XP

Facts

- Windows 2000 server with 2.0-GHz processor, 2 GB of memory, and 72-GB three-drive redundant array of independent disks (RAID) array
- Windows XP workstation with 2.8-GHz processor, 512 MB of memory, and 40-GB hard drive
- HP2000C network printer with dedicated external print server with the printer shared on the Windows 2000 server as \\server\hp2000c

Symptoms

An administrator was attempting to add a network printer on a Windows XP workstation. The workstation continually received the error message, "There is no printer driver available for this printer."

Questions to Ask

Q: Has anything changed? A: No. When attempting to install the printer on the workstation, the administrator received the error message.

Troubleshooting Steps

1. **Verify the problem.** When we attempted to install the printer, we received the same error message that there is no available printer driver for the printer.
2. **Check the XP printer drivers.** We had administrator rights on the workstation, so we knew that this was not a workstation rights issue. We checked the printer driver list on Windows XP and found that the printer driver HP2000C is included in Windows XP.
3. **Check Microsoft's knowledge base.** We went online to Microsoft's knowledge base and performed a search on the error message. We found the article *http://support.microsoft.com/default.aspx?scid=kb;en-us;282842&Product=winxp.*

Problem Resolution

We installed the printer driver as a local printer and selected LPT1 as the local port. We made sure that "Automatically detect and install the plug and play printer" was unchecked. After the printer was installed as a local printer, we modified the printer properties by right-clicking the printer and selecting Properties. Then, we clicked the Port tab and then clicked Add Port, Local Port, and finally New Port, where we entered the name \\server\hp2000c in the port name field.

After the printer port was changed, we were able to print to the HP2000C printer on the server.

Lessons Learned

If you are running Windows NT 4.0 and want to preload printer drivers for Windows 2000/XP on your NT 4.0 server, check out the Microsoft knowledge base article *http://support.microsoft.com/default.aspx?scid=kb;en-us;263090&Product=winxp*. This article describes how to install Windows 2000/XP printer drivers on an NT 4.0 server so that the workstations will not be prompted for the printer driver location when the printer is installed on the workstation. Note that these steps might not work with third-party drivers due to differences in driver names.

Scenario 2 USERS ARE UNABLE TO PRINT TO A NETWORK PRINTER

Facts

- Windows 2003 server with 3.0-GHz processor, 2 GB of memory, and 72-GB three-drive RAID 5 array
- 50 Windows XP workstations, each with a 2.8-GHz processor, 512 MB of memory, and 40-GB hard drive
- HP4000 printer with internal print server, printer shared on the server, the server configured to print to the printer via the print server at IP address 192.168.1.20
- Workstations configured to print to the HP4000 via the queue on the Windows 2003 server

Symptoms

On Monday morning, users were unable to print to the printer.

Questions to Ask

Q: Has anything changed? A: No. When users arrived in the morning, no one was able to print to the printer.

Q: Was it working before? A: Yes. Users were able to print as of the previous Friday.

Troubleshooting Steps

1. **Verify the problem.** When we attempted to print to the printer, no print jobs came out of the printer.
2. **Determine if there is a problem with the workstation or network.** To narrow down the location of the problem, we tried to print from another workstation. This workstation had the same results; that is, no printing. What did this tell us? Most likely, the problem was with the printer, print server, or Windows server because the problem was not workstation specific.
3. **Examine the printer queue.** We looked at the printer queue and saw that multiple jobs were backed up in the queue.
4. **Ping the print server.** We opened a command prompt and pinged the print server at 192.168.1.20. The print server did not respond to our ping requests. Most likely, the problem was with the print server itself, the IP address of the print server, or the cabling to the print server.
5. **Print a diagnostics page.** On most HP laser printers, you can print a test page that will display the IP address of the printer. When we printed the test page, we noticed that the IP address of the printer was no longer 192.168.1.20; it had changed to 192.168.1.30!
6. **Examine the print server configuration.** Closer examination of the printer test page revealed that the printer was configured to obtain an IP address from DHCP.
7. **Reconfigure the print server with a static IP address.** We reconfigured the IP address of the printer to a static address of 192.168.1.20 using the panel controls on the printer. We labeled the printer with the address of 192.168.1.20 for future reference. Evidently, the server was rebooted over the weekend and DHCP assigned a different IP address to the print server.

Problem Resolution

After the print server was assigned a fixed IP address, the printer started printing the backed-up jobs in the print queue.

Lessons Learned

We made sure to assign static IP addresses to all print servers. If the addresses are assigned an IP address via DHCP, a reset of the DHCP server can potentially cause all of the printers to stop working. We also like to label all network-attached printers with the IP address of the printer so we can quickly glance at the printer and learn the IP address of that printer.

Scenario 3 USERS CANNOT PRINT TO NETWORK PRINTERS

Facts

- Windows 2003 server with 3.0-GHz processor, 3 GB of memory, and 146-GB three-drive RAID 5 array
- 100 Windows XP workstations, each with a 3.2-GHz processor, 512 MB of memory, and 40-GB hard drive
- Multiple HP black-and-white printers and color laser printers with dedicated print servers configured with fixed IP addresses
- Workstations configured to print to the HP laser printers via multiple queues set up on the Windows 2003 server
- Workstations printing primarily heavy graphics and CAD drawings

Symptoms

During the middle of an extremely busy day, suddenly no one could print to any network printer.

Questions to Ask

Q: Has anything changed? A: No. Users were working as usual and suddenly no one could print to any network printer.

Q: Was it working before? A: Yes. Everyone was able to print in the morning.

Troubleshooting Steps

1. **Verify the problem.** When we attempted to print to the printer, no print jobs came out of the printer.
2. **Determine if there is a problem with the workstation or network.** To narrow down the location of the problem, we tried to print from another workstation. This workstation had the same results; that is, no printing. Most likely, the problem was located with the printer, print server, or Windows server because the problem was not workstation specific.
3. **Examine the printer queues.** We looked at the printer queues and saw that multiple jobs were backed up in the queue.
4. **Ping the print server.** We opened a command prompt and pinged the print server. The print server replied to our requests. Most HP printers have a built-in Web interface, so we opened Windows Explorer and examined the printer configuration. Everything appeared to be properly configured on the print server.
5. **Configure a workstation to print directly to the printer.** On one of the workstations, we set up another printer that printed directly to the IP ad-

dress of the print server. We ran a test print job from this workstation, and it came out fine. Because all of the workstations were configured to print through queues set up on the server, most likely there was a problem on the Windows 2003 server.

6. **Examine the Windows 2003 server Event Viewer.** A review of the Event Viewer revealed that the C: drive was out of disk space. We opened Windows Explorer to verify this.

Problem Resolution

By default, the spool location on a Windows 2003 server is located in C:\WINDOWS\system32\spool\PRINTERS. We changed the location to D:\windows\system32\spool\printers because the D: drive had plenty of room. Although initially the C: drive had a fair amount of free space, heavy printing during the day had filled the C: drive with print jobs.

To change the location of the spool files, click Start, then Settings, and then Printers. Then, right-click the white space in the Printers and Faxes window and select Server Properties. Click the Advanced tab at the top of the Print Server Properties window and change the location of the spool folder (see Figure 2.5).

FIGURE 2.5 Changing the location of the printer spool files on a Windows 2003 server.

Lessons Learned

When we set up a server, we typically create two drives: C: and D:. We use the C: drive primarily to hold the OS and applications, and the D: drive for data files. By default, the C: drive is used to spool print jobs. If your C: drive is already quite full and you anticipate heavy printer use, consider moving the print spool location to a drive that has more free space.

The primary reason why we set up two drives on the server is for Remote Installation Services (RIS). RIS is used to image a workstation or server and is very useful when duplicating multiple machines that have a similar hardware configuration. It's very similar to Symantec's Ghost(tm), but it's built into the Windows 2000/2003 server OS. RIS requires that the RIS images be stored on a drive separate from the host machine's OS.

Scenario 4

Users Receive a "Printer Installation Failed" Error Message When Attempting to Install a Printer From Their Web Browsers

Facts

- Windows 2003 server with 3.0-GHz processor, 3 GB of memory, and 72-GB three-drive RAID array
- 200 Windows 2000 workstations, each with a 2.0-GHz processor, 512 MB of memory, and 40-GB hard drive
- Web-based printing enabled on the server
- IE 6.0 used on workstations

Symptoms

When users attempt to install a printer from their Web browsers, they receive the error message "Printer installation failed. You do not have enough privilege to complete the printer installation on the local machine."

Questions to Ask

Q: Has anything changed? A: No. When users attempted to install the printer, they received the error message.

Troubleshooting Steps

1. **Verify the problem.** When logged in as a regular user, we received the same error message. Regular users do not have power user or administrator rights on their local machines.

2. **Determine if this is a problem with rights.** In this case, the error message was meaningful. The key word in the message was *privilege*. We suspected the user did not have enough rights to complete the installation. We logged off the workstation as the regular user and logged in as administrator. When we attempted to install the printer, it installed successfully without any problems. This confirmed that the regular user did not have enough rights on the local workstation to complete the printer installation.

Resolution

There are several ways to fix a rights problem. You can either make the user a member of the power users or administrators group or download a hotfix provided by Microsoft to address this problem. For more information, refer to knowledge base article *http://support.microsoft.com/default.aspx?scid=kb;en-us;826978&Product=win2000* on Microsoft's Web site. However, to obtain the fix, you must call Microsoft Product Support Services.

This problem can also occur if you do not have "Initialize and script ActiveX controls not marked as safe" set to enabled on your local intranet zone in IE.

Lessons Learned

Before rolling out any new technology, it's always a good idea to thoroughly test it before releasing it into production. In this particular scenario, Internet printing was tested, but it was tested when an administrator was logged in to the workstation, so the problem did not occur. Before you implement anything new, thoroughly test it with a group of technically savvy users to make sure all of the bugs are worked out. Thorough testing will ensure that an implementation is introduced with a minimum of disruption and aggravation for end users. For any major implementation, consider creating a test plan that takes into account all of the possible scenarios regarding how and where this technology will be used. This will save you many headaches during the implementation phase.

CHAPTER SUMMARY

Using dedicated print servers for all of the network printers is one of the best ways to reduce printing problems on a network. Dedicated print servers are fast and stable and require little, if any, maintenance. Make sure to size a printer for its intended application. Don't use a color ink jet printer that prints one page every three minutes and expect users to be happy with its performance. It's more a question of style, but we like to configure our network printers to print to a server queue rather than have each workstation print directly to the printer. This makes the printers easier to manage and gives you more flexibility if you have to change the IP address of a printer. If you're running Windows 2000/XP workstations, check out the article at *http://support.microsoft.com/default.aspx?scid=kb;en-us;314486&Product=winxp* to learn how to automate the setup of network printers on your workstations.

REVIEW QUESTIONS

1. What is the preferred way to set up a network printer? (Choose one.)
   a. Workstations print through a server queue, and the server prints to the printer connected to a local LPT1 port.
   b. Workstations print directly to a printer with a dedicated print server.
   c. Workstations print through a server queue, and the server prints to the printer connected to a dedicated print server.
   d. Workstations print to a shared printer connected to another workstation.
   e. All workstations have local printers.
2. What are possible causes of garbled print jobs? (Choose all that apply.)
   a. Corrupted printer driver
   b. Incorrect printer driver
   c. Server out of disk space
   d. Damaged cable run connected to the print server
   e. High printing volume
3. By default, where is the printer spool location on a Windows 2003 server? (Choose one.)
   a. C:\WINDOWS\system32\spool\PRINTERS
   b. C:\WINNT\system32\spool\printers
   c. C:\spool\printers
   d. C:\printers\spool
   e. D:\WINDOWS\system32\spool\PRINTERS
4. When configuring a print server, you should use what method to assign the IP address? (Choose one.)
   a. DHCP
   b. DNS
   c. RIS
   d. Manually assigned (static) IP address
   e. WUS

5. Which operating systems support Web-based printing? (Choose all that apply.)
   a. Windows 2000 server
   b. Windows NT 4.0 server
   c. Windows NT 3.51 server
   d. Windows 2003 server
   e. Windows 3.1

3 Workstation Troubleshooting

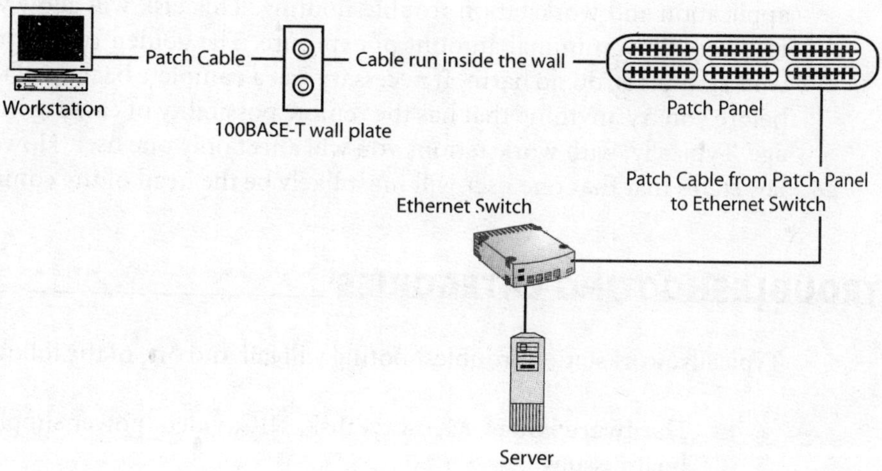

CHAPTER PREVIEW

The first part of this chapter focuses on workstation troubleshooting categories, the Windows OS, and basic network troubleshooting tools. The second part of the chapter examines some real-world troubleshooting scenarios that we've encountered in our daily consulting adventures. Some problem resolutions are rather obscure, whereas others are quite simple. In our opinion, the more obscure, the better.

We selected scenarios that are more difficult to challenge your troubleshooting skills. Pay close attention to the *Lessons Learned* sections because they should be helpful to you when fixing problems in the future. If you can solve these problems, you should be able to quickly solve the simple ones. Don't be discouraged if you can't figure out each scenario on your own. Remember, we're focusing on the process of troubleshooting, rather than the outcome. As you read each scenario, test yourself to see if you can predict the next logical step. Try to think about all of the items that can cause the problem. Try to predict the next step. You'll know you're getting good when you can predict the possible outcomes just by reading the symptoms of the problem.

Most likely, one of the first tasks you will be assigned as a network engineer is application and workstation troubleshooting. This task will allow you to get your feet wet with a minimal amount of exposure. The golden rule of troubleshooting workstations is, do no harm. If necessary, get a complete backup of the workstation before you try anything that has the remote possibility of causing irreversible damage. Typically, with workstations you will affect only one user. However, Murphy's law states that that one user will most likely be the head of the company.

TROUBLESHOOTING CATEGORIES

Typically, workstation troubleshooting will fall into one of the following categories:

- **Hardware issues.** Memory, disk, NIC, video, power supply, and motherboard issues
- **OS issues.** Workstation booting issues, service pack issues
- **Hardware issues.** Memory, disk, network interface card (NIC), video, power supply and motherboard issues.
- **Printing issues.** User cannot print, printing from different trays on a printer, printing comes out garbled
- **Application troubleshooting.** Troubleshooting applications such as Microsoft® Office Suite (Word, PowerPoint®, Excel, Access), Internet browsers (Netscape and IE), accounting applications, and Adobe® Photoshop®
- **Networking issues.** Connecting to the server, Internet, and other network resources
- **User issues.** Users blame the computer, but in reality require additional training

TROUBLESHOOTING THE WINDOWS OPERATING SYSTEM

The following are a few general guidelines when troubleshooting workstations.

Windows service packs. Try to stay current with Windows service packs. We monitor message boards and see the issues that arise when new service packs are released. We don't recommend installing service packs as soon as they are released; let someone else discover the problems first. Many patches address security issues, so it's probably a good idea to apply them to make your workstations (and servers) as secure as possible. After you are fairly comfortable that the service pack is not going to cause any major issues, go ahead and install it on a few workstations and test it in your environment. We don't recommend rolling it out to all workstations at the same time because if something goes wrong, you'll have a big mess on your hands. Consider a phased approach for any service pack rollout. When you do roll out a service pack, we suggest installing it on every workstation in the company within a relatively short period of time. In that way, you'll have consistency across all workstations at the OS level. It's one less item to think about when troubleshooting a problem. If you're running Windows 2000/XP on the desktop and have a Windows 2000/2003 server, consider using Software Update Services (SUS), soon to be Windows Update Services (WUS) to automate the service pack process. For more information on SUS/WUS, refer to *http://www.microsoft.com/windowsserversystem/sus/default.mspx.*

Firmware and drivers. If you suspect a problem with the hardware, consider upgrading the firmware and/or driver. In general, it's a good idea to upgrade both at the same time. Make sure to get a good backup of the current firmware and driver before attempting the update. If you have to call the hardware vendor for a problem, one of the first questions they'll ask is if you have the most recent driver. Try the driver upgrade first so when you call technical support, you will already have the driver installed. This should streamline the technical support call process.

Windows temporary files. It's a good idea to regularly clear out any old temporary files on the workstation. As you probably know, applications create a number of temporary files that are supposed to be deleted when the program shuts down. You can sort by the file creation date to determine the files that have been on the computer for a while. If we haven't touched a workstation for some time, we usually clear out the temporary files on the workstation as part of our maintenance routine. What does it mean if the workstation has a lot of temporary files (that is, 100+)? It's usually a good indicator that the workstation has been reset without a normal shutdown or an application has caused the workstation to freeze. If you notice a large amount of temporary files on the workstation, make sure the user properly shuts down the workstation and that the problem is not hardware related (bad memory or motherboard problems). Temporary files for Windows 9*x* workstations are usually located in C:\windows\temp and for Windows 2K/XP in C:\Documents and Settings\<*user_name*>\Local Settings\Temp. Try deleting the temporary files if the workstation is unstable and/or has poor performance. You can also obtain the location of the temporary files by opening a command prompt and typing "set" and press <Enter>. The environment variable TEMP will display the location of the workstation's temporary files.

Scandisk. Typically, we run a scandisk in conjunction with the deletion of temporary files to make sure there are no file issues on the hard drive. We find more file issues on Windows 9x than with Windows 2000/XP. This is primarily because Windows 9x uses FAT or FAT32 formatted drives, and Windows 2000/XP uses NTFS formatted drives. NTFS is more robust and usually has fewer problems than FAT/FAT32-based systems. If you're running Scandisk on a Windows 9*x* machine, we suggest restarting the machine. When the machine first boots, press F8 and select Command Prompt Only. Then, at the C:\> prompt, type `scandisk` and press <Enter>. By running scandisk at the command prompt, you eliminate the possibility of other processes causing a restart of scandisk.

IE temporary files and cookies. It's a good idea to clear out the temporary IE files on a regular basis. You can check the settings of IE temporary files by starting the browser and selecting Tools and then Options (see Figure 3.1). From this screen, you can Delete Cookies, Delete Temporary Internet Files, control your temporary file settings, and clear the history. Note that if you clear this information, some information must be reentered when you revisit certain Web pages, so make sure the user understands this. Try clearing out the temporary files if you have issues with surfing on the Internet.

BASIC WORKSTATION NETWORK TROUBLESHOOTING TOOLS

To diagnose network connection issues, you should be familiar with the following tools.

Ping/Pathping

Determines that a host is reachable. `Pathping` is a new utility in Windows 2000/XP that combines some of the features of the `ping` and `tracert` utilities. It also gathers packet statistics on the traffic to a target host.

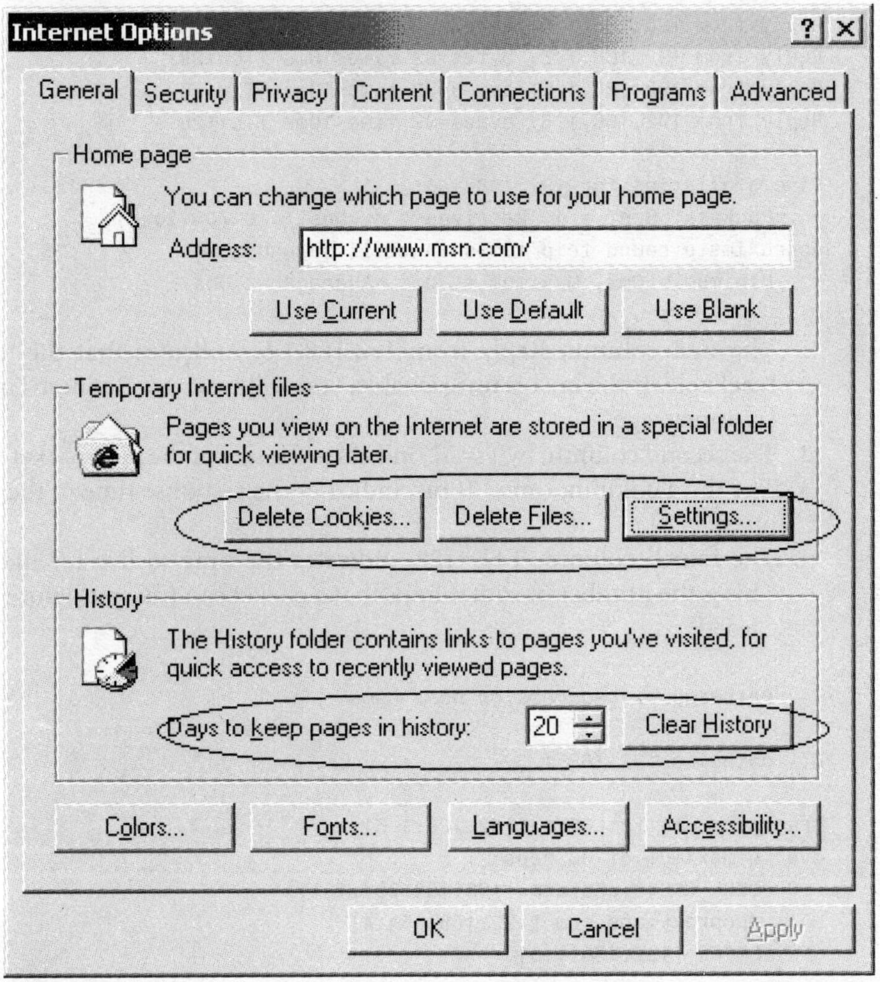

FIGURE 3.1 Temporary Internet file settings in IE.

Usage

```
    ping ip_address or host_name:
C:\:ping 192.168.1.6

Pinging 192.168.1.6 with 32 bytes of data:
```

```
Reply from 192.168.1.6: bytes=32 time<10ms TTL=128
Reply from 192.168.1.6: bytes=32 time<10ms TTL=128
Reply from 192.168.1.6: bytes=32 time<10ms TTL=128
Reply from 192.168.1.6: bytes=32 time<10ms TTL=128

Ping statistics for 192.168.1.6:
    Packets: Sent = 4, Received = 4, Lost = 0 (0% loss),
Approximate round trip times in milli-seconds:
    Minimum = 0ms, Maximum =  0ms, Average =  0ms
```

1. The first column, Reply from 192.168.1.6, indicates that the host was reachable. If the host is unreachable, you will receive a Request Timed out error message.
2. The second column, bytes=32, indicates the size of the `ping` packet in bytes.
3. The third column, time@10ms, indicates the response time of the `ping` request.
4. The fourth column, TTL=128, indicates the time-to-live for the packet. This is the number of router hops that a packet can traverse before it is discarded.

```
    PathPing <ip_address or host_name>

C:\>pathping 192.168.1.5

Tracing route to LBEX2 [192.168.1.5]
over a maximum of 30 hops:
  0  DELL_GX240.abc.com [192.168.254.101]
  1  abcproxy.abc.com [192.168.254.4]
  2  LBEX2 [192.168.1.5]

Computing statistics for 50 seconds...
                        Source to Here   This Node/Link
Hop  RTT    Lost/Sent = Pct  Lost/Sent = Pct  Address
  0                                           DELL_GX240.abc.com
[192.168.254.101]
                                0/ 100 =  0%   |
  1   0ms     0/ 100 =  0%      0/ 100 =  0%  abcproxy.abc.com
[192.168.254.4]
                                4/ 100 =  4%   |
  2   33ms    4/ 100 =  4%      0/ 100 =  0%  LBEX2  [192.168.1.5]

Trace complete.
```

1. The first column, Hop, indicates the number of router hops that the packet has traveled.
2. The second column, RTT, is the average response time.
3. The third column, Lost/Sent, indicates the number of lost and sent packets from the `pathping` source, with percentages.
4. The forth column, Lost/Sent, indicates the number of lost and sent packets to the `pathping` destination with percentages.
5. The fifth column, Address, is the name and IP address of the source, router, or destination.

Occurrences to Watch For When Running `Ping`

Following are some things you'll want to watch for when using `ping`.

- **Timeouts.** The host is unreachable. Always try to ping by *ip_address* first, then by *host_name.*
- **Ping packets blocked by the firewall.** Your firewall might block ping packets to the Internet. Make sure you are familiar with your firewall configuration before attempting to ping any address on the Internet.
- **You can ping by *ip_address,* but not by *host_name.*** This is possibly a name resolution issue; that is, a problem with DNS or Windows Internet Naming Service (WINS). Double check your DNS settings.
- *Wide variance in response times.* This indicates possible network traffic problems, either on the LAN or WAN.
- *Low time-to-live numbers.* There might be too many router hops between your computer and the host you are trying to contact.

Here are a couple of things to be aware of when using `pathping`.

- Verify that the packets are taking the intended route.
- Look for any dropped packets during the packet gathering process.

When to Use

Use `Ping/Pathping` to determine if a host is reachable. You can use `Pathping` even when a host is unreachable to determine where the packet dies. Make sure to ping by IP address first and then by name.

Ipconfig(NT, 2000, XP)/WinIPCfg(Win 9X)

You use the `ipconfig` and `winipcfg` utilities to display the IP configuration of a workstation.

Usage

```
C:\>ipconfig /all

Windows 2000 IP Configuration

        Host Name . . . . . . . . . . . . : DELL_GX240
        Primary DNS Suffix  . . . . . . . : abc.com
        Node Type . . . . . . . . . . . . : Hybrid
        IP Routing Enabled. . . . . . . . : No
        WINS Proxy Enabled. . . . . . . . : No
        DNS Suffix Search List. . . . . . : abc.com

Ethernet adapter Local Area Connection:

        Connection-specific DNS Suffix  . :
        Description . . . . . . . . . . . : 3Com 3C920 Integrated Fast
Ethernet
Controller (3C905C-TX Compatible)
        Physical Address. . . . . . . . . : 00-0A-99-23-31-A5
        DHCP Enabled. . . . . . . . . . . : No
        IP Address. . . . . . . . . . . . : 192.168.99.101
        Subnet Mask . . . . . . . . . . . : 255.255.255.0
        Default Gateway . . . . . . . . . : 192.168.99.8
        DNS Servers . . . . . . . . . . . : 192.168.99.100
```

Items to Watch For When Running `ipconfig /all`

Here are some actions to take to ensure success with `ipconfig`:

Verify you have a correct IP address and subnet mask. An incorrect IP address or subnet mask can cause connectivity problems.

If DHCP is enabled, make sure you can obtain an IP address. If you cannot get an IP address, you might have a problem with the DHCP server. An IP address that starts with 169.*x.x.x* usually indicates that the workstation was unable to obtain an IP address from the DHCP server. Verify that the DHCP server issuing the IP address is the correct server.

Verify the default gateway. An incorrect default gateway can cause connectivity issues to remote networks or the Internet. If you have multiple interfaces on the workstation, you should have a default gateway on only one interface. Multiple default gateways on different network interfaces can cause major IP routing problems.

Verify the DNS server(s). Windows 2000 and XP rely on DNS for name resolution. If the workstation is located in a Windows 2000/2003 server environment, the workstation should point to a Windows 2000/2003 server for DNS. The Windows 2000/2003 DNS server should be configured with root hints or forwarders to handle DNS requests for hosts outside of the Windows 2000/2003 domain.

When to Use

Use `ipconfig` when you have connectivity issues to the Internet or Windows 2000, which uses TCP/IP to communicate with the workstations. Double check the default gateway to make sure it has the correct IP address.

`IPConfig /flushdns` and `IPConfig /registerdns`

`ipconfig /flushdns` and `ipconfig /registerdns` flushes the DNS cache, refresh all DHCP leases, and re-register DNS names.

Usage

```
C:\>ipconfig /flushdns
Windows 2000 IP Configuration
Successfully flushed the DNS Resolver Cache.
C:\>ipconfig  /registerdns

Windows 2000 IP Configuration
Registration of the DNS resource records for all adapters of this
computer has been initiated. Any errors will be reported in the Event
Viewer in 15 minutes.
```

Occurrences to Watch For When Running `IPConfig`

- **Error messages.** Open the Event Viewer after 15 minutes to display any DNS errors associated with this command.

When to Use

Try this command whenever you have DNS name resolution problems. This is especially true when you make a DNS change that the workstation did not receive. Use this command when the name does not resolve to the correct IP address.

TROUBLESHOOTING SCENARIOS

The next part of this chapter consists of examples of real-world troubleshooting problems we have encountered with workstations. Don't forget the troubleshooting tools discussed earlier in this chapter. These scenarios should give you a good idea of how and when to use these tools.

Scenario 1 WORKSTATION CANNOT CONNECT TO WINDOWS SERVER

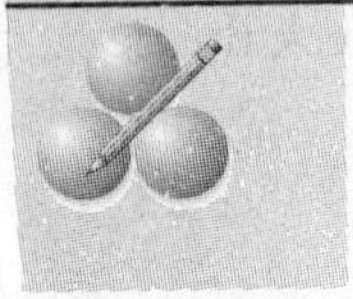

Facts

- XP workstation with Service Pack 1
- Dell workstation with Pentium 4, 2.8-GHz processor, and 512 MB of memory
- Workstation assigned IP address via DHCP
- Connected to a 10/100 24 port switch

Symptoms

When users attempt to log in to a server, they get the error message "No domain server was available to validate your password." Users have tried to reboot the workstations several times and still receive the same error message.

Questions to Ask

Q: Has anything changed? A: No.
Q: Was it working before the problem first occurred? A: Yes. I just turned on my machine this morning, and I received this error message.

Troubleshooting Steps

1. **Do a `ping` test.** Pinging the server at 192.168.1.1 results in:

```
C:\> ping 192.168.1.1
Pinging 192.168.1.1 with 32 bytes of data:
Destination host unreachable.
Destination host unreachable.
Destination host unreachable.
Destination host unreachable.

Ping statistics for 192.168.1.1:
    Packets: Sent = 4, Received = 0, Lost = 4 (100% loss)
```

We are unable to establish basic communication with the server, thereby indicating that something is wrong at a basic level.

2. **Run `ipconfig/all|more`.** Running `ipconfig/all|more` returns:

```
Windows IP Configuration

        Host Name . . . . . . . . . . . . : DAVEDELL28
         Primary Dns Suffix  . . . . . . . : abc.com

         Node Type . . . . . . . . . . . . : Hybrid

         IP Routing Enabled. . . . . . . . : Yes

         WINS Proxy Enabled. . . . . . . . : No


Ethernet adapter Local Area Connection:


         Media State . . . . . . . . . . . : Media disconnected
         Description . . . . . . . . . . . : Intel(R) PRO/100 VE
Network Connection

         Physical Address. . . . . . . . . : 00-08-0D-18-F6-5F
```

At this point, something should jump out at you. Notice the media state under "Ethernet adapter Local Area Connection." It indicates that the media is disconnected. It's no wonder the workstation cannot see the server. We know that the workstation is not physically plugged into the network. What are the possibilities? A typical workstation connects to the network with the following connections:

a. Patch cable from workstation to wall plate
b. Cable run from wall plate to patch panel
c. Patch cable from patch panel to hub or switch

Figure 3.2 depicts a workstation cabling run.

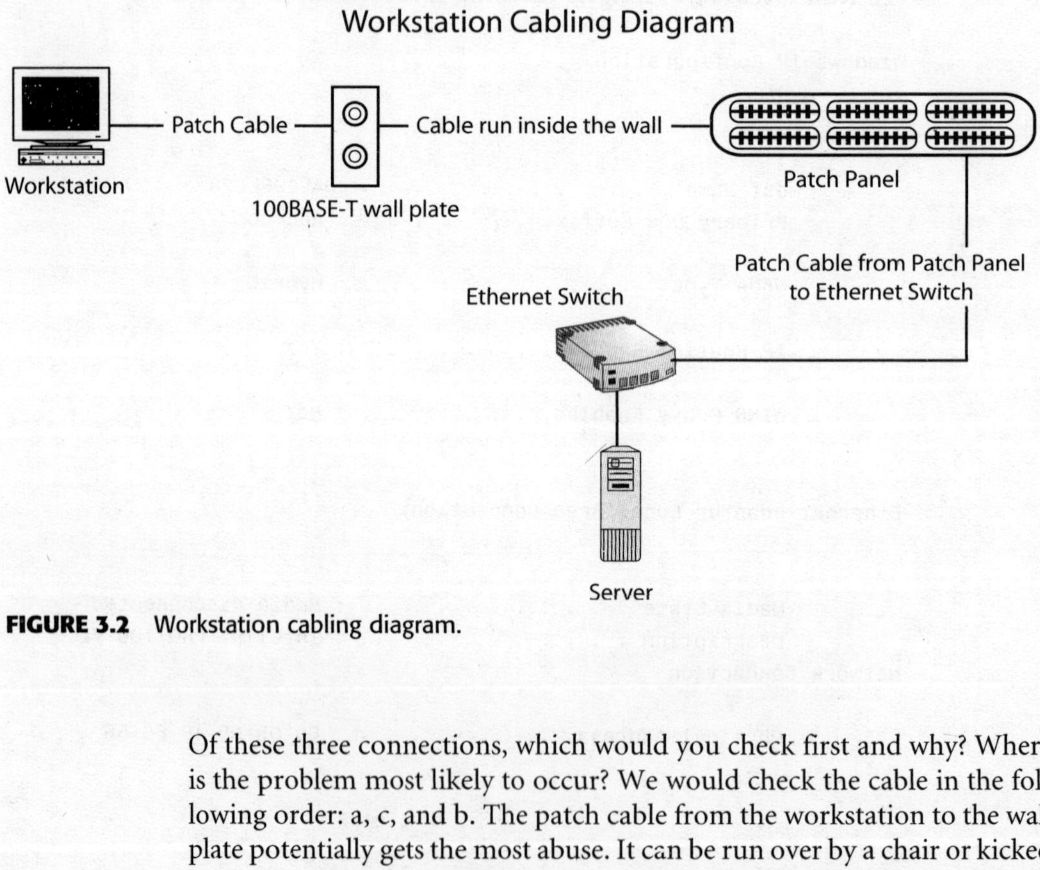

FIGURE 3.2 Workstation cabling diagram.

Of these three connections, which would you check first and why? Where is the problem most likely to occur? We would check the cable in the following order: a, c, and b. The patch cable from the workstation to the wall plate potentially gets the most abuse. It can be run over by a chair or kicked by a user. The patch cable from the patch panel to the hub or switch is the next place we would look. Usually, after the cable is dressed, it isn't moved around a lot. The cable in the wall is the last place we would look unless we knew that some recent construction or electrical work had been done in the wall or to the building.

3. Check the patch cable. An inspection of the patch cable from the workstation to the data jack reveals that the patch cable plug is not fully inserted into the wall plate. A visual inspection of the plug also reveals that the plastic retaining tab has broken off the plug.

Problem Resolution

We replace the patch cable with a cable that has good retaining tabs on both ends and reboot the workstation. The user can now get the login screen and can successfully log in to the network.

Lessons Learned

Check the obvious first! We always carry spare patch cords, including at least one very long patch cord and one that is a "crossover" cable. The pinouts for a crossover cable are listed in Table 3.1.

TABLE 3.1 Pinouts for a Crossover Cable

Pin	*Cable Color (Solid/Stripe)*	*Pin*	*Cable Color (Solid/Stripe)*
1	White/Orange	3	White/Green
2	Orange/White	6	Green/White
3	White/Green	1	White/Orange
4	Blue/White	4	Blue/White
5	White/Blue	5	White/Blue
6	Green/White	1	Orange/White
7	White/Brown	7	White/Brown
8	Brown/White	8	White/Brown

Ethernet transmits its signal on pins one, two, three, and six. Consider investing in a cable crimper to make and repair damaged patch cords, a punch down tool to connect cable to patch panels, a cable toner to locate cable drops, and a cable tester to ensure the cable has the appropriate signal quality.

Scenario 2 WORKSTATION CANNOT CONNECT TO WINDOWS SERVER

Facts

- XP workstation with Service Pack 1
- Dell workstation with Pentium 4, 2.8-GHz processor, and 512 MB of memory
- Workstation is assigned IP address via DHCP on a Windows 2000 server
- Connected to a 10/100 24-port switch

Symptoms

When users attempted to log in to a server, sometimes they succeeded and other times they received the error message "No domain server was available to validate your password." Sometimes the workstation got disconnected from the server or ran very slowly. Other workstations on the network were not experiencing any problems.

Questions to Ask

Q: Has anything changed? A: I don't think so, but I think someone was in the computer room making changes.

Q: Was it working before? A: Yes. I turned on my machine this morning, and I received this error message.

Q: Was anything recently installed on your computer? A: No.

Troubleshooting Steps

1. **Do a `ping` test.** An attempt to ping the server at 192.168.1.6 resulted in the following:

```
C:\>ping 192.168.1.6

Pinging 192.168.1.6 with 32 bytes of data:

Reply from 192.168.1.6: bytes=32 time<10ms TTL=128
Request timed out.
```

```
Reply from 192.168.1.6: bytes=32 time<10ms TTL=128
Request timed out.

Ping statistics for 192.168.1.6:
    Packets: Sent = 4, Received = 2, Lost = 2 (50% loss),
Approximate round trip times in milli-seconds:
    Minimum = 0ms, Maximum =  0ms, Average =  0ms
```

The results of the ping indicated that the problem was intermittent. We pinged several more times. Sometimes the ping was successful, and sometimes it would time out. Intermittent problems are the most difficult to resolve.

2. **Run `pathping`.** Windows 2000/XP includes a utility called `pathping`. `pathping` combines the best features of `ping` and `tracert` and gathers statistics on packets. Here are the results of running `pathping`:

```
C:\>pathping 192.168.254.6

Tracing route to ABCWEB1 [192.168.1.6]
over a maximum of 30 hops:
  0  DELL_GX240.abc.com [192.168.1.101]
  1  ABCWEB1 [192.168.1.6]

Computing statistics for 25 seconds...

             Source to Here   This Node/Link
Hop  RTT    Lost/Sent = Pct  Lost/Sent = Pct  Address
  0
@dis:DELL_GX240.abc.com [192.168.1.101]
                                           67/ 100 =   67%   |

  1     600ms     54/100 =   54% 56/ 100 =   56%  ABCWEB1 [192.168.1.6]

Trace complete.
```

From the results of `pathping`, you can see that roughly half of the packets were lost. What can cause lost packets on a network? Basically, anything in the path from the workstation to the target host can cause lost packets. Some possible causes include:

- Heavy network traffic
- Bad cabling
- Bad NIC either in the workstation or ping target
- Bad hub/switch

This particular network did not have a lot of traffic on it. How can you quickly verify this? One way is to physically look at the hub/switch and observe the traffic patterns. A heavily loaded network will show almost solid packet traffic lights on the switch, while on a lightly loaded network the packet lights will flash occasionally. On this particular network, the packet lights flashed only every four to five seconds, thereby indicating a light load.

How can you check the cabling? If you don't have a scanner, you can swap out the workstation with another workstation that's working fine. If the problem persists with the new workstation, you should suspect something specific with the cable run. If the new workstation can log in with no problems, suspect something that is workstation specific. If you don't have a network analyzer or managed switch, track down the cable run where the workstation is connected to the hub/switch. Observe the port light and look for heavy traffic on the port. Heavy traffic on the port (especially when the workstation is idle) is often a sign of a bad NIC in the workstation.

If you suspect a bad hub/switch, try connecting the workstation to a different port on the hub/switch. If the workstation starts functioning properly, the port on the hub/switch is probably bad. If the workstation continues to have problems, the hub/switch port is probably okay. If the entire switch fails, other users connected to the hub/switch will have problems connecting to the server. In this case, only a single workstation was having a problem, so the hub/switch is probably okay. A quick review of the hub/switch did not reveal any abnormal traffic patterns on any port. This leaves the cabling as a possible problem. If you don't have a cable tester handy, you can swap out the workstation with a working one. If after swapping the workstation the problem remains with the cable run, call in a cabling company to test the run.

Problem Resolution

When the cabling company tested the cable run, the tester indicated that pin six was broken on the cable run. From the last example, recall the pins that Ethernet transmits on: 1, 2, 3, and 6. Some work was performed in the computer room, and a patch panel was moved from a wall to a floor rack. When the panel was moved, a cable tie was cut and one cable was accidentally nicked. The cable was repaired, and this fixed the workstation connection.

Lessons Learned

Consider implementing an activity log for any work done in the computer room. The log can be a useful troubleshooting tool for fixing problems. Users are notorious for being vague ("It doesn't work!") when it comes to communicating the nature of a problem. Make sure not to take a user's answer to your question at face value.

Scenario 3 WORKSTATIONS DROP OFF THE NETWORK

Facts

- Windows 2000 workstations with Service Pack 3
- Dell workstations with Pentium 4, 2.8-GHz processor, and 512 MB of memory
- Workstation assigned IP address via DHCP
- Connected to a 100 MB/sec. 24-port hub

Symptoms

When users attempted to log in to a server, sometimes they can log in and other times they receive the error message "No domain server was available to validate your password." If the users successfully log in, the system will slow frequently and sometimes loses connection to the network entirely. Users are unable to browse the My Network Places and cannot surf the Internet. Sometimes a reboot helps, and other times it does not.

Questions to Ask

Q: Has anything changed? A: No.

Q: How long has this occurred? A: It's been going on for some time now. Some days it's worse than others, but I usually have the disconnect problem at least once a day and as many as 10 or more times a day.

Troubleshooting Steps

1. **Do a `ping` test.** An attempt to ping a local server at 192.168.1.1 resulted in the following:

```
Pinging 192.168.1.6 with 32 bytes of data:


Reply from 192.168.1.6: bytes=32 time<10ms TTL=128
Request timed out.
Reply from 192.168.1.6: bytes=32 time<10ms TTL=128
```

```
Request timed out.
Reply from 192.168.1.6: bytes=32 time<10ms TTL=128

Ping statistics for 192.168.1.6:
    Packets: Sent = 5, Received = 3, Lost = 2 (40% loss),
Approximate round trip times in milli-seconds:
    Minimum = 0ms, Maximum =  0ms, Average =  0ms
```

A second ping test revealed:

```
Pinging 192.168.1.6 with 32 bytes of data:


Reply from 192.168.1.6: bytes=32 time<10ms TTL=128
Reply from 192.168.1.6: bytes=32 time<10ms TTL=128
Reply from 192.168.1.6: bytes=32 time 600ms TTL=128
Reply from 192.168.1.6: bytes=32 time<10ms TTL=128
Reply from 192.168.1.6: bytes=32 time 1000ms TTL=128

Ping statistics for 192.168.1.6:
    Packets: Sent = 5, Received = 5, Lost = 0 (0% loss),
Approximate round trip times in milli-seconds:
    Minimum = 0ms, Maximum =  1000ms, Average =  326ms
Another ping test revealed:
```

A third ping test revealed:

```
192.168.1.6 with 32 bytes of data:

Request timed out.
Roquoct timed out.
Request timed out.
Request timed out.
Request timed out.

Ping statistics for 192.168.1.6:
    Packets: Sent = 5, Received = 0 Lost = 5 (100% loss),
Approximate round trip times in milli-seconds:
    Minimum = 0ms, Maximum =  0ms, Average =  0ms
```

From the answers the user gave us to our questions, we know that this problem is intermittent. Looking at the ping response, notice that:

- Ping sometimes responds normally with a response time of < 10 ms.
- Ping sometimes responds with a wide variance in response times.
- Ping sometimes times out completely.

Fortunately, we had an internal information technology (IT) person with us. He indicated that the problem occurred only on the fifth floor of the building; the building had six floors. What was the next step? Verify the obvious. Some quick ping tests and browsing My Network Places indicated that the workstations on other floors were working correctly. Therefore, the problem appeared to be related to the fifth floor. A review of the cable diagram indicated a fiber backbone that ran from the first, second, third, fourth, and sixth floors and then back down to the fifth. So, the fifth floor was at the end of the fiber backbone. A network diagram is shown in Figure 3.3.

All of the servers were located on the first floor. Based on Figure 3.3, what was the next step?

We know that only the users on the fifth floor are having trouble, so we should suspect either something wrong with the fiber run between the sixth and fifth floors or possibly a bad fiber card in either the sixth floor switch or fifth floor hub. How would you test this? The best way to test fiber is with an Optical Loss Meter. However, these meters are expensive, so we usually call in an outside cable company to test fiber runs. A certified fiber cable company was brought in to check the fiber run, and it tested out fine, so the fiber run was not the problem.

The next suspect was the fiber card in either the switch or hub. We removed the fiber cards from the first floor switch and swapped them with the cards from the sixth floor switch. If the cards were a problem, what should happen? If a card were bad, no one on floors two through six would be able to communicate with the servers located on the first floor. However, after swapping the cards, everyone was still able to connect, so a bad card in the switch was ruled out.

We've checked the areas in which the problem should have occurred, but we didn't find anything. On each floor, copper is used to connect a workstation with its respective switch/hub on each floor. Could all of the runs from the fifth floor hub to the workstations be bad? It's possible, but highly unlikely. If they are, we'd better get a new cable company. When we were walking by one of the cubicles, we noticed a small hub lying on the floor. We performed a quick trace of the wires. It appeared that as many as three hubs were daisy chained together. Evidently, whenever previous IT persons wanted to add workstations to the network, they would

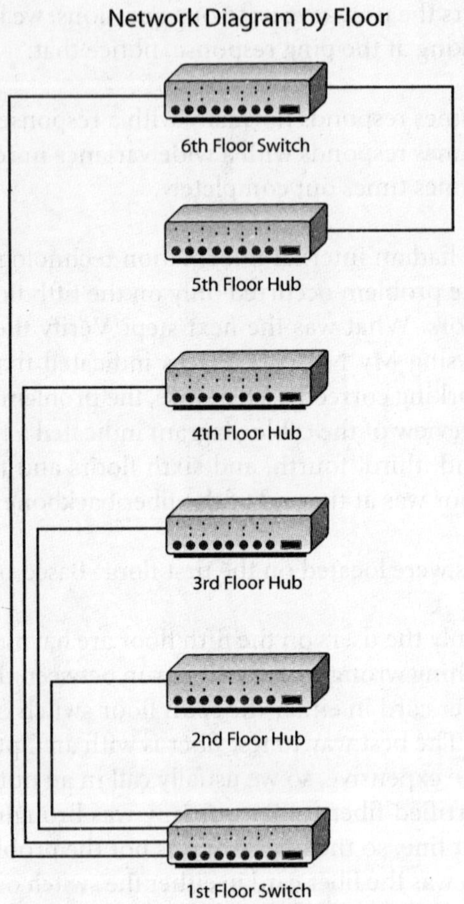

FIGURE 3.3 A network diagram by floor.

purchase a small hub to add more workstation runs. Figure 3.4 shows what the network diagram really looked like.

How many repeater hubs can you have with 100BaseT? You can only have two (0.46 ms. or less latency) repeater hops per segment on a 100BaseT network. From the diagram in Figure 3.4, we could tell that they were breaking the specification. Theoretically, the network shouldn't even run with that many repeater hops on the fifth floor.

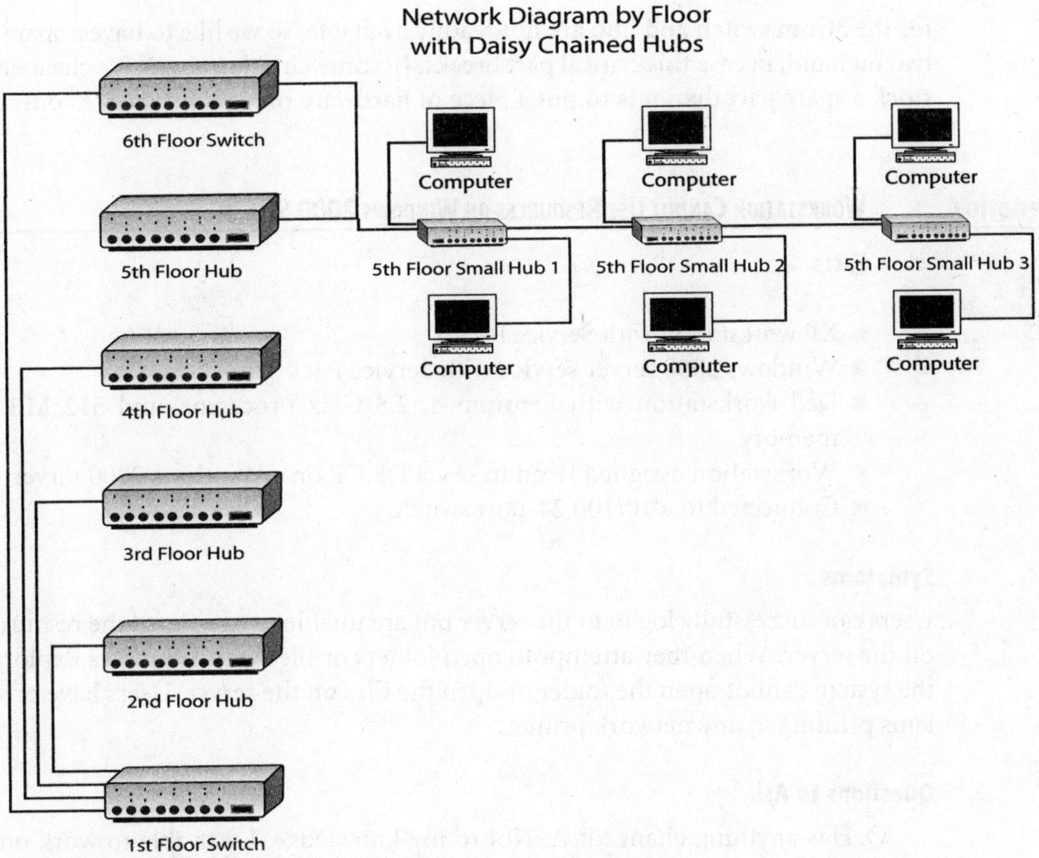

FIGURE 3.4 Network diagram by floor with daisy-chained hubs.

Problem Resolution

The small hubs were removed and all of the workstations on the small hubs were recabled to run directly from the main fifth floor hub. After the cabling was completed, the problem went away.

Lessons Learned

Resist the temptation to use small hubs. While convenient, do not consider hubs a permanent solution to add users to your network. We recommend staying away from daisy chaining any hubs because it's too easy to break the 100BaseT specification of two repeater hops, often without knowing it. Moreover, if you break the specification, it can be very difficult to diagnose the problem. We also suggest stocking spare parts for items that are hard to obtain. For example, the fiber cards for the 3Com switch and hub are not readily available, so we like to have a spare or two on hand, in case this critical part breaks. In some circumstances, it's cheaper to stock a spare part than it is to put a piece of hardware on a maintenance contract.

Scenario 4 WORKSTATION CANNOT USE RESOURCES ON WINDOWS 2000 SERVER

Facts

- XP workstation with Service Pack 1
- Windows 2000 server service with Service Pack 3
- Dell workstation with Pentium 4, 2.8-GHz processor, and 512 MB of memory
- Workstation assigned IP address via DHCP on a Windows 2000 server
- Connected to a 10/100 24-port switch

Symptoms

Users can successfully log in to the server but are unable to use any of the resources on the server. When they attempt to open folders or files with Windows Explorer, the system cannot open the folder or open the files on the server. Users have problems printing to any network printer.

Questions to Ask

Q: Has anything changed? A: Not to my knowledge. I was able to work on it yesterday, but now I can't access anything.

Q: Was it working before then? A: Yes, it was working fine yesterday.

Q: Was anything recently installed on your computer? A: No.

Troubleshooting Steps

1. **Verify the problem.** We can log in to the server, so most likely the workstation and server are communicating on a basic level. Because we can log in, a ping test probably won't reveal much. What's the next step? First we need to verify that the problem still exists. We attempt to log in with the user ID of the person having the problem. In this case, the problem was exactly how the user described it; that is, the user could log in to the server but could not use any of the resources on the server.

2. **Try a different user account.** One possible cause could be a corrupted user account, so we try to log in with the administrator account. Using the administrator account results in the same problem. This tells us that this problem is not specific to the user account, and most likely, the user account is not corrupted. Another way to verify this information is to log in to another workstation and see if the problem occurs with that workstation.
3. **Verify the location of the problem.** Both user accounts are able to log in to the server and access server resources from another workstation, so it appears that the problem is workstation specific. Since the user can't access data on the server, the next logical step is to examine the server for clues to the problem.
4. **Check the server.** After logging in to the server, we check to see if the problem exists on the server itself. From the server we are able to browse My Network Places and access resources, so it appears that this problem is workstation specific. In general, when troubleshooting any server-related problem, it's a good rule of thumb to check the Event Log for any events that might reveal a solution to the problem. When opening the Event Log, we notice a license error on the server indicating that the server is out of licenses.

Problem Resolution

The resolution to this problem depends on the type of licensing mode the server is in. The licensing applet is accessed by clicking Start and then Programs, Administrative Tools, and Licensing menu. There are two licensing modes on a Windows 2000 server: Per Seat and Per Server. Per Seat licensing is usually more attractive when a user has to access resources on multiple servers. Per Server licensing usually makes more sense if the company has only one server on the network. If the server is in Per Seat mode, you can revoke the Per Seat license of a user who no longer works for the company. Look at the Date Last used on the licensing screen to help determine whether a user that can have the license revoked (see Figure 3.5).

If the server is in Per Server mode, you can have a user log off and then another user can log on. Of course, the long-term solution is to purchase additional licenses for the appropriate applications running on the server and then increase the licenses using the licensing applet. This server is in Per Seat mode, and we are able to find a user who left the company and therefore no longer needs the license. After we revoke the user's license, the other user can log in and access all of the resources on the computer.

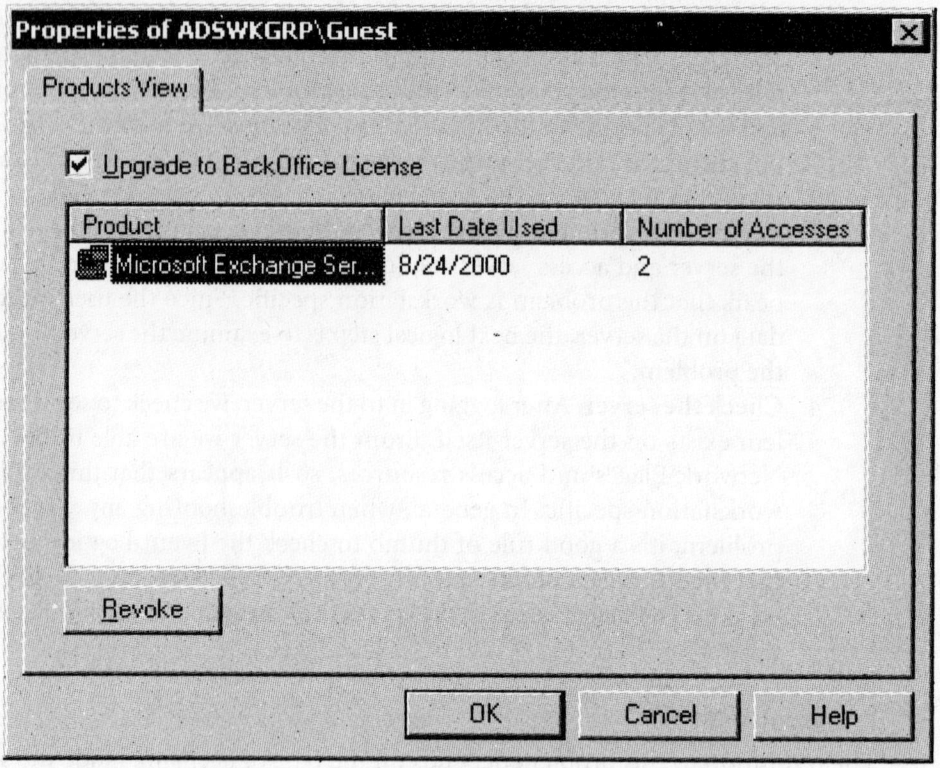

FIGURE 3.5 Date last used on the licensing screen.

Lessons Learned

Licensing issue symptoms can vary widely, from not being able to log in, to an inability to access server resources or other applications such as Exchange and SQL Server on the server. In most cases, the problem is not obvious until you check the Event Log on the server. For this reason, it's always a great idea to check the Event Viewer for any server-related problem. It's easy and fast to check and might provide excellent clues to help you resolve a problem. As part of your Network Management documentation, we suggest you develop procedures for adding a new hire to the network, as well as for removing a user from the network. Steps to add a user to your network might include:

1. Obtain the user's full name, position, and phone extension, add in the user, and inform him of his user ID.
2. Assign a password to the user, and optionally require the user to change it at the first login. Alternatively, request a password from the user that meets the company's password requirements for length and complexity.

3. Determine the group membership for the user and add it to the appropriate groups. In general, we suggest assigning rights to groups rather than to users and then making users members of groups. This makes the network easier to manage and usually prevents a reassigning of rights to existing folders. We suggest creating groups even if only one user will be assigned to this group. An exception to this rule is a personal area on the server. We like to create a user directory with the user's name off this directory and assign rights directly to the individual and to the administrator. Typically, we use this area of the server for a user's private files and for offline synchronization of files on Windows 2000 and XP workstations.
4. Enter a login script for the user. Usually, an existing login script can be used for the new user.
5. Set up a mail account on the Exchange server and inform the user of his Internet e-mail address. If necessary, grant the appropriate rights to Public Folders by adding a user to the appropriate user group. To assign rights to Public Folders with Groups, you must create a Universal Security Group (USG). USGs can be created only when a server is in Windows 2000 native mode (no pre-Windows 2000 domain controllers) and not mixed mode. A quick way to determine the operation mode of your domain is to open Active Directory Users and Computers. From Start, click Programs Administrative Tools, and then Active Directory Users and Computers. Right-click the domain and select Properties and then the General tab, which will display the domain operation mode (see Figure 3.6).
6. Create a personal folder for the user's data files and grant appropriate rights for the user in that area.
7. If the workstation is running Windows 2000/XP, configure the workstation to synchronize offline files with a specific folder on the server. Off-line files are especially handy for laptop users.
8. Set up the necessary printers for the user.
9. Test the new user account, and verify that it works properly. Additionally, verify that the user does not have access to any unauthorized areas on the server and does have access to the necessary areas on the server.

Steps to remove a user from your network might include:

1. Create backups of the user's data files.
2. Create a personal folders file (a .pst file) of the user's mail and archive the .pst file.
3. If necessary, forward the user's e-mail to another user.
4. Disable or delete the user account.

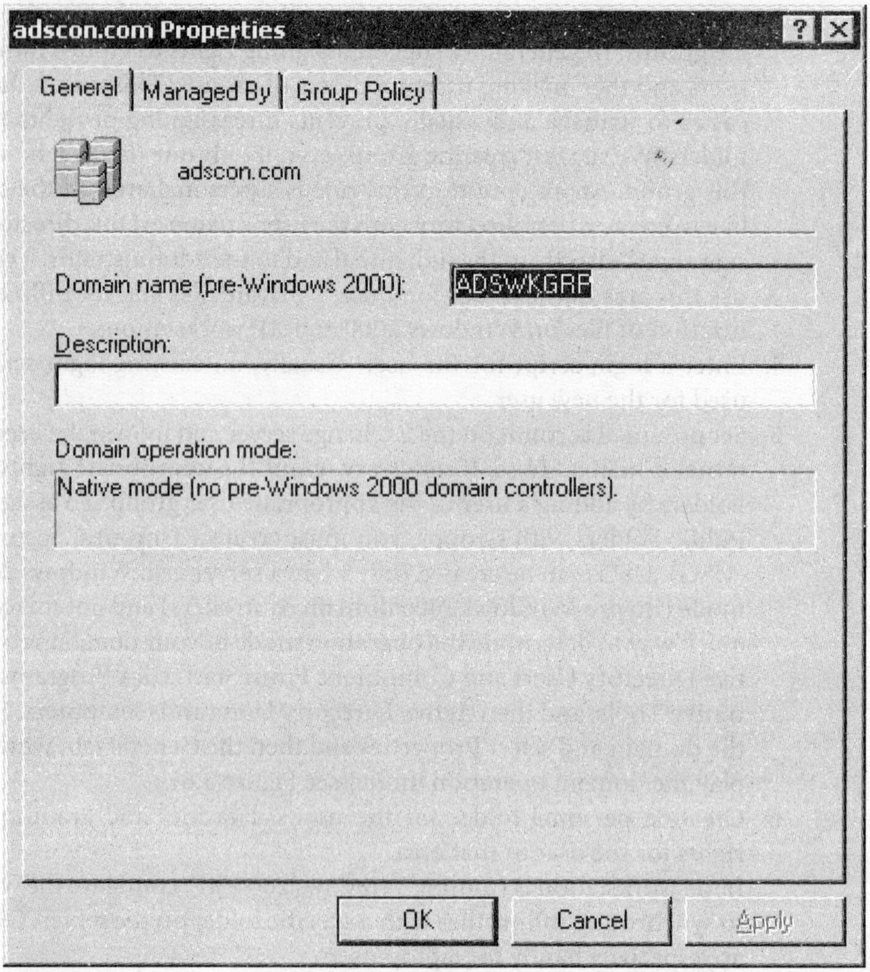

FIGURE 3.6 The General tab showing the domain operation mode.

5. Remove the user from the Exchange mailbox backup. If you're running Backup Exec with the Exchange 2000 add-on and delete a user's mailbox, the backup will fail because Backup Exec will be unable to locate the user's mailbox. This is due to a feature in Exchange 2000 that allows an administrator to recover a deleted mailbox for a specified time period.
6. Revoke the user's Per Seat license.

Of course, this is not a comprehensive list, but it should provide a good starting point.

Scenario 5 WORKSTATION CANNOT CONNECT TO THE NETWORK SERVER

Facts

- XP Workstation with Service Pack 1
- Windows 2000 server service with Service Pack 3
- Dell workstation with Pentium 4, 2.8-GHz processor, and 512 MB of memory
- Workstation assigned IP address via DHCP on a Windows 2000 server
- Connected to a 10/100 24-port switch
- SonicWALL Pro 230 with a T1 to the Internet

Symptoms

Monday morning, a user tries unsuccessfully both to log in to the network and to surf the Internet.

Questions to Ask

Q: Has anything changed? A: No, not that I'm aware of.

Q: Was it working before? A: Yes, it was working fine on Friday.

Q: Was anything recently installed on your computer? A: No.

Troubleshooting Steps

1. **Verify the problem.** We sit down at the user's computer and try to log in to the server. We cannot log in to the network and cannot surf the Internet. What's our next step? Obviously, something is very wrong if both the server and Internet connection appear to be down. What do these two items have in common? They both use TCP/IP.
2. **Run `ipconfig /all`.** The results of `ipconfig/all` are shown next.

```
C:\>ipconfig /all

Windows 2000 IP Configuration

Host Name . . . . . . . . . . . . : DELL_GX240
Primary DNS Suffix  . . . . . . . : abc.com
Node Type . . . . . . . . . . . . : Hybrid
IP Routing Enabled. . . . . . . . : No
WINS Proxy Enabled. . . . . . . . : No
```

```
Ethernet adapter Local Area Connection:

Connection-specific DNS Suffix  . :
Description . . . . . . . . . . . : 3Com 3C920 Integrated Fast Ethernet
Controller (3C905C-TX Compatible)
Physical Address. . . . . . . . . : 00-06-5B-5C-53-22
DHCP Enabled. . . . . . . . . . . : Yes
Autoconfiguration Enabled . . . . : Yes
Autoconfiguration IP Address. . . : 169.254.87.133
Subnet Mask . . . . . . . . . . . : 255.255.0.0
Default Gateway . . . . . . . . . :
DNS Servers . . . . . . . . . . . :
```

This workstation is using DHCP to automatically obtain an IP address from a Windows 2000 server. Notice the IP address (169.254.87.133) that was assigned to the workstation. When a workstation is unable to obtain an IP address from the server, it defaults to a 169.254.*xxx.xxx* address. In general, when you see an address starting with 169, the connection problem is usually related to the DHCP server. If you try to renew an IP address on the workstation with the `ipconfig /Renew` command, you will receive an error message that the workstation was unable to obtain an IP address. We suspect that the DHCP services are not working properly on the server.

3. **Determine if the problem is networkwide or workstation specific.** How can we verify that this is a global problem and not a problem specific to the workstation? One of the easiest ways is to try the `ipconfig /Renew` command on a different workstation. If we cannot obtain an IP address on another workstation, the problem is most likely some issue with the DHCP services. If we can obtain an IP address on the other workstation, the problem is most likely workstation specific. In this particular case, the other workstation could not obtain an IP address, so the next logical step is to investigate the DHCP services on the server.
4. **Examine the DHCP server.** Where is the first place we should look on the server to start troubleshooting the DHCP services on a Windows 2000 server? The Event Viewer is probably one of the first items to look at for this scenario. A review of the Event Viewer indicates that the DHCP services were stopped on the server at 2:00 A.M. on Thursday. What's the fastest way to verify this? Simply click Start, Programs, and the Administrative Tools Services applet and look at the DHCP server service to verify that it is not running. In this case, when the DHCP services were reviewed, the service

was stopped. For various reasons, we have seen the DHCP services stop responding on a Windows 2000 server. Sometimes an error message is recorded in the Event Viewer and sometimes it is not. Usually, a simple restart of the services or reboot of the server will fix the problem. In rare cases, the DHCP database will become corrupted and must be reinitialized. Refer to Microsoft's Web site to knowledgebase article *http://support.microsoft.com/default.aspx?scid=kb;en-us;173396&Product=win2000* for information on restoring a corrupted DHCP database.

Problem Resolution

In this case, a simple restart of the DHCP services fixed the problem. However, what if the restart of the services failed? How could we recover? We could restart the server, but that would require all users to disconnect from the server before we can restart it. What's a better temporary solution? If we have a router, other Windows 2000/2003 server, firewall, or any other device capable of running DHCP services, we could quickly configure that machine to issue IP addresses and then take Windows 2000 down after hours, fix the problem, and move the DHCP services back to the original server.

Lessons Learned

If multiple workstations on the network are unable to obtain an IP address from a DHCP server, take a look at the DHCP services. Usually, a simple restart of the services or reboot of the server will fix the problem. Consider moving the services to another machine or device to prevent a disruption in services.

Scenario 6 WORKSTATION CANNOT CONNECT TO THE NETWORK SERVER

Facts

- XP workstation with Service Pack 1
- Windows Server 2003
- Dell workstation with Pentium 4, 2.8-GHz processor, 512 MB of memory
- Workstation assigned IP address via DHCP on a Windows 2000 server
- Connected to a 10/100 24-port switch with 12-port hubs

Symptoms

Monday morning, a user tries unsuccessfully to log in to the network and to surf the Internet.

Questions to Ask

Q: Has anything changed? A: No, not that I'm aware of.

Q: Was it working before? A: Yes, it was working fine on Friday.

Q: Was anything recently installed on your computer? A: No.

Troubleshooting Steps

1. **Verify the problem.** We sit down at the user's computer and try to log in to the server. We cannot log in to the network or surf the Internet.
2. **Run `ipconfig`.** The `ipconfig` command reveals the following results:

```
C:\>ipconfig /all

Windows 2000 IP Configuration

Host Name . . . . . . . . . . . . : DELL_GX240
Primary DNS Suffix  . . . . . . . : abc.com
Node Type . . . . . . . . . . . . : Hybrid
IP Routing Enabled. . . . . . . . : No
WINS Proxy Enabled. . . . . . . . : No

Ethernet adapter Local Area Connection:

Connection-specific DNS Suffix  . :
Description . . . . . . . . . . . : 3Com 3C920 Integrated Fast Ethernet
Controller (3C905C-TX Compatible)
Physical Address. . . . . . . . . : 00-06-5B-5C-53-22
DHCP Enabled. . . . . . . . . . . : Yes
Autoconfiguration Enabled . . . . : Yes
Autoconfiguration IP Address. . . : 169.254.87.133
Subnet Mask . . . . . . . . . . . : 255.255.0.0
Default Gateway . . . . . . . . . :
DNS Servers . . . . . . . . . . . :
```

3. **IP Address 169.254.87.133.** We know that the 169.254.xxx.*xxx* address usually means that the DHCP server is unavailable. Therefore, we suspect the server. A quick check of another workstation also reveals it cannot obtain an IP address from the server. We look at the Event Viewer on the server and the DHCP services seem fine. Ping tests to another server on the network first by IP address and then by name to verify that the IP stack is functioning on a basic level. Assume we restart the DHCP services and the

server, but the problem persists. What does this mean? Most likely, the problem is not related to DHCP services on the network. What is another way to verify this? A quick way is to manually assign a static IP address to the original workstation to see if the workstation can connect. We do this, but it still can't connect. An `ipconfig` displays the following information after we assign a static IP address to the workstation:

```
C:\>ipconfig
Windows IP Configuration

Ethernet adapter Local Area Connection:

Connection-specific DNS Suffix  . :
IP Address. . . . . . . . . . . . : 10.1.3.100
Subnet Mask . . . . . . . . . . . : 255.255.255.0
Default Gateway . . . . . . . . . : 10.1.3.10
```

4. **Ping the server.** A ping to the DHCP Windows 2000 server on 10.1.3.1 reveals:

```
C:\ >ping 10.1.3.1
Pinging 10.1.3.1 with 32 bytes of data:
Request timed out.
Request timed out.
Request timed out.
Request timed out.

Ping statistics for 10.1.3.1:
Packets: Sent = 4, Received = 0, Lost = 4 (100% loss),
```

What do these tests indicate? We cannot ping the server or obtain an IP address from the server. Something must be wrong at a very basic level.

5. **Isolate the problem.** We could swap out the broken workstation with a working one to see if the problem is drop specific, but we already know that another workstation cannot connect to the server, so the problem is affecting more than one workstation. What's the next step? A network diagram is shown in Figure 3.7.

We know that this problem affects more than one workstation. At this point, we try to connect from a third workstation. The third workstation can connect to the server with no problems and works fine. The two workstations having problems

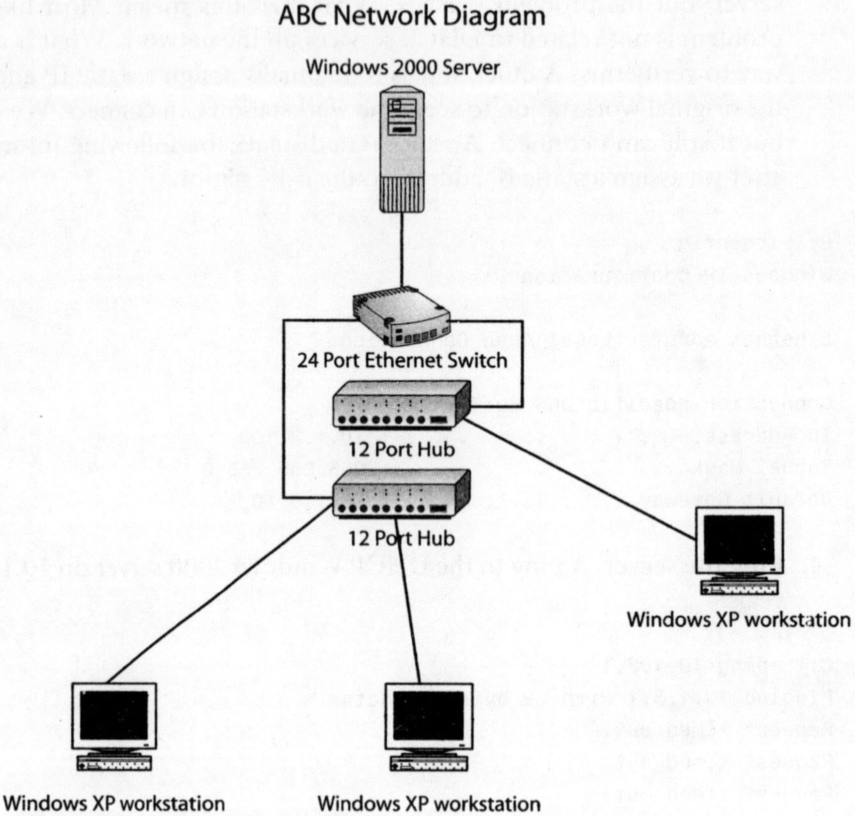

FIGURE 3.7 ABC network diagram.

are connected to the bottom hub, and the workstation having no problems is connected to the middle hub. Notice anything? The problem appears to be hub specific. How can we test this? One quick way is to move a workstation from the bottom hub to the middle hub and see if we can connect.

Problem Resolution

Moving the workstation from the bottom to the middle hub resulted in the workstation working fine. What does this tell us? Most likely, the hub is bad. If we have some extra ports on the good hub or switch, we could move key workstations from the bad hub to the working hub or switch. Assume that we order a new hub and install it over the weekend. Just to make sure, we test the workstations on the new hub to make sure we can connect. In this particular case, the workstations work fine. However, what if the workstations were unable to connect to the server? What could be the problem? One obvious problem is that the MDI-X port is not properly set, but the newer hubs and switches are auto-detecting. Assuming that the MDI-X and crossover cables are properly installed, what could be the problem? The new hub could be bad. What would be a fast way to test this? One way is to connect the workstation directly to the switch port that was daisy-chained to the hub. If the workstation works, the problem is most likely a problem with the new hub. What if the workstation does not work? The problem is most likely a bad switch port on the switch. How could we test for this? A quick way is to plug the workstation into another port on the switch. If the workstation can connect, the problem is most likely a bad switch port. If the switch port is not working, we suggest resetting the switch to see if the port starts working again. Sometimes, a simple power cycle of the switch can solve the problem.

Lessons Learned

We always stress keeping good network documentation. Having an accurate and current network diagram can save hours of troubleshooting time. This particular problem is a classic case of problem isolation. Once the problem is isolated, it is relatively easy to fix. However, without the skills to isolate the problem, you might never be able to fix the problem. If your network is wired with hubs connected to switch ports, consider using a different color patch cable to quickly identify the uplink connects from the hub to the switch. Always make sure to test new hardware after it is installed, no matter how confident you are that it will work. Sometimes what you think is the problem might not be the problem. In fact, it's always better to assume that your fix will not work and must be tested. In that way, you can prevent panic the next morning if it doesn't work. Even after you've tested the network, we suggest always having someone available the next morning to handle any issues that might arise. This is especially important after any major upgrade or infrastructure change.

Scenario 7 WORKSTATION TAKES A LONG TIME TO LOG IN TO THE SERVER

Facts

- Toshiba Laptop Satellite Pro running Windows XP workstation with Service Pack 1
- Windows server 2000 service with Service Pack 3 with TCP/IP and IPX
- NetWare server 5.0 with TCP/IP and IPX
- Workstation is assigned IP address via DHCP on a Windows 2000 server
- Connected to a 10/100 24-port switch
- SonicWALL Pro 230 with a T1 to the Internet

Symptoms

When a user tries to log in to the network, the system pauses for two minutes and then finally allows the login.

Questions to Ask

Q: Has anything changed? A: No, not that I'm aware of.

Q: Was it working before? A: Yes, last time I connected, it logged in fine.

Q: Was anything recently installed on your computer? A: No.

Troubleshooting Steps

1. **Verify the problem.** We sit down at the user's computer and try to log in to the server. There is a noticeable delay of roughly two minutes, and then the machine finally logs in to the network. The main issue with laptops is that they can be used in a variety of environments because of their portability. This particular laptop belonged to an accounting firm, and the laptop was used off-site at a client's location. Remember that end users are notorious for excluding information or giving the wrong information. Because of these facts, make sure to check the obvious when troubleshooting any laptop.
2. **Verify the network configuration.** We should probably verify the network configuration to see if anything has changed. An `ipconfig` reveals:

```
C:\>ipconfig /all

Windows IP Configuration

    Host Name . . . . . . . . . . . . : SATPROM10
    Primary Dns Suffix  . . . . . . . : abc.com
    Node Type . . . . . . . . . . . . : Hybrid
    IP Routing Enabled. . . . . . . . : Yes
    WINS Proxy Enabled. . . . . . . . : No
    DNS Suffix Search List. . . . . . : abc.com

    Ethernet adapter Local Area Connection:

    Description . . . . . . . . . . . : Intel(R) PRO/100 VE Network
    Connection
    Physical Address. . . . . . . . . : 00-08-0D-18-F6-5F
    Dhcp Enabled. . . . . . . . . . . : No
    IP Address. . . . . . . . . . . . : 10.1.0.55
    Subnet Mask . . . . . . . . . . . : 255.255.0.0
```

```
Default Gateway . . . . . . . . . . : 10.1.0.1
DNS Servers . . . . . . . . . . . . : 208.29.225.20
```

Notice anything? DHCP is disabled, but the laptop is supposed to be assigned an IP address from the DHCP server. This network was set up on a 192.168.1.0 255.255.255.0 IP scheme that doesn't match the 10.1.0.0 255.255.0.0 scheme of the workstation.

3. **Change the IP configuration.** Simply change the IP configuration back on the laptop to automatically obtain an IP address. This is done by clicking Start, Settings, Control Panel, and then Network Connections. Next, right-click the appropriate network connection and select Properties. Scroll down in the Local Area Connection properties and click Internet Protocol (TCP/IP) and click Properties (see Figure 3.8).

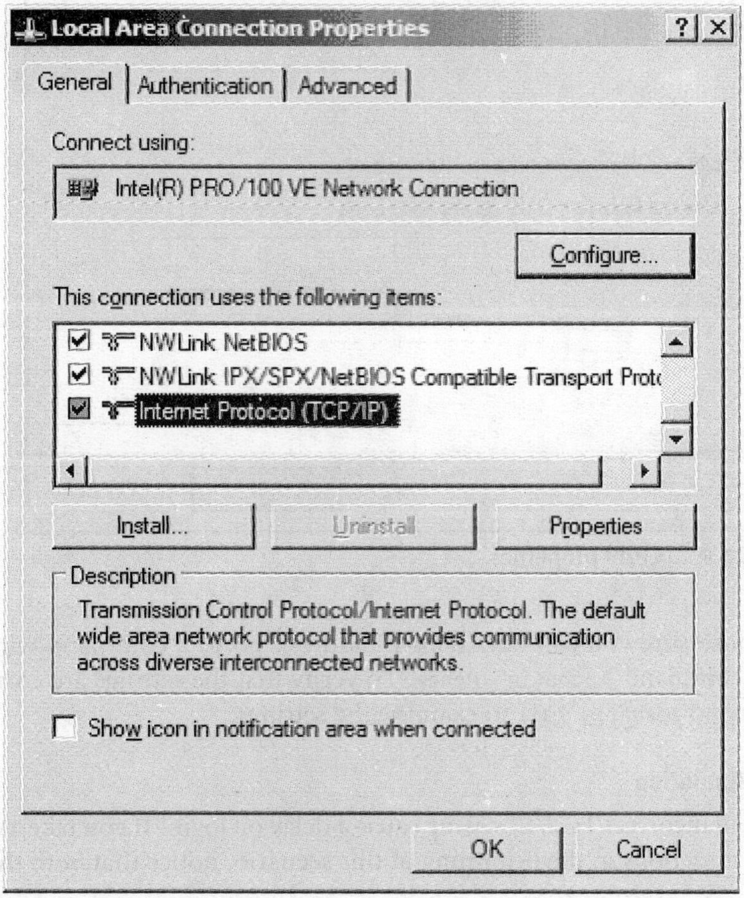

FIGURE 3.8 Local Area Connection Properties general screen.

Make sure "Obtain an IP address automatically" and "Obtain DNS server addresses automatically" are selected, as shown in Figure 3.9, and click OK twice to accept the change.

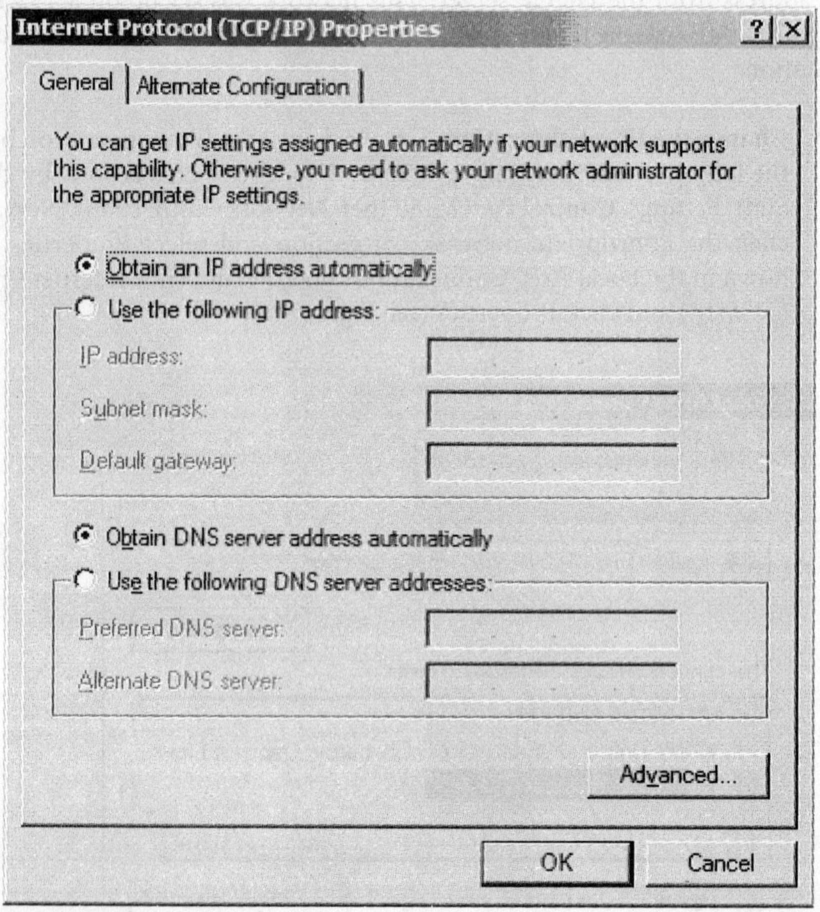

FIGURE 3.9 TCP/IP properties.

To make sure you can obtain an IP address, go to a command window and issue the command `ipconfig /Renew`. To verify that the settings are correct, issue the command `ipconfig /all` to examine the settings.

Problem Resolution

How can an incorrect TCP/IP setting cause a delay on login? If you take a close look at the *Facts* sections in the beginning of this scenario, notice that both the TCP/IP and IPX stacks were loaded. Upon login, the system defaults to the TCP/IP protocol stack, and it takes some time for TCP/IP to time out. After TCP/IP times out, the workstation will try the IPX protocol stack, and that's what is used to connect to the network. What is another symptom, assuming that this network has an Internet connection? If the TCP/IP settings are not correct, the user will be able to connect to the internal servers but unable to surf the Internet because TCP/IP was not properly configured.

Lessons Learned

This particular laptop was used in an environment in which the client required the use of static IP addresses. If possible, train your end users to restore their original network settings to prevent problems when they reconnect to your network. If you don't feel comfortable training your end users to restore the TCP/IP settings, at least train them to notify you that their laptop configuration has changed, in order to connect to the client's network.

Scenario 8 WORKSTATION IS UNABLE TO SURF THE INTERNET

Facts

- Dell workstation running Windows 95
- Windows 2000 server service with Service Pack 3 with TCP/IP
- Workstation is assigned IP address via DHCP on a Windows 2000 server
- Connected to a 10/100 24-port switch
- Internet Explorer 5.0
- SonicWALL Pro 230 with a T1 to the Internet

Symptoms

Users open IE and cannot get their home page or any other home page.

Questions to Ask

Q: Has anything changed? A: No, not that I'm aware of.

Q: Was it working before? A: Yes, yesterday it worked fine.

Q: Was anything recently installed on your computer? A: I'm not sure.

Troubleshooting Steps

1. **Verify the problem.** We sit down at a user's computer and open IE, and it does not open the home page.

2. **Determine if the problem is workstation specific or networkwide.** We log in to another computer and try to connect to the Internet, and it works fine. The workstation having the problem can access the server and open files with no problem. It appears that this problem is workstation specific, preventing the workstation from accessing the Internet.
3. **Run `WinIpCfg`.** Since the Internet uses TCP/IP to communicate, we examine the Windows 95 TCP/IP configuration by running the command `WinIpCfg`. We receive an error message of "Fatal Error, cannot read IP configuration." It looks like something is damaged on the TCP/IP stack.
4. **Reinstall network components.** Often, removing the network components and reinstalling will fix most network protocol issues. In this scenario, however, after we removed the network components, rebooted the computer, and reinstalled the components, the problem persisted. We contact *www.google.com* and perform a search on the error message "Fatal Error, cannot read IP configuration." The problem turns out to be corrupted Winsock 2 files.

Problem Resolution

To fix this problem, we restart the computer in safe mode. To start the Windows 95 machine in safe mode, we hold the left Shift key down as the computer boots. After the machine starts up in safe mode, we click Start and Run, and then run `C:\windows\Ws2Bakup\WS2Bakup.Bat` to restore the Winsock configuration.

Lessons Learned

If you receive a specific error message and after completing some basic troubleshooting steps, you might want to try searching for the message on *www.google.com* or *www.microsoft.com*. In this scenario, we could have saved some time by searching the Internet before reinstalling the network components.

Other symptoms of a corrupted TCP/IP stack include the ability to ping a host by IP address but not by the FQDN, receiving an error message when pinging, and the inability to connect to the server. This problem can also affect Windows 98/Me, although the fix is slightly different on these workstations. For more information, refer to Microsoft's Web site to reach the knowledgebase report at *http://support.microsoft.com/default.aspx?scid=KB;en-us;286748&*.

Scenario 9 WORKSTATION IS GENERALLY UNSTABLE

Facts

- Dell workstation running Windows 98 with 256 MB memory
- Windows 2000 server service with Service Pack 3 with TCP/IP

- Workstation assigned IP address via DHCP on a Windows 2000 server
- Running Office 97
- Connected to a 10/100 24-port switch

Symptoms

A user complains of the workstation freezing often. The user has to reboot the workstation at least twice a day, sometimes more often.

Questions to Ask

Q: Has anything changed? A: No, not that I'm aware of.

Q: Was it working before? A: Not really, it's been acting up for some time.

Q: Was anything recently installed on your computer? A: No.

Troubleshooting Steps

1. **Verify the problem.** We open Word and Excel and attempt to open a few documents in those programs. After we use the computer for about five minutes, it freezes and we have to shut it down by powering it off. Scandisk is set to run after an improper shutdown, so we let it run. Scandisk finds a couple of lost file links, which it fixed, but otherwise finds no major problems. If a machine is not shut down properly, what is one of the first items you should examine? The Windows temporary folder, because there should be many files there.
2. **Examine the temporary files.** When we examine this folder, we find that it contains more than 300 MB of files.

Problem Resolution

We delete all of the files in the temporary folder and reboot the machine. After the reboot, the machine is stable and performs better.

Lessons Learned

Explain to the user that Windows creates temporary files whenever an application is started on the machine. Have the user delete any files in the c:\windows\temp folder whenever the computer is not shut down properly. Alternatively, you can add a statement to the autoexec.bat file or login script that deletes any files in the temporary folder when the computer is started. Deleting the temporary files on a regular basis can reduce future help desk calls.

Scenario 10 — Unable to Add a Networked HP2000C Printer to a Windows XP Workstation

Facts

- Dell workstation running Windows XP, 3.2-GHz processor, 512 MB memory, and Service Pack 1
- Windows server 2000 service with Service Pack 3
- Workstation assigned an IP address via DHCP on a Windows 2000 server
- Office XP Professional
- Connected to a 10/100 24-port switch
- Connected to a networked HP2000C printer

Symptoms

This is a brand new workstation. This user wants to use a HP2000C color printer that is networked via an HP External Jet Direct Card. When trying to add the HP2000C networked printer, the use gets the error message "No suitable drivers were found for this printer."

Questions to Ask

Q: Has anything changed? A: Yes, everything. This is a brand new computer.

Troubleshooting Steps

1. **Install additional printer drivers on the Windows 2000 server.** On Windows 2000 servers, we can install additional drivers for Windows 2000 and earlier OSs by clicking Start, Settings, and Printers and Faxes, and then right-clicking the printer. Next, click Properties, the Sharing tab, and Additional Drivers (see Figure 3.10).

There is no way to add a printer driver for Windows XP on a Windows 2000 server. When you try to add the networked printer, you get the error message "No suitable drivers were found for this printer."

2. **Search *www.microsoft.com* for a workable driver.** We searched *www.microsoft.com* under the product name Windows XP with the search text "No suitable drivers were found" and came up with this link to a knowledge base article: *http://support.microsoft.com/default.aspx?scid=kb;en-us;282842&Product=winxp.*

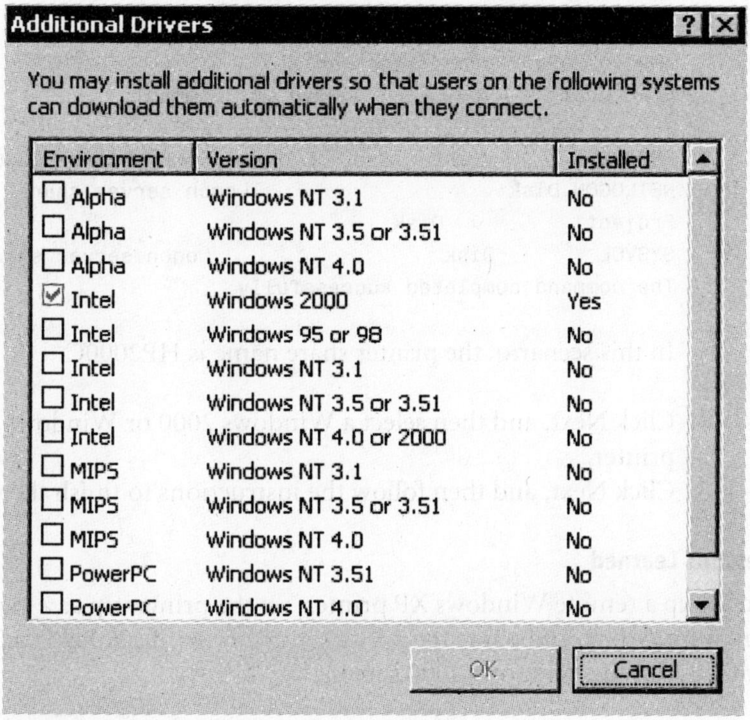

FIGURE 3.10 Installing additional drivers.

Problem Resolution

We install this printer by setting up the printer as a local printer:

1. Click Start, Settings, Control Panel, Printers and Other Hardware, and then click Printers and Faxes.
2. Click Add Printer to start the Add Printer Wizard, and then click Next.
3. Click Local printer, click to clear the "Automatically detect and install" check box, and then click Next.
4. Click "Create a new port," and then click Local Port in the Port type section.
5. In the Port Name box, type the path to the printer in the following format, where server is the name of the print server and *printer* is the name of the printer: `\\server\printer`.
6. If you don't know the name of the printer, open a command prompt by clicking Start and Run and then type `cmd` in the open field and click OK. At the command prompt, type:

```
c:\>net view \\server1
Shared resources at \\server1
Share name   Type        Used as   Comment
------------------------------------------
HP2000C      Print                HP LaserJet 2000C
NETLOGON Disk                   Logon server share
Project1          Disk
SYSVOL       Disk                 Logon server share
The command completed successfully.
```

In this scenario, the printer share name is HP2000C.

7. Click Next, and then select a Windows 2000 or Windows XP driver for the printer.
8. Click Next, and then follow the instructions to finish the wizard.

Lessons Learned

To set up a remote Windows XP printer, set the printer up as a local printer, create a new local port, and name the *port \\server\printer* if a suitable printer driver does not exist on the Windows 2000 server.

Scenario 11 — In Outlook 2002, Typing a Partial Name in the To: Field Defaults to the Wrong User

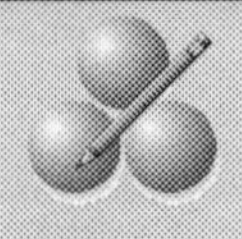

Facts

- Workstation running Windows XP Service Pack 1 and 512 MB memory
- Windows 2000 Server Service with Service Pack 4 and TCP/IP
- Workstation assigned an IP address via DHCP on a Windows 2000 server
- Running Office XP
- Connected to a 10/100 24-port switch

Symptoms

A user creating a new message in Outlook types the first few letters of the recipient's name in the To: field, but an incorrect name is displayed, causing a message to be sent to the incorrect person.

Questions to Ask

Q: Has anything changed? A: Yes, Service Pack 2 for Office XP was just installed.

Q: Was it working before the installation? A: Yes, it was fine yesterday.

Troubleshooting Steps

1. **Search for issues with Office XP Service Pack 2.** Because Service Pack 2 for Office XP was installed just before the problem began, we suspect that the installation possibly reset some of the settings of Outlook 2000. We searched at *www.microsoft.com* and *www.google.com* for possible issues and solutions regarding Service Pack 2 but did not find anything. Outlook 2002 can use different address lists to resolve names in the To: field depending on a user's preferences. We found this Microsoft knowledge base article *http://support.microsoft.com/default.aspx?scid=kb;en-us;296948&Product=ol2002* that explains how to change the order in which address lists are read. In this particular scenario, the user wanted to pull names first from the Global Address List (GAL) and then from the Contacts list. After the address lists are reordered, the user's names are still not coming up in the correct order. Evidently, the names that come up in the bubble after a partial name is typed in the To: field is controlled by something else. We suspect that these names are possibly cached somehow in Outlook 2002.
2. **Search *www.microsoft.com* for an Outlook 2002 name cache.** We searched *www.microsoft.com* for the product name Outlook 2002 and the keywords "name cache." This led us to an article in Microsoft's knowledge base at *http://support.microsoft.com/default.aspx?scid=kb;en-us;287623&Product=ol2002*. Evidently, the addresses that appear in the bubble list are stored in a different file, one ending with the extension NK2.

Problem Resolution

We search the user's hard drive for any files with the NK2 extension. We rename these files and load Outlook 2002. Because the name cache is gone, the user has to send a message to the desired person so that the person's name can be cached again. Alternatively, the user can highlight the incorrect username and press the Delete key to remove that name from the cache. Once the mail is sent to the recipient, the cache pulls the correct person. Most likely, the cause of this problem was that the user sent out a mass mailing just before this problem started, and another user with the same first name was placed in the cache. Once cached, this caused the incorrect name to appear when the user partially typed the intended recipient's name.

Lessons Learned

In this particular scenario, it's easy to assume that a recent change made to the workstation caused the problem. That assumption is a good place to start troubleshooting, but don't assume it will fix the problem. For each general rule, there are always exceptions. If it looks like the recent change did not cause the problem, regroup and look at other possibilities.

Scenario 12 USER IS UNABLE TO INSTALL NAV CORPORATE EDITION ON A WORKSTATION

Facts

- Dell workstation running Windows 2000 Professional Service Pack 4 with 512 MB memory
- Windows 2000 Server service with Service Pack 4 running NAV Corporate Edition 8.6
- Workstation assigned an IP address via DHCP on a Windows 2000 server
- Connected to a 10/100 24-port switch

Symptoms

When attempting to install the NAV Corporate Edition 8.6 on a Windows 2000 workstation, the user receives the error message "An Error has occurred that prevents this installation from completing. This error was received from the WindowsInstaller program msiexec.exe."

Questions to Ask

Q: Has anything changed? A: No. We're just trying to upgrade NAV on the workstation.

Troubleshooting Steps

1. **Try installing in safe mode.** Whenever we roll out an upgrade of NAV Corporate, it seems at least one workstation fails during the installation process. In the past, we have been successful installing NAV on problem machines by using safe mode. Therefore, in this particular scenario, we reboot the machine in safe mode and retry the installation. It failed.
2. **Search *www.symantec.com* for assistance.** We searched *www.symantec.com* and found this link: *http://service1.symantec.com/SUPPORT/ent-security.nsf/d04e6f2f2dfad5de88256c910079502c/6633557e2e0bfcc388256c400071a463?OpenDocument&src=bar_sch_nam*. We try each suggestion, but the last idea in the tech note of running c:\winnt\system32\msiexec.exe /regserver

produced the error message "Unspecified error." After trying each of the items suggested in the tech note, we still receive the same error message.

3. **Check the Windows installer program msiexec.exe.** Because msiexec.exe was at least giving us an error, we suspect that this file might have been corrupted. Running Winver on the workstation reveals that this workstation is running Windows 2000 Professional with Service Pack 4.
4. **Expand Service Pack 4 for Windows 2000 Professional.** By downloading the Network Install for any Windows service pack, we can expand the service pack by typing <service_pack_name> -x. The -x expands the service pack to a selected folder. This is helpful for two reasons: to view the service pack files and to slipstream the service pack files into the \i386 setup directory. For more information on slipstreaming service pack files, refer to Chapter 4. After expanding the Service Pack 4 files and using the expand utility, we compare the file sizes of msiexec.exe from the service pack file and the one located in the c:\winnt\system32 directory. Guess what? The files are different! Now we're on to something! We could try to copy msiexec.exe to the c:\winnt\system32 directory, but chances are if this file is different, other files likely weren't properly updated during the service pack process. Just to be on the safe side, we reapplied Service Pack 4 to this workstation.

Problem Resolution

After reapplying Service Pack 4 and rebooting the workstation, we can successfully install NAV correctly.

Lessons Learned

Initially, it appeared as though NAV was causing the problem because it didn't install properly. In NAV's defense, it was just displaying a symptom of a larger problem with msiexec.exe and a service pack that did not install properly. Although it's a good idea to look for the problem where the message is received, remember that it can be just a symptom of a larger problem. Remember, finding the actual location of the problem is at least half the battle.

CHAPTER SUMMARY

Most workstation problems fall into operating system, hardware, application, or networking categories. Some complex problems may be a combination of more than one problem. Remember to verify the obvious and cut the problem in half to quickly fix workstation problems. Don't forget `ping`, `pathping`, and `ipconfig` to help you solve workstation networking problems. When cabling your network, make sure that the cable vendor fully tests all of the cable runs, provides documentation of each test, and a diagram of drop numbers. This will ensure your cabling is within the 100BaseT specification. Don't feel discouraged if you didn't get any of the troubleshooting scenarios correct; we're focusing on the process rather than the outcome. As you acquire more experience, reread this chapter to see if you can determine the cause of the problem dealt with in each scenario. If you're a troubleshooting newbie, try writing down all of your troubleshooting experiences and review them from time to time. By reviewing your past troubleshooting experiences, you should be able to quickly build critical mass and find it easier to solve future problems.

REVIEW QUESTIONS

1. What's the maximum cable length for a 100BaseT run?
   a. 10 meters.
   b. 1000 meters.
   c. 100 meters.
   d. 320 meters.
   e. There is no maximum length.
2. What pins does Ethernet transmit on by default? (Choose one.)
   a. 1 and 2.
   b. 3 and 4.
   c. 1, 2, 3, and 4.
   d. 1, 2, 3, and 6.
   e. 5, 6, 7, and 8.
3. When faced with a network connection problem on a workstation, what should you determine first?
   a. Search on the Internet for possible solutions.
   b. Determine if the problem is networkwide or workstation specific.
   c. Run a cable scan on the workstation run.
   d. Install the latest service pack on the workstation.
   e. Reload the operating system.
4. When should `ping` be used? (Choose three.)
   a. To determine if a host is reachable.
   b. To trace the path the network packets take on the network.
   c. To verify that a name can resolve to an IP address.
   d. To examine the workstation's IP address configuration.
   e. To see if a problem is cable related.

5. A large number of Temporary files can indicate (choose two):
   a. The workstation does not have the latest service pack.
   b. The workstation often freezes.
   c. The workstation has network connection problems.
   d. The workstation needs more memory.
   e. The operating system should be reinstalled.

4 Windows Server Troubleshooting

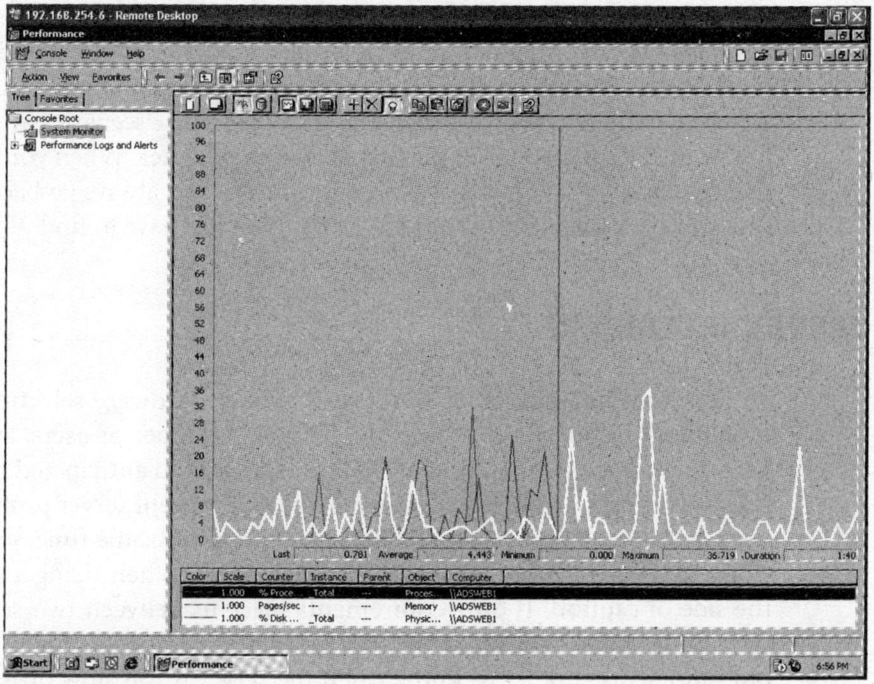

CHAPTER PREVIEW

If you run a server for any length of time, eventually you will have a problem. Hardware failures, power outages, viruses, network traffic, misbehaving applications, and user error can and will cause problems on your server. Out of all of the suggestions in this chapter, if you remember only one, let it be this: Have a good backup strategy! Even if your server catches fire, with a good backup you can always recover from any server problem. In addition to making full daily backups, we have a standing policy to run an incremental backup before we perform any type of hardware upgrade, application installation, or other major change on the server. Always plan for the worse-case scenario: having to rebuild the server from scratch. Proper server configuration and installation will minimize any server problems in the future. Make sure the server is properly sized for your application. Make sure you have enough processor, memory, and disk capacity for your present and future growth needs. The expected life of a server is roughly four to five years, so plan your hardware upgrades accordingly.

In the first part of this chapter, we look at server hardware and software, operating system (OS) configuration, server problems, server troubleshooting, and recovery tools. In the second part, we include real-world server troubleshooting scenarios that we've encountered on our clients' servers. Often, these scenarios are the result of not following the suggestions in the first part of the chapter. When you're stuck in a difficult situation, don't panic. Take a deep breath, and always go back to the troubleshooting basics. The solution is out there—you just have to find it.

SERVER HARDWARE

A stable and reliable server starts with proper hardware selection. After the requirements of the server are clearly defined—number of users, applications, network load, storage requirements, fault tolerance, and anticipated future expansion needs—proper hardware selection is critical to prevent server problems. You don't need a dragster to go to the grocery store, but at the same time, you don't want to ride a skateboard from Los Angeles to New York. When sizing a server, we err on the side of caution. If our requirements place us between two server models, we typically go with the larger server. We never hear complaints that a server is too fast, but our clients sure let us know when the server is too slow or unstable. We recommend staying with name-brand servers, such as Hewlett Packard (HP)/Compaq and Dell, because they are usually more reliable and more people are familiar with them. We also suggest standardizing on one vendor's servers—if you start with Dell, stick with Dell. Often, parts are interchangeable between servers; this gives you the option to steal parts from one machine to install in another in an emergency. Each vendor's servers have their own quirks. By standardizing on one vendor's brand of server, you can become familiar with their technical support procedures, part numbers, BIOS settings, and driver installation routines. For mission-critical servers, consider placing the server on maintenance with short turnaround times to minimize downtime if you have a hardware failure.

Disk Configuration

For any Windows server, we recommend some type of disk redundancy. Hard drive failure is the most common hardware reason for downtime on a server. The following sections review common RAID configurations found in file servers. Hard drive performance has a significant influence on overall file server performance.

RAID 0

Figure 4.1 shows a RAID 0 disk configuration. In this configuration, the server has no hard disk fault tolerance. If the hard drive fails, the server will go down. We don't suggest this configuration on any file server.

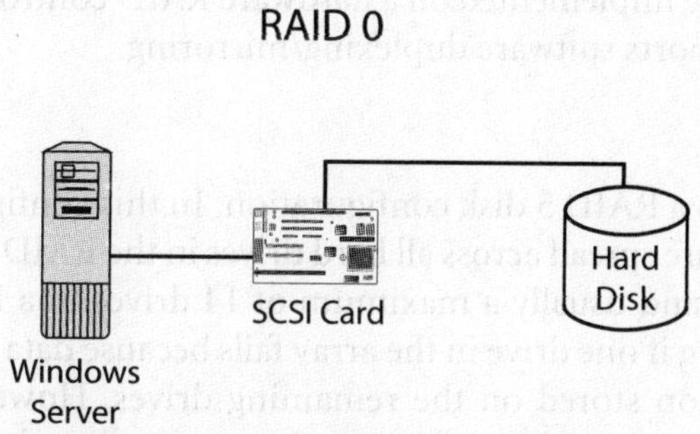

FIGURE 4.1 RAID 0 disk configuration.

RAID 1

Figure 4.2 shows a RAID 1 disk configuration. RAID 1 is also known as *drive mirroring* or *duplexing*. Drive mirroring connects the drives on the same SCSI bus, while drive duplexing connects each drive on a separate SCSI bus. The same information is stored on both drives, so you can continue working in the event of a hard disk failure. The usable space on a duplexed system is half of the total disk space. For example, if you have two 72-GB SCSI drives, your server will have 72 GB of usable space.

If you decide to use this configuration in your server, we strongly suggest placing the primary and mirrored drives on separate SCSI channels. Figure 4.2 shows a single SCSI controller with two SCSI channels (drive duplexing). If the drives share the same SCSI channel, you will take a big performance hit because data must be written serially and not in parallel. With drive mirroring, writes take twice as long and reads are roughly 10-percent faster compared to a RAID 0 configuration. With drive duplexing, writes are 10-percent faster and reads are 50-percent faster than a RAID 0 configuration. The bottom line is: always duplex, never mirror. Ideally,

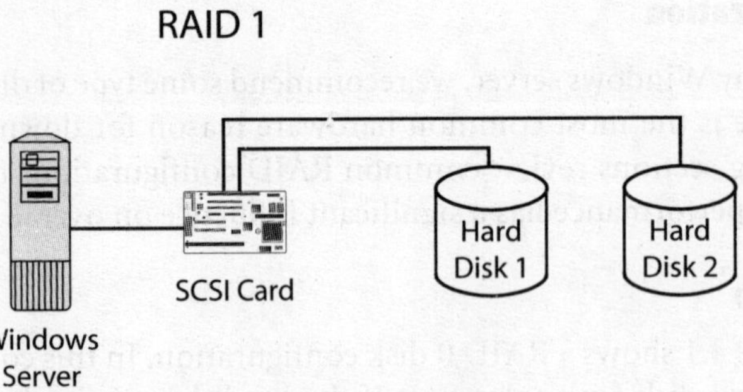

FIGURE 4.2 RAID 1 disk configuration.

RAID 1 should be implemented on a hardware RAID controller; however, the Windows server supports software duplexing/mirroring.

RAID 5

Figure 4.3 shows a RAID 5 disk configuration. In this configuration, data and parity information are spread across all hard drives in the RAID 5 array. You must have at least 3 drives and usually a maximum of 14 drives in a RAID 5 array. You can continue working if one drive in the array fails because data can be rebuilt from the parity information stored on the remaining drives. However, if more than one drive fails in the array at the same time, the array will go down.

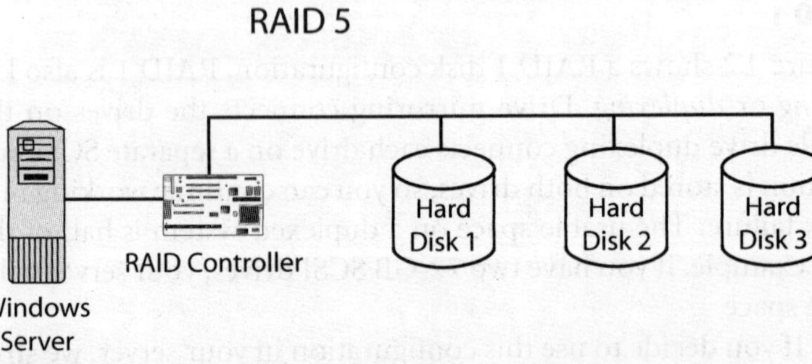

FIGURE 4.3 RAID 5 disk configuration.

The capacity of each drive in the array must be identical. The usable space is the total capacity of the drives minus the capacity of a single drive. For example, if you had a four-drive RAID array using 146-GB SCSI drives, the usable space would be 438 GB ((146 x 4) – 146). RAID 5 arrays are probably the most common drive configuration in today's servers. They offer a good compromise of fault tolerance, performance, and value. Some RAID controllers allow you to designate a drive as a "hot spare"; that is, this drive will automatically take the place of a failed drive in the array. Using a hot spare, you can have two drives simultaneously fail in the array without losing the array.

RAID 1+0

Figure 4.4 shows a RAID 1+0 disk configuration. In this configuration, data are striped and duplexed across two SCSI channels. Multiple hard drives are combined to create one logical drive.

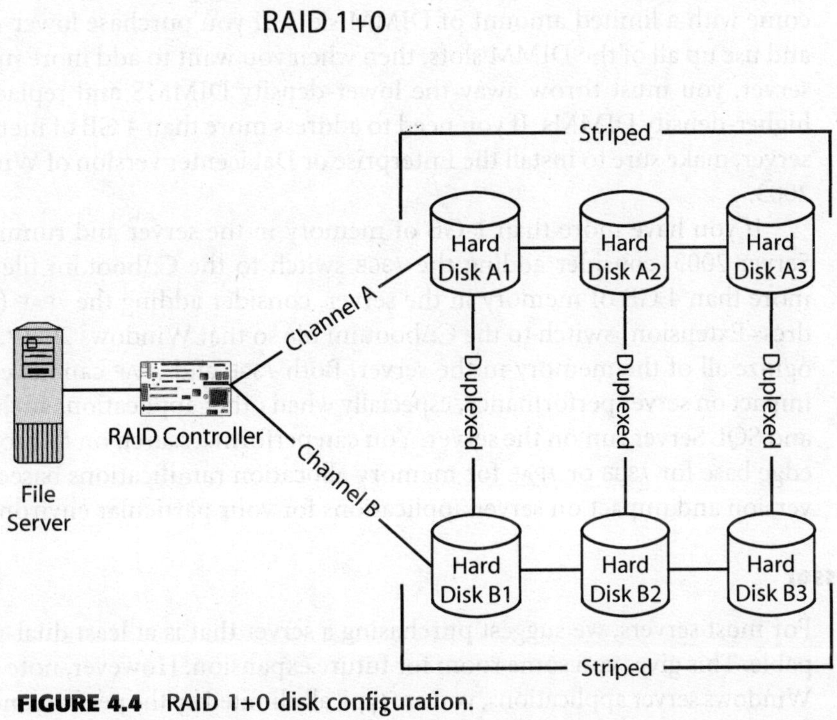

FIGURE 4.4 RAID 1+0 disk configuration.

Assume that each of the drives in Figure 4.4 is 72 GB. To implement a RAID 1+0 configuration, you need six 72-GB hard drives. This will give you 216 GB of usable space. RAID 1+0 is usually configured on the RAID hardware controller. After the configuration, the OS sees the RAID 1+0 array as one 216-GB hard disk.

This configuration is the fastest, most fault tolerant, and most expensive of all of the RAID configurations. Half of the drives can fail in the array and it will stay up. Short of a storage area network (SAN), this drive configuration is the best performing disk array you can install in a server. Unlike RAID 5, you can mix and match drive sizes as long as the duplexed drive pairs are the same size. For example, drive pairs for hard disk1 could be 36 GB, drive pairs for hard disk2 could be 72 GB, and drive pairs for hard disk3 could be 146 GB.

Memory

For Windows 2000/2003, we suggest a minimum of 1 GB of memory. When selecting a server, always check the maximum amount of memory the server will support, for future expansion. When purchasing Dual Inline Memory Module (DIMM) chips, we always try to purchase the highest-density DIMM chips that the server will support. This gives us room for future expansion. Most current servers come with a limited amount of DIMM slots. If you purchase lower-density chips and use up all of the DIMM slots, then when you want to add more memory to the server, you must throw away the lower-density DIMMS and replace them with higher-density DIMMs. If you need to address more than 4 GB of memory on your server, make sure to install the Enterprise or Datacenter version of Windows Server 2003.

If you have more than 1 GB of memory in the server and running Windows Server 2003, consider adding the `/3GB` switch to the C:\boot.ini file. If you have more than 4 GB of memory in the server, consider adding the `/PAE` (Physical Address Extension) switch to the C:\boot.ini file so that Windows 2000/2003 will recognize all of the memory in the server. Both `/3GB` and `/PAE` can have a significant impact on server performance, especially when other applications such as Exchange and SQL Server run on the server. You can perform a search on Microsoft's knowledge base for `/3GB` or `/PAE` for memory allocation ramifications based on your OS version and impact on server applications for your particular environment.

Processor

For most servers, we suggest purchasing a server that is at least dual-processor capable. This gives you some room for future expansion. However, note that for most Windows server applications, you are typically limited by the performance of the hard disks and not by the processor speed on the server. Exceptions to this are SQL Server, Terminal Server, or any other server application that is processor intensive. On a properly running file and print server, the processor utilization is relatively low, usually averaging below 20 percent. Table 4.1 lists the processor and memory support for the different versions of Windows Server.

Table 4.1 Summary of Processor and Memory Support for Different Versions of Windows Server

Operating System	Maximum Processors	Maximum Memory
Windows NT 4.0	4	4 GB
Windows NT 4.0 Enterprise	8	4 GB
Windows 2000 Standard	4	4 GB
Windows 2000 Advanced	8	8 GB
Windows 2000 Datacenter	32	32 GB
Windows 2003 Standard	4	4 GB
Windows 2003 Enterprise	8	32 GB with the 32-bit version
		64 GB with the 64-bit version
Windows 2003 Datacenter	64	64 GB with the 32-bit version
		512 GB with the 64-bit version

Uninterruptible Power Supply (UPS)

We consider a UPS a mandatory piece of equipment for any server. If the server suddenly loses power, data can be lost or corrupted. The first time a UPS prevents this from happening, it will pay for itself. Make sure to select a UPS that supports a graceful shutdown of the OS in case the power goes out when you're not around.

Most UPS software can test the condition of the battery on a regular basis to make sure it can handle the server load. It's a bad time to find out when you have a power outage that the UPS battery is bad. Battery life on a UPS is typically three to five years.

We suggest a UPS with a rating of 1000 to 1500 volt/amps (VA) for most small to mid-range servers. The higher the VA rating on the UPS, the longer the runtime. For installations with diesel generators, UPS are still needed to provide power while the generator starts up. Make sure to plug the monitor as well as any other server devices into the UPS.

SERVER SOFTWARE

At the very least, you need an OS to run on the server, but don't forget other critical packages that we feel are necessary to run on the server. At a minimum, this includes anti-virus software and backup software. We will not put a server into production without having these critical components installed.

Operating System

Of course, you must install an OS on the server to make it work. Make sure your requirements are clearly laid out before selecting the server hardware and software.

Disk Partitions

This is more an issue of style, but we like to set up two disk partitions on a Windows server. If we have a disk size of 72 GB, we'll typically create a C: drive of 10 to 20 GB and leave the rest of the disk for the D: drive. This usually gives us enough room to install the OS, swap file, and applications on the C: drive and leave the D: drive for data files. Of course, if your server has a lot of memory, you might want to create a larger C: drive, because Windows tends to create a larger swap file when there is more memory installed in the server.

By keeping the OS separate from the data, you can install other services such as Remote Installation Services (RIS) in the future. RIS allows you to clone workstation images and push these images down to other workstations. It's very handy when you have to set up a lot of workstations at the same time that have the identical or similar hardware configuration. RIS requires that the workstation images are stored on a separate partition than the host OS. It's similar to Symantec's Ghost, but it is built into the Windows 2000/2003 OS.

By separating the OS from the data, you have a greater chance of recovering data in case the C: drive becomes corrupted. We've run into situations where a C: drive becomes corrupted, but the D: drive is still okay, and we were able to rescue the data on the D: drive. If you store both the OS and data on the same partition and C: becomes damaged, you are usually out of luck.

i386 Setup Files and Service Pack Integration

Whenever we install a new Windows 2000/2003 server, we copy the i386 setup files to the hard drive. Then, when new services are installed on the server, the setup files are readily available and we don't have to search for the Windows CD-ROM. Anytime the server is service packed, we slipstream the service pack files into the i386 directory. Slipstreaming integrates the service pack with the i386 setup files.

To slipstream the service pack files into the i386 directory:

1. Extract the service pack files by typing <*service_pack_name*> -x. You will be prompted for a location to which to extract the files.
2. Use update to slipstream the files. In the <*service_pack_directory*>\i386\update directory, type update –s:<*i386_ file_ location*>. This is a little tricky because the i386 file location is actually one directory level up from where the i386 files are located. For example, if the i386 files are located in C:\i386, you would type update –s:c: because C: is one level up from C:\i386.

By slipstreaming the service pack files, you avoid the irritating prompts that ping pong back and forth from the i386 to the current service pack location when you install new services on the server. We copy the i386 files to every server so that they are readily available if the server experiences an OS problem. If we have to run the Recovery Console, we have convenient access to the i386 setup files in case they are needed.

Terminal Server in Remote Administration Mode

One of the nicest features in Windows 2000/2003 is the Terminal Server in remote administration mode. This allows you to remotely control a server from any other computer that has Terminal Services Client installed on it. If you have to manage a remote server across a WAN, this is a great feature.

To install Terminal Server in remote administration mode on a Windows 2000 server:

1. Click Start, Settings, Control Panel, and Add/Remove Programs.
2. Click Add/Remove Windows Components.
3. Scroll down, select Terminal Services, and click Next. When prompted, select Terminal Services in Remote Administration Mode. This allows two users to connect to the server for remote administration. If you do not select the remote administration mode, you must provide licensing services for Terminal Server.

To install Terminal Services on a Windows 2003 server:

1. Right-click My Computer and select Properties.
2. Click the Remote tab.
3. Check the section "Allow users to connect remotely to this computer" in the Remote Desktop. If you want to assist other users from this computer, check the section "Turn on remote assistance and allow invitations to be sent from this computer" in the Remote Assistance.

Terminal Server makes it extremely easy to remotely administer a Windows server; however, it does have some risks. By default, Terminal Server communicates on port TCP 3389. *Never* open this port on a firewall, even for a specific IP address or range. We view this as a serious security risk. If you need remote Terminal Server access to a server, establish a virtual private network (VPN) tunnel to the network and then start your Terminal Server session. If you do not establish a VPN, it makes it too easy for hacker to trap Terminal Server packets as they travel across the Internet because they are not encrypted. Even if the packets are encrypted, a hacker can compromise a remote computer accessing the Terminal server and gain access to your network. If a hacker obtains a username and password, he can access your server, install a few back doors, and wreak havoc on your network. At this point, the server belongs to the hacker and not to you. The only way to ensure that all of the hacking programs are removed is to format the hard drive and reinstall the OS from scratch. It's not worth the risk. If you need remote Terminal Server access, establish a VPN first.

Domain Controllers

If you have more than one server, we suggest making both servers domain controllers (DCs) and DNS servers. This gives you greater fault tolerance for Active Directory (AD) authentication and DNS services in case one of the servers goes down. If you have a WAN, with multiple users at the remote sites, consider placing a DC at the remote location to speed up the AD authentication process and reduce WAN traffic. If you are using the single AD domain model, make the remote DC a Global Catalog (GC) server. A GC contains all of the global information about the domain. By creating more than one GC server, you increase the fault tolerance of AD and improve the AD authentication across the WAN. To make a DC a GC:

1. On the DC you want to make a GC, click Start, Programs, Administrative Tools, and Active Directory Sites and Services.
2. Click Sites, *<sitename>*, and Servers, *<server_name>*.
3. Right-click NTDS settings, and select Properties.
4. On the General tab, select the Global Catalog check box and restart the DC.

This process is shown in Figure 4.5.

DNS Configuration

Windows 2000/2003 uses DNS for name resolution. In our experience, DNS is more stable than WINS as long as it's properly configured. An improper DNS configuration in a Windows 2000/2003 network is one of the most common errors we see with Windows 2000/2003. Common symptoms include workstations and servers that

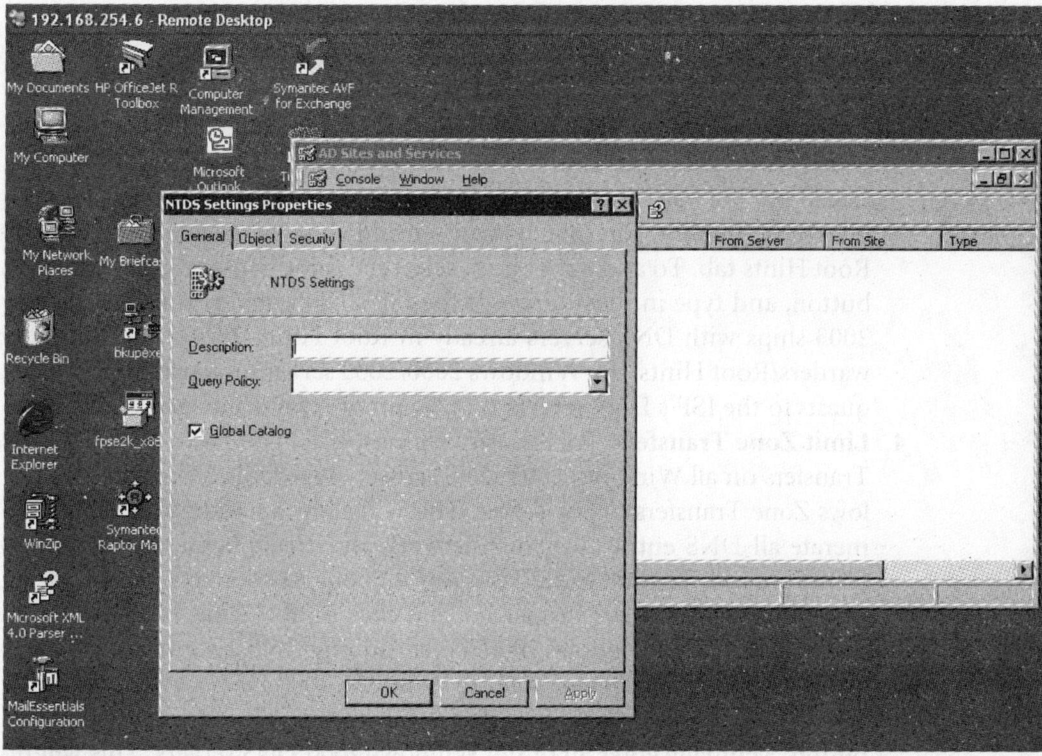

FIGURE 4.5 Making a DC a GC server.

disappear and reappear randomly on the network, difficulty logging in to the network, and basic network instability. If you set up DNS with Windows 2000/2003 as you did with Windows NT, you will have major problems.

To properly set up DNS on Windows 2000/2003:

1. **Make sure DNS is installed on the server.** If it is not installed, click on Start, Settings, Control Panel, Add/Remove Programs. In the left column, click on Add/Remove Window Components. Scroll down and highlight Network Services, and then click on Details. Select the DNS and click OK. If this server is configured as an AD DC, DNS should already be installed.
2. **For domains without child domains, make sure the DNS server is installed in the root.** Open the DNS manager by clicking on Start, Programs, Administrative Tools, DNS. You should see your server with your AD name listed under the Forward Lookup Zones. If you see a domain with a ".." name, then your server is not in the root. Typically, for a single AD domain you should have at least one server in the root. If your server is not in

the root directory, you will not be able to configure forwarders/root hints, which is crucial to proper DNS setup.

3. **Configure forwarders/root hints.** Right-click on your DNS server, select Properties, and then click on the Forwarders tab. Check the Enable Forwarders box and enter your ISP's DNS servers in the IP address box. Click OK. If the Forwarders check box is grayed out, your DNS server is probably not in the root. Alternately, you can add your ISP's DNS servers to the Root Hints tab. To add a root hint, select the Root Hints tab, click the Add button, and type in the address of the ISP's DNS server. Windows Server 2003 ships with DNS servers already in Root Hints. By configuring Forwarders/Root Hints, the Windows 2000/2003 server forwards any DNS requests to the ISP's DNS servers that it cannot resolve internally.
4. **Limit Zone Transfers.** For security reasons, it's a good idea to limit Zone Transfers on all Windows 2000 DNS servers. By default, Windows 2000 allows Zone Transfers to any server. This will allow a hacker to quickly enumerate all DNS entries on your network and create bogus entries if it is compromised. To limit Zone Transfers for your AD domain, right-click on your AD domain, select Properties, and click on the Zone Transfers tab. If you only have one Windows 2000 server running DNS, clear the Allow Zone Transfers box. If you have multiple Windows 2000 DNS servers, check the Allow Zone Transfers box and select "Only to the following servers" option button. Manually enter all of the Windows 2000 DNS servers. This will restrict Zone Transfers to authorized Windows 2000 DNS servers.
5. **Change the Windows 2000/2003 DNS server.** Right-click on My Network Places, Select Properties, Local Area Connection, and Properties. Click on Internet Protocol (TCP/IP) and click on Properties. In the Preferred DNS server, enter the IP address of the server itself. If you have another Windows 2000 DNS server, enter its IP address in the Alternate DNS server field. You might think it's a good idea to use your ISP's DNS server as an alternate DNS server. Do not do this! This will cause problems if the Windows 2000 DNS server does not respond immediately; the server will use your ISP's DNS server to try to find local Windows 2000 resources. This will cause intermittent problems with name resolution as the server flips between itself and your ISP's DNS servers. Make sure to change the DNS configuration for every server running on the network.
6. **Reset DNS.** Open a command window and enter:

```
ipconfig /flushdns
ipconfig /registerdns
```

7. **Update DHCP.** If you are running DHCP, change the DNS servers to point to the internal Windows 2000/2003 servers instead of the ISP's DNS servers.

> You can force an update of the DNS information by reducing the lease time of the IP addresses. If you are in a single server environment and you take the Windows server down, you will be unable to surf the Internet because the workstations will not be able to name resolve. To work around this, set up another Windows 2000 server running DNS as a backup, or temporarily change the DNS entries on the workstation to the ISP's DNS server until the Windows 2000 server comes back up.

Workstations and servers now use the internal DNS servers for name resolution. If the DNS query is a local request, it is directly handled by the internal DNS server. If the request cannot be resolved locally, the query is forwarded to the ISP's DNS server for resolution either by using forwarders or root hints. This ensures that local computers are resolved using the internal DNS server rather than an ISP's DNS server.

IP Addresses and DHCP Servers

Most likely, you'll want to install Dynamic Host Configuration Protocol (DHCP) on one of your Windows servers to automatically assign IP addresses to workstations. When you create a scope, make sure to reserve enough IP addresses for devices that require a fixed IP address. For a 192.168.1.0 255.255.255.0 network, we typically start the DHCP range at 192.168.1.51, and reserve the first 50 addresses for manually assigned IP addresses. It's not a bad idea to create a text file or Excel spreadsheet that tracks all of the manually assigned IP addresses. The following devices should have manually assigned IP addresses:

- Servers
- Printers
- Routers
- Firewalls
- Switches
- Video Conference Units
- Any other device that requires a fix IP address

Although the preceding list is pretty obvious, we commonly see printers that are dynamically assigned an IP address. Everything works fine, until the server is rebooted and the printer IP address changes. Suddenly no one can print, and we get a call.

We suggest purchasing a label printer, and labeling each device (server, router, firewall, printer, etc.) that has a fixed IP address so you can quickly determine the IP address of the device without going into any management interface.

Virus Protection

We consider virus protection mandatory for any network installation. We suggest using a virus package that is designed to work in a network environment like Symantec's Anti-Virus™ Corporate Edition. These packages are designed to work in networked environments, and have central virus management and pattern distribution features. If you are running Exchange or other internal e-mail server, it is very important to get a virus scanner that will scan e-mail messages and attachments in addition to the workstation and server virus protection. With most new viruses spreading via e-mail worms, it's important to train your users not to open messages and attachments that look suspicious or are from unknown users. Of course, make sure the patterns are updated on a regular basis—the virus software is only as good as its latest pattern. We suggest checking for pattern updates at least daily, or more often when a new virus is released. The first time that the virus software catches a virus or prevents it from spreading, it will pay for itself. Older virus software often cannot catch the newer viruses, so it's important to stay current with the latest virus software as well as the patterns. Consider placing the virus software on annual support so you receive the latest version of the anti-virus software.

Server Backup

A good backup strategy is vital for a smooth-running network. Don't get a false sense of security just because you have disk fault tolerance built into your servers. If a user accidentally deletes a file or a file becomes corrupted, it will be nicely duplicated across all of the hard drives. We suggest full daily backups on all servers and key workstations. We suggest at least a two-week rotation of tapes with a monthly archive of a backup. You might not discover that a file is corrupted for more than one week. If you overwrite a backup tape weekly, you eliminate the possibility of restoring an uncorrupted version of the file. We suggest installing the tape drive directly on the server and using server-based backup software like Veritas' Backup Exec or Computer Associates' ARCserve for server backup. A less desirable and less expensive alternative to full daily backups is a full backup over the weekend, with differential backups during the week. Differential backups do not reset the archive bit on a file when it's backed up, so each differential backup backs up all files since the last full backup. This is important during a restore, because you only have to restore from the last full backup, and then the latest differential backup.

We do not recommend incremental backups, because too many things can go wrong that can result in data loss. Consider the following scenario. It's Friday afternoon and you're looking forward to that out-of-town trip you've been planning for the last four months. You suddenly get a phone call that no one can access the server. You rush into the server room to find all of the hard drives smoking in the server. However, you planned ahead and have a four-hour response for your server.

You make a call to the server vendor, and the hard drives arrive one hour later. You have a backup strategy of full backups on weekends with incremental backups Monday through Friday. You install the hard drives, install the OS, install the tape backup software, and start the restore from the last full backup. So far, so good. As the tape is restoring, you suddenly remember that you accidentally overwrote the incremental backup from Monday. By not having Monday's incremental backup, you cannot restore any of the incremental backups from Tuesday, Wednesday, and Thursday without risking data integrity problems on the server. Instead of restoring the server as of Thursday night, you can only restore the server as of Monday morning. Your company has just lost an entire week's worth of work, because of a simple mistake on your part. Hardware has the uncanny ability to fail at the worse times, in the worst situations. Make sure you do not fall into this trap—stay away from incremental backups! It's bad enough you have to cancel your out-of-town trip, but now you might be looking for a new job. Some people claim that their company does not have the budget to purchase a bigger tape drive. It's your job to educate management that they can't afford *not* to have a good backup plan. If they still refuse to purchase the tape drive, make sure that you get it in writing, so if (when) something does goes wrong you can gently remind them that you predicted that this would happen and they chose to ignore it.

If you store any of the tapes on-site, make sure they are in a data-approved fire safe. At least one of the tapes should be taken off-site weekly, in case of fire or theft. Insurance can cover the replacement cost of the hardware, but it cannot recover any lost data for your company.

When sizing a tape drive for the server, consider purchasing a tape drive that has a capacity equal to or greater than the hard drive capacity on the server. That way, you can back up the entire server on one tape. Be aware that many tape drive manufacturers specify their tape drive capacity assuming a 2:1 compression ratio on the tape. Often, this higher number is a "marketing" number, because you typically do not get the advertised storage capacity on the tape drive. For example, HP sells a DAT 72 tape drive that assumes a 2:1 compression ratio and a capacity of 72 GB. In reality, expect roughly 39 GB to 45 GB of backup capacity with this tape drive, unless your file server contains mostly text files. For companies with larger backup requirements, consider multiple tape drives, autochangers, or tape libraries as part of your backup strategy. You can never be too careful when it comes to tape backup. According to the National Archives & Records Administration in Washington, 93 percent of the companies that lost their data center for 10 days or more filed for bankruptcy within one year. We find that the companies that have the best backup practices are ones that have suffered some type of data loss in the past. Learn from other company's disasters, and back up your data!

Anytime you open, install a service pack, or perform a major upgrade on the server, make sure you at least get an incremental backup of the server. This is the only situation where we feel an incremental backup is okay. If you do perform an incremental backup and not a full backup, make sure you have access to the latest full backup. That way, if anything goes wrong, you have a fallback position to quickly restore the server.

SERVER PROBLEM CATEGORIES

Most server problems tend to fall into the following categories.

Hardware problems. In our experience, disk failures are the most common hardware problem on a server, followed by power supplies, memory, motherboard, and processor failures. Keep this in mind when you suspect a hardware problem on a server. The server manufacturer's hardware diagnostics can be helpful when troubleshooting a hardware problem; however, they can often report that a hardware component is fine, when in fact it has failed. This is especially true with intermittent failures. When troubleshooting a suspected hardware problem, make sure that you have the latest firmware and drivers installed on the server before contacting technical support. One of the first questions they will ask you is, "Do you have the latest drivers?" By installing them ahead of time, you save everyone's time.

Operating system problems. Symptoms of OS problems are instability, poor performance, and blue screens. OS problems are usually server specific. We usually wait a few months or so after a service pack is released before installing it on a server, unless the service pack addresses an immediate security threat or other major concern. We monitor newsgroups and other Web forums to identify issues that others have found with a service pack release. Before installing a service pack, make sure that you have a current backup of your server. Ideally, you should test the service pack in a test lab before installing it on all of your servers. If you can't afford a test lab, at least consider a phased approach when rolling out a new service pack.

Application problems. Sometimes, a misbehaved or corrupted application running on the server can cause performance problems, or server instability. If you suspect that an application or service is causing a problem, stop/unload the application and see if the server stabilizes.

Network problems. Beaconing hubs, switches, bad cabling, and bad network cards can cause serious performance problems on the server. Network problems typically affect an entire network segment or group of computers and are usually not isolated to one server. If you suspect a network problem, take a quick glance at your switches and hubs. Beaconing hubs and switches usually generate a significant amount of network traffic. If your switches have management, check the switch for fragmented packets and abnormally high traffic. The Network Monitor that comes with Windows NT/2000/2003 is a useful tool when diagnosing network and protocol problems.

SERVER TROUBLESHOOTING TOOLS

When you have problems with your server, consider using one of the following tools to isolate the problem. Remember that problem isolation is key to resolving the problem. The Performance Monitor can provide clues to server performance issues. Get familiar with the Performance Monitor before you have to use it. You don't want to bump up against a learning curve with the Performance Monitor, while trying to fix a problem at the same time.

Server Event Viewer

The Windows Event Viewer is a good place to start when troubleshooting any server problem. You can get to the Event Viewer by clicking on Start, Programs, Administrative Tools, Event Viewer. We suggest reviewing the Event Viewer messages on a regular basis, so you get used to typical messages generated by the server. This will give you a good "feel" for what is normal and what is not. Whenever we log in to a server, we make an effort to check the Event Viewer, just to make sure there are no critical errors on the server. Depending on the logging level of the server, the amount of messages the server generates can become overwhelming. For networks with multiple servers, consider monitoring software that notifies you of critical errors via e-mail. This allows you to become proactive in your server management without the burden of checking the event logs on a regular basis. When troubleshooting specific error messages, Microsoft's knowledge base is an excellent source for determining the cause of specific server events. Another good resource is searching *www.google.com* or other search engines for the event error message text and error number.

Task Manager

The Windows Task Manager is a good resource for troubleshooting Windows performance problems. Bring up the Task Manager by right-clicking on the Windows task bar and select Task Manager. If the server is running slowly, check the CPU utilization on the Performance tab. If the CPU utilization stays above 50 percent for more than a minute, you might have a problem, unless the server is busy running a SQL Stored Procedure, virus scan, or backup. Click on the Processes tab and on

CPU to sort the processes by CPU utilization. The System Idle Process should take up most of the CPU cycles, but you can view any other processes on the server that are taking up CPU cycles. If the server is running slowly, you can try killing a process that is hogging CPU cycles. Note that this might make the server unstable, so we suggest troubleshooting this type of problem after hours. If the server instantly speeds up, you know that the process you just killed has something to do with the poor server performance.

Performance Monitor

The Performance Monitor is a good tool for tracking down performance issues. It can monitor almost every aspect of server performance, including processor, disk, application, network, and services. Use it to help you isolate and diagnose server problems. We consider the Performance Monitor a great "level two" troubleshooting tool—one to help you narrow down a performance problem on the server or used as a server optimization tool. For example, you might notice poor performance on your server, but what will speed it up? More memory, faster processor, faster hard disks, Gigabit Ethernet upgrade, or all four? The Performance Monitor can help you answer these questions. It can determine what upgrades will give you the most bang for the buck, or help determine the optimum configuration with your existing hardware. You should become familiar with the Performance Monitor before you have to use it. That way, you can leverage this excellent tool to its fullest extent.

When to Use

When you have a performance issue on the server, use the Performance Monitor to determine where the bottleneck on the server resides. Historical Performance Monitor captures can identify trends on server usage. This will allow you to become proactive and address any performance issues on the server before users notice a decrease in performance.

Troubleshooting Server Performance

Let's suppose that you notice that your server is running slower than usual. Taking a quick glance at the server, you notice that the hard disk's access lights are on solid. Just by this simple observation, you notice that the server is probably disk bound, or is it? High disk utilization can be a symptom of any one of the following:

Disk hardware problems—disk or SCSI transmission errors. Disk hardware problems can cause excessive reads and writes on a disk. Usually, hardware errors of this type are accompanied by error messages in the System Event Viewer.

Misbehaved application(s) or virus. A misbehaved application or virus can cause excessive disk access, either by causing a memory leak that in turn causes excessive page file access, or by a self-replicating virus that causes excessive disk access.

Not enough memory in the server. Inadequate memory on the server can cause excessive page file access. Ideally, a server should only use the physical memory on the server with minimal page file access.

Excessive page file access. This can be caused by inadequate memory on the server, or by allocating too much memory to applications running on the server such as SQL Server or Exchange.

Slow/overworked disks. Assuming that the server has adequate Processor and Memory resources, the server really could be disk bound. Defragmenting the disk, adding an additional RAID array, replacing the current disks with faster disks, or moving to a SAN may be solutions for your disk performance problem.

This is why we call the Performance Monitor a great "level two" troubleshooting tool. It can help you narrow down the root cause of the server performance problem. Proper use of the Performance Monitor can help you determine the best strategy to improve your server's performance. Each of these scenarios can be diagnosed by using the Performance Monitor.

Establish Server Baselines

By using the Logging feature in the Performance Monitor, you can establish baseline data for any server. This baseline data is extremely useful when troubleshooting a server performance problem. Is it "normal" to have the processor utilization at 60 percent? Did the service pack we just applied cause a problem with a network card driver? Is the recent increase in network traffic a trend, or just a blip on the radar? A proactive approach to server management can help you identify bottlenecks and address them, before any users notice the performance hit.

Set Alerts and Thresholds

The Performance Monitor has the capability to set alerts and thresholds for any item that it can monitor. For example, you can be notified when the disk space on your main server drops below a certain percentage. This allows you to address the situation before a critical file becomes corrupted and takes down the server.

How to Use

The next section explains how to use the Performance Monitor. In general don't leave the Performance Monitor running unless you establishing some baseline numbers. The Performance Monitor itself can place a significant load on the server, especially if you are tracking multiple counters.

Using the Performance Monitor

To start the Performance Monitor, click on Start, Programs Administrative Tools, Performance (see Figure 4.6).

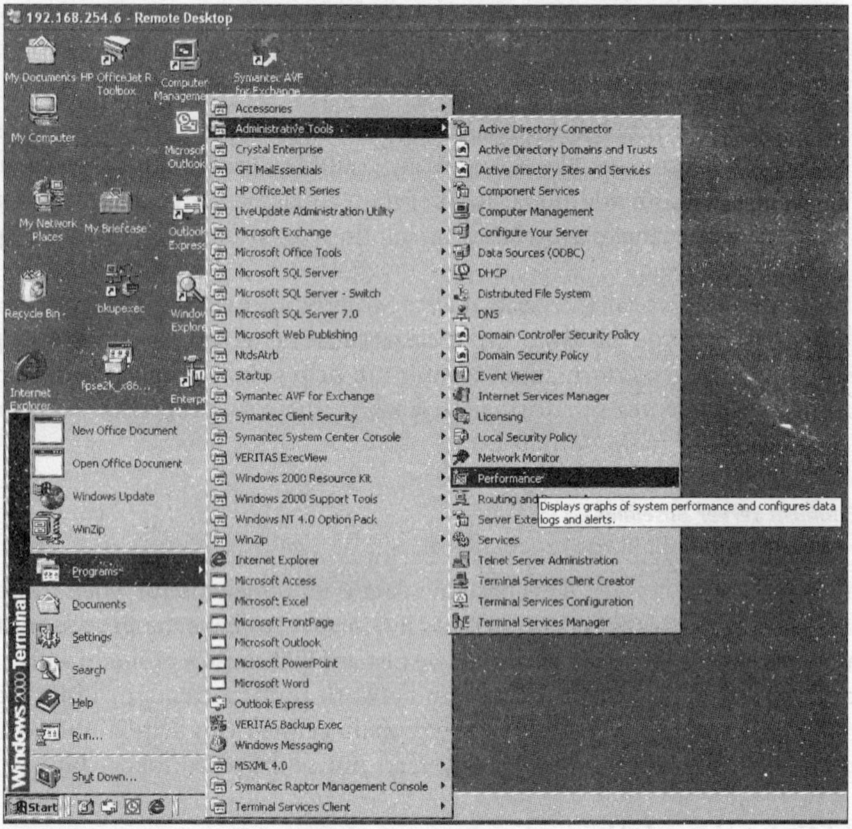

FIGURE 4.6 Starting the Performance Monitor.

When you start the Performance Monitor, the screen in Figure 4.7 will appear.

To add counters to the Performance Monitor, simply click on the "+" from the icons at the top of the screen. This allows you to add any parameter that you want to monitor. When the Add Counters window appears, click the Explain button to display a description of the monitored parameter. In Figure 4.8, we're adding the % Processor Time from the Performance Object Processor.

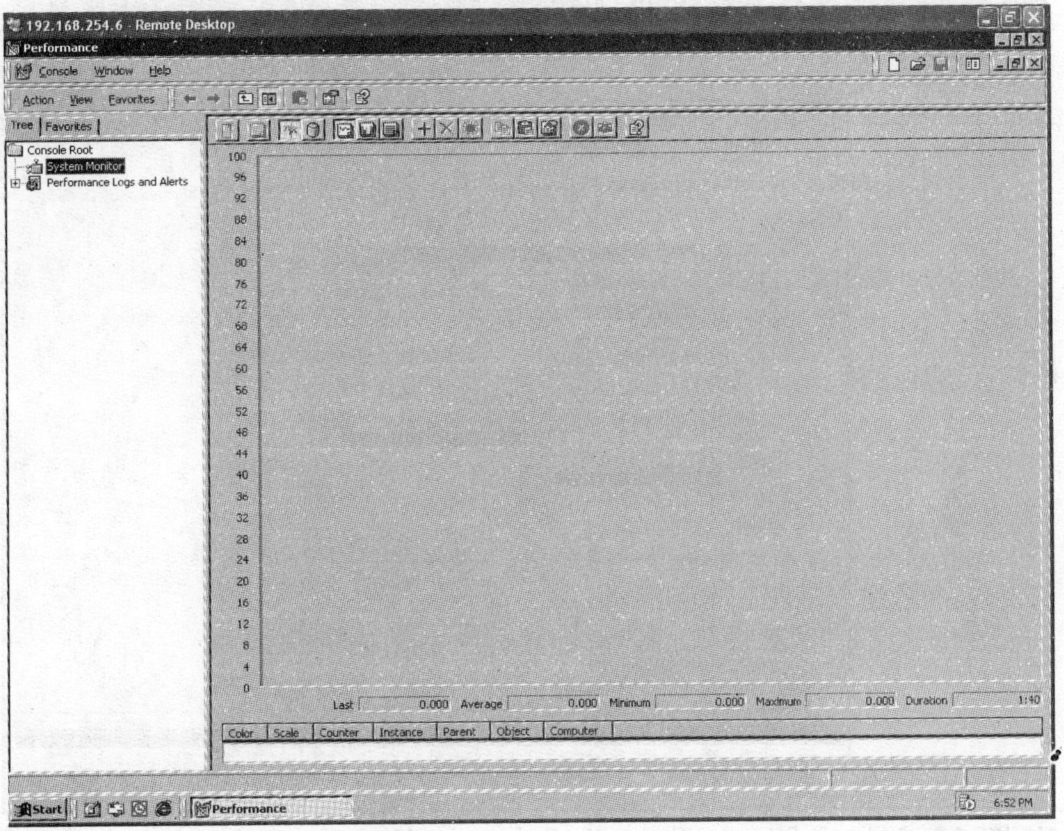

FIGURE 4.7 Performance Monitor screen.

When you click the Add button, the selected parameter will be added to the Performance Monitor. For this example, we will add the following parameters:

Performance Object	***Counter***	***Instances***
Processor	% Processor Time	_Total
Memory	Pages/Sec	
Physical Disk	% Disk Time	_Total

After the parameters are added, click the Close button to close the Add Counters window. Often, when you add multiple counters it's difficult to tell what line corresponds with a given parameter. Clicking on the "Light Bulb" icon to the right of the "X" icon will highlight in white the parameter selected at the bottom of the Performance Monitor. In Figure 4.9, the screen below the % Processor Time is dis-

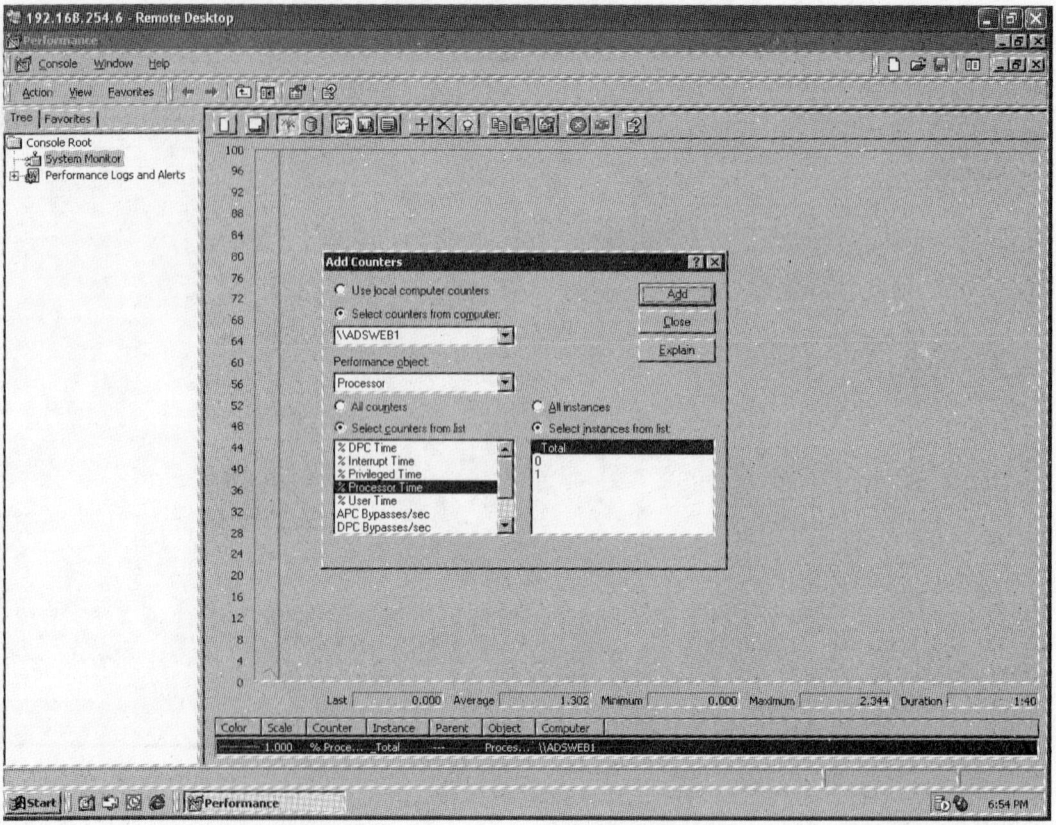

FIGURE 4.8 Adding % Processor Time to the Performance Monitor.

played in white, because this parameter is selected at the bottom of the Performance Monitor.

You can save your monitoring parameters by clicking on Console, Save As, and assigning a name to the Monitoring Configuration.

What to Monitor

When you use the Performance Monitor, we suggest monitoring a number of server parameters. The specific combination of parameters depends on the nature of the problem you are troubleshooting.

Memory

There are several critical items to monitor when troubleshooting memory issues on your server. You should look at several of these indicators to determine if you need to add more memory in the server, increase the page file size, or reallocate more/less memory to an application running on the server. A quick way to determine the

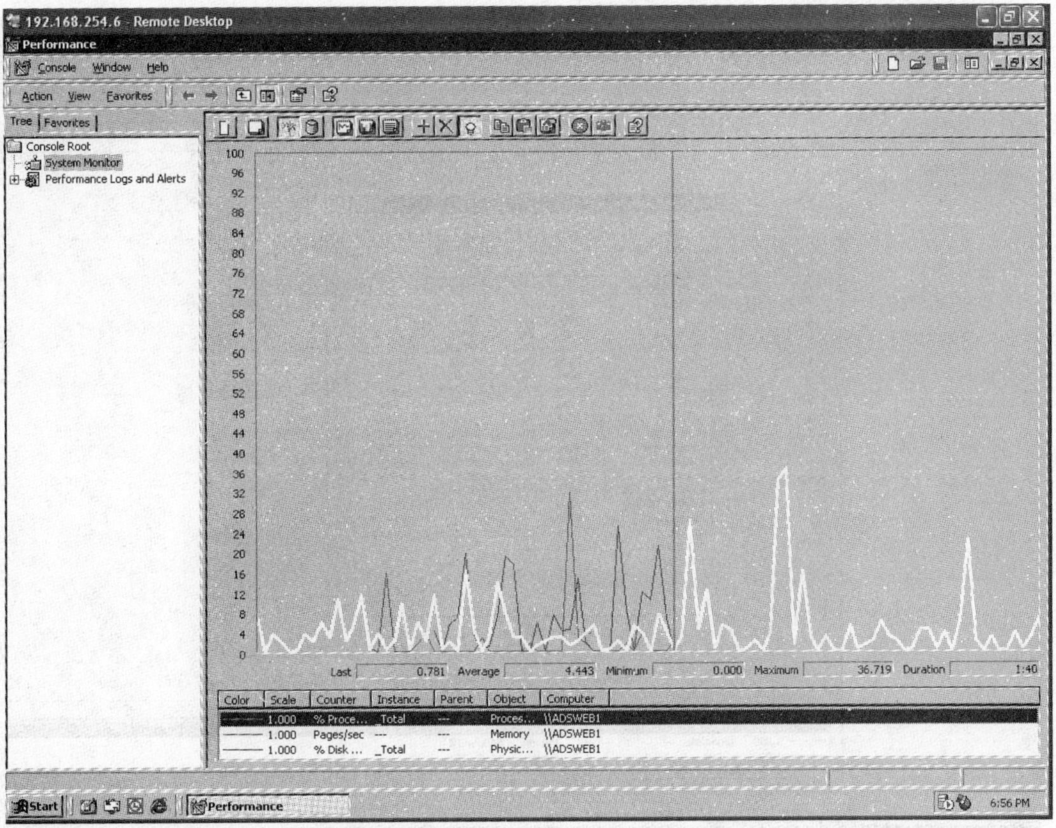

FIGURE 4.9 Performance Monitor with % Processor Time, Pages/Sec, and % Disk Time.

amount of memory used by an application is to pull up the Task Manager, click on the Processes tab, and sort the Processes by Memory Usage by clicking on the Mem Usage tab (see Figure 4.10).

Pages/Sec in the Memory Performance Object. This is the pages/sec written to or read from the hard disk to resolve hard page faults. A hard page fault occurs when information is required that is not available in memory and must be retrieved from the physical disk. This counter should average below 25 pages/sec, although on a busy server it might be as high as 50 pages/sec. Check the Available Bytes in the Memory Performance Object before concluding that you need more memory in the server.

Pages/Sec (Memory) * Avg. Disk sec/Transfer (Physical Disk). The product of these two counters should be below 10 percent. These counters measure the amount of time that the disk is used to access the paging file.

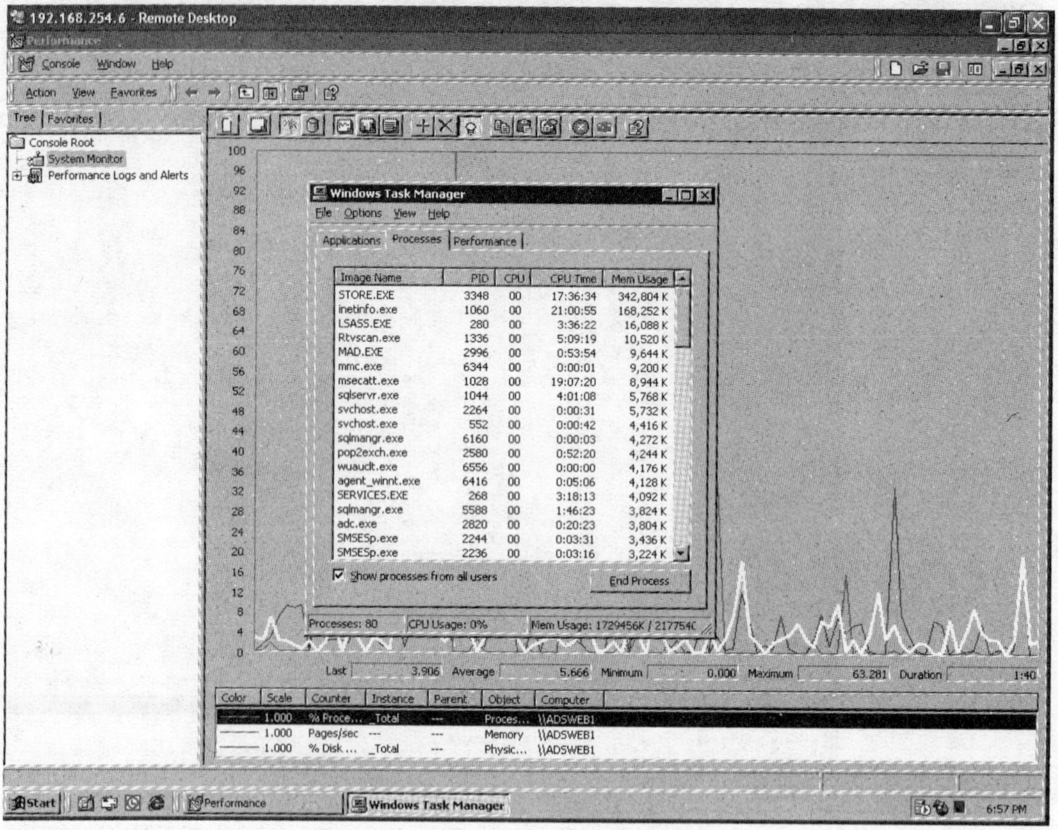

FIGURE 4.10 Sorting current server processes by memory usage.

Pool Nonpaged Failures in the Server Performance Object. This should be zero or close to zero. Any value in this counter typically indicates that the server needs more memory.

Pool Pages Failures in the Server Performance Object. This indicates that either physical memory or a paging file is close to its capacity. Increasing physical memory, the paging file, or both should fix this problem.

Physical/Logical Disk

Besides memory, disk performance can be a limiting factor on a server. Assuming that the server has adequate memory, most servers are disk bound. However, a server that is short on memory typically will access the paging file more frequently than a comparable server with adequate memory will. You can somewhat compensate for slower hard drives by making sure your server has enough system/file/

application cache to minimize unnecessary disk access. On Windows 2000 servers, the Logical Disk System Performance Object is not enabled by default. To monitor this parameter issue the command:

```
DiskPerf –Y
```

and reboot the server. The overhead to monitor Logical Disk Activity is minimal, so we suggest turning this parameter on before you need it, because you have to reboot the server to enable it. On Windows 2003 servers, Logical Disk Monitoring is enabled by default.

% Disk Time in the Physical Disk System Performance Object. This is the percentage of time that the disk is busy. Sustained average values over 85 percent indicate a serious disk bottleneck.

Disk Queue Length in the Physical Disk System Performance Object. This is the queue length for disk requests. If the % Disk Time is above 85 percent and the disk queue length is over 2, you probably have a disk bottleneck on the server.

Average Disk sec/Transfer in the Physical Disk System Performance Object. Average consistent values over 0.3 seconds can indicate a disk or hardware problem. A disk defragmentation might also help to increase the disk transfer rate.

% Free Space in the Logical Disk System Performance Object. This is a good parameter to set up as an alert. You can configure the Performance Monitor to issue an alert when the percentage of free space on a logical disk drops below a certain percentage.

Fixing disk bottlenecks on the server is not an easy task. If you suspect that the disk is highly fragmented, run a defragmentation on the disk, or purchase third-party software like Diskeeper® (*www.softwareshelf.com/products/display_enterprise.asp?p=5*) to automate the process. Assuming your disk is not fragmented and you have adequate memory on the server, you have some tough decisions to improve disk performance on the server. Before you attempt to upgrade the disk subsystem on your server, make absolutely sure that your server has enough memory and that it is optimized for your environment. Memory upgrades are relatively easy, compared to upgrading the disk subsystem on your server. These disk upgrade suggestions are listed from the least to most expensive:

1. **Duplex server hard drives.** If you only have one hard drive or your hard drives are mirrored (both drives are on the same SCSI channel), consider duplexing the drives instead. Duplexing puts each drive on its own SCSI channel, thereby reducing/eliminating SCSI bus contention. Ideally, the

drive duplexing should be done in hardware using a RAID controller, and not in software using Windows 2000/2003 support for drive mirroring. Disk reads are twice as fast and writes are 10-percent faster than a non-duplexed system. For a server that performs a majority of disk reads (most servers do), expect roughly double the disk performance compared to a single drive, or mirrored system. (Approximate cost of $1,500 for the additional disk and installation.)

2. **Increase the cache on your RAID or replace the RAID controller.** Some RAID controllers have the capability to hold additional cache on the controller. This is a good solution if your disk access has many spikes, because the cache can compensate for slower hard drives and the controller will have time to flush the cache during low-usage periods. If your disk load is constant, additional cache on the controller will probably not help, because the cache will quickly fill up and the server will be limited to the speed of the hard drives. The greater the amount of cache on the RAID controller, the more important it is to get a controller that has battery backup to retain the data in the cache in the event of a sudden power loss like a power supply failure on the server. If the cache on the RAID controller does not have a chance to properly flush to the hard disks, you risk serious corruption of the RAID array. (Approximate cost of $2,000 for RAID controller and installation.)
3. **Reconfigure your disk arrays.** If you have an existing RAID 5 array with more than six disks, consider purchasing a multichannel RAID controller and run multiple RAID arrays on the server. This will reduce the amount of SCSI bus contention of the array. (Approximate cost of $3,000 for the RAID controller and installation.)
4. **Purchase faster SCSI controllers/hard disks.** Replace your existing array controller and hard drives with the newer Ultra-320 SCSI hard drives. To take advantage of the faster drives, make sure that your SCSI controller can handle the Ultra-320 SCSI drives, or purchase a new controller. Most of the new Ultra-320 SCSI controllers conform to the PCI-X standard, so make sure that your server can handle the PCI-X controller for maximum throughput. (Approximate cost of $5,000 for the additional hard disks and installation.)
5. **Move to RAID 10 (or RAID 1+0) Array.** If you are running RAID 5 or below, consider reconfiguring your server to run RAID 10. RAID 10 uses mirroring and striping. Typically, two SCSI channels are used, and you must purchase double the amount of drive for a RAID 10 solution. For example if you had six 72-GB hard drives, using RAID 10 would give you a 216-GB volume (see Figure 4.11).

This is the one of the fastest, most fault tolerant, and most expensive drive configurations you can install in a server. (Approximate cost of $6,000 and up for the additional disks, RAID controller and installation.)

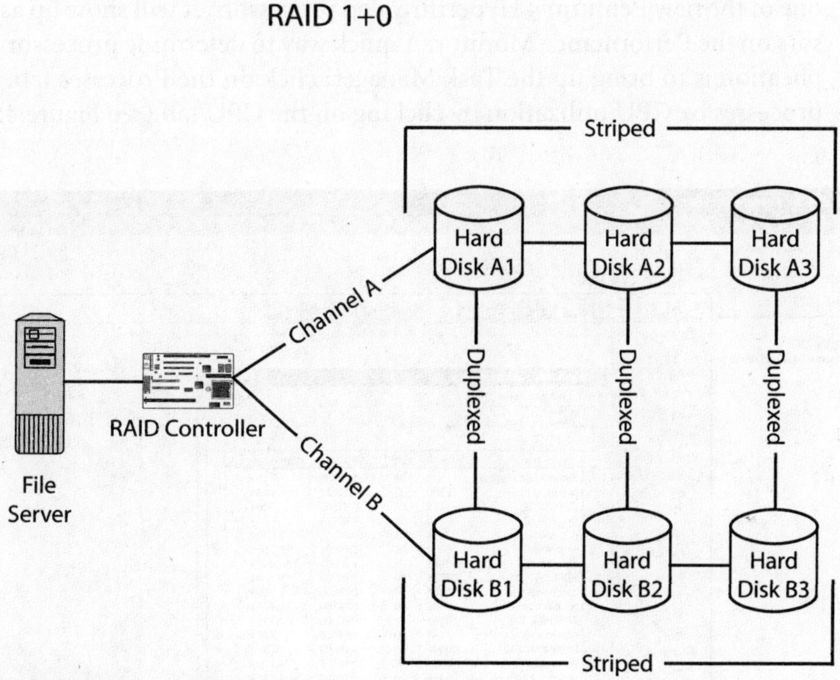

FIGURE 4.11 RAID 1+0 disk configuration.

6. **Move an application to another server**. If your server is getting hammered because you are running Exchange, SQL Server, IIS, Terminal Server, and File/Print services on the same server, consider purchasing a new server and moving some of the applications to another server to balance the load of the servers. (Approximate cost $8,000 and up.)
7. **Move to a storage area network (SAN)**. If you really feel the need for speed, purchase a SAN. Most SAN solutions use fibre-channel and a fabric of storage devices that are commonly shared among two or more servers. These solutions are highly scaleable and fault tolerant. Because of their shared storage architecture, SANs are ideal for server clustering. (Approximate cost $20,000 and up.)

Processor

The server processor can be a bottleneck on the server. Typically, the processor is not a bottleneck unless you are running very processor-intensive applications on the server like SQL Server with stored procedures, or Terminal Server. If you have one of the new Pentium 4 Hyperthreaded processors, it will show up as two processors on the Performance Monitor. A quick way to determine processor usage by application is to bring up the Task Manager, click on the Processes tab, and sort the processes by CPU utilization by clicking on the CPU tab (see Figure 4.12).

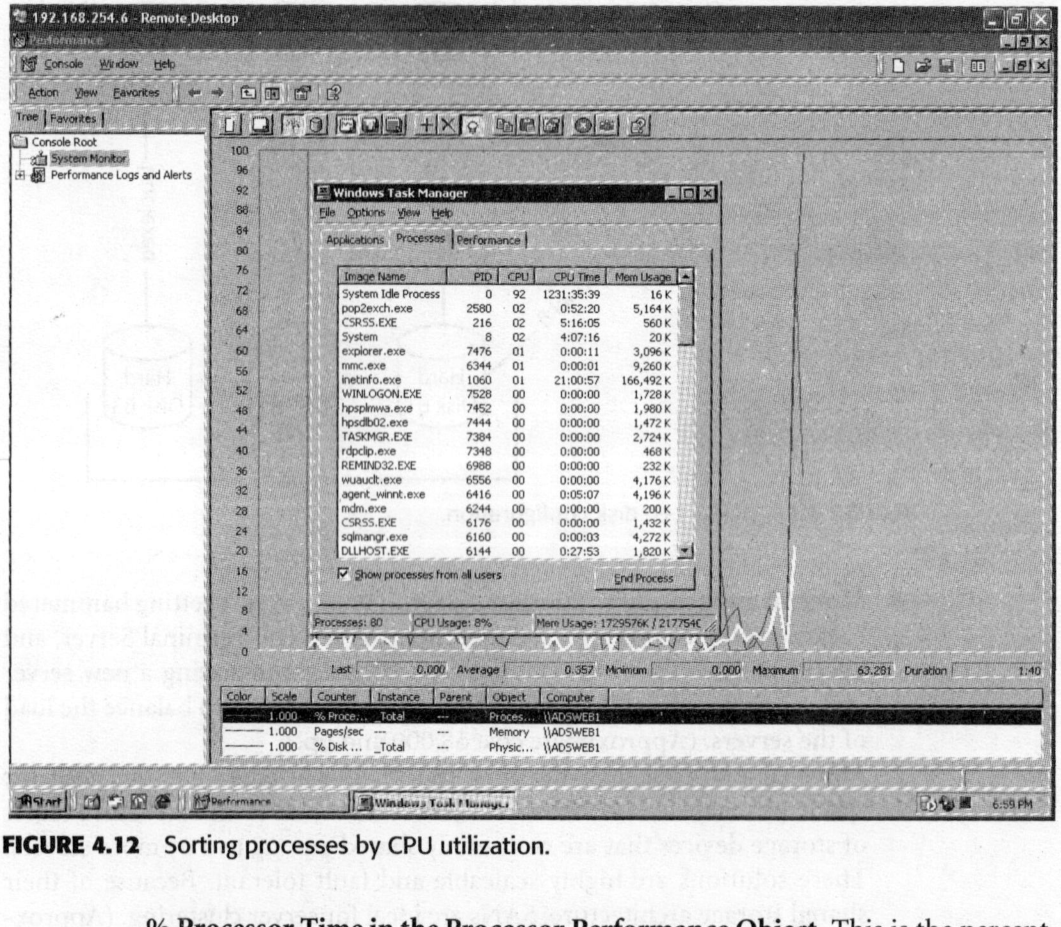

FIGURE 4.12 Sorting processes by CPU utilization.

% Processor Time in the Processor Performance Object. This is the percentage of time that the processor is used. Usually, the processor is not a bottleneck until the utilization is over 80 percent for sustained periods of time. If you have high CPU utilization on the server, you can use the Performance Monitor to view which application is "hogging" all of the CPU cycles. In the Performance

Monitor, click on the "+" icon to Add Counters. In the Performance Object window, select Process and % Processor Time from the Select Counters list. Select the option button "Select instances from list," and use Ctrl-Click to select all of the Processes in the window, excluding the _Total and the Idle instances. Click the Add button to add these counters, and then Close to close the Add Counters window. To get a better view of the CPU utilization, change the graph range from 0 to 20 by right-clicking on the graph and selecting Properties. Click on the Graph tab and change the Vertical Scale Maximum value to 20. A sample of this Performance Monitor is shown in Figure 4.13.

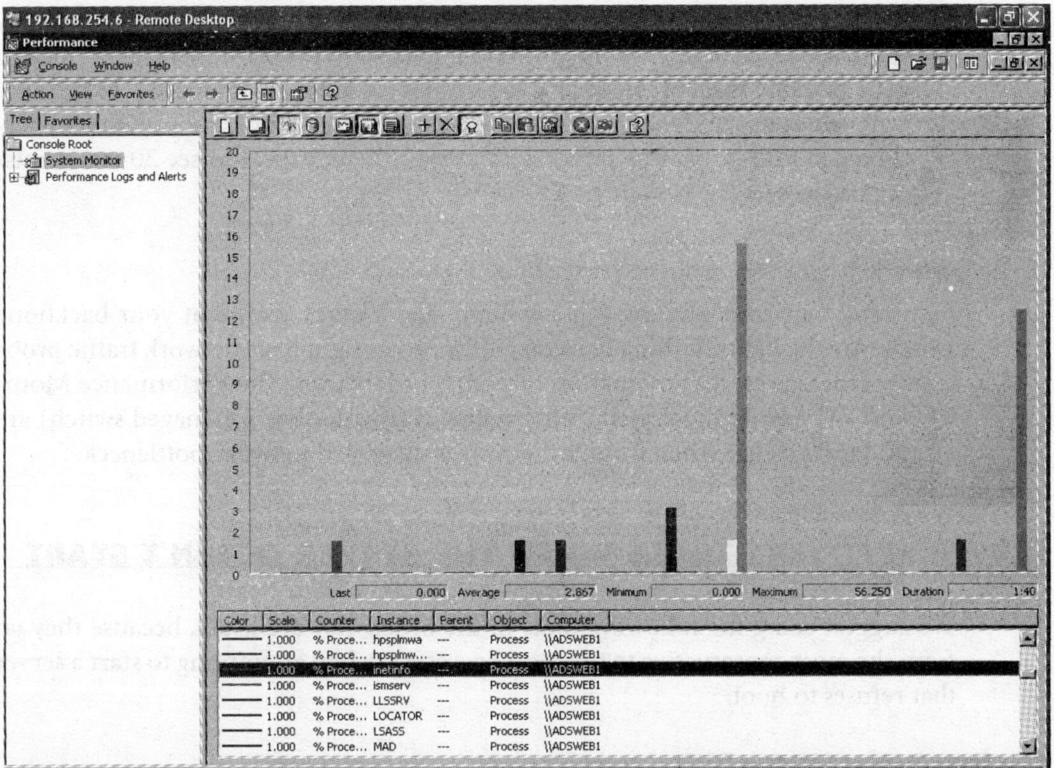

FIGURE 4.13 Performance Monitor using bar graphs.

Don't forget to use the Lightbulb button to make it easier to identify the current highlighted process. Once you have found the process that is taking up all of the processor cycles, you can troubleshoot that specific process. It might be a legitimate process, a process that is accessing a corrupted data file, or a virus.

Processor Queue Length in the System Performance Object. These are requests waiting to be processed by the processor. If the average queue length is consistently more than 2, you probably have a processor bottleneck on the server.

Total Interrupts/sec in the Processor Performance Object. This is the number of interrupts per second that require the processor's attention. Devices that require interrupts are typically SCSI controllers, system clock, mouse, network card, and other peripherals. Note that this counter is measured in 0.01 increments, so a value of 2500 is really 25 interrupts per second. This number is dependent upon the number of processors in the server, and the current load on the server. If you have a dramatic increase in processor interrupts without any other server changes, you might have a hardware problem. It's a good idea to get a baseline measurement of this number, so you can compare it to the current values to see if they're in line with normal server operations. On a hyper-threaded four-processor server with a heavy load, expect to see 30 interrupts/sec on the server.

Network

Assuming that your server is on a switch, take a quick glance at your backbone switch. Are the lights flashing like crazy? If so, you might have network traffic problems on the server. A combination of switch observation, the Performance Monitor, and a review of the switch traffic statistics (if you have a managed switch) are all good tools to use when troubleshooting a suspected network bottleneck.

SERVER RECOVERY TOOLS WHEN THE SERVER DOESN'T START

We suggest using the following tools in the order they are listed, because they go from the most conservative to the most aggressive when attempting to start a server that refuses to boot.

Windows Server Startup Disk

Sometimes, a server might not start, because the boot.ini, boot record, or OS files become corrupted. You can create a Windows Server 2003 startup disk to get the server up and running if there is a problem with the boot record or boot files. To create a Windows 2003 boot floppy:

1. Format a blank floppy, and insert it into the floppy drive. Right-click on Start, and select Explore. Click on My Computer, right-click on the floppy

drive, and select Format. In the Format window under Format Options, check the Quick Format box and click OK.

2. Copy the following files to the A: drive. Click on Start, Run, type `cmd` in the Open box, and click OK. This example assumes your boot files are located on the C: drive, and your floppy drive is A:. At the command prompt, type:

```
xcopy c:\boot.ini a:\ /h <ENTER>
xcopy c:\ntdetect.com a:\ /h <ENTER>
xcopy c:\ntldr a:\ /h <ENTER>
If bootsect.dos exists, xcopy c:\bootsect.dos a:\ /h <ENTER>
If ntbootdd.sys exists, xcopy c:\ntbootdd.sys a:\ /h <ENTER>
attrib a:\*.* -r –h –s <ENTER>. This removes the Read only, Hidden
  and System attributes from all files in the root of A:.
```

3. Make sure to test the startup disk by placing the disk in the floppy drive, and then restart the server and verify that the server starts properly. Label the disk as the Windows Server 2003 startup disk with the server name and date it was created. Make sure to update this disk if you change the disk configuration in the server.

Refer to *http://support.microsoft.com/default.aspx?scid=kb;en-us;325879&Product=winsvr2003* for more information on creating a boot floppy for a Windows 2003 server. If you did not create the boot floppy ahead of time, you can create it from another server running Windows Server 2003 or from a setup of XP setup disks. You might have to adjust the boot.ini file to get the floppy to properly work. Refer to *http://support.microsoft.com/default.aspx?scid=kb;en-us;317526* for more information on editing boot.ini files.

Safe Mode

Windows 2000/2003 can be started in safe mode by pressing F8 at startup and selecting Safe Mode. Try booting the server in safe mode when applications refuse to install, uninstall, or the server fails to boot and gets stuck on the Windows startup splash screen. Safe mode loads with a minimal amount of services and drivers. Often, you can boot the server in safe mode, remove the offending driver, and start the server normally. Table 4.2 lists the Safe Mode options.

Whenever you make a major change to a server, we suggest restarting the server to verify that it properly starts. If it does not, you can use safe mode to reverse the changes you just made. If you wait until a later date to restart the server, it will not be obvious that an updated driver or program is the cause of a failed restart on the server. This will make it much more difficult to troubleshoot a restart problem, because it could be months before the server is restarted.

TABLE 4.2 Safe Mode Options

Safe Mode Options	*When to Use*
Safe Mode	Remove offending program, driver, or service that prevents Windows Server 2003 from starting.
Safe Mode with Networking Support	Use to verify that network components are working properly.
Safe Mode with Command Prompt	Use to run command-line utilities only. After login, only a command prompt is displayed. Try running if safe mode does not work.

Last Known Good Configuration

Sometimes you can use the Last Known Good Configuration (LKGC) to start a server. This restores the information for the registry subkey HKEY_LOCAL_MACHINE\SYSTEM\CurrentControlSet. Any updated drivers are restored to the previous version if you use the LKGC. Be aware that starting the server in this mode might cause the server to revert to a much earlier configuration than anticipated. To access the LKGC, press F8 before the Windows Server 2000/2003 splash screen appears and select Last Known Good Configuration.

Recovery Console

Use the Recovery Console when the startup disk, safe mode, and LKGC fail to start the server. The Recovery Console in Windows Server 2000/2003 gives you a command line that can be used for the following:

- Enable/disable services that prevent Windows Server 2003 from properly starting.
- Read/write/copy files on a local drive. The Recovery Console enforces NTFS permissions.
- Format hard disks.
- Repair a boot sector.

To use the Recovery Console, you must log in to the server with the local Administrator account. You can either preinstall the Recovery Console or run it directly from the Windows Server 2000/2003 CD-ROM. To install the Recovery Console:

1. Insert the Windows CD-ROM into the server.
2. Click on Start, Run. In the Open field, type

```
<CD_Rom_Letter>:\i386\winnt32 /cmdcons.
```

When the server is restarted, the Recovery Console should appear as an option in the Start menu. Quite honestly, if the server requires you to run the Recovery Console, it's probably in pretty bad shape already, and you might not be able to get it to even display the Start menu. For this reason, we feel that installing the Recovery Console on the server has limited value. Fortunately, you can also run the Recovery Console directly from the Windows CD-ROM:

1. Insert the Windows CD-ROM in the server.
2. If necessary, press a key to boot from the CD-ROM.
3. Press R to select the Repair/Recover option.
4. Select the Recovery Console.

Logging in to the Recovery Console

To log in to the Recovery Console:

1. Enter the Windows installation you want (usually 1).
2. Enter the password for the local Administrator account.

Recovery Console Commands

Type `help` to display a list of Recovery Console commands. Table 4.3 lists the Recovery Console commands.

TABLE 4.3 Recovery Console Commands

Command	***Description***	***Syntax***
ATTRIB	Display/set file attributes	`ATTRIB -R|+R|-S|+S|-H|+H|-C|+C` *`filename`* + Sets an attribute. - Clears an attribute. `R` Read-only file attribute. `S` System file attribute. `H` Hidden file attribute. `C` Compressed file attribute. To view attributes, use the `DIR` command.

(continued)

TABLE 4.3 *(continued)*

Command	*Description*	*Syntax*
BATCH	Execute commands in a text file	BATCH Inputfile [Outputfile] InputFile. Specifies the text file that contains the list of commands to be executed. OutputFile. If specified, contains the output of the specified commands. If not specified, the output is displayed on the screen.
BOOTCFG	Repair boot configuration and recovery	BOOTCFG /ADD BOOTCFG /REBUILD BOOTCFG /SCAN BOOTCFG /LIST BOOTCFG /DISABLEEMS BOOTCFG /EMS [PORT BAUDRATE] | [useBiosSettings] /SCAN Scan all disks for Windows installations and display the results. /ADD Add a Windows installation to the boot list. /REBUILD Iterate through all Windows installations and allow the user to choose which to add. /DEFAULT Set the default boot entry. /LIST List the entries already in the boot list. /DISABLEEMS Disable redirection in the boot loader. /EMS Enable redirection in the boot loader with the specified configuration. example: bootcfg /ems com1 115200 bootcfg /ems useBiosSettings
CD (CHDIR)	Displays the name of the current directory or changes to another directory	CD [path] CD [..] CD [drive:] CD .. Specifies that you want to change to the parent directory.

Command	*Description*	*Syntax*
		Type `CD drive:` to display the current directory in the specified drive. Type `CD` without parameters to display the current drive and directory. The `CD` command treats spaces as delimiters. Use quotation marks around a directory name containing spaces. For example: `cd "\windows\profiles\username\programs"` `CD` only operates within the system directories of the current Windows installation, removable media, the root directory of any hard disk partition, or the local installation sources.
CHKDSK	Checks a disk and display a status report	`CHKDSK [drive:] [/P] [/R]` `[drive:]` Specifies the drive to check. `/P` Check even if the drive is not flagged dirty. `/R` Locates bad sectors and recovers readable information (implies `/P`). `CHKDSK` can be used without any parameters, in which case the current drive is checked with no switches. You can specify the listed switches. `CHKDSK` requires the AUTOCHK.EXE file. `CHKDSK` automatically locates AUTOCHK.EXE in the startup (boot) directory. If it cannot be found in the startup directory, `CHKDSK` will attempt to locate the Windows installation CD-ROM. If it cannot be found, `CHKDSK` prompts for the location of AUTOCHK.EXE.
CLS	Clears the screen	`CLS`
COPY	Copies a single file to another location	`COPY source [destination]` `source` Specifies the file to be copied. `destination` Specifies the directory and/or filename for the new file.

TABLE 4.3 *(continued)*

Command	***Description***	***Syntax***
		The source might be removable media, any directory within the system directories of the current Windows installation, the root of any drive, the local installation sources, or the Cmdcons directory.
		The destination might be any directory within the system directories of the current Windows installation, the root of any drive, the local installation sources, or the cmdcons directory. The destination cannot be removable media. If a destination is not specified, it defaults to the current directory. `COPY` does not support wildcards. `COPY` prompts if the destination file already exists. A compressed file from the Windows installation CD-ROM is automatically decompressed as it is copied.
`DEL` `(DELETE)`	Deletes one or more files	`DEL [drive:][path]filename` `[drive:][path]filename` Specifies the file to delete. `DELETE` only operates within the system directories of the current Windows installation, removable media, the root directory of any hard disk partition, or the local installation sources.
`DIR`	Displays a list of files and sub-directories in a directory	`DIR [drive:][path][filename]` `[drive:][path][filename]` Specifies drive, directory, and/or files to list. `DIR` lists all files, including hidden and system files. Files might have the following attributes: `D` Directory `R` Read-only `H` Hidden file `A` Files ready for archiving

Command	***Description***	***Syntax***
		S System file C Compressed E Encrypted P Reparse Point DIR only operates within the system directories of the current Windows installation, removable media, the root directory of any hard disk partition, or the local installation sources.

DISABLE	Disable a system service or device driver	`DISABLE servicename`
		`servicename` The name of the service or driver to be disabled.
		DISABLE prints the old `start_type` of the service before resetting it to `SERVICE_DISABLED`. You should make a note of the old `start_type`, in case you need to enable the service again.
		The `start_type` values that the DISABLE command displays are:
		`SERVICE_DISABLED`
		`SERVICE_BOOT_START`
		`SERVICE_SYSTEM_START`
		`SERVICE_AUTO_START`
		`SERVICE_DEMAND_START`

DISKPART	Manage partitions on your hard drive	`DISKPART [/add|/delete] [device-name|drive-name|partition-name] [size]` `/ADD` Create a new partition. `/DELETE` Delete an existing partition. `device-name` Device name for creating a new partition. The name can be obtained from the output of the MAP command. An example of a good device name is \Device\HardDisk0. `drive-name` This is a drive letter-based name for deleting an existing partition. An example of a good drive name is D:. `partition-name` This is a partition-based name for deleting an existing partition

(continued)

TABLE 4.3 *(continued)*

Command	***Description***	***Syntax***
		and can be used in place of the `drive-name` argument. An example of a good partition name is \Device\HardDisk0\Partition1. Note: If you use the `DISKPART` command with no arguments, a user interface for managing your partitions appears.

ENABLE	Enable a system service or device driver	`ENABLE servicename [start_type]`
		`servicename` The name of the service or driver to be enabled.
		`start_type` Valid start_type values are:
		`SERVICE_BOOT_START`
		`SERVICE_SYSTEM_START`
		`SERVICE_AUTO_START`
		`SERVICE_DEMAND_START`
		`ENABLE` prints the old `start_type` of the service before resetting it to the new value. You should make a note of the old value, in case it is necessary to restore the `start_type` of the service.
		If you do not specify a new `start_type`, `ENABLE` prints the old `start_type` for you.
		The `start_type` values that the `DISABLE` command displays are:
		`SERVICE_DISABLED`
		`SERVICE_BOOT_START`
		`SERVICE_SYSTEM_START`
		`SERVICE_AUTO_START`
		`SERVICE_DEMAND_START`

EXIT	Exit Recovery Console and restart the computer	`EXIT`

EXPAND	Expands a compressed file	`EXPAND source [/F:filespec] [destination] [/Y]`
		`EXPAND source [/F:filespec] /D`
		`source` Specifies the file to be expanded. Cannot include wildcards.

Command	Description	Syntax
		destination Specifies the directory for the new file. Default is the current directory. /Y Do not prompt before overwriting an existing file. /F:filespec If the source contains more than one file, this parameter is required to identify the specific file(s) to be expanded. Can include wildcards. /D Do not expand; only display a directory of the files that are contained in the source. The destination can be any directory within the system directories of the current Windows installation, the root of any drive, the local installation sources, or the cmdcons directory. The destination cannot be removable media. The destination file cannot be read-only. Use the ATTRIB command to remove the read-only attribute. EXPAND prompts if the destination file already exists unless /Y is used.
FIXBOOT	Writes a new boot sector onto the system partition	FIXBOOT [drive:] [drive:] Specifies the drive to which a boot sector will be written, overriding the default choice of the system boot partition. FIXBOOT is only supported on x86-based computers.
FIXMBR	Repairs the Master Boot Record (MBR) of the partition boot sector	FIXMBR [device-name] device-name Optional name that specifies the device that will be updated with a new MBR. If this is left blank, the boot device is used. FIXMBR is only supported on x86-based computers.

(continued)

TABLE 4.3 *(continued)*

Command	***Description***	***Syntax***
FORMAT	Formats a disk	FORMAT [drive:] [/Q] [/FS:file-system] [drive:] Specifies the drive to format. /Q Performs a quick format. /FS:file-system Specifies the file system to use (FAT, FAT32, or NTFS).
HELP	Displays list of Recovery Console commands	HELP
LISTSVC	Lists all available services and drivers on the computer	LISTSVC
LOGON	Logs in to Windows Server 2003	LOGON
MAP	Display drive letter mappings	MAP [arc] The arc parameter tells MAP to use ARC paths instead of Windows device paths.
MD (MKDIR)	Creates a directory	MD [drive:]path MD only operates within the system directories of the current Windows installation, removable media, the root directory of any hard disk partition, or the local installation sources.
MORE	Displays a text file to screen	MORE filename or TYPE filename
RD (RMDIR)	Remote a directory	RD [drive:]path RD only operates within the system directories of the current Windows installation, removable media, the root directory of any hard disk partition, or the local installation sources.
REN (RENAME)	Renames a single file	REN [drive:][path]filename1 filename2 You cannot specify a new drive or path for your destination file.

Command	Description	Syntax
		RENAME will only operate within the system directories of the current Windows installation, removable media, the root directory of any hard disk partition, or the local installation sources.
SYSTEMROOT	Sets the current folder to the systemroot folder	SYSTEMROOT
TYPE	Displays a text file to screen	TYPE filename

Restoring a Windows Server

Unfortunately, there are times when the server has to be restored from tape. This is especially true when you lose a hard disk, the server is compromised by a hacker, or have some other type of catastrophic hardware failure. When you have to rebuild the server, you typically reinstall the OS, the tape backup software, catalog the tape, and restore from backup. Some tape backup software has a feature that allows you to directly restore from tape without having to preinstall the OS and tape backup software. This involves creating a bootable CD-ROM, which loads an OS and allows the restore of the server. This one-step solution works fine, as long as you are restoring to the identical hardware; however, if you have to replace a server or critical piece (SCSI controller) of hardware because the old part in no longer available, this can cause the one-step restore solution to fail. For mission-critical servers it's a good idea to purchase the one-step restore option; however, you should always be familiar with the "manual" restore process in case you have to restore the data to different hardware. Make sure to follow the backup software recommendations for a full server recovery. For a DC restore using Backup Exec software, they suggest placing the server into a workgroup, and then running the complete restore. Before starting any restore procedure, download any knowledge base articles from the backup software manufacturer. Completely restoring a server from tape is a tricky process, especially if a server is a domain controller.

TROUBLESHOOTING SCENARIOS

If you follow the guidelines suggested in the first half of this chapter, you can avoid some of the server problems. However, when servers go down because of a hardware failure, a good backup strategy is your "safety" net to get the server quickly back up and running. The following scenarios are some real-world examples of troubleshooting adventures we've experienced getting servers back up and running.

Scenario 1 — DATA FACTION SERVER DOES NOT BOOT

Facts

- Clone server Pentium 3 with 256 MB of RAM
- Running Linux and Pick OS with Datafaction software

Symptoms

This client was recently hit by a series of power surges. After a recent surge, the server was shut down properly to see if there was any damage to the server. When the user attempted to turn on the server, the server was completely dead—nothing happened when the power switch was turned on.

Questions to Ask

Q: What happened? A: After the server was shut down properly, we tried to turn it on, but nothing happened.

Q: Has anything changed? A: Nothing on the server, but there was a series of recent power surges.

Troubleshooting Steps

1. **Verify the problem.** When we arrived on site, we tried to start the server and it was dead. No activity from the power supply, fans, or lights.
2. **Verify the obvious.** The server was plugged into an APC Back UPS 650. Just to ensure the UPS was not bad, we plugged the server into an outlet that was known to have good power—still nothing.
3. **Causes of a dead server—power supply and switch.** When you turn on a server and nothing happens, it's usually one of two problems: a bad power supply or bad power switch—in that order. We've seen power switches go out, but it's fairly rare. First, verify the type of power supply in the machine. For PCs, there are basically two different types of power supplies: AT and

ATX. AT power supplies were used on 486 and some early Pentiums, and ATX power supplies are typically used on Pentium II and later machines. The connectors for a typical ATX power supply are shown in Figure 4.14.

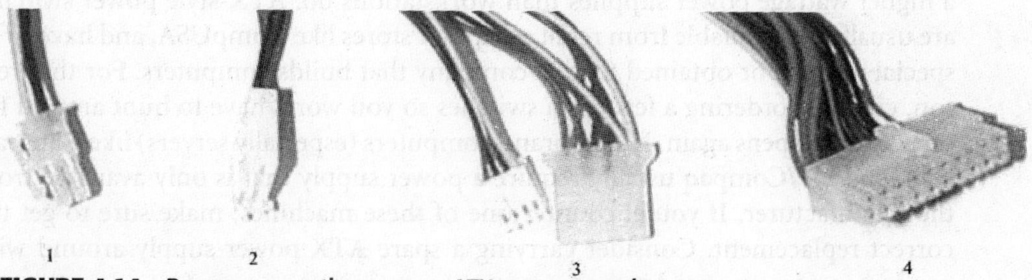

FIGURE 4.14 Power connections on an ATX power supply.

The first connector is typically used for a cooling fan on Pentium 4 machines. The second AUX connector is for a Pentium 4 motherboard. It supplies 12 volts directly to the processor. The third connectors are for hard, tape, and floppy drives. The fourth connector is the main power to the motherboard. An AT power supply typically has two single-row connectors for main power to the motherboard. That's one way to tell if you have an AT versus an ATX power supply. After pulling the power supply from the computer, it indicated that it was a 300-watt power supply. The power supply wattage in this server was higher than a typical workstation, which usually has a ~250-watt power supply. This particular power supply did not have the AUX power 12V connector because it came from a Pentium 3 machine. We tested the on/off switch with a volt meter to test it for resistance. An ATX power switch sends a "message" to the motherboard to turn on. Set a volt meter to the "ohms" setting. With a volt meter connected to the two switch leads, you should see a brief change in resistance. We went to a computer store and purchased a replacement power supply and power switch. Unfortunately, the store only had the older style AT power switch with four connectors, as opposed to the newer two-connector ATX power switch—we purchased the AT switch anyway.

Resolution

When we installed the power supply, the machine started, but the switch would not shut off the computer. We thought maybe the switch was bad, so we replaced it with the AT-style switch. The computer would turn on, but then shut off after about four seconds. However, if you press the switch twice quickly, the machine stayed on. We got the machine back up and running by pressing the switch twice, and ordered a replacement ATX switch for the computer.

Lessons Learned

If you are replacing a power supply on a PC, make sure you purchase the correct type (AT versus ATX). As a rule, make sure that the replacement power supply has the same or higher wattage than the one you are replacing. Usually, servers require a higher wattage power supplies than workstations do. ATX-style power switches are usually not available from retail computer stores like CompUSA, and have to be special ordered or obtained from a company that builds computers. For that reason, consider ordering a few extra switches so you won't have to hunt around for one if this happens again. Name-brand computers (especially servers) like Gateway, Dell, and HP/Compaq usually require a power supply that is only available from the manufacturer. If you encounter one of these machines, make sure to get the correct replacement. Consider carrying a spare ATX power supply around with you just in case you need it.

Scenario 2 UNABLE TO ACCESS FILES FROM A WINDOWS 2003 SERVER

Facts

- HP/Compaq ML350 with one 2.0-GHz processor, 2 GB of memory, with 72 GB of storage.
- Windows Server 2003

Symptoms

Over the weekend, the server was possibly hacked. There was an unauthorized user in the Administrators group, and some rights were missing from certain folders.

Questions to Ask

Q: What happened? A: Certain folders are inaccessible.

Q: Has anything changed? A: Possibly a hacker changed rights on the servers.

Troubleshooting Steps

1. **Verify the problem.** When a user tries to access the folders, they are unavailable.
2. **Look at the server.** An unauthorized user was found in AD. The unauthorized user was deleted from the Administrators group, and the deleted from Active Directory Users and Computers.
3. **Review the Event Log.** A good hacker will clear the Event Viewer to remove traces of his activities. The Event Viewer was still intact; however, it appeared the hacker tampered with the Security Log. The other Event Logs appeared to be intact.

4. **Review rights on the folders.** When we right-clicked on the folder, selected Properties, and tried to click on the Security tab, we received a message that we did not have permission to view or edit the current permission settings. When we attempted to add a user and grant rights to the folder, we received an "access denied" error message.
5. **Take ownership of a folder.** To grant rights to a folder, when you do not have any rights, you must take ownership of the folder. Most likely, the hacker added himself as the owner of the folder and then simply removed all of the rights to certain folders. Logged in as Administrator, the Administrator took ownership of the folder. This was done by right-clicking on the folder, selecting Properties, the Security tab, and clicking the Advanced button (see Figure 4.15).

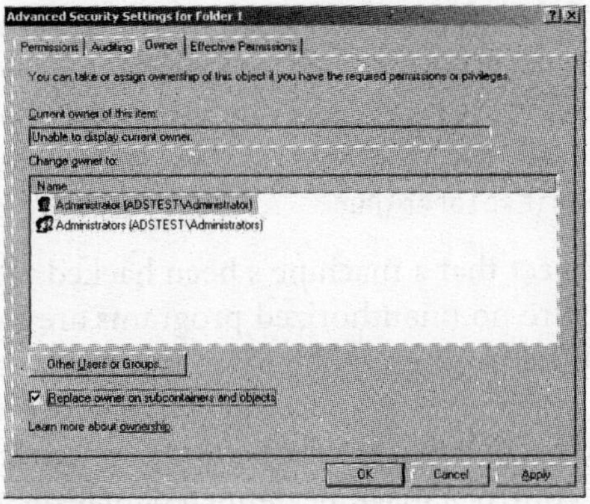

FIGURE 4.15 Taking ownership of a folder.

In this case, we granted ownership to the Administrator. Make sure to check "Replace owner on subcontainers and objects" and click Apply.

Resolution

After the Administrator was granted ownership of folder, we could grants rights normally.

Lessons Learned

The loss of rights on the folder were just a symptom of a larger problem. The hacker probably wanted us to know that he could get into the system. When you suspect a security breach, we suggest that you:

1. **Disconnect external lines.** Although this might not be practical, it's the only protection from the hacker while you're trying to figure out where the

breach came from. This also assumes that the hack came from an external source, although this might not always be the case. To further isolate the problem, consider disconnecting any external line(s) coming into your network, including private frame connections. Perform a wireless sweep to detect any rouge wireless access points.

2. **Check the public perimeter servers.** Start with the obvious. If you suspect that the hack came from an external source, this is a good place to start. This particular client had two public servers in their DMZ: a Web server that housed their Web and FTP site, and a front-end server that accessed a SQL server database on the LAN side. The front-end server was used by the client to enter time records. We checked the following registry keys on both servers:

```
HKEY_LOCAL_MACHINE\SOFTWARE\Microsoft\Windows\CurrentVersion\Run
HKEY_LOCAL_MACHINE\SOFTWARE\Microsoft\Windows\CurrentVersion\RunOnce
HKEY_CURRENT_USER\Software\Microsoft\Windows\CurrentVersion\Run
HKEY_CURRENT_USER\Software\Microsoft\Windows\CurrentVersion\RunOnce
KEY_LOCAL_MACHINE\SOFTWARE\Microsoft\Windows\CurrentVersion\
  Policies\Explorer\Run
```

If you suspect that a machine's been hacked, you should check these keys to make sure no unauthorized programs are loaded. The Web server was okay, but the front-end server was severely compromised. It had multiple root kits installed on it, and a rouge FTP program on it. Root kits are hacking problems that run at the operating system level and allow the hacker to remotely control a machine, launch denial-of-service (DoS) attacks, and a host of other hacking activities. They are often not caught by anti-virus software, because they are not considered viruses. The server was being used to distribute illegal copies of software and MP3s. Most likely, the hacker exploited a named pipe vulnerability with the SQL server or exploited a weakness in the front-end application. Refer to *www.microsoft.com/technet/security/bulletin/MS00-053.mspx* for more information on the named pipe vulnerability. This server was running Windows 2000 with Service Pack 2. We attempted to repair this server, but the machine was so compromised that it hacked our machine while we attempted to repair it.

3. **Rebuild the server.** When a machine is hacked, it is no longer yours. The only real way to make sure it's clean is to format the hard drives and reload the OS. Ideally, if a machine is hacked, the hard drives should be preserved for future forensic analysis. We wanted to perform a more in-depth investigation of the machine, but we needed to get the machine up and running again. Previously, the front-end server was in the DMZ, with SQL server traffic on port 1433 allowed into the back-end SQL server. Traffic was only

allowed from the front-end server in the DMZ to the back-end server on the LAN, but the machine was still hacked. We could have hardened the front-end server by installing an SSL certificate on it, installing the latest patches, and setting up a SSL Proxy server, but not that many people used the front-end server outside of the company to justify the additional cost. Therefore, the hard drives were formatted and the machine was rebuilt from scratch. We were unsure if the application running on the front-end server had other vulnerabilities, so it was decided to move the front-end server to the LAN side. We installed the latest service packs and critical updates on the server. If users require access to the front-end server in the future, they must establish a VPN to connect to the internal network.

Lessons Learned

Make sure to keep up to date with the latest service packs and critical updates on all servers. This is especially important for any public server accessible from the Internet. Consider formulating a "hacking recovery" plan for your company, similar to a disaster recovery plan. It's very difficult to keep a clear head when you're in panic mode and attempting to get a mission-critical server back online. Here is a suggested outline for a hacking recovery plan:

1. **Install an intrusion detection system (IDS) and/or have procedures in place to detect compromised machines.** Of course, not everyone can afford a full-blown IDS, but there are some changes you can make on your server to notify you of suspicious activity. Refer to *www.sans.org/resources/idfaq/* for information on IDSs. We suggest establishing an Account Lockout policy and enabling Account Management Auditing with Domain Controller Group Policy. The Account Lockout policy under the Domain Controller Group Policy, Security Settings, Account Policies, allows you to specify a threshold for incorrect login attempts, duration of the lockout period, and a reset of the account lockout period. This will notify you if a user has a number of unsuccessful login attempts that is greater than the threshold specified in the Group Policy setting. The Account Management setting under the Domain Controller Group Policy, Security Settings, Local Policies, Audit Policy allows you to log any add/modify/delete activity for accounts in AD. A common hacker tactic is to create a rouge user in AD with escalated privileges, and use that user to authenticate to your mail server to relay Spam and further compromise your system. After these setting are configured, you can use the link at *www.winnetmag.com/WindowsSecurity/Article/ArticleID/22297/22297.html* to configure your server to e-mail you notifications about critical security

events. Make sure each user has a description. If a hacker enters a rouge user, he typically does not enter a description for the user, making that user stand out. A quick way to check for rouge users, is to start Active Directory Users and Computers and sort the user list by Description. This will bring all of the accounts without descriptions to the top of the list, making it easier to identify an unauthorized user. Of course, firewall logs should be reviewed on a regular basis for any unusual activity. Periodically, key machines, especially ones in the DMZ, should be checked for hacking activity. Check the Run and Run Once keys for unauthorized software. Check these machines for suspicious *.bat files at the root of C:\, c:\winnt\, c:\windows\, c:\winnt\system32, and c:\windows\system32 folders. Many root kits create batch files in these directories to compromise the system. Run full virus scans on all machines on a regular basis and keep up to date with the latest critical security patches. Some hacking tools reside in hidden folders located off the Recycler Bin folder. Make sure to review this area of the hard drive and verify that no hacking tools are installed. Review the server's Event Viewer on a regular basis. In addition to monitoring hacking activity, it's a great idea to review these logs for overall health of the server. Keeping hackers out in the first place or detecting hacking activity shortly after a machine is compromised will help you contain the damage that a hacker is able to inflict on your network and make it much easier to repair any damage.

2. **Disconnect external lines.** If you suspect that a hacker has compromised your network, disconnect any external WAN lines coming into your network. If the attack came from the Internet, taking down external lines will make it more difficult for the hacker to further compromise any machines, and hopefully prevent the hacker from compromising any remote systems.
3. **Perform a wireless sweep.** With the advent of wireless networking, it's relatively simple to set up rouge access points and perform hacks from the parking lot. Airscanner™, Airsnort, Airosniff, NetStumbler, and APSniff are just some of the available wireless sniffers that will locate access points in the immediate area. Install one of these sniffers on a laptop or other mobile device before you need to use it to make sure it's working properly. The sniffer should be installed on a card that supports all of the current wireless standards: 802.11a, 802.11b, and 802.11g.
4. **Scan for compromised machines.** Multiple machines can be compromised. Make sure that every machine that has the potential to be hacked is checked for compromises.
5. **Disable/delete rogue users.** Review AD for any rogue users. Disable/delete the users as necessary.

6. **Change passwords.** Change all passwords for every account on the network, especially the Administrator account and accounts that are used to start up services on the server.
7. **Preserve the data.** If possible, purchase replacement hard drives for the hacked computers to preserve the hacking activity on the compromised computer. After the network is restored, you can review this information to gain more information about the hack.
8. **Identify and address the vulnerability.** This is often easier said than done. Make sure you know how the hacker accessed the network in the first place. If you do not address the vulnerability, you must start from the beginning.
9. **Rebuild the machine.** Once a machine is hacked, it's almost impossible to completely clean it. All you need to do is leave just one hacking tool, and the hacker will be able to gain access to the machine. The only way to make sure the machine is "clean" is to format the hard drives and rebuild the machine from scratch. If you have to restore data on the computer, make sure not to accidentally restore any previously installed hacking tools. Make sure not to restore the registry, any OS files, or programs from tape. All applications should be installed manually.
10. **Bring the network back up.** Reconnect the WAN lines and carefully monitor them. Make sure you have closed any holes on your network, to make sure the hacker does not return.
11. **Perform forensic analysis on the hard drives.** After the network is running again, you might want to install the hacked drives on a stand-alone computer to gain more information about the hack. Often, hackers will spoof their IP addresses, but for tracking down the source, the IP address is a good place to start. You can get a list of IP address allocations from *www.iana.org*. Document each hacking tool that you find on a computer. It's very difficult to track down hackers, especially if they've covered their tracks. Often, you must catch them when the hack is occurring. You might want to leave the tracking of the hacker to the appropriate authorities.
12. **Notify authorities.** Most FBI field offices have Cyber Action Teams (CATS) and run the Internet Fraud Complaint Center (*www.ifccfbi.gov/ index.asp*) to report suspicious activity on the Internet. To contact your local FBI office, refer to *www.fbi.gov/contact/fo/fo.htm*. People don't like to admit they've been hacked, but notifying the proper authorities is the first step to prevent a hacker from doing more damage. The more information that you can provide about the attack, the more likely the FBI can capture the hacker.

These suggestions should help you get started with a hacking recovery plan, but they are just the beginning. These suggestions should be custom tailored to each company and integrated into your company's disaster recovery plan.

Scenario 3 INACCESSIBLE BOOT DEVICE ERROR STOP 0000007B

Facts

- HP/Compaq Proliant ML350 1-GHz processor with duplexed 36-GB hard drives. Hard drives are connected to a dual-port SCSI controller on the server feature board. Hard drives are software mirrored using the Windows 2000 Disk Administrator. The drives are formatted with NTFS.
- HP DAT 40 connected to Compaq dual-port SCSI3 controller. The server is running Backup Exec 8.6 with the Exchange Agent. Last good backup was three days ago.
- Windows Server 2000 with Service Pack 3, and Exchange 2000 Service Pack 3.

Symptoms

When the server boots, it pauses at the Windows 2000 splash screen and eventually times out and blue screens with an "Inaccessible boot device" error message.

Questions to Ask

Q: What happened? A: The server was running slowly, so it was rebooted. When the server was restarted, the client received the error message.

Q: Has anything changed? A: No.

Troubleshooting Steps

1. **Verify the problem.** When we arrived, we attempted to start the server and received the "Inaccessible boot device" error message. During the boot process, we received an error message that the primary mirror drive was about to fail.
2. **Create a bootable disk for an NTFS partition.** Since the primary mirror drive indicated it was about to fail, we attempted to boot off the mirror drive, hoping that it was still good. Since the drive was still under warranty, we had HP send us a replacement drive. Unfortunately, the replacement drive was on back order and would not arrive for two weeks. To boot off a mirror drive, you must first create a boot floppy. Refer to *http://support.microsoft.com/default.aspx?scid=kb;EN-US;119467* for instructions on how to create a boot floppy for an NTFS partition.
3. **Attempt to boot from mirror drive.** After the boot floppy was created, we swapped the SCSI connectors and placed the mirror drive on the primary SCSI port. We inserted the boot floppy and attempted to boot off the mirror. At approximately the same place, the server blue screened and dis-

played the dreaded "Inaccessible boot device" error message. At this point, we might have two bad hard drives, or a bad SCSI controller.

4. **Test the SCSI controllers.** This server had two SCSI controllers with two SCSI ports on each controller (a total of four ports). One SCSI controller was on the server feature board, and the other SCSI controller was connected to an external tape drive. We temporarily disconnected the tape drive to eliminate it as a variable. On the ML350, you can change the boot controller order by pressing F9 during startup and then selecting the desired boot controller order. We connected the secondary mirror drive to the second port on the server feature board and changed the boot controller order to boot off the second port. We received the same error message when we attempted to boot off the second SCSI port. We also tried the two ports on the second SCSI controller that had the tape drive connected to it by connecting the secondary mirror drive to each port, and changed the controller boot order. We also tried booting off the primary mirror on all four SCSI ports. On all boot attempts, we still received the same "Inaccessible boot device" error message. What does this tell us? It appears as though the problem was following the hard drives. Because the SCSI controllers could "see" the drives and started the booting process, it seemed as though the SCSI controllers were okay. The probability of having all four SCSI ports go bad simultaneously were pretty small, and the fact they could at least "see" the drives and started the boot process led us to focus on the hard drives.
5. **Run the Recovery Console.** Windows 2000/2003 has a feature called the Recovery Console. The Recovery Console allows you to access an NTFS partition and has utilities that allow you to copy files, format drivers, repair the Master Boot Record (MBR), and fix partitions. You can install the Recovery Console on the hard drive, or run it directly from the Windows 2000 CD-ROM. In this case, the Recovery Console was not installed, so we ran it from the Windows 2000 CD-ROM. Considering the condition of the hard drives, there was a good chance the Recovery Console would not have run from the hard drives, even if it were installed. To run the Recovery Console:

    a. **Insert the Windows 2000 CD-ROM and boot the server.** If necessary, press F6 during the Windows 2000 startup to load a third-party driver.
    b. **Select "Repair a Windows 2000 installation."**
    c. **Select the Recovery Console.** Normally, after you select the Recovery Console, you are prompted for a Windows 2000 installation to log in to and are prompted for the Administrator login. When we

attempted to run the Recovery Console on this computer, the screen froze and the computer did not respond. We also tried the primary mirror drive and received the same results.

6. **Attempt a manual repair of Windows 2000.** Windows 2000 also has an option to attempt to repair the Windows 2000 installation. The procedure is similar to starting the Recovery Console, except you select the Repair the Windows 2000 installation instead of the Recovery Console. When you run a repair, the system will prompt you for a Windows 2000 emergency repair disk (ERD). Unfortunately, the client did not have an ERD. If you do not have an ERD, Windows 2000 can search for a Windows 2000 installation on the hard drive to repair. Unfortunately, Windows 2000 Repair could not locate a valid Windows 2000 installation on either hard disk. At this point, we theorized that the primary mirror hard drive had failed, but in the process of failing, the secondary mirror mirrored the corrupt data on the primary drive. This left both drives inaccessible. We knew that this installation consisted of two NTFS partitions: a C: and D: drive.
7. **Purchase a new hard drive.** We prepared the client for the fact they would probably have to restore from their backup of three days ago. We purchased a new SCSI hard drive to replace the damaged ones. We installed a clean copy of Windows 2000 Server on the new hard drive. As you probably know, you can install a hard drive with an NTFS partition on an existing server and read the information off the drive. In an attempt to save the data on the secondary mirror drive, we installed this drive on the second port of the SCSI controller after the new install of Windows 2000 Server was completed. You might wonder why we just didn't install the secondary mirror in an existing server (the client had three other servers on site), and went through the hassle of installing a clean OS on a new hard drive? The simple answer is conservatism. We didn't want to risk (however small) installing the secondary mirror drive in a production server, have something go wrong, and have that server go down as well. After we installed the secondary mirror drive in the new Windows 2000 Server installation, the old partitions showed up as drives F: and G:. F: corresponded to the old C: drive, and G: corresponded to the old D: drive. We were able to access the data on the G: drive; however, the data on F: was not accessible. This explains why we were unable to boot to the secondary mirror drive, run the Recovery Console, and Repair the Windows 2000 installation—because we could not access C:.

Resolution

As a last attempt to recover the data from the secondary mirror, we ran `ChkDsk f: /f`. The `/f` switch attempts to fix any errors on f:. The `ChkDsk` utility found numerous errors on F: and fixed them. After it ran the first time, we ran it again to see if it caught all of the errors (it did). After running `ChkDsk` twice, we were able to access the information on F:. Since the drive was now accessible, we shut down the server and placed the secondary mirror on the boot controller primary port and the server came back up. Of course, because we were booting to the secondary mirror we still had to use the boot disk we created in step 2 of the Troubleshooting steps to boot the server. We tested the server and all of the data was recovered up to the point when the server went down. We decided to leave the server in this configuration until we received the replacement hard drive from HP.

Lessons Learned

If you run into a situation in which the secondary or primary mirror is inaccessible, try installing the hard drive in another Windows 2000 server and run the `ChkDsk` utility. If it's successful, you will save a lot of time and have many grateful users. You might wonder why we didn't use a RAID controller and a hardware mirror as opposed to using the software mirror in Windows 2000. We decided to use software mirroring for two reasons:

Each drive on a separate controller. By using the software mirror, we could attach each drive to a separate controller. This eliminates any SCSI bus contention because each drive is on a separate SCSI bus. This particular server came standard with a dual-port SCSI controller already on the server.

Breaking the mirror still leaves the drives readable. On most hardware RAID controllers configured for RAID 1 or RAID 5, the controller does a great job recognizing when a drive fails. However, sometimes when the array does fail, the hardware array repair utility fails to repair the array. When this happens, it sometimes leaves all drives in the array unusable. At that point, the array has to be rebuilt from scratch.

With software mirroring, sometimes you can recover the data off the mirror drive using the Recovery Console, Windows 2000 Repair, and the `ChkDsk` utility. Don't get us wrong, we like hardware RAID, but for this particular installation, we felt that this configuration gave the client the best performance and fault tolerance for their dollar.

Scenario 4

AFTER A COMPLETE SYSTEM RESTORE, NET VIEW, NET USE, AND BROWSING MY NETWORK PLACES DO NOT WORK (CONTINUATION FROM SCENARIO 3)

Facts

- HP/Compaq Proliant ML350 1-GHz processor with duplexed 36-GB hard drives. Hard drives are connected to dual-port SCSI controller on the server feature board. Hard drives are software mirrored using the Windows 2000 Disk Administrator. The mirrored drives are formatted with NTFS.
- HP DAT 40 connected to Compaq dual-port SCSI3 controller. The server is running Backup Exec 8.6 with the Exchange Agent.
- Windows Server 2000 with Service Pack 3, and Exchange 2000 Service Pack 3.
- This server was the only DC for the AD domain.
- Primary mirror drive failed, and the server was rebuilt to restore the original configuration.

Symptoms

After a complete system restore, the `net use` command, `net view` command, and browsing My Network Places do not work.

Questions to Ask

Q: What happened? A: The primary mirror drive on the server failed, and we wanted to restore the server to its original duplexed configuration, and avoid booting the server from floppy.

Troubleshooting Steps

1. **Back up the server.** A complete backup of the server was run and verified.
2. **Run the Recovery Console.** We attempted to run the Recovery Console and the commands `Fixboot` and `FixMbr`. Unfortunately, after running these commands the server did not boot from the hard drive, and also refused to boot from the floppy. Most likely, this happened because we attempted to run a `Fixboot` and `FixMbr` on a drive that was originally designated as the secondary mirror, not the primary mirror.
3. **Reinstall Windows 2000 Server.** At this point, we decided to rebuild the server. Since we had a complete backup of the server, we formatted the hard drive and installed a clean copy of Windows 2000 Server. When preparing for a full system restore, Backup Exec suggests leaving the server in a workgroup, and avoid joining the domain.
4. **Install Backup Exec and run a full restore.** After installing Windows 2000 Server in a workgroup, we installed Backup Exec and cataloged the most

recent backup. After the tape was cataloged, we performed a full system restore of the registry, system state, and data. When the server was restarted, AD and the data were restored, but we were unable to use the `net view` command, `net use` command, and browse My Network Places. Shares on this server were inaccessible, both by this server and other servers. This server was also unable to connect to any remote shares on other servers. Internet access was working.

5. **Call Veritas technical support.** We called Veritas for suggestions. We decided to attempt another system restore, because we thought that the first one was unsuccessful. We started the server in Active Directory Restore Mode and attempted to run a system restore. As soon as the job was run, it was placed "On hold." A review of the backup exec log indicated that access was denied and Backup Exec was able to attach to the server. At this point, the Veritas technical support person was out of ideas. We reviewed the restore steps of the server, and Veritas agreed that we had followed the proper restore steps. We decided to install a clean copy of Windows 2000 again and try the restore. At this point, we ended the call with Veritas support. We have successfully restored numerous servers in the past following these exact steps, without any of these problems.
6. **Attempt another system restore.** We installed a clean copy of Windows 2000, and performed a complete restore of the server, including the system state, AD, and data. When the server was rebooted, we had the same problem again—no `net view`, `net use`, or browsing My Network Places.
7. **Call Microsoft technical support.** We decided to call Microsoft tech support. When we clicked on My Computer and looked at the server name, it was missing the fully qualified domain name (FQDN). Because this server was a DC, it should have the name <server_name>.<windows_2000_domain>.com. In this case, the server name was only <server_name>. Microsoft sent us a VBS script to fix this entry error. The registry keys to fix this problem are located in:

   HKLM\SYSTEM\CurrentControlSet\Services\Tcpip\Parameters\Domain
   HKLM\SYSTEM\CurrentControlSet\Services\Tcpip\Parameters\NV Domain
   HKLM\SYSTEM\CurrentControlSet\Services\Tcpip\Parameters\SyncDomainWithMembership

   After the server name was fixed, we still had the `net view` problem. We checked the values in HKLM\SYSTEM\CurrentControlSet\Services\Tcpip\Parameters\Interfaces.

   When you check the entries off this key (there should be a couple), each entry corresponds to a network device on the computer. The hex value corresponds to the Globally Unique Identifier (GUID) of the network device. Each of these entries was checked to determine which GUID matched the network card on the server, by examining the IP address of each GUID.

We then checked the values of keys in:

HKLM\SYSTEM\CurrentControlSet\Services\NetBIOS\Linkage\Bind

HKLM\SYSTEM\CurrentControlSet\Services\NetBT\Linkage\Bind

Each of the bind entries should have a corresponding entry in HKLM\SYSTEM\CurrentControlSet\Services\Tcpip\Parameters\Interfaces

However, the GUID that corresponded to the network card was missing in the NetBIOS and NetBT keys. There was another GUID in NetBIOS and NetBT that probably corresponded to the GUID of the clean Windows 2000 Server installation. Somehow, during the system restore process, the GUID for the network card was not properly bound to the correct network card. This caused `net use`, `net view`, and network browsing to fail, because all of these services use NetBIOS. This most likely caused the failure of the system restore in step 5, because the server must connect to the system state via NetBIOS.

Resolution

After it was determined that NetBIOS was not properly bound to the network card in the server, we:

1. Uninstalled the card from the server using the Device Manager, and shut down the server.
2. Removed the card from the server and restarted it.
3. Shut down the server and installed the card again.
4. After the card was installed, plug and play installed the drivers for the card and restored the network settings. Fortunately, this time the NetBIOS and NetBT properly bound to the network card. By removing the card, we forced Windows 2000 to assign a new GUID to the network card. This was verified by checking the registry key settings.

At this point `net view`, `net use`, and browsing worked. We have successfully restored many servers using Veritas, but this was the first time we ran into this issue.

Lessons Learned

In retrospect, it seems pretty obvious that we had a NetBIOS problem because `net view`, `net use`, and browsing My Network Places didn't work. Fortunately, we attempted this rebuild over a weekend because we spent over 35 hours getting this server back up and running, but everyone was able to work on Monday morning. It was particularly difficult to restore this server, because it was the only DC for their domain, and we wanted to avoid rebuilding Active Directory from scratch. The client decided to purchase another server to serve as an additional DC and dedicated this server to run Exchange. The original server is now used only for file and print services. This particular job was difficult because at one point we were unsure that we could get the server up and running again. Persistence will pay off. Just keep reminding yourself at 3:00 A.M. that you *will* get this server up and running again.

Scenario 5 SERVER DISAPPEARS AND REAPPEARS IN MY NETWORK PLACES

Facts

- Windows Server 2003 running an HP Proliant ML370 G3 with a 3.0-GHz processor and three-drive RAID 5 array with 72-GB hard drives. This new server was recently introduced into the network to replace an aging NT server.
- The server is a domain controller and is running DNS and DHCP services.
- Workstations are a mix of Windows 2000 and Windows XP workstations.
- The network has a T1 to the Internet going through a SonicWALL Pro 3060 firewall.

Symptoms

The server in the My Network Places randomly disappears and reappears. Mapped drives are sometimes accessible and sometimes inaccessible.

Questions to Ask

Q: What has changed? A: A Windows 2003 server was recently installed on the network to replace an aging NT server.

Q: Is the problem reproducible? A: It seems to happen randomly for no apparent reason.

Troubleshooting Steps

1. **Verify the problem.** After browsing My Network Places for about five minutes, the Windows 2003 server disappeared.
2. **Review the Windows 2000 Professional Workstation IP configuration.** We opened a command prompt on a workstation and issued the command:

```
ipconfig /all
```

We reviewed the IP configuration and noticed that the workstation was using the client's ISP's DNS server. Windows 2000 and later use DNS for name resolution. Evidently, the network's DNS configuration setup was similar to the old Windows NT server.

Resolution

To properly configure DNS in a Windows 2000/2003 server environment:

1. **Verify that DNS is installed on the Windows 2003 server.** On this server, DNS was already installed, but if it's not installed, click on Start, Settings, Control Panel, Add/Remove Programs. In the left column, click on Add/Remove Window Components. Scroll down and highlight Network Services, and then click on Details. Select the Domain Name System (DNS) and click OK.
2. **Configure forwarders or root hints.** On the server, we started the DNS Manager, right-clicked on the DNS server, selected Properties, and clicked on the Forwarders tab. We checked the Enable Forwarders box, entered the ISP's DNS servers in the IP address box, and clicked OK. Alternately, you can click on the Root Hints tab and enter the ISP's DNS servers in this window. Root hints are used to find other DNS servers on the network.
3. **Limit Zone Transfers.** For security reasons, it's a good idea to limit Zone Transfers on all Windows 2000/2003 DNS servers. By default, Windows 2000/2003 allows Zone Transfers to any server. This can allow a hacker to quickly enumerate all DNS entries on your network and create bogus entries if the network is compromised. Since this was the only Windows 2003 server on the network, we cleared the Allow Zone Transfers box.
4. **Change the DNS server on the Windows 2003 server.** We right-clicked on My Network Places, selected Properties, right-clicked on Local Area Connection, and selected Properties. We clicked on Internet Protocol (TCP/IP) and clicked on Properties. In the Preferred DNS server field, we entered the IP address of the server. Don't enter your ISP's DNS server in the Alternate DNS server field, because this can cause serious name resolution problems. If the Windows 2003 DNS server does not respond immediately, the server will use the ISP's DNS server to resolve local Windows 2000/2003 resources. This will also generate 5774 error messages in the Server's Event Viewer.
5. **Flush the DNS cache on the server.** We opened a command window and issued the commands:

```
ipconfig /flushdns
ipconfig /registerdns
```

This clears all cached entries on the server and reregisters the server in DNS.

6. **Update DHCP.** The workstations were getting their IP addresses from the Windows 2003 server via DHCP. We started the DHCP Manager and changed the DNS servers in the Scope options to point to the Windows 2003 server instead of the ISP's DNS servers.
7. **Update the IP addresses on the workstation.** We issued the commands

```
ipconfig /release
ipconfig /renew
```

   to push the DHCP changes down to the workstation. Alternately, you can expire all of the leases from the DHCP Manager, but this might cause network interruptions on the workstations.
8. **Test.** After these changes were made, we tested the workstations and the network was stable. Now, when a workstation tries to find a local Windows Server 2003 resource, it queries the Windows 2003 DNS server for local resources. If the Windows 2003 DNS server cannot resolve the request locally, it uses forwarders or root hints to forward the request to the ISP's DNS servers.

Lessons Learned

Make sure to have to the proper DNS configuration on a Windows 2003 server. With the proper configuration, the network should be very stable, but if you try to use the "old" NT way of configuring DNS, your network will be very unstable.

Scenario 6 Users Cannot Connect to the Server

Facts

- Compaq DL740 with four processors, and 32 GB of memory running Windows Server 2003 Enterprise Server. The server has a RAID 10 array with eight 146-GB hard drives, and five Ultrium 460 external tape drives. Workstations are a mix of Windows 2000 and Windows XP workstations.
- This server has dual Gigabit Ethernet cards installed on the motherboard.
- The server is connected to a 3Com 24-port Gigabit Ethernet Switch 4924 with a Category 6 patch cable.
- This server is the company's main file and print server for 200 users.

Symptoms

Some users cannot log in, and other users can log in but the server is extremely slow.

Questions to Ask

Q: What has changed? A: One of the drives in the array failed, and it was replaced one day ago. A review of the Event Viewer indicated that the drive was successfully synchronized.

Q: Only certain users are affected? A: It appears to be random. Some users cannot log in at all, other users can log in but run slow, and still other users run fine. For some users, the server disappears and reappears at random.

Q: Has this happened before? A: No. The server was running fine yesterday.

Troubleshooting Steps

1. **Review the server and Event Viewer.** We logged in to the server and reviewed the Event Viewer. The drive that was replaced the previous day was successfully synchronized.
2. **Review the teaming properties of the NICs.** This particular server has two Gigabit NICs installed on the motherboard. Using the HP NIC driver, this server was configured for NIC teaming. Teaming allows for a number of different NIC configurations. The server in its current configuration was set up for load balancing so each NIC would equally share in the network load.
3. **NIC teaming icon displays error.** When NIC teaming is active, an icon appears in the System Tray. This icon displayed a "!" notice. We pulled up the teaming management interface and it indicated that one of the NICs had failed. We noted that no errors were reported in the Event Viewer, even though the NIC had failed.
4. **Disable teaming.** We made a note of the bad NIC and unteamed the NICs. We activated the good NIC and restarted the server. We double-checked the statistics on the switch and it did not record any errors on either server port.
5. **Upgrade drivers.** We updated all of the HP drivers on the server by downloading the latest support pack for the DL740 from HP's Web site. Often, when you call technical support, one of the first questions they ask you is, "Do you have the latest drivers?"
6. **Call HP technical support.** When we called HP technical support, they wanted us to run some diagnostics test on the server. Since this was a production machine, we had to wait until the end of the day to run the tests. After we ran the tests on the NIC, it did not report any errors. They suggested upgrading the firmware on the NIC. We tried their suggestion, but for some reason the server did not boot after the firmware was upgraded. We went into safe mode, removed the NIC, and reinstalled the drivers. After reinstalling the drivers, the server booted normally. We located a later version of the NIC driver, so we installed this upgraded driver as well.

Just to make sure the server would reboot successfully the next time, we restarted the server, and it started fine.

7. **Place NICs in Fault Tolerance Mode.** After the firmware was updated, we configured the NICs in Fault Tolerance Mode using the HP Utility, placing the known good NIC as the primary card. The server was run for a week in this configuration successfully, and then we switched the primary NIC to the suspect NIC. It ran fine for a while, but after a week or so, the server started showing the same symptoms as the original problem.
8. **Call HP technical support.** It was obvious to us that we had an intermittent NIC on the server. When we called HP technical support, we explained all of the previous steps we had tried, but still had the same problem. At this point, it was our goal to get a replacement motherboard. After explaining the situation, they agreed to send us a new motherboard.

Resolution

When the motherboard arrived, we performed an incremental backup on the server and replaced the motherboard. We agreed to install the motherboard, because we could only take down this server after hours. After the motherboard was installed, we double-checked the NIC teaming configuration and placed it back in load-balancing mode. The server has remained stable since we replaced the motherboard on the server.

Lessons Learned

Try to anticipate what technical support will ask you to do before you call them. Typically, if it's a hardware problem, they will ask you to update the drivers to the latest version, update the computer BIOS, and possibly update the firmware for the problem hardware device. One of these updates might solve the problem, avoiding the need to call technical support in the first place. If technical support gives you a suggestion that you don't agree with, politely ask them why they want you to perform the task. If you think their suggestion is a bad idea (too aggressive, not relevant, has the potential to lose data, or cause more downtime), don't be afraid to refuse their request. If you feel that the person is incompetent, or is just guessing at the resolution; either call back, or ask the technical support person to escalate the call to the next level of technical support. Troubleshooting problems over the phone is probably one of the most difficult ways to solve a technical problem. Sometimes, it helps to mention an item that you notice on the server, even though you might not think it's relevant. After the second call to technical support, we were determined to get a replacement motherboard, after trying all of their previous suggestions. Fortunately, it wasn't too difficult to convince them this time to send us a replacement motherboard. Be aware that intermittent problems are the most difficult to solve. Usually, the problem will not show up on any diagnostic test. It's just like taking your car to the mechanic complaining of a noise, going for a ride with the mechanic, and the car runs perfectly. Knowing how to answer technical support's questions will help you get the replacement part that you need. Of course, it's their job to make sure they are not replacing perfectly good parts, but in this case, the replacement motherboard did solve the problem.

Scenario 7 USERS COMPLAIN OF SLOW SERVER PERFORMANCE

Facts

- HP ML370 with one 2.0-GHz processor, 512 MB of memory, and a three-drive RAID array using 72-GB hard disks. This is the only server on the network.
- The server was running Windows Server 2003 and Exchange 2003.
- This network has 30 users.

Symptoms

Users were complaining of server pauses and timeouts. Server performance was especially slow on Monday mornings.

Questions to Ask

Q: Has this happened before? A: Not really. The server was installed a few months ago. It was working fine, but has become increasingly slower over time.

Q: What has changed? A: No recent changes were made on the network.

Troubleshooting Steps

1. **Log in to the server.** When we arrived at the server, we noticed that it was difficult even to log in to the server. There was a noticeable pause on the server when we logged in. Server performance overall was very slow.
2. **Observe disk activity.** We noticed that the hard drive access lights on the server were constantly solid. The server was experiencing heavy disk activity.
3. **Check the Task Manager.** We pressed Ctrl-Alt-Delete and brought up the Task Manager. We clicked on the Performance tab and noticed that the Available Physical memory was down to 64 MB.
4. **Open the Performance Monitor.** We started the Performance Monitor and added the pages/sec in the Memory Performance Object. The pages/sec were averaging over 100 pages/sec with spikes well above the average.

Resolution

The combination of only 64 MB of available physical memory and the high number of pages/sec indicated that the server clearly needed more memory. Because the server was forced to frequently access the page file, disk activity was very heavy. We decided to increase the memory by 2 GB. After the memory was installed, the server ran much faster. Disk activity was greatly reduced, because the page file was rarely accessed.

Lessons Learned

For any new server installation, we start the server with at least 1 GB of memory, and 2 GB of memory if the server is running Exchange. Memory is relatively cheap and a simple way to increase server performance. When deciding on the amount of memory for the server, always err on the side of caution—too much memory is better than not enough. Be aware that the standard version of Windows 2000/2003 server has a 4-GB memory limit. If you anticipate the amount of memory you need in the server will be more than 4 GB, install the Enterprise Edition of Windows 2003 (32-bit), or Datacenter edition of Windows 2003 (32 bit), which can address 32 GB or 64 GB of memory, respectively.

Scenario 8 SCSI Bus Timeout Errors on HP DLT 70 Tape Drive

Facts

- HP ML370 with one 1.2-GHz processor, 3 GB of memory, and a three-drive RAID array using 72-GB hard disks. The server is running Windows Server 2003 and Exchange 2003.
- The server has three external tape drives connected on a separate SCSI controller: an HP Ultrium 230, an HP DLT 70, and an HP DAT 24 tape drive, in that order. A terminator is installed on a DAT 24 drive. Veritas Backup Exec 9.1 is used to back up the server.
- This network has 50 users.

Symptoms

This server was installed to replace an old Exchange 2000 server. The HP DLT70 and HP DAT 24 were moved from the old Exchange 2000 server and installed on the new Exchange 2003 server along with a new Ultrium 230 tape drive. After the tape drives were installed, a test backup was run on the DLT and Ultrium drive. The Ultrium drive backed up the server with no errors, but shortly after the DLT drive started backing up a remote server, Backup Exec reported a SCSI bus error on the tape drive and aborted the backup.

Questions to Ask

Q: What has changed? A: Three external tape drives were added to the server.

Q: Was this working before? A: The DLT and DAT tape drives were working on the old Exchange 2000 server with no problems.

Troubleshooting Steps

1. **Double-check the SCSI connections.** Incorrect SCSI termination can cause SCSI bus errors, so we double-checked the cable connections. The drives were daisy-chained in the following order: HP Ultrium 230, HP DLT 70, and HP DAT 24. All of the connections were tight and the SCSI bus was properly terminated on the HP DAT 24 drive.
2. **Reboot the server.** Sometimes, errors on the SCSI bus can occur, and a cold boot of the server will fix the problem. We tried shutting down the server, turning off the tape drives, and then restarting everything with a cold boot of the server. We carefully watched the server to make sure that all of the devices were recognized by the SCSI controller (they were). When the server restarted, we ran the test backup again, but shortly after it started, the same SCSI bus error appeared on the DLT drive. We were using the latest Veritas Tape drivers for each tape drive, because we just downloaded the latest version from Veritas' Web site.
3. **Examine the SCSI connectors.** According to HP's Web site, the Ultrium 230 is an Ultra2 SCSI device, the DLT 70 is a FastWide SCSI device, and the DAT 24 is a SCSI-2 device. The Ultrium 230 and DLT 70 have 68-pin connectors, and the DAT 24 has a Centronics 50-pin connector. Table 4.4 lists the SCSI specifications.

As you can see, the Ultra 2 SCSI interface used on the Ultrium 230 drive cannot use a single-ended terminator that was on the HP DAT 24. We wanted to install the DAT 24 to restore files that were backed up using this tape drive; however, the most recent files on the DAT tapes were over one-year old.

Resolution

As a test, we shut down the server, removed the HP DAT 24 from the SCSI bus, and restarted the server. With the DAT 24 removed from the SCSI bus, both the Ultrium and DLT drive were able to successfully complete their backup jobs. We decided to leave the DAT 24 off the server permanently because the chance of having to restore a file from a DAT tape was very small. If we have to restore a file using the DAT drive, we can install a separate SCSI controller in the server, or remove the Ultrium drive from the server and install the DAT drive.

where the database crashed (with the proper backup strategy), it is better suited for mission-critical applications.

SQL Server Versions

Although there are several versions of SQL Server, including the Personal, Developer, Evaluation, Windows CE, and Desktop editions, most companies install the Standard or Enterprise edition of SQL Server. The Standard edition can address up to 2 GB of memory and use four processors. If you need the fault tolerance of a SQL server cluster, need to address more than 2 GB of memory, or must use more than four processors, you must purchase the Enterprise Edition of SQL Server. Either version of SQL Server can be purchased in an unlimited user version based on the number of processors in the SQL server, or number of users connecting to SQL Server. Determine the number of users, servers, and processors in the SQL server before making the final purchase decision on the version of SQL Server. For more information on selecting a version of SQL Server that is right for your company, go to *www.microsoft.com/sql/techinfo/planning/SQLResKChooseEd.asp* and click on the ChoosEd.doc link on the right side of the window.

Hardware Selection

Unlike the typical file server, the processor on a SQL server sees higher utilization. For dedicated SQL servers, we try to purchase the faster processor available at the time and select a machine that has the capacity for two or more processors. Processor utilization can be high especially if you plan to run many stored procedures on the SQL server. If you're on a tight budget and don't have that many users, you can install SQL Server on the same machine as your file and print server. However, if you plan to have more than 20 or 30 users on the SQL server, consider making the SQL server a dedicated server. This will increase the fault tolerance and give you better performance.

Make sure to have an adequate amount of memory on the SQL server. For dedicated SQL servers, we suggest starting with at least 2 GB of memory or more depending on the potential load of the SQL server. Remember, if you want SQL Server itself to use more than 2 GB of memory, you must purchase the Enterprise version of SQL Server. If you want SQL Server Enterprise to use more than 4 GB of memory, you must run SQL Server on top of Windows 2003 Enterprise Server or Windows 2003 Datacenter Server, because the Windows 2003 Server Standard can only address a maximum of 4 GB and four processors. SQL Server by default dynamically configures memory usage on the server. Usually, this setting works fine. However, if you have enough memory in the server, you can reserve a set amount of memory for SQL server queries. This can improve performance if your SQL server is under a heavy load.

If the SQL Server application is mission critical, with a large database consider implementing a SQL server cluster with a storage area network (SAN) for redundancy. Of course, you will need the Enterprise version for clustering. For any SQL server, we consider some type of disk fault tolerance mandatory. This can be a RAID 1, 5, or 10 depending on the SQL server load and budget constraints. If your server does not have any disk fault tolerance, make sure to install the data and log partitions of the database on separate physical drives. If you want better disk performance on your SQL server, but aren't ready to use a SAN, set up two or more RAID 5 or 10 disk arrays and store the log and database files on separate arrays on the server.

If you plan to upload/download a large amount of data on your SQL server, make sure that the backbone connection on your network is up to the task. If this is a potential bottleneck, consider upgrading your network backbone to Gigabit or 10-Gigabit Ethernet to reduce the data transfer time of any upload/download.

SQL Server Structure

Figure 5.1 shows the basic hierarchy of a SQL server using the SQL Server Enterprise Manager.

The SQL Server Enterprise Manager is the primary interface for maintaining and managing a SQL server. At the highest level, you have SQL server groups. Servers can be logically grouped together to form groups. Below the groups are the actual SQL servers. Each SQL server contains databases. A SQL server database is a grouping of tables, views, and other objects. Several system databases are contained in SQL Server.

- **Master.** Other than the database(s) that will hold your company's data, master is probably the most important database. It contains the entire SQL server configuration and login accounts for the SQL server. It must be backed up on a regular basis. If you lose the master database, it will be very difficult to restore data back onto the SQL server in the event of a system crash.
- **Model.** This database contains template information that is used to create new databases. This database should be backed up on a regular basis.
- **Msdb.** This database is used for scheduling alerts, jobs, and recording operators. This database should be backed up on a regular basis.
- **Tempdb.** This is a temporary database that is used to store temporary tables and temporary stored procedures. It is recreated every time the SQL server is restarted using the template information from the model database. Initially, tempdb is relatively small (8 MB) and is configured to grow dynamically. For larger SQL Server installations, 8 MB might be ridiculously small. To avoid the overhead of growing tempdb, use the `alter database` command to make the initial size of tempdb more appropriate for your organization.

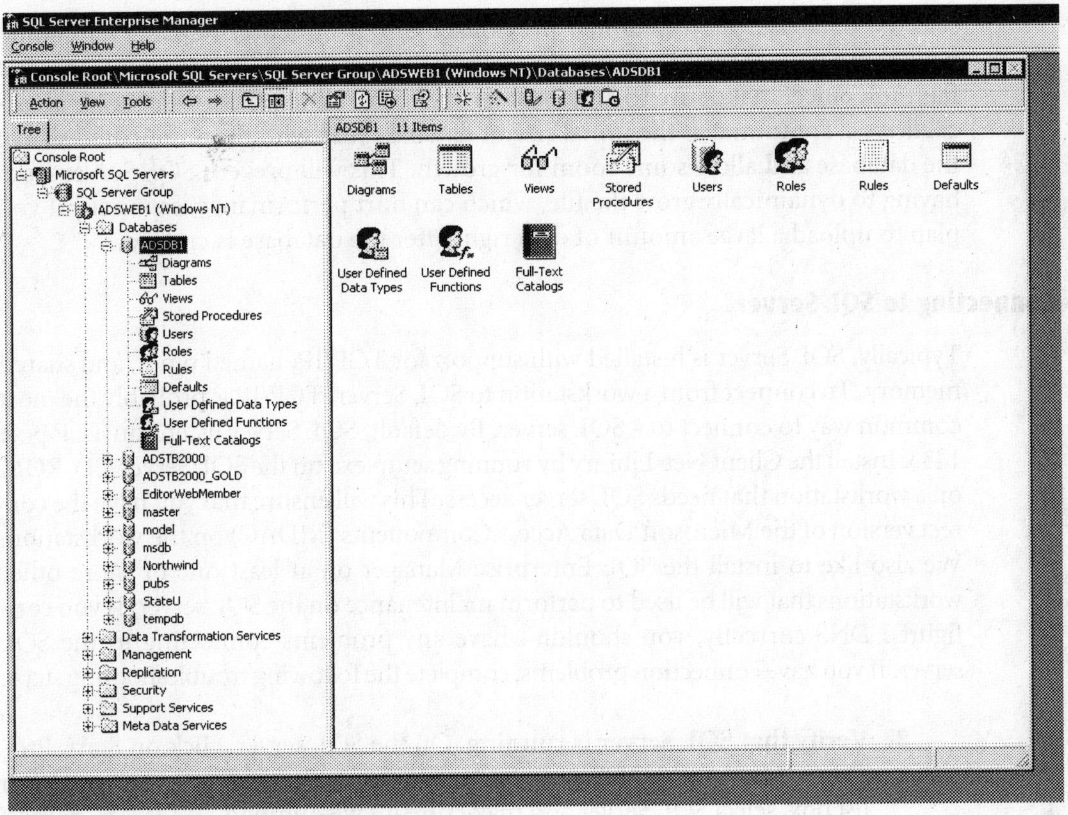

FIGURE 5.1 SQL Server Enterprise Manager.

The SQL server can also contain two sample databases: Pubs and Northwind. These databases can be easily recreated, and are not necessary to back up. On a production machine where they are not needed, consider dropping (deleting) these databases. If you need to recreate these databases, you can run the instpubs.sql and instnwind.sql scripts located in the install folder on the SQL Server CD-ROM.

Physical File Location for Databases

Databases are stored in two physical files: the data and log files. The data file contains the actual database information. The log file contains a record of every change that was made to the database since the last full backup. This file can be used to recreate data stored in the database in the event of a major system crash. You can right-click on any database, select Properties, and select the Data Files and Transaction Log tabs to determine the physical location of the data and log files for the selected database. As mentioned previously, any production SQL server should have some type of disk fault tolerance on the server. If you do not have any disk fault tolerance, make sure to at least store the data and log files on separate physical drives. Try to match the initial size of database files with the anticipated size of the database and allow some room for growth. This will prevent SQL Server from having to dynamically grow the file, which can hurt performance, especially if you plan to upload a large amount of data right after the database is created.

Connecting to SQL Server

Typically, SQL Server is installed with support for TCP/IP, named pipes, and shared memory. To connect from a workstation to SQL Server, TCP/IP is probably the most common way to connect to a SQL server. By default, SQL Server listens on TCP port 1433. Install the Client Net-Library by running setup.exe on the SQL Server CD-ROM on a workstation that needs SQL server access. This will ensure that you have the correct version of the Microsoft Data Access Components (MDAC) on the workstation. We also like to install the SQL Enterprise Manager on at least one or more other workstations that will be used to perform maintenance on the SQL server. If you configured DNS correctly, you shouldn't have any problems connecting to the SQL server. If you have connection problems, complete the following troubleshooting steps:

1. **Verify that SQL Server is running.** On the SQL server, click on Start, Programs, Microsoft SQL Server, Service Manager. In the Services drop-down list box, select SQL Server and make sure it says Running - \\<server_name> - MSSQLServer at the bottom (see Figure 5.2).

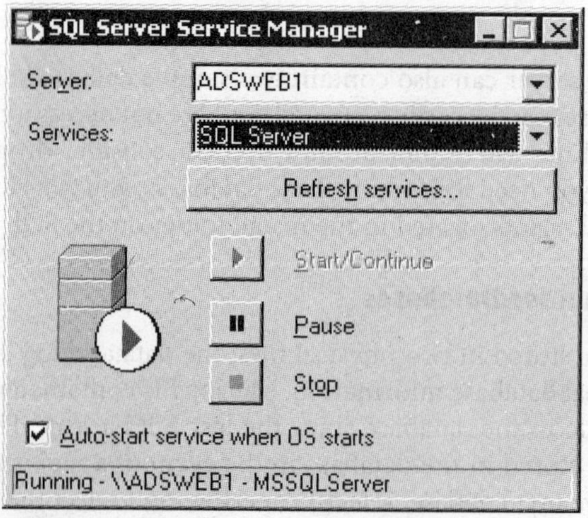

FIGURE 5.2 SQL Server Service Manager.

If the SQL server is not running, click on the Start/Continue button to start the service. Make sure "Auto-start service when OS starts" is checked if you want SQL Server to start when the server is rebooted. If the SQL server fails to start, check the Event Viewer to see if SQL Server logged an error during startup.

2. **Ping the server.** Obtain the IP address of the SQL server and try pinging by IP address by issuing the command ping <sql_server_ip_address>. If you cannot reach the SQL server, verify that you have the correct IP address and that the workstation's address has the correct IP address. If you cannot reach the server by IP address, use the trace route utility (tracert <sql_server_ip_address>) to determine where the ping packet dies. If you can ping by IP address, then ping by the name of the SQL server by running ping <sql_server_name>. If you can ping by IP address, but not by name, you probably have a DNS problem.
3. **Verify the SQL Server protocols.** From a workstation, click on Start, Programs, Microsoft SQL Server, Client Network Utility, and click on the General tab. Figure 5.3 will appear.

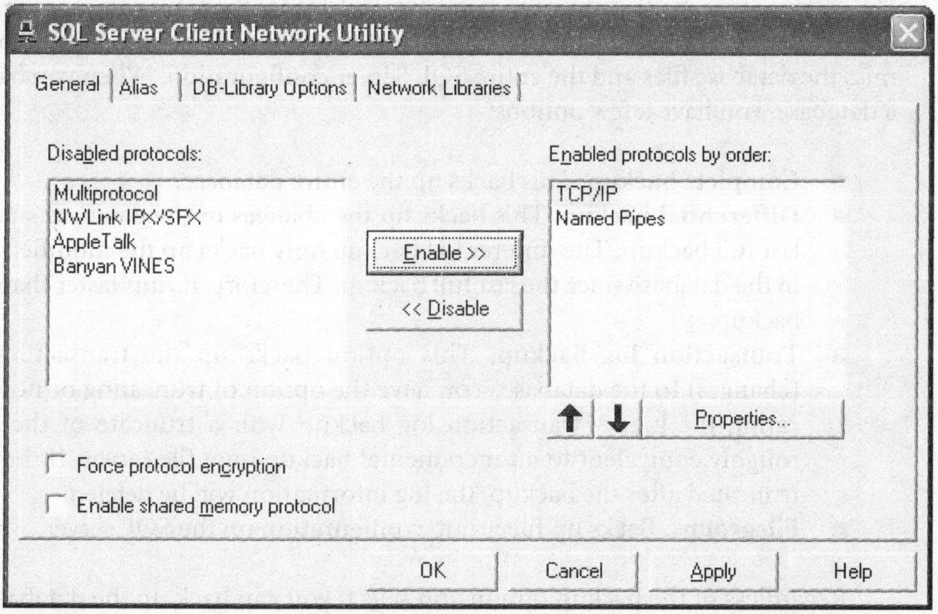

FIGURE 5.3 SQL Server Client Network Utility.

Make sure that TCP/IP and Named Pipes are enabled in the right window. Click on the Alias tab and verify that any aliases are properly set up.

4. **Login problem.** SQL Server can be configured for Windows Integrated Authentication only or Windows Integrated Authentication and SQL Server Authentication. We suggest only using Windows Integrated Authentication because it is more secure than SQL Server Authentication. To view the type of authentication, start the SQL Enterprise Manager, right-click on the server, and click on the Security tab. Make sure that you are using a valid username and password to connect to the SQL server based on the authentication method allowed on your SQL server.

BACKUP/MAINTENANCE OF SQL SERVER

As with any other server on your network, backup and maintenance of the SQL server are vital to a smooth-running database server. Here are some suggestions to help you formulate a backup strategy and maintenance plan.

Backup Types

Because the database is always running, the database files are in use. To back up a SQL server, you must dump the database and transaction files to tape or other backup device. If you back up the SQL server just like any other file server, you will miss the database files and the entire SQL Server configuration. When you back up a database, you have a few options:

- **Complete backup.** This backs up the entire database.
- **Differential backup.** This backs up the changes in the database since the last full backup. The differential backup only backs up the modified pages in the database since the last full backup. Therefore, it runs faster than a full backup.
- **Transaction log backup.** This option backs up the transaction logs (changes) to the database. You have the option of truncating or not truncating the log. A transaction log backup with a truncate of the log is roughly equivalent to an incremental backup on a file server. If the log is truncated after the backup, the log information will be deleted.
- **Filegroups.** Backs up file group configuration on the SQL server.

Regardless of the backup option you select, you can back up the database to a disk device or tape device. We suggest performing a test restore on one of the sample databases (pubs or Northwind) to verify that your backup is working properly.

Backup Strategy

For SQL Server, we suggest performing a full database backup on a daily basis. This includes a backup of the master, model, msdb, filegroups, and your production databases. We suggest backing the database to tape instead of disk, because the tape can be easily taken off site in the event of fire or other major disaster. The tape drive should be located on a SCSI bus that is separate from the disk drives. For the full backup, we set the backup job to overwrite. Usually, this full backup takes place after hours. During the day, we schedule a backup of the transaction log (no truncate) every hour to tape, this time appending to the tape. At the end of the day, the tape is swapped out and the cycle repeats. This backup strategy allows us to recover data at specific times throughout the day. Let's assume that the server crashes at 5:30 P.M. Let's also assume we have a tape that has a complete backup of last night and transaction log backups starting at 8:00 A.M. and then every hour until 5:00 P.M. Using this tape, we would restore the full backup from last night, and then restore the transaction log from 5:00 P.M. We only have to restore one transaction log because we did not truncate the log when we backed it up. Then, we would use the `restore log` command to roll forward the transactions from the full restore until 5:00 P.M. The users would have to create the data that was entered into the system from 5:00 P.M. to 5:30 P.M.; however, a majority of the data entry would be recovered from the transaction logs. We prefer to use Backup Exec with the SQL Server agent to back up our SQL servers; however, the backups can be run using the SQL Enterprise Manager.

Differential versus Transaction Log Backups

We could also use a differential backup on the database instead of a transaction log backup; however, a differential backup backs up the modified pages in a database, so you don't have the flexibility of performing a point-in-time restore when using a transaction log backup. Let's assume that a user accidentally deletes a large amount of critical records in the database at 4:31 P.M. If we used a differential backup every hour, we could restore the database as of 4:00 P.M. With a transaction log backup, we could perform a point-in-time restore as of 4:30. P.M, because we can roll the transactions forward just before the user accidentally deleted the records in the database. The main advantage of differential backups is that they tend to be smaller than transaction log backups, and take less time to restore. Another alternative is to use a combination of differential backups supplemented with transaction log backups. This is a good strategy if your database has many transactions but relatively few modified pages. You can run a differential backup every hour, and then a transaction log backup every 15 minutes. If the server crashed at 4:20 P.M., you could restore the full backup from the previous night, the differential backup as of 4:00 P.M. and then transaction log at 4:15 P.M. You would only lose five minutes of transactions on the SQL server with this backup strategy.

Of course, you must decide for yourself the best backup strategy for your SQL server based on the transaction load, data recovery requirements, speed of the SQL server, capacity of the tape drive, and database size. Although you can automate the backup of SQL Server with a database maintenance plan, we still like to use Veritas' Backup Exec SQL Server agent to perform backups. This gives us a single interface to check the backup status of all servers.

Database Maintenance Plans

Your backup strategy and database maintenance can be incorporated into a database maintenance plan. You can create a new maintenance plan by using the SQL Server Enterprise Manager. Click on SQL Server Group, <SQL_Server_Name>, Management, right-click on the Database Maintenance Plan, and select New Maintenance Plan. The wizard will guide you through the creation of the maintenance plan. Select the databases you want to include in the plan. The wizard will ask you the following questions to formulate your maintenance plan:

- **Reorganize data and index pages.** This is roughly equivalent to a defragmentation of files on a hard drive, except for a database. This process can be potentially processor and disk intensive, so we suggest running this on weekends.
- **Update statistics.** This process gathers information about the data contained in the database. This information is then used by the query analyzer to determine the best approach when performing a query. We suggest running update statistics whenever you add/remove a large amount of data on the database or at least once a week.
- **Remove unused space from DB files.** This option will shrink the physical size of the database files. Normally, the data on SQL Server grows. This can be a potentially disk- and processor-intensive process, but if you're short on disk space, you can free up some room by running this process. Run this process after hours or on weekends to minimize the effect on SQL Server users.
- **Check DB integrity.** We suggest running this on a weekly basis or more often if you have experienced data integrity problems in the past on your SQL server. It's important to know that your SQL server database integrity is sound; otherwise, you might have trouble restoring data from backup because the database backups are corrupted.
- **Back up databases.** Refer to our suggestions in the *Backup/Maintenance* section of this chapter for database backup strategies.
- **Back up transaction logs.** Refer to our suggestions in the *Backup/Maintenance* section of this chapter for database transaction log backup strategies.

- **Reports.** This option allows you to configure where the maintenance reports are stored, how long they are kept, whom to e-mail the report to, and where to write the history reports.

BEST PRACTICES ANALYZER

Microsoft released a SQL Server Best Practices Analyzer that looks at more than 70 parameters on your SQL server. This tool can be downloaded from *www.microsoft.com/downloads/details.aspx?FamilyId=B352EB1F-D3CA-44EE-893E-9E07339C1F22&displaylang=en.* This is great tool to run against your SQL server to increase performance, review stored procedures, review select statements, and review your backup/recovery model on the SQL server. We strongly recommend you download this tool and follow any suggestions to ensure that your SQL server is running optimally.

SQL SERVER SECURITY

Just like SQL Server itself, entire books have been written about SQL Server security. With increased levels of hacking activity, you must take SQL Server security seriously. Here are some suggestions that we follow when installing a SQL server:

Keep up to date with service packs and critical updates. This is especially important for servers that are accessed from the public Internet. Consider installing any critical updates automatically.

Keep IIS and SQL Server on separate servers. If you have a public Web server that will access SQL Server data, place the Web server in the demilitarized zone (DMZ) and create a rule to only allow SQL Server traffic on port 1433 from the IIS server to the SQL server located on the protected (LAN) side of the firewall (see Figure 5.4).

Use Integrated Windows Authentication only. SQL Server 2000 supports SQL Server authentication for backward compatibility. Unfortunately, when this authentication method is used, users and passwords are stored on the SQL server, and usernames and password are sent across the network for authentication. If you must use SQL Server authentication, make sure to change the sa (System Administrator) password, and delete the guest account.

Separate service accounts for IIS and SQL Server. Create separate IIS and SQL Server service accounts for starting up these services on the servers. Do *not* use the Administrator account to start IIS or SQL Server services! There is a chance

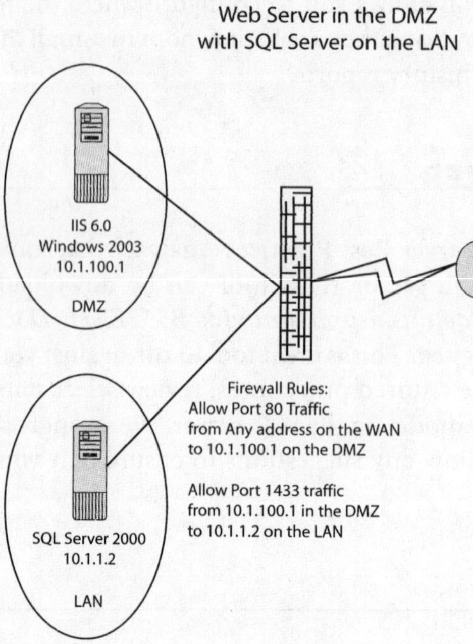

FIGURE 5.4 IIS in the DMZ accessing a SQL server on the LAN.

that a hacker can take advantage of rights granted to the service account if the SQL server or IIS machine is compromised.

Do not use a user ID and password in your ADO connection string to connect to SQL Server. Use the trusted_connection=Yes option to connect to SQL Server that forces Windows authentication. If you specify a user ID and password in your connection string, a hacker can obtain the code and obtain a valid user ID and password to the SQL server.

Install virus software on the SQL server. Install virus software on the SQL server, but exclude the SQL databases from virus scans.

Disable the guest account. Disable the guest account in Active Directory. Drop the guest account from any database on the SQL server.

Upgrade IIS to 6.0. If you're using IIS 5.0 with SQL Server for a backend database, consider upgrading to IIS 6.0. IIS 6.0 is more secure than IIS 5.0 because most services are disabled by default. If you must stay with IIS 5.0, run the lockdown tool located at *www.microsoft.com/downloads/details.aspx?FamilyID=DDE9EFC0-BB30-47EB-9A61-FD755D23CDEC&displaylang=en* to identify any security holes on your IIS server.

Install an SSL certificate for your Web applications. Purchase an SSL certificate from an SSL provider, or issue one from Windows 2000/2003 by installing certificate services. The SSL certificate will encrypt any data traveling from the IIS server to a client workstation.

Use Stored Procedures to access data from a Web application. Never issue SQL statements from an IIS server. Instead, create stored procedures for all data access and then grant the Web application rights to the stored procedures. Do not allow the Web application to execute dynamic SQL statements.

DATABASE ADMINISTRATORS

For any serious development effort, considering hiring a full/part time database administrator (DBA). A good DBA can make the difference between a successful development effort and a disastrous one. DBAs ensure that database structures meet the third normal form, create stored procedures, know how to improve the performance of the SQL server, and can devise elegant solutions for complex data models. They are typically responsible for backup and restore of the database, security, performance, and table structures on the SQL server.

TROUBLESHOOTING SCENARIOS

This section includes some real-world SQL Server issues that we've experienced during our consulting adventures. As with almost anything else on computers, make sure you have a good backup and that you can restore data from a test backup. As long as you have the backup, you should be able to recover from almost any type of SQL Server disaster.

Scenario 1 — USERS CANNOT ACCESS THE SQL SERVER

Facts

- HP SQL Server 2000 (Service Pack 3a) with four-drive RAID 5 array running over Windows Server 2003.
- Server has a 3.0-GHz processor with 3 GB of memory.
- Forty users connected to the SQL server.
- SQL Server runs internal reports and accounting system.
- Server is backed up with Veritas' Backup Exec 9.1 using the SQL Server Agent.

Symptoms

We received a call from the client that no one can access the SQL server and the Accounting system is down.

Questions to Ask

Q: Has anything changed? A: No.

Q: Was it working before? A: Yes, all of a sudden, no one could get in to the SQL server.

Troubleshooting Steps

1. **Verify the problem.** When we arrived on site, we tried to access the SQL server and received an error that the SQL server was unavailable.
2. **Check the SQL server.** When we checked, the SQL server was not running. We tried to restart the server, but when it booted we received the "Inaccessible boot device" error when we tried to start the server. We suspected that one of the drives in the RAID 5 array was bad.
3. **Run Server Diagnostics.** We ran the Server Diagnostics from the HP Smart Start CD-ROM. It identified two of the drives as bad. Although RAID 5 can recover from one hard drive failure, more than one will cause the RAID 5 array to go down.

Resolution

After it was determined that the drives were bad on the server, we placed a call to HP for replacement hard drives. To get the SQL server back up and running:

1. **Swap out the hard drives.** The hard drives arrived the next day, and we swapped them out for the failed hard drives.
2. **Install Windows Server 2003.** We performed a clean installation of Windows Server 2003, with the same drive configuration as the original server with all of the critical updates.
3. **Install SQL Server 2000.** We performed a clean install of SQL Server 2000, and installed Service Pack 3a.
4. **Install virus software.** We reinstalled the Corporate Edition of Norton Anti-Virus, excluding the SQL Server database files.
5. **Install Backup Exec.** We installed Backup Exec 9.1 with the SQL Server agent.
6. **Catalog the latest backup tape.** We cataloged the tape from the latest backup. This particular SQL server was backed up with a full backup from the previous night, and transaction log backups (with no truncate) were appended to the tape every hour during working hours from 8 A.M. to 5 P.M.

7. **Restore the master database.** We stopped the MSSQLSERVER service and started the SQL server in single-user mode by adding a `–m` in the `start` parameter. We selected the master database for restore. We selected the options under the Settings, SQL Restore options shown in Figure 5.5.

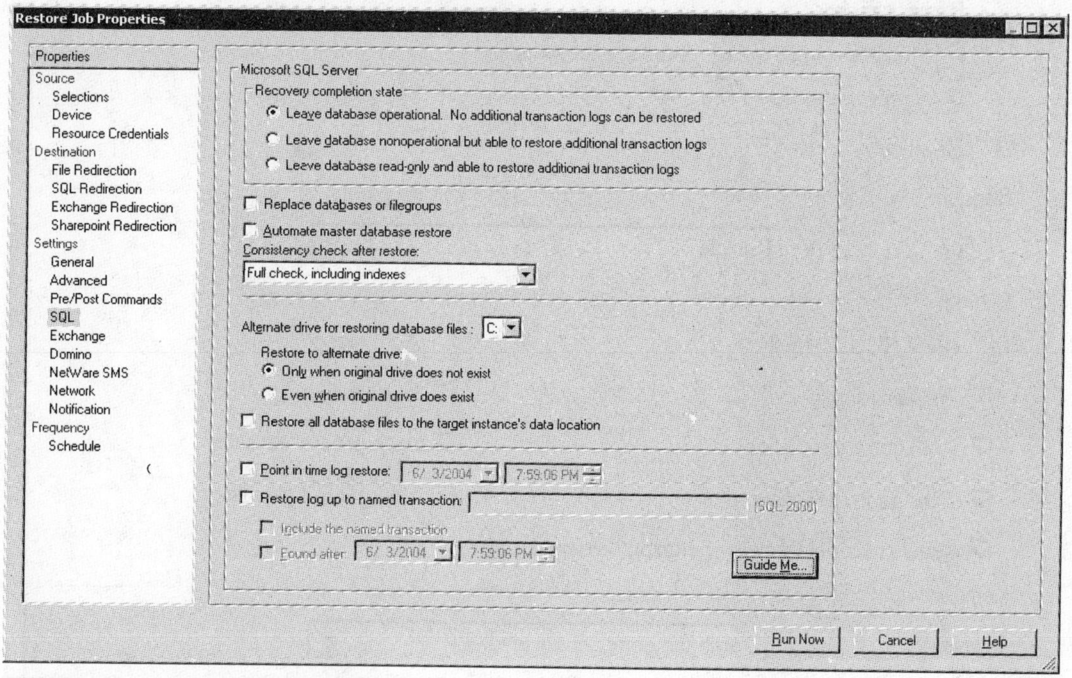

FIGURE 5.5 SQL Restore settings.

No changes to the master had taken place since the last backup, so we selected to leave the database operational. No additional transaction logs can be restored, and we performed a full consistency check on the master after the restore. After the master was restored, we restarted the MSSQLSERVER service in multi-user mode by removing the `–m` startup parameter.

8. **Restore the msdb database.** Before restoring the msdb database, we set the database in single-user mode, using the SQL Enterprise Manager. Right-click on the msdb database, select Properties, and click on the Options tab. Figure 5.6 will appear.

   Using Backup Exec, we selected the msdb database for restore. We selected the same SQL Restore options as the master when we restored the msdb database.

9. **Restore the model database.** We restored the model database using the same procedure as the msdb database.

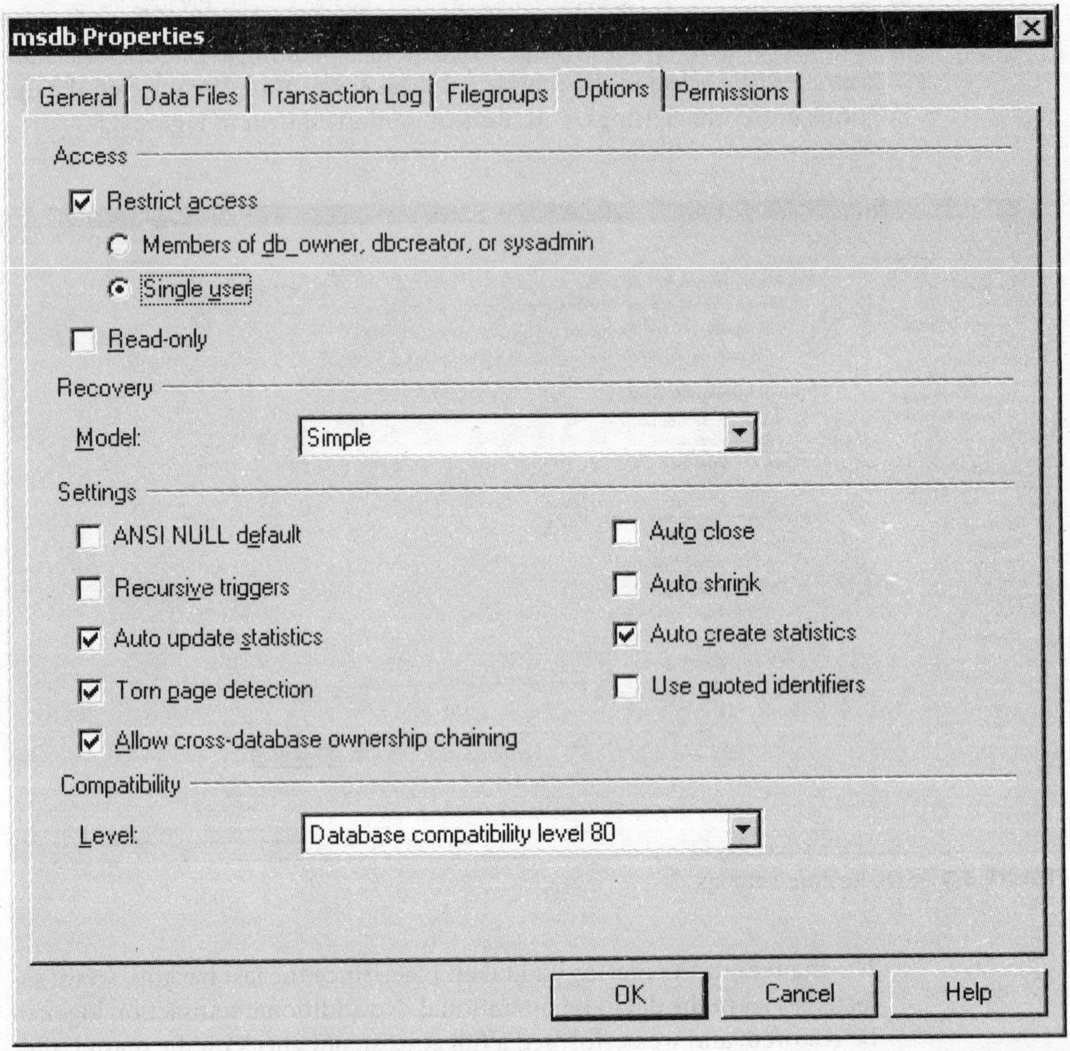

FIGURE 5.6 Setting msdb to single-user mode.

10. **Restore the main company database.** At this point, we were ready to restore the client's main database. We set the database to single-user mode using the SQL Enterprise Manager. We then used Backup Exec to restore the main company database. We had transaction log backups that we wanted to restore after the database restore was completed, so we selected the SQL Restore options shown in Figure 5.7.

    We selected the "Leave database nonoperational, but able to restore additional transaction logs" option because we want to restore the transaction logs after the database restore.

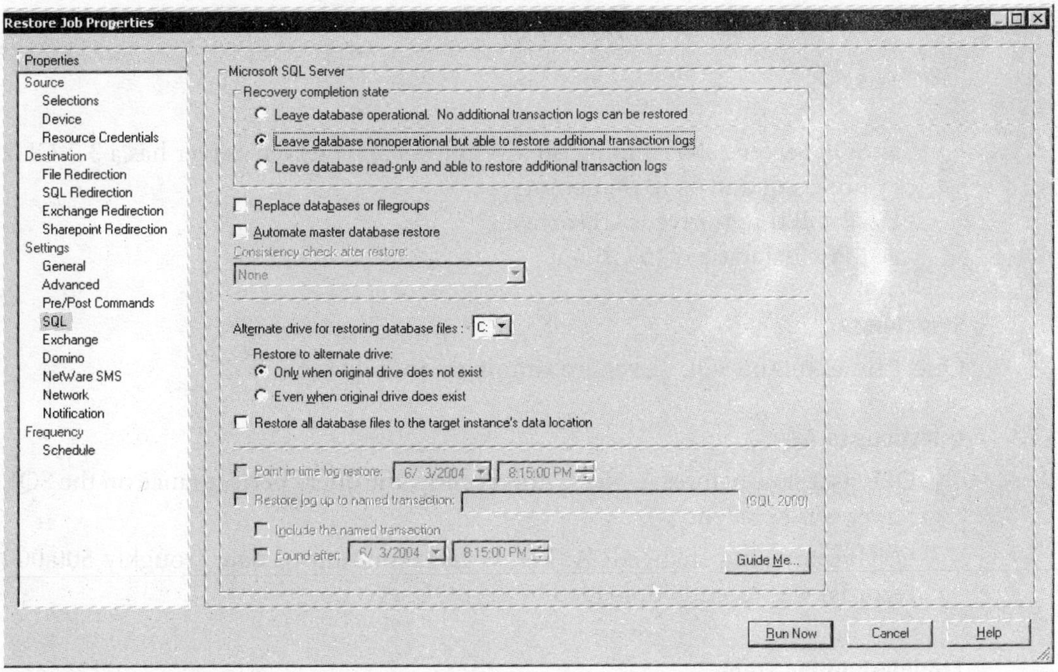

FIGURE 5.7 SQL Restore options for the main company database.

11. **Restore transaction log for main company database.** We selected the last available transaction log backup from the tape for restore. Because the transaction logs were not truncated, the last transaction log backup had all of the database changes since the last full database backup. This time, in the SQL Restore options of Backup Exec, we selected the "Leave database operational" option. No additional transaction logs can be restored.
12. **Place all databases in multi-user mode.** After the restore process was complete, we placed all of the databases in multi-user mode using SQL Enterprise Manager by removing the Restore Access check box on the Options tab of the database properties.
13. **Test.** After the SQL server was recovered, we verified that all of the data was recovered based on the time of the transaction log backup.

Lessons Learned

If more than one drive in a RAID 5 array fails, the entire array will crash. With the HP RAID (and other controllers), you can specify one drive in the array as a hot spare. This will allow you to lose up to two drives in the array, and it will still stay up. For additional fault tolerance, consider using RAID 10 because half of the drives in the array can fail and the array will still stay up. For the highest level of fault tolerance, configure a SQL server cluster and a RAID 10 SAN.

Scenario 2 Poor Performance on the SQL Server

Facts

- SQL Server 2000 running on a Windows 2003 server. Server has a 3.2-GHz processor and 4 GB of memory.
- 72-GB three-drive RAID array.
- Main database is 10 GB.

Symptoms

Query times on the SQL server are running unusually slow.

Questions to Ask

Q: Was it slow before? A: No. Until recently, the query performance on the SQL server was excellent.

Q: Has anything changed? A: Yes. A large amount of data (roughly 500,000 records) was recently uploaded to the SQL server.

Troubleshooting Steps

1. **Verify the problem.** We performed a few queries against the SQL server, and it was performing slower than normal.
2. **What has changed?** When we asked what had changed, we learned that a large amount of data was recently uploaded to the SQL server.

Resolution

Since we had run into this problem before, we already knew what the fix was. Whenever a large amount of data is added/removed from a table, you should run Update Statistics <table_name>. This command forces the SQL server to update distribution statistics for all table indexes. We determined what tables were affected by the upload, and issued the command for these tables. By running the command manually, we didn't have to wait for the database maintenance plan to run the command at the end of the week.

Lessons Learned

Make sure to train your DBA to run the Update Statistics command anytime they add/delete a large amount of data to any table.

Scenario 3 SQL Server Runs Especially Slow When Restarted, and Has Poor Overall Performance

Facts

- SQL Server 2000 standard running on Windows 2003 Standard.
- 1 GB of memory.
- Three-drive RAID 5 array with 72-GB disks.
- Single 3.0-GHz processor on the SQL server.
- 60 SQL server users.
- 70-GB database used for data warehousing.
- Symptoms.

The SQL server runs slow, especially when it is restarted. Queries run especially slow, when there are many users on the system.

Questions to Ask

Q: Has anything changed? A: Not really. Although, the system is more heavily used now than it was when the server was first installed.

Q: When is it slow? A: All of the time, but it's especially slow when the server is restarted. It's also slow when there are many users on the system.

Troubleshooting Steps

1. **Verify the problem.** When we ran a few queries against the database, response times were slow. Any report run from this server was especially slow. The performance of add/modify/delete of single records was a little better.
2. **Observe hard disks.** We logged in to the server, which took an unusually long time. We observed that the hard disk lights on RAID 5 array were on solid. Obviously, something was causing very heavy disk utilization.
3. **Review tempdb.** We looked at tempdb and noticed that it was over 600 MB in size. We made a mental note of this.
4. **Load Performance Monitor.** We loaded the Performance Monitor by clicking on Start, Programs, Administrative Tools, and Performance. We added the following parameters:

    a. **Memory Pages/sec.** This is the amount of hard page faults per second that the server had to read/write from/to the hard drive because the requested information was not in memory. A busy server should have no more than 50 pages/sec. This server was averaging over 100 pages/sec.
    b. **% Disk Time on the Physical Disk.** On a busy server, this should read below 70 percent. On this server, it was over 90 percent.

c. **Disk Queue Length on the Physical Disk.** A busy server should have no more than a queue length of 2. This server had a queue length of 5.
d. **% Processor Time.** This was relatively good, averaging 50 percent.

Obviously, we had some serious performance problems on this server, but what's the correct fix?

Resolution

We knew that the server was disk bound, but it was severely short on memory as well. The lack of memory in the server can cause a high amount of page faults as the server swaps virtual memory to/from the hard disk instead of performing an operation in RAM. Because they were running the Standard version of both SQL Server and Windows Server 2003, the SQL server could only use a maximum of 2 GB of memory, and Windows Server 2003 can address 4 GB of memory. We decided to increase the memory in the server to 4 GB as a first step, because it's a relatively easy and cheap fix. We warned the client that we would probably have to make additional modifications to the server. Since this was a dedicated SQL server, we allocated 2 GB of memory to SQL Server, leaving the remaining 2 GB for the operating system and disk cache.

After we added the memory, the server performance was improved, but disk activity was still heavy. We loaded the Performance Monitor and observed that the % disk time was still over 85 percent. We still had a serious disk bottleneck. The RAID controller was a single-channel controller. We purchased a dual-channel RAID controller and external drive subsystem. We then purchased six 72-GB hard drives and set up two additional three-drive RAID 5 arrays on the server. We placed the log files on one of the new arrays, and tempdb by itself on the third RAID 5 array. We used the `alter database` command to set the initial size of tempdb to 700 MB. Tempdb is initialized every time the server is restarted. Because tempdb grew so much during the normal running of the server, the server had to deal with increasing the size of tempdb, causing an even heavier load on the SQL server. After we made these changes, the SQL server performance improved dramatically. Just for kicks, we loaded the Performance Monitor and observed the % Disk Time and Disk Queue Length. The % Disk Time was now down to 40 percent, and the Disk Queue Length was either zero or one on the busiest array.

Lessons Learned

Make sure to have an adequate amount of memory and disk capacity on the SQL server. We might have been able to get by with just one additional RAID array, using it for both the transaction logs and tempdb; however, this database was going to grow significantly over the next few years. In general, we like to build our servers for growth and give the client some room for growth. We warned the client that the next step was to upgrade to the Enterprise versions of both SQL Server and Windows Server 2003 so we could take advantage of more memory and server clustering with a SAN if the database grew too large.

Scenario 4 ACCESS APPLICATION CANNOT UPDATE RECORDS ON SQL SERVER 2000

Facts

- Application migrated from Access 97 to Access XP.
- SQL Server upgraded from 7.0 to SQL 2000 with Service Pack 3a.
- New SQL server is a HP Proliant ML370 with 2.8-GHz processor, 2.5 GB of memory, and three-drive 72-GB RAID array.
- 5-GB database with 30 users.

Symptoms

We performed the upgrade of the client's network from Windows NT, Exchange 5.5, and SQL Server 7.0 to Windows 2000, Exchange 2000, and SQL Server 2000. All of the workstations were also upgraded to Windows XP with Service Pack 1. After the network upgrades were completed, the client's internal database application was migrated from Access 97 and SQL Server 7.0 to Access XP and SQL Server 2000. This migration was performed by another consultant. Evidently, whenever anyone tried to save data to the main customer table, Access XP would report that the update was unsuccessful. The developer was working on this particular problem for three weeks. We received a call from the client asking if we could come in and help.

Questions to Ask

Q: Has anything changed? A: Yes. This application was migrated from Access 97 and SQL Server 7.0 to Access XP and SQL Server 2000.

Q: What troubleshooting steps were completed? A: A careful review of the update statement revealed that it was using the correct syntax and table. A case was opened with Microsoft, and a copy of the entire database and application were sent to Microsoft. However, Microsoft was unable to duplicate the problem and it has remained unresolved for three weeks.

Troubleshooting Steps

1. **Verify the problem.** We started the application and received an error message whenever we tried to modify a customer record and save it.
2. **SQL Server 7.0.** When the new version of the application was run with SQL Server 7.0, the application worked fine. Because of this, and the fact that

Microsoft could not recreate the problem in their location, the developer wanted us to reinstall SQL Server 2000 on the new server. We didn't really feel that this would solve the problem, but we reinstalled it anyway. After the SQL server was completely reinstalled from scratch, they still had the same problem. At this point, the developer wanted us to wipe the server, reinstall Windows 2000, and SQL Server. We gently suggested that we should look at other areas before performing a complete reinstallation of the server. At this point, we did not feel that a reinstall would fix the problem. The network was stable since the upgrades were performed, and the Event Viewers on all servers did not reveal any problems with any of the servers.

3. **Run `update` command in SQL Query Analyzer.** We ran the raw `update` command in the SQL Query Analyzer that was used by the Access application, and the `update` command did not run successfully. Because the `update` command failed both in the Access application and with the SQL Query Analyzer, we figured that the problem was most likely with the SQL server itself, and not specific to that application.
4. **Use SQL Profiler.** We monitored the SQL server using the SQL Profiler. You can start the SQL Profiler by clicking on Start, Programs, Microsoft SQL Server, Profiler. SQL Profiler works similarly to the Network Monitor in Windows 2000 Server, but instead of monitoring network packets, it can monitor almost any event on the SQL server. It's a great tool for troubleshooting slow performance or errors on the SQL server. For more information on Profiler, refer to:

   http://techrepublic.com.com/5100-6329-5054787.html
   http://vyaskn.tripod.com/analyzing_profiler_output.htm
   www.sql-server-performance.com/sql_server_profiler_tips.asp

   Since we were experiencing problems with an update on one particular table, we set up a Trace Template to track all TSQL events, for the database in question. Unfortunately, even when we ran the `update` statement in Access or used the SQL Query Analyzer, the Profiler did not display any error messages.
5. **Review database.** We did install SQL Server on the new server; however, we did not upload the data from the old to the new server. Since we suspected that the problem was something related to SQL Server, we reviewed the structures, indexes, stored procedures, backup plan, security, and database maintenance plan on the SQL server.

Resolution

We paid careful attention to the table we were unable to update. We verified that we had enough rights to update the table. We reviewed and noticed that a primary key was defined on the table, but the index associated with the primary key was not a clustered index. A clustered index determines the physical sort of the database. To view the indexes associated with a table, right-click on the table in SQL Enterprise Manager and select All Tasks, Manage Indexes. Normally, when you create a primary key, a clustered index is created automatically on the primary key field, unless a clustered index already exists on the table or you explicitly specify not to use a clustered index. We made the index associated with the primary key a clustered index. Once we made this change, we were able to run the update statement without any problems.

Lessons Learned

When we create tables on the SQL server, we always define a primary key and clustered index associated with the primary key. A clustered index causes the SQL server to physically sort the table based on the value in the clustered index key. Therefore, a table can only have one clustered index. After the clustered index is created, we create any other indexes on the table as necessary. If you are uploading a large table to SQL Server, presort the table in the primary key order. This will speed up the creation of the clustered index and prevent the SQL server from having to sort the table after it's imported. It took us a day and a half to solve this problem. Because we were able to solve this problem relatively quickly, we were able to get future development work for this system.

CHAPTER SUMMARY

As we mentioned before, there have been entire books written on SQL Server. The goal of this chapter was to describe the basics of SQL Server from a network administrator's point of view. The most important topic of this chapter is to develop a sound backup strategy, based on your company's data requirements. With a good backup, you can quickly recover from almost any disaster. A combination of full, differential, and transaction log backups will ensure you can recover SQL Server data, often to the point just before the server crashed.

REVIEW QUESTIONS

1. What's the maximum amount of memory that SQL Server standard can use?
   a. 4 GB
   b. 2 GB
   c. 8 GB
   d. 16 GB
   e. 32 GB
2. During disaster recovery, what SQL commands would you use to roll forward transactions after a full database restore?
   a. Roll forward
   b. Roll log
   c. Restore database
   d. Restore log
   e. Restore transactions
3. In addition to your company's database, what SQL Server system databases should you back up on a regular basis?
   a. Pubs
   b. Master
   c. Msdb
   d. model
   e. tempdb
4. What tool can be used to perform a SQL Trace?
   a. Performance Monitor
   b. Profiler
   c. Network Monitor
   d. dbcc
   e. Update statistics
5. How should you access data from a SQL server using IIS running a Web-based application?
   a. Issue select statements from IIS with only the columns that are necessary.
   b. Use integrated Windows authentication.
   c. Use SQL Server authentication.
   d. Obtain data using only stored procedures.
   e. Include the username and password in your SQL connect string.

6 Exchange Server Troubleshooting

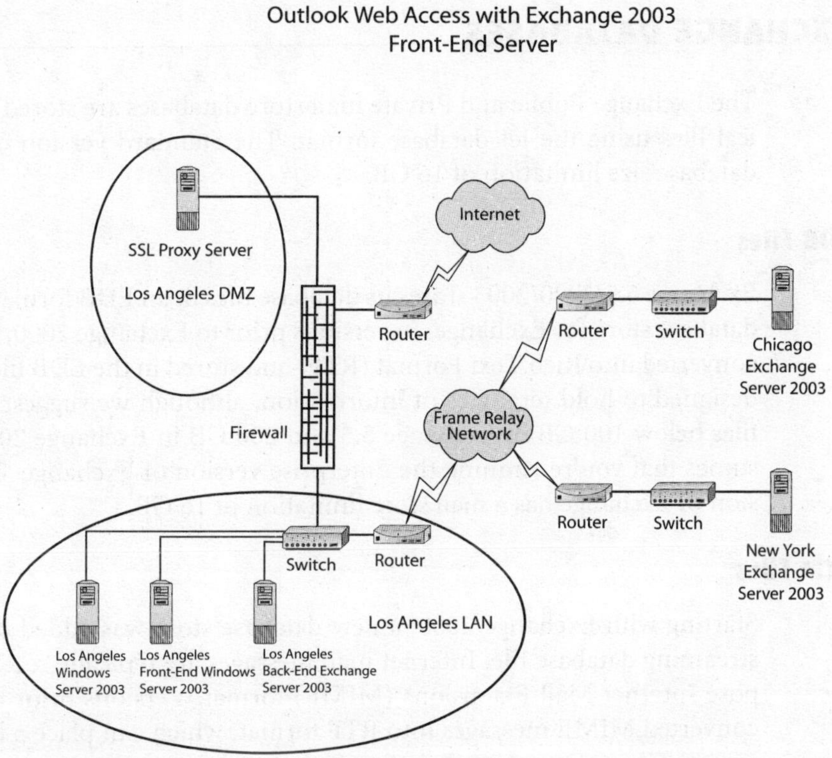

CHAPTER PREVIEW

If you use Windows Server on your network, chances are you use Exchange for your e-mail, scheduling, contacts, and tasks. Like any other server on your network, proper planning and configuration can prevent most Exchange problems from occurring in the first place. In the first part of this chapter, we examine the Exchange database structure and storage limitations. A familiarity with the databases will assist you if you ever have to recover an Exchange message store. We'll examine the proper Exchange server design, placement, backup, virus protection, Internet mail, and Outlook Web Access (OWA). Like any other installation, proper planning and design will prevent problems from occurring in the first place. The second half of the chapter is devoted to real-world troubleshooting scenarios. Many of the issues that we run into with Exchange can be prevented with proper planning, maintenance, and monitoring of the Exchange server.

EXCHANGE DATABASES

The Exchange Public and Private mail store databases are stored in different physical files using the Jet database format. The Standard version of Exchange has a database size limitation of 16 GB.

EDB Files

Exchange 5.5/2000/2003 stores its database files in an EDB format. This is the main database store for Exchange. In versions prior to Exchange 2000, mail messages are converted into Rich Text Format (RTF) and stored in the EDB file. This database is designed to hold terabytes of information, although we suggest keeping the EDB files below 100 GB in Exchange 5.5 and 200 GB in Exchange 2000/2003. This assumes that you're running the Enterprise version of Exchange. The standard version of Exchange has a mail store limitation of 16 GB.

STM Files

Starting with Exchange 2000, a new database store was added called the STM or streaming database file. Internet mail messages are typically received in Multipurpose Internet Mail Extensions (MIME) format. Versions prior to Exchange 2000 converted MIME messages into RTF format, which can place a heavy load on the server. To increase the efficiency of the mail server, Exchange 2000/2003 stores messages received in MIME format in the STM database. Because the messages are not converted to RTF format, this decreases the load on the mail server. A pointer is added to the EDB database that references the actual message stored in the STM database.

Log Files

As transactions are processed on the Exchange Server, a 5-MB log file is created. When the log file reaches the 5-MB limit, another log file is created. These log files contain a history of every transaction that occurred on the mail server. If it is necessary to restore the Exchange database from a tape backup, these log files can be used to rebuild the missing data since the last full backup. When creating an incremental backup, most backup software backs up only these log files.

16-GB Database Limitation for the Standard Version of Exchange

The standard version of Exchange 5.5/2000/2003 has a mail store limitation of 16 GB. With increased mail traffic, spam, and large attachments, it's not too difficult to have a mail store that's larger than 16 GB. With Exchange 2000/2003, you must add the size of the EDB and STM databases to come up with the total size of the mail store. For example, if you have a priv.edb that was 7 GB and a priv.stm that was 5 GB, Exchange 2000/2003 considers this mail store 12 GB. Unfortunately, you typically do not receive an error message that the mail store is reaching the 16-GB limitation. You usually find out when it's too late. If the mail store exceeds 16 GB, it usually becomes corrupted, users cannot access their mail, and you have to restore from backup or at least run an Exchange Repair Utility (EDBUtil in 5.5 or ESEUtil 5.5/2000/2003) to recover the databases. It's important to carefully monitor the size of your Exchange databases to prevent corruption of the mail store. If you need to store more than 16 GB in your private mail folders, you must upgrade to the Enterprise Edition. A comparison of the storage capacity of Exchange 2003 Standard and Enterprise Edition is shown in Table 6.1.

TABLE 6.1 Storage Comparison of Exchange 2003 Standard and Enterprise Versions

Feature	***Exchange 2003 Standard Edition***	***Exchange 2003 Enterprise Edition***
Storage groups support	1 storage group	4 storage groups
Number of databases per storage group	2 databases	5 databases
Individual database size	16 gigabytes (GB)	Maximum 8 terabytes, limited only by hardware
Exchange Clustering	Not supported	Supported
X.400 connector	Not included	Included

With the Enterprise version, you can have up to four storage groups and five databases within each storage group. This allows you to have a maximum of 20 Exchange databases on one server. If you do exceed the 16-GB limit and are running

Exchange 2000/2003, you can temporarily mount a mail store that exceeds the 16-GB limit by following the instructions in *http://support.microsoft.com/default.aspx?scid=kb;en-us;828070&Product=exch2003*. This will temporarily allow you to mount a mail store up to 17 GB, but the size limitation of 16 GB will return as soon as the Exchange Services are restarted. This temporary workaround is designed to allow you to delete messages from your mail store to reduce the size below 16 GB.

Exchange 2000/2003 Enterprise Edition: Distribute the Mail Store Across Several Physical Databases

If your mail store is large enough to require the Enterprise Edition, consider breaking up the private mail store (public mail store too if it's large) across several databases. Instead of having one large 200-GB private mail store and one 20-GB public mail store, consider breaking these mail stores into smaller databases. In this scenario, you might have four private mail stores of 50 GB and one public store of 20 GB. The smaller mail databases make it easier to defragment the mail store and run a recovery process in the event of the mail database corruption. The mail store should be more stable because there is a lower probability of a database corruption with a smaller physical database. There is less chance of corrupting the entire mail store if you have the mail databases spread across multiple physical databases.

Exchange Server Performance

Exchange is a very disk-intensive application. A virus scanner and anti-spam filter can place an increased load on an Exchange server. Assuming that you have adequate memory and processing power in the server, an Exchange server is usually disk bound. Carefully pick your disk subsystem! We suggest a RAID 5 array for most small to medium Exchange servers (10 to 300) users. For larger installations, consider multiple RAID 5 arrays, RAID 1+0, or a storage area network (SAN) for your database store. The speed of your disk subsystem will often be the limiting factor in your Exchange server's performance. If you are experiencing slow performance on the Exchange server, use the Performance Monitor to identify bottlenecks in server performance. If your Exchange server's hard disk access lights are on solid, consider upgrading your disk array to faster hard drives, additional drive arrays, additional servers, or a SAN.

Monitor Disk Space

It sounds simple, but the amount of disk space that Exchange requires can sneak up on you. Make sure you have enough space for log files and mail store growth. If the mail server runs out of space, you risk corrupting the mail store, and no one will be able to access his or her mail. If you do run out of space, free up disk space on the server, and restart the server. If the mail stores do not mount when the server restarts, back up the mail store database and try running `EseUtil /p /g <database_name>` to repair the Exchange database. The `/p /g` option checks the database for consistency and then prompts to begin the repair process.

PROPER EXCHANGE SERVER PLACEMENT

Proper Exchange Server Placement is vital to a stable, well performing Exchange implementation. Be sure to consider the number of users on each Exchange server, anticipated load of the users, WAN bandwidth links and fault tolerance requirements when designing your Exchange Infrastructure.

Exchange Server Placement on a WAN

If your company has a WAN, consider placing an Exchange server in every location where you have more than 20 users, a slow WAN link, or users who send/receive mail with a large number of attachments. If an Exchange server is not local to the user, the messages and attachments must be transferred over the WAN, taking up precious WAN bandwidth. If the user has a local Exchange server, the message (and attachment) is transferred to the local server, and the messages are accessed locally. If the WAN goes down and the Exchange server is in a remote location, the users' mail will go down. If the Exchange server is local, and the WAN goes down, users can still access their mail, and send to/receive from other local users. Of course, sending to/receiving from remote locations will be down until the WAN connection is restored. Having an Exchange server local to the users provides some fault tolerance in case the WAN goes down.

A possible exception to this is Exchange 2003 with Outlook 2003. Outlook 2003 with Exchange 2003 supports a disconnected client that reduces the load on slow WAN links by locally caching mailbox information.

Exchange Clustering

For a larger number of users (300+), consider establishing an Exchange cluster for improved fault tolerance. An Exchange cluster uses two or more servers for fault tolerance in case one of the servers goes down. You must have the Enterprise Version of Exchange to perform clustering. Exchange Enterprise 5.5 supports two-node clustering. Exchange Enterprise 2000 supports up to four-node clustering. Exchange Enterprise 2003 supports up to eight-node clustering. Table 6.2 lists the Exchange version and the operating systems (OSs) on which it will run.

TABLE 6.2 Exchange Versions and Their Operating Systems

Exchange Version	Supported Operating Systems
Exchange 2003 Enterprise	Windows 2000 Server, Advanced Server, or Datacenter Server with SP3 or later.
	Windows Server 2003 Standard, Enterprise, or Datacenter.
Exchange 2003 Standard	Windows 2000 Server or Advanced Server, with SP3 or later.
	Windows Server 2003 Standard or Enterprise.
Exchange 2000 Enterprise	Windows 2000 Server, Advanced Server, or Datacenter Server.
Exchange 2000 Standard	Windows 2000 Server or Advanced Server.

BACK IT UP!

Having a good, reliable, and complete backup of the Exchange server will allow you to gracefully recover from most disasters. We strongly recommend purchasing third-party backup software like Veritas' Backup Exec with the Exchange Server agent to ensure you have a good backup of the Exchange server. Backup Exec allows you to back up both the mail store and individual mailboxes. This allows you to restore a single mailbox without having to restore the entire mail store. We suggest full complete backups on a daily basis of both the server itself and the mail store. For mission-critical mail servers, consider backing up the log files every couple of hours to tape. This will allow you to restore the full mail server backup and use the log files to recreate the lost transactions that occurred after the full backup.

VIRUS PROTECTION

Most new viruses are spread via e-mail. We consider good virus scanning software a mandatory part of any Exchange installation. Symantec Mail Security for Exchange and Trend's ScanMail make anti-virus packages that specifically scan inside each mail message and attachment on the server. It's important to have anti-virus software on every Exchange server, not just the server that send/receives Internet mail. Although this server is the most vulnerable, other Exchange servers in your organization can become infected with a virus and cause major damage before it's discovered. One common way of infecting an Exchange server that is not used as a main Internet mail gateway is from a user who accesses a POP3 mail account from the Internet. If the user downloads mail from a POP3 Internet server that is infected, the user can quickly infect your internal mail server and can spread to other unprotected Exchange servers in your organization. Unless your users absolutely need POP3 access to another mail server, we suggest using your firewall to block POP3 traffic to the Internet. Additionally, your main Internet mail gateway might receive a new virus that the virus pattern does not check for and spread it to other Exchange servers in your organization. Bottom line: install virus protection on each Exchange server in your organization.

EXCHANGE SERVER AND INTERNET MAIL

Most companies that have an internal Exchange server use it for Internet mail. Ideally, your main Internet gateway should be on a separate server that does not contain a mail store. If you do not have the budget for a dedicated e-mail gateway, you can forward the Internet mail to one of your Exchange servers.

Register Your Domain

To receive mail on your company's domain, you must register the domain name with a domain provider such as *www.verisign.com* or *www.register.com*. By registering your domain, you are ensured exclusive rights to that domain name for the length of the registration period.

Mail Exchange (MX) Records

After you've registered your domain, you must create a Mail Exchange (MX) record for your domain. Typically, this is set up on your ISP's DNS server. Most ISPs require an e-mail from an authorized contact before they will set up the MX record and other DNS entries for your domain. When establishing an MX record, make sure the ISP creates a Reverse DNS (PTR) entry for your mail server. The PTR record resolves a fully qualified domain name (FQDN) to an IP address. A reverse record is important, because many ISP and other Internet mail servers run anti-spam software that perform a reverse lookup when mail is delivered to their server. If a reverse record is missing for your mail server, the mail will be rejected. In addition to the reverse record, make sure the ISP also creates a record for the domain itself. Typically, this should resolve to your Web page, although it can resolve to your mail server if you don't have a Web page. Again, some ISPs and mail servers look for the existence of a DNS domain entry when receiving mail. If you do not have any entry for the domain, the mail will be rejected. If you have problems sending mail to certain domains and the mail server is not blacklisted as an open relay, check with your ISP to ensure that these DNS records are in place for your domain.

Internet Mail Connector in Exchange 5.5

If you're running Exchange 5.5, you must create an Internet Mail Connector in order to send and receive Internet mail. In the Exchange 5.5 Administrator, click on File, New Other, Internet Mail Service, and configure the parameters as necessary. Exchange 2000/2003 does not need an Internet Mail Connector, because it uses SMTP as the native protocol to send and receive all mail to the Internet and to other Exchange servers in the organization.

Firewall Configuration

If you're running NAT, you must create a static NAT mapping between a public address (where the MX record points) and your private mail server. Ideally, this should be to a front-end Exchange server that does not have a mail store on it. After you create the static NAT, allow TCP port 25 traffic to pass both to and from the Exchange server.

Telnet to Exchange Server on Port 25 for Testing

After you configured the Exchange server for Internet mail, you can test it by using Telnet on port 25 to verify the mail service is properly responding. Refer to *http://support.microsoft.com/default.aspx?scid=kb;en-us;153119&Product=ech* for detailed steps to perform this test. The Telnet test can be a useful tool when troubleshooting incoming Internet mail problems.

Setup Authoritative Name Servers

When you request that these DNS entries are entered for your domain, ask your ISP which DNS servers should be used as the authoritative name servers for your domain. Alternately, you can host your own DNS servers and make them the authoritative server for your domain. Typically, the ISP will provide two DNS servers for this task. An authoritative name server has the "last word" on where your DNS records should point. When you've verified that all of the DNS records are in place for your domain, change the authoritative name servers with the company you used (VeriSign or Register) to point to the name servers that were provided by your ISP. After these changes take place, you must wait for these changes to propagate throughout the Internet. This typically takes 4 to 16 hours.

SPAM

Spam becomes more of a problem every day. There are several anti-spam solutions available for Exchange. We now suggest an anti-spam filter as part of any Exchange implementation. Make sure your server is not an open relay that spammers are using to send junk e-mail.

Anti-Spam Filtering

Unfortunately, spam or junk e-mail is a way of life. It is increasing at an alarming rate. Consider installing anti-spam filtering software on the Exchange server to reduce the amount of junk e-mail in your inbox. Be aware that anti-spam software installed on the Exchange server will increase the load on your Exchange server. If your server is already heavily loaded, consider installing the anti-spam software on a separate server, or sign up for an anti-spam service that filters the junk mail before it reaches your server. Several anti-spam packages work with Exchange. One of our favorites is GFI Mail Essentials. This package uses a combination of Bayesian filtering, whitelists, blacklists, keyword searches, and open-relay checking to reduce the amount of spam.

Bayesian filtering. Bayesian filtering uses a fuzzy logic to determine if a message is spam. It runs an analysis of your outgoing mail and gathers statistics on the type of mail your company sends. It uses this information to analyze incoming mail to determine if it's spam.

Whitelists. If an e-mail address is on the whitelist, the message is not blocked regardless of the message characteristics. Whitelists are primarily used to reduce false positives.

Blacklists. Blacklists are the opposite of whitelists. If a sender's e-mail address is on the blacklist, the message is treated as spam regardless of the content.

Keyword searches. If a message contains a keyword, it is treated as spam. Spammers get around keyword searches by misspelling words, or using graphics in their spam.

Open-relay checking. Mail servers are checked against open-relay databases on the Internet such as *www.ordb.org/lookup/*. If a message is received from a server marked as an open relay, it is treated as spam.

GFI can be installed on an existing Exchange server or dedicated anti-spam server.

A higher-end solution that usually requires a dedicated server is sender validation or challenge response. This spam-filtering method gives the sender a challenge: enter a secret code, click on a hyperlink, or reply to an e-mail. If the challenge is completed correctly, the sender is added to the recipient's "approved list." After a sender is added to the "approved list," mail is accepted by the server without further steps. The main drawback of sender validation is the increased cost, because it usually requires a dedicated server, and a sender must be validated before his mail is accepted by the server. However, sender validation has the potential to block 100-percent of spam. SpamLion™ and MailFrontier are two sender validation packages that work with Exchange. If you decide to implement a sender validation package, make sure the package will allow you to preload an "approved list" before the spam filtering is activated to reduce the number of false positives. For more information on implementing a sender validation solution, refer to *http://cc.realtimepublishers.com/publicationhome.asp?pid=3.*

Is Your Exchange Server an Open Relay? •

Make sure your mail server is not an open relay. An open relay is a mail server that spammers can use to relay messages off your server to send spam. If enough people complain that they receive spam from a specific server, the server can be added to one or more of the open-relay databases on the Internet. If your server gets marked as an open relay, you might have problems sending mail, and difficulty getting off the open-relay database. Exchange 2000/2003 by default does not allow mail relaying. Relay control features were first added to Exchange 5.5 in Service Pack 1. However, you should be running the latest service pack for Exchange 5.5, which, as of this writing, is Service Pack 4. Exchange 5.0 does not include any relay control features. Your firewall might have some anti-relay control features built into it. Refer to your firewall's documentation for more information. Several sites on the Internet allow you to test your mail server to see if it's an open relay. One we often use is *www.ordb.org/submit/*. Because of the increase in spam, some companies check if a sender's mail server is listed in one or more of these open-relay databases. If the server is listed, the mail is treated as spam and is rejected. Make sure your mail server is not an open relay to avoid getting in one or more of these open-relay databases.

What If My Server Is Marked as an Open Relay?

If your server is marked as an open relay, you must first close it, and submit it for testing. Unfortunately, there are many databases that track open mail relays. Some of the more popular databases are listed in Table 6.3.

Of course, this is a small subset of all of the open-relay databases on the Internet. Refer to *http://rbls.org/* for a more extensive list of open-relay databases. Some sites like *www.ordb.org* allow you to perform lookups on other open-relay databases to see if your mail server is listed. If your server is listed in multiple databases and your mail server is not an open relay, you must submit a separate test for each

TABLE 6.3 Open-Relay Databases

Name	*URL to see if you're listed*
Spambag.org	*www.spambag.org/query.html*
Njabl.org	*http://dnsbl.njabl.org/lookup.html*
Ordb.org	*www.ordb.org/lookup/*
Spamhaus	*www.spamhaus.org/sbl/*
Spamcop	*www.spamcop.net/bl.shtml*

open-relay database. Some sites regularly retest servers listed in their open-relay databases to verify if they are closed. If the server is not an open relay, the server is automatically removed from their database. Unfortunately, most databases require you to submit a test manually. We experienced certain situations where a mail relay was closed, the server retested and verified as closed, but the mail server still remained in the open-relay database! One workaround to this problem is to change the IP address of your mail server. Unfortunately, this requires an MX record change, and time for the change to propagate throughout the Internet. If your Exchange server has problems sending mail to certain domains, check if your server is marked as an open relay. If you suspect that someone is blocking your mail because your server is in an open-relay database, temporarily change the public IP address of your mail server, and see if you can send mail to the problem location. If you are successful, then most likely your server is listed in an open-relay database.

OUTLOOK WEB ACCESS

Outlook Web Access (OWA) is a feature that is installed by default on Exchange 2000 and 2003. It must be installed separately on Exchange 5.5. OWA allows a user to access his e-mail via a Web interface. OWA works best with Internet Explorer, ideally 6.0 or later, but it will work with versions as early as 4.0. Although the interface is similar to Outlook, OWA might require additional end-user training in order for users to use the full functionality of the product. One exception might be OWA on Exchange 2003. The interface of OWA running on Exchange 2003 is greatly improved, and is very close to the Outlook interface.

Install Secure Sockets Layer Certificate on OWA

If you plan to use OWA from the Internet, we strongly suggest installing a Secure Sockets Layer (SSL) certificate on the Exchange server. This will ensure that the communication between the front-end OWA server and the Web client will be encrypted. If you do not install an SSL certificate on the server, a hacker can capture packets in an OWA session and read information in the packets. You can either set up Certificate Services on Windows 2000/2003 or purchase an SSL certificate from an SSL vendor. We suggest purchasing an SSL certificate from a vendor; otherwise, users will be prompted to view and accept the "untrusted" SSL certificate every time they log in to OWA. For a list of SSL providers, refer to *www.whichssl.com*. You can purchase an SSL certificate for as little as $38.00 per year. To use SSL with OWA, you must install the certificate on Internet Information Server (IIS). Ideally, your MX record should match your server name before you make the request. If your MX record for your server and the internal server name do not match, the certificate might not work correctly, or you might have trouble getting the certificate to work. If they don't match, contact your DNS provider and have them change the name of the MX record to match the name of your server. To obtain and install the SSL certificate:

1. **Issue an SSL request from IIS.** Refer to *http://support.microsoft.com/default.aspx?scid=kb;EN-US;228821* for instructions on how to issue an SSL request from IIS 5.0.
2. **Submit the Certificate Request File to the online authority.** When you've decided on your SSL provider, send them the Certificate Request File generated in the previous step. When you're approved, the SSL provider will issue you an SSL certificate.
3. **Install the SSL certificate on IIS.** Refer to *http://support.microsoft.com/default.aspx?scid=kb;en-us;228836&Product=iis50* for instructions on how to install an SSL certificate on IIS 5.0.
4. **Turn on SSL for OWA.** Refer to *http://support.microsoft.com/default.aspx?scid=kb;en-us;320291&Product=exch2k* for instructions on how to turn on SSL with OWA.

All of these steps should be completed before anyone is allowed to access OWA from the Internet.

OWA Architecture

If you plan to use OWA, make sure to install all of the latest patches for Windows Server and Exchange. If you are running Exchange 5.5, Exchange 2000 Enterprise Edition, or Exchange 2003, you can set up a front-end server in a DMZ to handle

OWA requests. This configuration is more secure than directly accessing an Exchange server with a mail store on it. A front-end/back-end OWA configuration is shown in Figure 6.1.

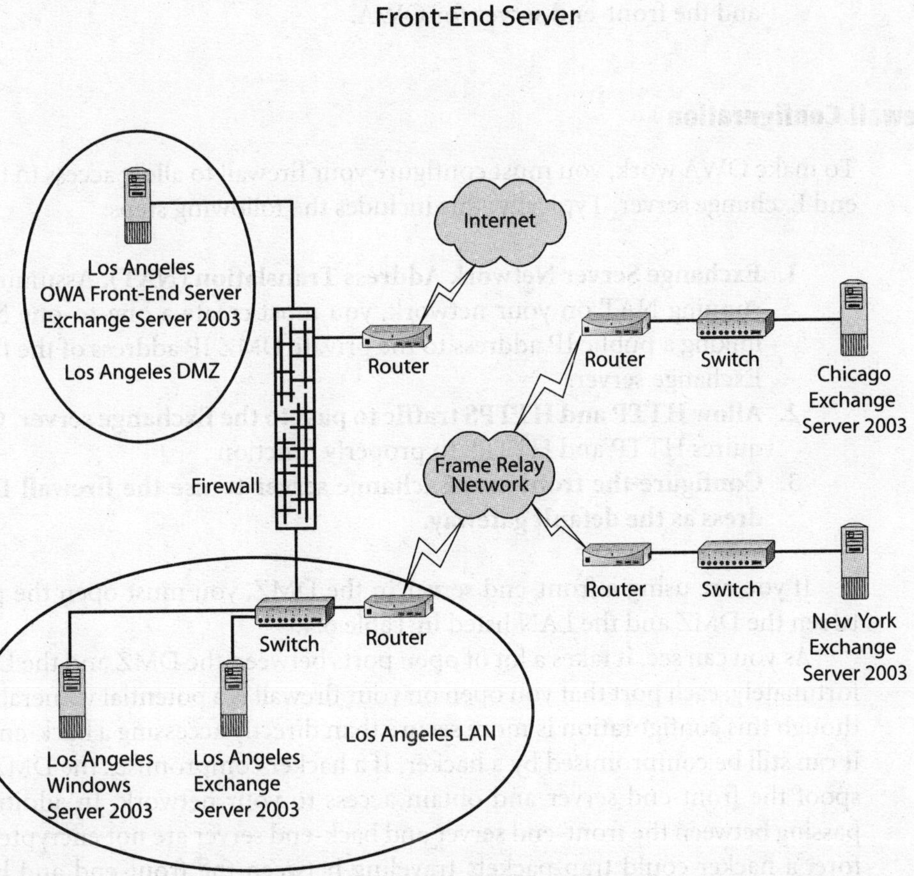

FIGURE 6.1 OWA in a front-end/back-end configuration.

Using this configuration, OWA users access the front-end Exchange server in the Los Angeles DMZ. Users are redirected to a back-end server in Los Angeles, Chicago, or New York depending on where their mailbox is located. If the Exchange server in the DMZ is hacked, only the front-end server is compromised, and no mail or critical file information resides on this server. Note that if you are using Exchange 2000, only the Enterprise Edition of Exchange 2000 supports this front-end/back-end configuration. In larger installations, this configuration is preferable over accessing the back-end server directly because:

- You only have a single entry point into the DMZ.
- If the front-end server is hacked, there is no mail store or critical file data on the server.
- Reduced load on the back-end servers.
- You can optionally use the front-end server as your Internet mail gateway and the front-end server for OWA.

Firewall Configuration

To make OWA work, you must configure your firewall to allow access to the front-end Exchange server. Typically, this includes the following steps:

1. **Exchange Server Network Address Translation (NAT).** Assuming you're running NAT on your network, you must create a one-to-one NAT rule linking a public IP address to the private DMZ IP address of the front-end Exchange server.
2. **Allow HTTP and HTTPS traffic to pass to the Exchange server.** OWA requires HTTP and HTTPS to properly function .
3. **Configure the front-end Exchange server to use the firewall DMZ address as the default gateway.**

If you are using a front-end server in the DMZ, you must open the ports between the DMZ and the LAN listed in Table 6.4.

As you can see, it takes a lot of open ports between the DMZ and the LAN. Unfortunately, each port that you open on your firewall is a potential vulnerability. Although this configuration is more secure than directly accessing a back-end server, it can still be compromised by a hacker. If a hacker compromises the DMZ, he can spoof the front-end server and obtain access to your network. In addition, data passing between the front-end server and back-end server are not encrypted; therefore, a hacker could trap packets traveling between the front-end and back-end servers and read this information.

OWA with an SSL Proxy

Instead of accessing the front-end server in the DMZ, consider moving the front-end server into the LAN and install an SSL Proxy server in the DMZ. With this configuration, users access the SSL Proxy server and pass the SSL request to the front-end server on the LAN (see Figure 6.2).

In this configuration, only TCP port 443 (HTTPS) is necessary between the DMZ and LAN. Even if a hacker compromises the DMZ, the data are still encrypted between the SSL Proxy and the front-end server. Microsoft's Internet Security and

TABLE 6.4 Necessary Ports for Front-End Server in the DMZ to Back-End Servers on the LAN

Source	*Port*	*Protocol*	*Description*
Back-end server	80	TCP	Relayed HTTP traffic
Front-end server	80	TCP	Communicate with back-end server
Back-end server	389	TCP	Windows Active Directory (AD)
Front-end server	389	TCP	Windows AD
Back-end server	3268	TCP	Windows 2000 AD/Global Catalog
Front-end server	3268	TCP	Windows 2000 AD/Global Catalog
Back-end server	88	TCP and UDP	Windows AD
Front-end server	88	TCP and UDP	Windows AD
Back-end server	53	TCP and UDP	DNS
Front-end server	53	TCP and UDP	DNS
Back-end server	135	TCP	Remote Procedure Call (RPC)
Front-end server	135	TCP	RPC
Back-end server	1127	TCP	Windows AD. Fixed port assigned in the registry.
Front-end server	1127	TCP	Windows AD. Fixed port assigned in the registry.
Back-end server	445	TCP	Server Message Block (SMB)
Front-end server	445	TCP	SMB
Back-end server	123	TCP	Network Time Protocol (NTP)
Front-end server	123	TCP	NTP

Acceleration (ISA) server, or Symantec Enterprise Firewall with a crypto-accelerator card can perform the SSL proxy duties. These solutions are good for up to 300 OWA users. If you need to support more users, consider purchasing an SSL appliance. Nortel, Cisco, F5 Networks, and Radware all have SSL/TLS proxy server appliances. The higher appliances are capable of supporting 15,000 users. However, these appliances are expensive. Expect to pay $15,000 to $60,000 depending on the performance and features. These appliances have the added benefit of increasing throughput on the front-end server, because the front-end only has to manage an SSL session between the SSL proxy and itself for each user. The SSL Proxy server,

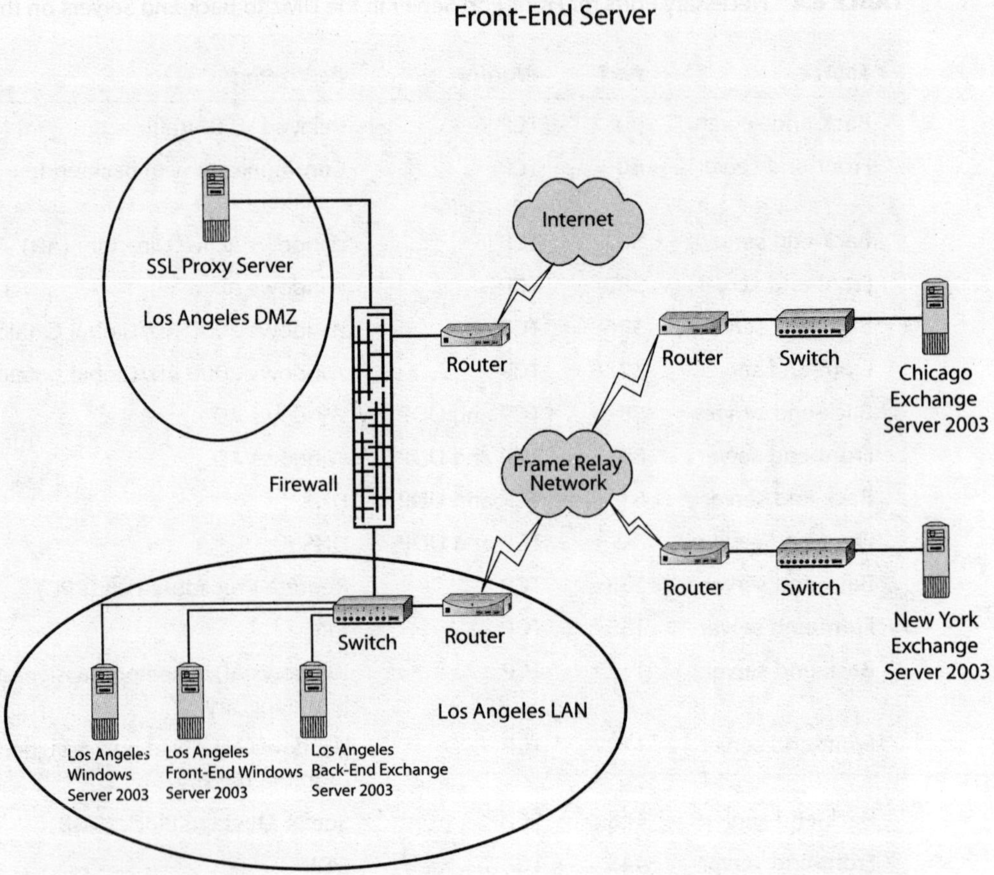

FIGURE 6.2 OWA with an SSL Proxy server.

however, must manage handshaking for many cryptographic key pairs for each client; thus, it bears a majority of the SSL load.

Make Sure Your Firewall Supports WebDAV for Exchange 2000/2003

If you plan to use OWA with Exchange 2000/2003 and don't use an SSL Proxy server, make sure that your firewall supports WebDAV. Most of the later firewalls support WebDAV; however, if you have an earlier firewall, you might experience problems. You can modify the settings in OWA by following the tech note at *http://support.microsoft.com/default.aspx?scid=kb;en-us;296232&Product=exch2k*. Note that if you make this change, you will lose some of the functionality of OWA. In light of the recent increase is hacking activity, we suggest upgrading your firewall to one that supports WebDAV.

TROUBLESHOOTING SCENARIOS

If you follow the guidelines suggested in the first half of this chapter, you can avoid most Exchange problems. The following scenarios are real-world examples of some of the problems we've encountered in our Exchange troubleshooting adventures.

Scenario 1 EXCHANGE SERVER IS RUNNING VERY SLOW

Facts

- HP/Compaq ML350 with one 1.0-GHz processor, 1.1 GB of memory, with 72 GB of storage.
- Running Windows Server 2000 with Service Pack 3 and Exchange 2000 with Service Pack 3.
- Three remote sites using a VPN mobile client for remote network access.

Symptoms

We received a call that an Exchange server was running very slow and backup was failing. We initially dismissed the performance issue, because this user was known to complain about server performance, even when the server was running fine.

Questions to Ask

Q: What has happened? A: Sending mail is very slow.

Q: Has anything changed? A: No.

Q: Is the entire server slow or just Exchange? A: Exchange is very slow and the server itself seems a bit sluggish.

Q: When did the backup start failing? A: About a week ago, it started failing.

Troubleshooting Steps

1. **Verify the problem.** We logged in to the server, and noticed that it was running very slow. Even clicking on the Start button took awhile for the menu to appear. There was a lot of drive activity on the server and the CPU utilization was very high.
2. **Review Task Manager.** We pressed Ctrl-Alt-Delete and sorted the processes by CPU utilization and noted that Store.exe and inetinfo.exe were taking up most the of the CPU cycles. Store.exe is an Exchange Service, and inetinfo.exe is tied to IIS 5.0. You can find the executable name of

the service by opening up Services and double-clicking on the service. The executable name is listed on the details of the service (see Figure 6.3).

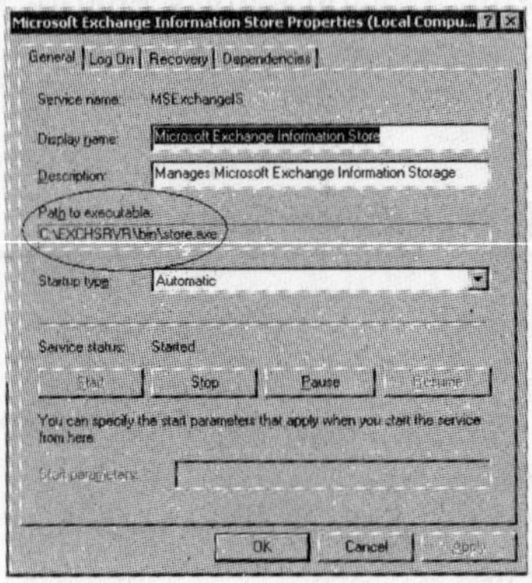

FIGURE 6.3 Displaying the service executable name under Services.

Most likely, inetinfo.exe was tied to the SMTP service running on the server. Corrupted mail store? Large mail volume? This particular client was not a heavy e-mail user and only had 15 users connected to the server. Corrupted mail stores tend to happen on Exchange servers with a larger (50 or more) number of users and/or larger (40 GB or more) mail databases.

3. **Start the Exchange System Manager.** We started the Exchange System Manager (which took a long time to load) and reviewed the mail configuration. We looked at the Administrative Groups, <*Admin_Group_Name*>, Servers, <*Server_Name*>, Protocols, SMTP, Default SMTP Virtual Server, Current Sessions and noticed there were six connections connected to the SMTP virtual server for more than five minutes. This was the first clue that something was very wrong on the server. Typically, a session on the Exchange server will only connect for a few seconds at most, unless the connection is sending/receiving an e-mail with a large attachment. We then looked at the queues on the default SMTP virtual server and noticed that there were over 50 queues in various states of sending or waiting for a retry to send mail.
4. **Mail server an open relay?** Obviously, someone was using the mail server as a relay. But how? As you know, Exchange 2000 is not an open relay by default. The server was serviced packed with the latest versions (Service Pack 4 for Windows 2000 and Service Pack 3 for Exchange with the hotfixes) and had the latest critical updates. We reviewed the relay settings to ensure that the relay was closed. Just to make sure, we used the *www.ordb.org* open-relay test, and the server did not test as an open relay.

Resolution

1. **Clear current connections.** Whenever we tried to clear a connection on the default SMTP virtual server, it would reappear, usually with a different domain name, but from the same IP source.
2. **Determine the location of the source IP address.** After noting the source IP address ranges, we performed a lookup on the Internet Assigned Numbers Authority at *www.iana.org/ipaddress/ip-addresses.htm.* This site contains links to worldwide sources to determine what ISP has been assigned a block of IP addresses. This information is helpful when you're tracking down an IP address in the event of a hack or other inappropriate use of the Internet. You have to take the IP address at face value, because the hacker will often spoof the IP address of the attack or compromise a machine and launch that attack from an infected machine, but the source IP address is a good place to start. The IP ranges in question were traced back to a block allocated to an ISP in China.
3. **Sending mail by authenticating to the server.** After concluding that the server was not an open relay, we figured that someone was probably authenticating to the server and sending mail.
4. **Reason for failed backup.** It was no wonder that the backup was failing because it was attempting to back up all of the messages the spammer was trying to send. In addition, the server was taking such a severe performance hit that it caused the server backup to grind to a halt.
5. **Review Active Directory User and Computers.** Since we suspected that the spammer was using a valid username and password to send mail, we checked Active Directory (AD) for a rogue user. With the client's help, we deleted several user accounts of people who had left the company. We checked the Administrator group and discovered there were users who didn't belong in this group. The unauthorized users were removed. After all unnecessary users were deleted from AD, the passwords were reset for the remaining users.
6. **Review the server for hacking tools.** Since it looked like there was some hacking activity on the server, we checked the run keys in the registry to see if any hacking programs were loaded in:

   HKEY_LOCAL_MACHINE\SOFTWARE\Microsoft\Windows\CurrentVersion\RunHKEY_CURRENT_USER\Software\Microsoft\Windows\CurrentVersion\Run

   KEY_LOCAL_MACHINE\SOFTWARE\Microsoft\Windows\Current Version\Policies\Explorer\Run

All of these keys turned out to be clean. We also ran a virus scan on the server, and the server was clean. At least from the surface, it looked like the server was free from any hacking tools.

7. **Clean up spam.** We wanted to prevent the spammer from relaying any more messages, so we disconnected the firewall from the Internet and cleared the connections to the default SMTP server. We tried to delete the messages from the queues using the System Manager, but this was taking forever! We stopped all of the Exchange services, opened up a command prompt, and deleted the messages from the directory d:\exchsrvr\mailroot\vsi 1\queue. As soon as the Exchange services were stopped, the performance on the server greatly improved. Even deleting the messages from the command prompt took over one hour—there were over 10,000 messages waiting in various queues. We also looked at the bad mail directory in d:\exchsrvr\mailroot\vsi 1\badmail. There were so many messages in this directory that we couldn't even view the number of files in this directory. We started a delete of all files from a command prompt, which took approximately eight hours!
8. **Firewall rule to block traffic.** We created a rule on the firewall to deny traffic from the IP ranges where the spam originated. This prevented spam from coming from these IP ranges in the future.
9. **Reconnect firewall to the Internet.** We reconnected the firewall to the Internet and closely monitored the server. Fortunately, this time, the spam connection did not reappear. This particular network had a couple of remote sites running VPN tunnels. When the sites were first brought up, we suggested that they use "mini" firewalls to protect the remote users and perform the VPN encryption, but they decided to use the mobile clients instead to save money. Because of the spam incident, they were convinced to purchase the firewalls to protect the remote connections.
10. **Review remote sites.** Because of the hacking activity, we went out to the remote sites to review the computers. The first remote site we reviewed had quite a few hacking tools installed:
    - Bat.mumu.A.worm
    - Hacktool
    - W32.valla.2048
    - w32.HLLW.lovegate.J@mm
    - Bat.Boohoo.worm
    - MSBlast

    This computer was left on all of the time, with the VPN tunnel active, and no firewall to protect it from the Internet, so it was just a matter of time before it was hacked. We always recommend that the remote clients sit behind a firewall for this reason, especially if they are using a broadband connection (this computer was using a DSL Internet connection). If you have to use a mobile VPN client, make sure your users turn off the computer when it's not in use, and disable the tunnel if they do not need access to the corporate network.

11. **Rebuild hacked workstation.** We strongly suggest completely rebuilding a machine whenever you suspect that it's been hacked. Often, you can remove most of the hacking programs, but if you miss just one tool, the hacker will be able to gain access to the computer again, and you have to start the cleaning process from the beginning. After backing up the data files, we formatted the hard drive and installed the operating system from scratch. This is the only way to ensure that you removed all of the hacking tools on the computer. We installed the latest service pack and critical patches. Fortunately for this client, the hacker only wanted to use the server for spam. If he wanted to, he could have caused much more damage.

Lessons Learned

Protect your remote VPN users. A network is only as secure as its weakest point. If you have any users who use mobile VPN clients, make sure they are protected by a firewall (see Figure 6.4).

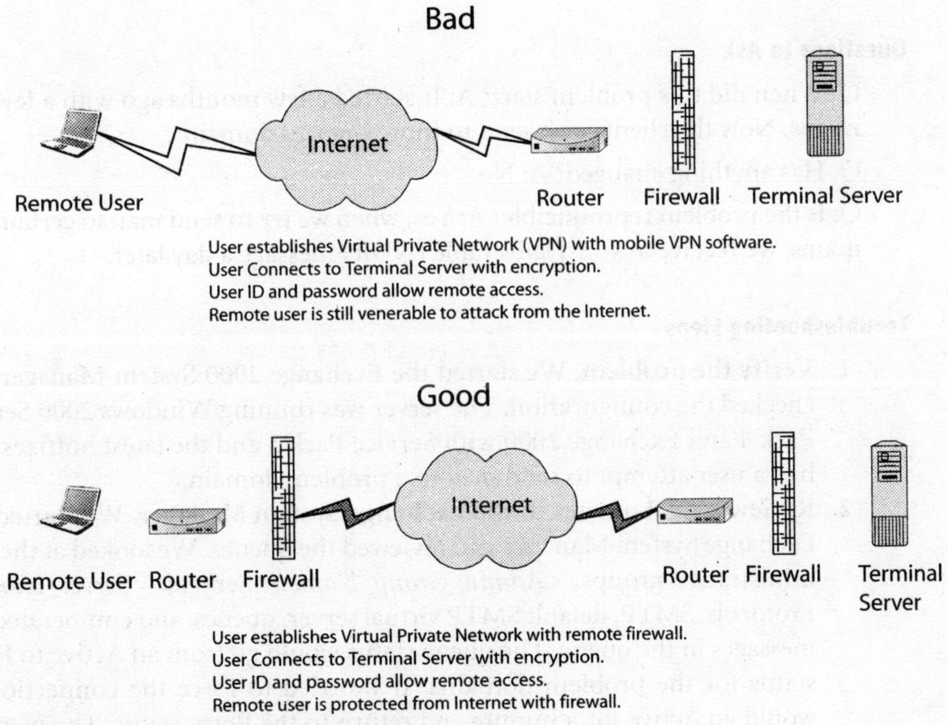

FIGURE 6.4 Remote VPN access configuration.

If the user cannot be placed behind a firewall, make sure that the user disables the VPN tunnel when it's not is use. Make sure users turn off their computers when not in use. Don't think you're not a target just because you do not work for a high-profile company. If you have a faster connection (384k+) to the Internet, you *are* a target, because of your bandwidth automatically makes you a target. Make sure to stay current on all patches that come out for your operating system.

Scenario 2 EXCHANGE 2000 SERVER UNABLE TO DELIVER MAIL TO SPECIFIC DOMAINS

Facts

- HP/Compaq ML350 with one 1.0-GHz processor, 1.5 GB of memory with 36 GB of storage.
- Running Windows Server 2000 and Exchange 2000.

Symptoms

Users cannot send e-mail messages to certain domains. After 24 hours, they are notified by the Exchange server that their message was not delivered.

Questions to Ask

Q: When did this problem start? A: It started a few months ago with a few domains. Now the client can't send to more than 10 domains.

Q: Has anything changed? A: No.

Q: Is the problem reproducible? A: Yes, when we try to send mail to certain domains, we receive a Non-Deliverable (NDR) message a day later.

Troubleshooting Steps

1. **Verify the problem.** We started the Exchange 2000 System Manager and checked the configuration. The server was running Windows 2000 Service Pack 4 and Exchange 2000 with Service Pack 3 and the latest hotfixes. We had a user attempt to send mail to a problem domain.
2. **Review SMTP queues in the Exchange System Manager.** We started the Exchange System Manager and reviewed the queues. We looked at the Administrative groups, *<Admin_Group_Name>*, Servers, *<Server_Name>*, Protocols, SMTP, default SMTP virtual server, queues, and enumerated the messages in the queue. The queue status would go from an Active to Retry status for the problem domains. If we tried to force the connection, it would go Active for a minute and return to the Retry status. The message

would stay in an outgoing queue and retry periodically until the retry count was exceeded. Then, the user would get the NDR message.

3. **Mail server blacklisted?** Whenever a server has a problem sending mail, one of the first places we check is to see if the server is listed as an open relay in any of the open-relay databases. A good source for this is *www.ordb.org/lookup/*. You can see if the server is listed not only in their database, but other databases as well—yes, there's approximately 30 of these databases on the Internet. Some companies and ISPs use anti-spam software that checks if the mail server is listed in an open-relay database, and rejects the mail if the server is listed as an open relay. The server was listed in two lesser known open-relay databases: *www.blackholes.us/* and *www.agk.nnov.ru/drbl/*. *www.blackholes.us/* looked like it was wholesale blocking entire ISP address ranges, and the *www.agk.nnov.ru/drbl/* was in Russian. Nothing really to worry about, because both of these databases are some of the lesser known blacklist databases.
4. **Change the outside IP address of the mail server.** Just to make sure the IP address wasn't being blocked, we modified the Network Address Translation (NAT) rule on the firewall to a different IP address assigned by the ISP. After changing the mail server's IP address, the problem still occurred. Therefore, we reversed the changes so they could receive incoming mail.
5. **Mail server an open relay?** Using the open-relay test at *www.ordb.org/submit/*, we submitted the outside IP address of the mail server to verify it was not an open relay. The test results confirmed that the server was not an open relay.
6. **Reverse DNS record.** Some anti-spam software has the capability of performing a reverse record lookup to verify that the sender's domain matches the server. We discourage this practice because it can cause many false positives, especially for domains that have multiple mail servers. The following steps show how to look up an MX record for the sample domain *cnn.com* with Nslookup (Name Server Lookup) and verify that the correct reverse DNS (PTR) record exists.

    a. **Open a command prompt.** On Windows 2000 and XP, click on Start, Run, type `cmd` in the Open: field, and click OK.
    b. **Type `NSLookup <enter>`.** Items in bold are typed in. Items not bolded are responses from NSLookup. Items in parentheses are comments.

```
> set type=mx <enter> (Set query type to Mail Exchange —MX)
> cnn.com <enter> (Lookup MX record for cnn.com)
Server: adsntproxy.adscon.com
Address: 192.168.254.4
```

```
Non-authoritative answer:
cnn.com MX preference = 10, mail exchanger =
atlmail4.turner.com
cnn.com MX preference = 10, mail exchanger =
atlmail1.turner.com
cnn.com MX preference = 30, mail exchanger =
nymail1.turner.com
cnn.com MX preference = 20, mail exchanger =
atlmail2.turner.com
(cnn.com has four mail servers handling their Internet mail,
the lower the MX preference, the higher the priority)
> set type=a <enter> (Set query type to a to find the ip
address of the mail server)
> atlmail4.turner.com <enter> (first mail server listed in MX
query)
Server: adsntproxy.adscon.com
Address: 192.168.254.4
Non-authoritative answer:
Name:  atlmail4.turner.com
Address: 64.236.221.5 (This is the IP address of
atlmail4.turner.com)
> set type=ptr <enter> (Set query type to ptr for reverse
lookup)
> 64.236.221.5 <enter>
Server: adsntproxy.adscon.com
Address: 192.168.254.4
Non-authoritative answer:
5.221.236.64.in-addr.arpa    name = atlmail4.turner.com
(The PTR record should display the IP address of the server in
reverse and should include the name of the server)
```

After completing these steps for the client's domain, we verified that the reverse DNS record was correctly set up.

7. **Telnet into the problem domain mail servers.** Using NSLookup, we obtained the IP addresses of one of the problem domain's mail server. Using Telnet *<ip_address_of_mail_server>* 25, we verified that mail server was running and responding on TCP port 25 (SMTP). We looked at two other problem domain mail servers to see if they had something in common. One item we noticed was that two of the servers were running Sendmail.
8. **ESMTP support.** Sendmail and Exchange talk ESMTP by default. ESMTP has an enhanced instruction set compared to the basic SMTP commands.

Could this be the fix? The client's firewall used an SMTP daemon that didn't use ESMTP by default. We enabled the ESMTP support on the firewall. Unfortunately, the messages still remained in the queue.

9. **What now?** At this point, we were running out of ideas. We knew that most likely there was something in common with all of the problem domains, but what? Something was causing the server to reject our messages, but what? We were pretty confident that everything was properly configured on our end.

Resolution

We contacted the ISP that was hosting the e-mail for one of the problem domains. We asked if they were doing anything to block e-mail traffic from our server. Fortunately, we reached someone who was familiar with their mail server configuration. He explained that they were checking for a DNS record for the sender's domain as an anti-spam measure. He said they just checked for the existence of the record, not the IP address to which the domain resolved. He performed a quick test, and sure enough, the DNS record was missing for the client's domain. To use the *cnn.com* example, start NSLookup and perform the following steps:

```
> cnn.com <enter> (The domain you want to query)
Server: UnKnown
Address: 192.168.254.6

Non-authoritative answer:
Name:      cnn.com
Addresses:  64.236.16.116, 64.236.16.84, 64.236.16.52, 64.236.16.20
            64.236.24.28, 64.236.24.20, 64.236.24.12, 64.236.24.4
```

We contacted the company hosting the client's DNS and had them create a DNS record for the domain. We had this domain record point to the same IP address as the MX record. As soon as the record updated on the Internet, the client could send mail to all of the problem domains.

Lessons Learned

Make sure you have both a reverse lookup and DNS entry for your domain. The most frustrating thing about this problem is that most DNS hosting companies will automatically enter a record for the domain when they create the MX record. Sometimes, we have to ask specifically for a reverse lookup, but this is the first time we had to specifically request a record for the domain itself.

Scenario 3 WINDOWS 2003 SERVER EVENT VIEWER DISPLAYS EVENT 9582

Facts

- HP/Compaq ML350 with one 1.0-GHz processor, 2.0 GB of memory, with three 36-GB RAID 5 arrays.
- Running Windows Server 2003 with Service Pack 3 and Exchange 2000 with Service Pack 2.
- 40 users connected to the system who use file, print, and e-mail services on this server.

Symptoms

Event 9582 states that "The virtual memory necessary to run your Exchange server is fragmented in such a way that performance may be affected. It is highly recommended that you restart all Exchange services to correct this issue." This error message appears in the Event log every one to three hours.

Questions to Ask

Q: When did this problem start? A: It started one month ago. The server has been in production for approximately two years.

Q: Do the users notice any slowdown? A: No, the users do not notice any slowdown on the server.

Troubleshooting Steps

1. **Verify the problem.** We pulled up the Event Viewer and confirmed that the 9582 error was still occurring on the server.
2. **Restart the server.** Since the error message indicated that the Exchange Services should be restarted, we decided to reboot the server.
3. **Apply latest service packs.** The error message returned shortly after the server was rebooted. The server was behind on service packs both for Windows and Exchange. We applied Service Pack 3 for Exchange 2000 with the appropriate critical updates.
4. **Search *support.microsoft.com*.** After applying the service packs and rebooting the server, the error returned. We performed a search on Microsoft's site for 9582 under Exchange 2000. This returned the article *http://support.microsoft.com/default.aspx?scid=kb;en-us;325044&Product=exch2003.*

Resolution

The following steps fixed the error message:

1. Add the /3GB switch to the boot.ini. The boot.ini is located in the root directory of the boot drive, typically c:\. Open a command prompt and complete the following steps:
    a. c: <enter>
    b. cd\ <enter>
    c. attrib boot.ini –s –r –h <enter>
    d. edit boot.ini <enter>. At the end the of the [Operating Systems] section, add the /3GB after the /fastdetect switch. A sample of this boot.ini section is show here:

    [Operating Systems]
    ```
    multi(0)disk(0)rdisk(0)partition(2)\WINDOWS="Microsoft Windows 2003
    Server" /fastdetect /3GB
    ```

2. Save the file, and exit edit.

    ```
    attrib boot.ini +s +r +h <enter>
    ```
3. Change the registry key HKLM\SYSTEM\CurrentControlSet\Control\Session Manager\HeapDeCommitFreeBlockThreshold=40000.
4. Change the registry key HKLM\SYSTEM\CurrentControlSet\Control\Session Manager\Memory Management\System Pages=30000.
5. Reboot the server.

Lessons Learned

As the mail store grows, the load on a file server grows and increases the probability of memory fragmentation. This most likely explains why we did not get this error message until the server was in production for two years. If you're running Windows 2003 and have more than 1 GB of memory in the server, consider using the /3GB switch in the boot.ini file when you first install the server to avoid this problem.

Scenario 4 — Exchange Is Unable to Receive Internet Mail

Facts

- HP/Compaq ML350 with one 1.0-GHz processor, 1.0 GB of memory with mirrored 36-GB drives.
- Running Windows 2000 with Service Pack 4 and Exchange 2000 with Service Pack 3.

Symptoms

We received a call from the client that they were unable to receive Internet mail.

Questions to Ask

Q: When did this problem start? A: About two days ago.

Q: Has anything changed on the network? A: No.

Troubleshooting Steps

1. **Verify the problem.** We tried to send a test message from our server to the client's, but it was not delivered. A test of outgoing mail worked fine.
2. **Check the MX record.** Using the name server lookup (nslookup.exe) tool, we performed a lookup on their domain name. In this example, we're using the domain *cnn.com.*

```
C:\nslookup                       Start NSlookup
> set type=mx                     Set the query type to Mail eXchange
> cnn.com                         Enter the domain.  In this case
cnn.com
Server:  UnKnown
Address:  192.168.254.6
Non-authoritative answer:
cnn.com MX preference = 10, mail exchanger = atlmail4.turner.com
cnn.com MX preference = 10, mail exchanger = atlmail1.turner.com
cnn.com MX preference = 30, mail exchanger = nymail1.turner.com
cnn.com MX preference = 20, mail exchanger = atlmail2.turner.com
```

   In this particular example, the domain *cnn.com* has four mail servers. When we performed the same lookup for the client, nslookup verified that the MX record was pointing to the correct address of the Exchange server.
3. **Telnet into the Exchange server on port 25.** From the Internet, we used Telnet to connect to the Exchange server to verify the firewall and Ex-

change server were properly configured to accept Internet mail. To Telnet in, use the command:

```
telnet <server ip address> 25
```

At this point, you should receive a message like 220 <*server_name*> Microsoft ESMTP MAIL Service, Version: 5.0.2195.6713 ready. This indicates that the mail server is ready to accept Internet mail messages. Refer to article *http://support.microsoft.com/default.aspx?scid=kb;en-us;153119&Product=ech* for more information on testing a mail server with Telnet. Be aware that some firewalls are smart enough to detect an attempt to connect to a mail server using Telnet and will block the request. If this is the case, disable this feature on the firewall, or at least run the Telnet test from the LAN side of the network. Using the Telnet utility, we were able to connect to the Exchange server and send a test message that was received by a user.

4. **Check the authoritative DNS.** Even though the MX query was responding with the correct answer, we decided to verify the DNS servers responsible for this domain. You can use the `nslookup` utility to perform this task by completing the following steps:

```
C:\nslookup                      Start NSlookup
> set type=soa                   Set the query type to Start of
Authority
> cnn.com                        Enter the domain.  In this case
cnn.com
    primary name server = bender.turner.com
    responsible mail addr = hostmaster.tbsnames.turner.com
    serial  = 2004012001
    refresh = 900 (15 mins)
    retry   = 300 (5 mins)
    expire  = 604800 (7 days)
    default TTL = 900 (15 mins)
```

Using the *cnn.com* domain as an example, *bender.turner.com* is the authoritative DNS server for this domain. When we used the `nslookup` utility, the SOA record was correct for our client.

5. **Where now?** At this point, we were a little frustrated, because one of these troubleshooting steps should have revealed the reason why incoming mail was not working. We knew that the MX record was correct, Exchange was correctly configured to allow incoming Internet mail, the firewall was properly configured to allow mail into the server, and the authoritative DNS was correct. What else is left?

6. **Contact VeriSign.** This client's domain was registered with VeriSign, so we decided to contact them. This was the only item left in this puzzle. After we gave them the domain name, they indicated that the domain name has expired.

Resolution

An emergency payment was made to VeriSign to reinstate their domain name. Somehow, the paperwork for the domain renewal was misplaced, and the domain name was never renewed. After the domain was renewed, incoming Internet mail started working again.

Lessons Learned

Besides the obvious risk of having a cyber squatter steal your domain name, you run the risk of taking down your e-mail and Web site if the domain name is not renewed on time. Even after the payment was made to VeriSign, we had difficulty getting the domain name reestablished, and had to call back a couple of times before mail started working again. Always be conscious of your domain name expiration date, and make sure to renew the domain before it expires.

Scenario 5 — USERS ARE UNABLE TO OPEN THEIR MESSAGES ON EXCHANGE 2003

Facts

- HP/Compaq ML370 with one 3.2-GHz processor, 5 GB of memory with three 146-GB drive RAID 5 arrays.
- Running Windows Enterprise Server 2003 and Exchange Enterprise Server 2003.
- 200 users are using this mail server.
- The mail store is approximately 150 GB.
- Running Symantec Mail Security 4.0.10.458.
- Running Norton Anti-Virus Corporate Edition 8.0.

Symptoms

When a user tries to access her messages on Outlook, her mailbox appears, but if she attempts to open a message, Outlook freezes, and the message details are not displayed. Outlook must be forced close using the "End Task." The same problem happens with OWA.

Questions to Ask

Q: How long has the server been in place? A: The server was brought into production last week.

Q: When does this problem occur? A: It seems to happen when the server has a heavy load on it.

Troubleshooting Steps

1. **Verify the problem.** When users were unable to access their messages, we started Outlook. Outlook started okay, and displayed messages in the user's inbox. However, when we double-clicked on the message to view it, the system was unresponsive. We had to use the "End Task" on Outlook to close it. The problem only seemed to happen when the server was under a heavy load.
2. **Outlook Web Access.** We also tested OWA, and received the same problem. We could log in to the Exchange 2003 server, but when we double-clicked on a message, OWA would freeze and the message would not appear.
3. **Check the Event log.** We checked the Event log on the server for any error messages. The server did receive this event:

   ```
   Type: Error
   User: N/A
   Computer: Exchange2003
   Source Symantec Mail Security
   Category: Error
   Event ID: 104
   Error 0x8E1 occurred sending alert to NT server "Exchange2003"
   ```

   This error occurred roughly every 30 minutes. Because it happened many times without the server crashing, we didn't think this error caused the Exchange server to become unresponsive.
4. **Check the Exchange Services.** We checked all of the Exchange Services on the server and they were still running. We also sorted the services by status to verify that none of the services set to Automatic Startup was stopped. All services set to automatically start up were still running.
5. **Restart the server.** Even with the Exchange services running and no significant errors in the Event log, users could not access their mail. At this point, we needed to get the server running again, so we decided to cold boot the server. When the server came back up, users were able to access their mail and all of the services started normally.

6. **Task Manager.** We took a look at the Task Manager, clicked on the Performance tab, and reviewed the memory utilization, and processor utilization. Although the server was certainly under a load, we did not notice anything abnormal. Available physical memory was still at 3.5 GB, with the System Cache using roughly 400 MB. The CPU utilization averaged about 5 percent. On the Processes tab, we noted that store.exe was using about 1 GB of memory. Sorting the processes by CPU utilization, the SAVFMSFSp.exe (Symantec Mail Security) process occasionally took up 5 percent of the CPU time. Most of the CPU time was taken up by the System Idle Process.
7. **Optimize memory on the Exchange server.** We downloaded Microsoft's Knowledge Base Article 815372 for optimizing memory in Exchange Server 2003 and followed the directions. In addition to the `/3GB` and `/USERVA 3030` switches in the boot.ini, we added the `/PAE` (Physical Address Extension) switch because this server had more than 4 GB of memory and was running Windows 2003 Enterprise Server (Enterprise server can address up to 32 GB of memory). After these changes were made, we restarted the server to activate these changes.
8. **Exchange server stops responding.** After we made the boot.ini changes, approximately one hour later the Exchange server stopped responding again. When this server was initially installed, we did not install the Symantec Mail Security because the CD-ROM did not arrive. We remembered that the server started having problems after the Symantec Mail Security was installed. We had incoming mail routed through an Exchange 2000 server, that was protected by NAV for Exchange, so we were somewhat protected.
9. **Check Symantec's Web site.** We found a Tech Note on Symantec's site about a new release. We downloaded version 4.0.10.459 and ran reinstall.bat to install it over the previous version. Unfortunately, after the update the server still continued to crash.
10. **Disable Symantec Mail Security.** To test our theory about Symantec Mail Security, we stopped the services and disabled real-time protection. The server continued to stay up after we disabled Symantec Mail Security.
11. **Novarg virus hits.** Unfortunately, shortly after we disabled the Symantec Mail Security, the Novarg virus hit. This is a particularly nasty virus that can cause a lot of damage. We had no choice but to re-enable Symantec Mail Security.
12. **Contact Symantec support.** We contacted Symantec support to see if they had any suggestions. They suggested a complete uninstall and reinstall of Symantec Mail Security, which we performed. We also disabled a rescan of the mail store after a new pattern was received, background scanning, and reduced the number of scanning threads from five to three. Symantec recommends the number of scanning threads by adding the number of proces-

sors + 1. This server had one hyperthreaded processor. In Windows 2003, hyperthreaded processors will incorrectly show up as two processors. Symantec support verified that we had excluded certain files from scanning with Norton Anti-Virus Corporate Edition (NAVCE). You must prevent NAVCE from scanning Exchange files;, otherwise, it will conflict with Symantec Mail Security.

13. **Server crashes again.** The server stayed up for two days after we performed the clean install of Symantec mail security. However, after two days the server crashed again. We reviewed the Event log to see if we could correlate any event with the server crashes. One item we did notice was that Symantec Mail Security checked or uploaded a new pattern file shortly before the mail server stopped responding. Symantec Mail Security was currently configured to check for a new virus pattern every four hours.
14. **Contact Symantec.** At this point, we theorized that the Live Update process was causing the server to crash when it was under a heavy load. The NAVCE also checks the parent server for pattern updates as well. This could also be a potential conflict. We decided to change the Live Update Process to every day at 2:00 A.M. instead of every four hours. We had not experienced this problem with previous versions of Symantec Mail Security, although the check for virus patterns every *x* hours is a new feature added to this version of the software. Previously, you could only specify the day of the week and time of day when the server would check for a new virus pattern.
15. **Will the server stay up?** If the server remains stable, this is most likely a bug with the Live Update process when the server is under a heavy load. Symantec sent us a tech note to turn on capture debugging information on the server. If the server crashes again, we will send the debugging log to Symantec. At this point, we theorize that Live Update might be conflicting with NAV Corporate Edition, when checking for new patterns.

Resolution

Symantec sent us a new version of Symantec Mail Security 4.0 version 4.10.461. Since we installed this version, the server has remained stable. Evidently, this problem would only happen on a heavily loaded server with more than 150 users accessing the server.

Lessons Learned

We typically wait for products to be released for several months, so that other people can find the bugs. In this case, the client really needed the enhanced features of Exchange 2003. When faced with a complex troubleshooting task, remember to eliminate the variables. When we disabled the Symantec Mail Security and the server stabilized, we were pretty confident that this software was causing the problem, and the Exchange 2003. Moreover, Exchange 2003 has been out for several months, and a check of Microsoft's knowledge base did not reveal any problem of this nature, so we're pretty confident that Symantec Mail Security is the source of the server crash.

Scenario 6 USERS CANNOT SEND SCHEDULING INFORMATION TO EACH OTHER

Facts

- HP/Compaq ML370 with one 2.0-GHz processor, 2.0 GB of memory, with a three-drive 36-GB RAID 5 array.
- Running Windows Server 2000 with Service Pack 4 and Exchange 2000 with Service Pack 3.
- 50 users connected to the system who use file, print, and e-mail services on this server.

Symptoms

When users send scheduling information to other users, they do not receive it.

Questions to Ask

Q: Was it working before? A: It was working fine, until about an hour ago.

Q: Has anything changed? A: No, nothing has changed on the network.

Troubleshooting Steps

1. **Verify the problem.** We started Outlook and tried to send a schedule to another user, but he did not receive it.
2. **Send a test message.** Logged in as Administrator, we tried to send a test message to Administrator, but we did not receive it. At this point, we know that something is seriously wrong with the Exchange server.
3. **Check the Event Viewer.** We tried to check the Event Viewer, but it was blank, although the Event Viewer indicated that events existed.
4. **Restart the server.** We thought a restart of the server would fix Exchange and the Event Viewer problem. When the server restarted, we noticed that it took a long time for the server to reboot. No one could send messages after the server was restarted. We opened the Event Viewer, but it was still blank.

5. **Clear Event logs.** We thought there was a corrupted Event message preventing the display of the events. We cleared the Event logs, and messages started to appear. ESE in the Application log shows event 445, with the following error message:

```
Information Store (3156)  The database c:\program files\Exchsrvr\
mdbdata\priv1.edb has reached it maximum size of 16383MB.  If the
database cannot be restarted, an offline defragmentation may be
performed to reduce its size.
```

Fix

1. **Shut down Exchange Services.** We stopped the Exchange Services on the server and copied the priv1.edb and priv1.stm to another server. Make sure you have enough space on the target server before making a backup of the mail store. Note that the combined size of .edb and .stm files is used to calculate the mail store size. As a maintenance task, we deleted all of the files in c:\exchsrvr\mailroot\vsi 1\badmail.
2. **Delete mail.** After we had Exchange backed up, we started the Exchange Services and had all of the users delete their unwanted mail. We had the users delete their messages from their deleted items folder, sent items folder, and empty the trash. Luckily, users were able to still access their mailboxes. Typically, when the mail store exceeds 16 GB, you have to restore from backup, or run the Eseutil /p /g *<exchange_database_name>* to recover the database.
3. **Run Eseutil /d.** After the users deleted their mail, we stopped the Exchange services and ran Eseutil /d *<exchange_database_name>* to defragment the mail store.
4. **Upgrade or set mail store limits.** The client was notified that they must either upgrade to Exchange Enterprise or set limits on their mail store to prevent this problem in the future.

Lessons Learned

Keep a close eye on the Exchange mail store. It's not a bad idea to run an offline defrag with Eseutil every now and then. Remember, the combined size of the STM and EDB files is used to compute the maximum mail store size. Consider limiting the mailbox size for each user, or upgrade to Exchange Enterprise.

Scenario 7 Outlook Web Access Inbox Is Empty

Facts

- HP/Compaq ML350 with one 1.0-GHz processor, 2.0 GB of memory, with mirrored 36-GB hard drives.
- Running Windows Server 2000 with Service Pack 4 and Exchange 2000 with Service Pack 3.
- Symantec Enterprise Firewall 6.5.2 with a T1 connection to the Internet.

Symptoms

When users attempt to access their mail with Outlook Web Access (OWA), their inbox is empty.

Questions to Ask

Q: When did this problem start? A: After Exchange 2000 was installed, users could no longer access their inbox with OWA.

Q: Was OWA ever working on Exchange 2000? A: No.

Troubleshooting Steps

1. **Verify the problem.** When we attempted to log in to a user's mailbox using OWA, the inbox was blank. The user was allowed to enter his username and password, but OWA displayed a blank inbox after the user logged in.
2. **Access OWA from the LAN.** After failing to access OWA from the Internet, we attempted to access OWA from the LAN. When logging in to OWA from the LAN, the inbox and all other OWA features worked. What does this tell us? Most likely, there is a configuration error on the firewall, because OWA works from the LAN, but not from the Internet.
3. **Search Microsoft Knowledgebase.** On Microsoft's knowledgebase we searched for Exchange 2000 and "empty inbox" and found the article *http://support.microsoft.com/default.aspx?scid=kb;en-us;296232&Product=exch2k* "Empty Inbox When Using Internet Explorer 5 and Later to Gain Access to OWA."

Resolution

Following the instructions on the KB article, we completed the following steps:

1. Start Registry Editor (Regedt32.exe).
2. Migrate to the registry key: HKEY_LOCAL_MACHINE\SYSTEM\CurrentControlSet\Services\MsExchangeWEB.

3. On the Edit menu, click Add Key.
4. In the Key Name box, type OWA, and then click OK.
5. Click the OWA key that you just created.
6. On the Edit menu, click Add Value, and then add the following registry value:
   Value name: ForceClientsDownLevel
   Data type: REG_DWORD
   Value data: 1
7. Quit the Registry Editor.
8. Restart the World Wide Web Publishing Service on the Exchange 2000 computer.

   If you make this change, it reduces the functionality of OWA. OWA on Exchange 2000/2003 uses WebDAV, and the Symantec Enterprise Firewall 6.5.2 does not support WebDAV. By modifying the registry, you prevent OWA from using WebDAV.

Lessons Learned

The other resolution to this problem is to upgrade the firewall, or replace the current firewall with one that supports WebDAV. The Symantec Enterprise Firewall 7.0.4 and later support WebDAV.

Scenario 8 — EXCHANGE SERVER IS UNAVAILABLE

Facts

- HP/Compaq ML370 with one 3.0-GHz processor, 4.0 GB of memory, with three 72-GB RAID 5 arrays.
- Running Windows Server 2000 with Service Pack 4 and Exchange Enterprise 2000 with Service Pack 3.
- 200 users use this server for e-mail.
- The mail private mail store is 40 GB.

Symptoms

When users attempt to start Outlook, they receive an error message that the Exchange server is unavailable.

Questions to Ask

Q: When did this problem start? A: It started 10 minutes ago.

Q: Has anything changed? A: No.

Q: Was it working okay before? A: Yes.

Troubleshooting Steps

1. **Verify the problem.** When we started Outlook, we received an error message that the Exchange server was unavailable.
2. **Check the Exchange Services.** We looked at the Exchange Services; the Exchange System Attendant and the Exchange Information services were stopped. We attempted to start them, but they failed to restart.
3. **Check the Event Viewer.** We reviewed the messages in the Event Viewer to determine the reason why the Exchange Services did not start. At this point, we noticed an error message that the server was out of disk space. This was most likely the cause of the Exchange server crash.
4. **Free up disk space.** We deleted the files in \exchsrvr\mailroot\vsi 1\BadMail. Then, we copied the log files from \exchsrvr\mdbdata to another server. This freed up about 1 GB of space on the server.
5. **Restart the server.** When the server came up, we checked the services, and all of the Exchange services properly started. We started the Exchange System Manager and noticed that the private mail store did not mount. We tried to mount the private store manually, but it failed to mount.
6. **Run `EseUtil /p /g`.** We copied the private mail store to another server that had more room and ran `eseutil /p /g` <*database name*> to repair the database. Because the private mail store was 40 GB, this took several hours to run.

Resolution

After `Eseutil` completed, we were able to mount the store and users were able to access their mail.

Lessons Learned

Keep a close eye on disk space on the Exchange server. The Exchange log files and bad mail directories can quickly fill a server. This is especially true if the server has a heavy load on it. The Enterprise Edition of Exchange can have up to four Storage Groups and five information stores in each storage group, so we decided to create four additional private mail store databases. We separated each group by the following e-mail usernames:

- Private store A–F
- Private store G–L
- Private store M–S
- Private information store
- Public store

After the groups were created, we used the Exchange System Manager to move the users' mailboxes to the correct mail store. After all of the mailboxes were moved, we renamed the Private information store to Private store T–Z. This gave us four private mail store databases of approximately 10 GB each, instead of one large 40-GB mail store. In the event of a mail store corruption, `Eseutil` will run much faster because each mail store is smaller. In addition, the Exchange server is more fault tolerant, because the chances of corrupting each mail store simultaneously is fairly remote. Even if each mail store became corrupted at the same time, we could copy each database to a different server and run `Eseutil`. This will allow us to recover the Exchange server much faster (theoretically four times faster) than running `Eseutil` against one 40-GB mail store.

Scenario 9 PUBLIC FOLDERS DO NOT FULLY REPLICATE ON EXCHANGE 2000 SERVER

Facts

- HP/Compaq ML370 with one 2.0-GHz processor, 4.0 GB of memory, with three 72-GB RAID 5 arrays.
- Running Windows Server 2000 with Service Pack 4 and Exchange Enterprise 2000 with Service Pack 3.
- 200 users use this server for e-mail.
- Migrating from an Exchange 5.5 server.
- Symantec Anti-Virus/Filtering for Exchange 3.04.10.101.

Symptoms

A new Exchange 2000 server was introduced into the network to replace an aging Exchange 5.5 server. All of the user mailboxes were transferred over to the new Exchange 2000 server using the Exchange 2000 System Manager with no problems. Replicas of the Exchange 5.5 public folders were created using the Exchange 5.5 Manager; however, when the size and the number of items were compared for each public folder, the new server was missing items in many public folders.

Questions to Ask

Q: How big is the public folder store? A: About 10 GB.

Q: Are any public folders fully replicated? A: Yes, but about half are not fully replicated.

Q: How long has public folder replication been working? A: About one week.

Troubleshooting Steps

1. **Verify the problem.** Using the Exchange 5.5 Administrator, we compared the size and number of the items in each public folder. Approximately half of the public folders on the Exchange 2000 server were not completely replicated.
2. **Check the Event Viewer.** A review of the Event Viewer did not indicate anything out of the ordinary.
3. **Attempt replication again.** We removed the Exchange 2000 replicas on 10 public folders and recreated the replicas again. We waited for 24 hours, but the public folders were still not properly replicating.
4. **Search Microsoft Knowledgebase.** We performed a search for "public folder replication" on Microsoft's site and found the article *http://support.microsoft.com/default.aspx?scid=kb;en-us;817187&Product=exch2k*. We applied the post Service Pack 3 patch, but the problem still persisted.
5. **Search *www.google.com*.** We performed a search for "public folder replication Exchange 2000," but the search did not reveal any relevant articles. What's the next step? At this point, we know that something is preventing the public folders from properly replicating, but what could it be? During the replication process, the public folder information is copied to the new server. What process could prevent this from happening?

Resolution

As a test, we decided to disable the Symantec Virus protection, and replicated a few public folders again. We waited an hour and checked the status of the replication. The size and item count were correct on the Exchange 2000 server. Evidentially, the virus software was preventing proper public folder replication.

Lessons Learned

When you move a large amount of data from one Exchange server to another, you might have to disable virus scanning in order to move the data. The danger, of course, is copying a virus to the new server. If you have to disable the virus software, make sure to perform a complete scan on the server with the latest virus pattern after hours, when the migration is complete. This should catch any viruses that were moved to the new server.

CHAPTER SUMMARY

Proper maintenance of Exchange is vital to ensure a fast and stable mail server. Make sure to monitor disk space closely on the Exchange server to prevent running out of disk space and risk a mail database corruption. If you're running the Standard version of Exchange 2000/2003, remember that it's the combined total of the .EDB and .STM files when calculating the 16-GB mail store limit. It's not too difficult to hit this limit with as few as 25 users who store a lot of attachments on the mail server. If you're coming close to the limit, set up storage restrictions on each user's mailbox or upgrade to the Enterprise version of Exchange.

As you can see from the troubleshooting scenarios, what first appears to be an Exchange issue might be a symptom of a larger problem. Keep an open mind when troubleshooting Exchange problems. Otherwise, you can become easily frustrated, looking for an Exchange resolution to the problem when the answer might not be related to Exchange. Make sure to have a good virus package, backup strategy, and anti-spam filtering on the server to prevent problems from occurring in the first place. For larger installations (300+ users) of Exchange, remember that performance of your server will only be as fast as the disk subsystem. If you have a larger number of users to support, consider installing multiple Exchange servers, or implement a SAN to prevent disk bottlenecks. E-mail still continues to be the "killer" application on the network. Users used to get upset when the file server went down, but now they're ready to revolt if e-mail goes down. By practicing preventative maintenance, and careful monitoring, you can minimize downtime on an Exchange server.

REVIEW QUESTIONS

1. What is the mail database limitation for the standard version of Exchange 5.5/2000/2003?
   a. 16 GB
   b. 160 GB
   c. 160 MB
   d. 1.6 GB
   e. 16 TB
2. What versions of Exchange use an .edb and .stm file for their database store?
   a. Exchange 5.0
   b. Exchange 5.5
   c. Exchange 2000
   d. Exchange 2003
   e. Exchange 4.0
3. On an Exchange 2003 server with 500 users, what factor will most likely have the greatest impact on performance?
   a. Speed of the processors.
   b. Number of processors.

c. Speed of the network connection.
d. Speed of the disk subsystem.
e. Speed of the server PCI bus.

4. On an Exchange 2003 server with 2 GB of memory, what command should be added to the boot.ini to ensure that the Exchange server memory is optimized?
   a. /PAE
   b. /3GB
   c. /USERVA 4030
   d. /2GB
   e. /Fastdetect
5. Which of the following tasks are necessary to set up Internet e-mail on an Exchange 2003 server? (Choose all that apply.)
   a. Register a domain with a domain provider such as VeriSign or Register.com.
   b. Have your ISP create an MX record for your mail server.
   c. List your ISP's DNS servers as the authoritative record for your domain.
   d. Configure your firewall to allow port 25 traffic to flow into your mail server.
   e. Configure the firewall to create a static NAT between the private and public address of your mail server.

7 Wide Area Networks and IP Routing

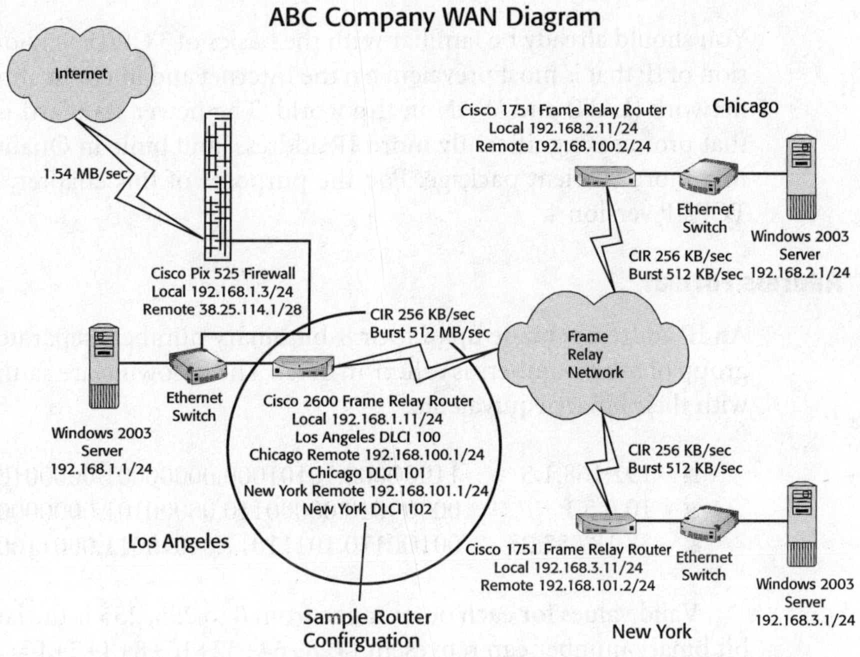

CHAPTER PREVIEW

In this chapter, we start with a basic review of TCP/IP. It helps to have a thorough understanding of TCP/IP and IP routing before you bring up a wide area network (WAN). We'll examine the different WAN technologies and the advantages and disadvantages of each WAN topology and factors that should guide you to a WAN solution that is the best fit for your company. When you use Active Directory over a WAN, proper configuration of site connectors is vital to ensure timely and efficient replication over relatively slow and expensive WAN links. We'll look at IP routing and static versus dynamic routes, Cisco routers, and some basic Cisco IOS command and troubleshooting procedures. The last half of the chapter is dedicated to real-world troubleshooting scenarios.

TCP/IP BASICS

You should already be familiar with the basics of TCP/IP version 4. This is the version of IP that is most prevalent on the Internet and in use in almost every local area network (LAN) and WAN in the world. The newer standard is TCP/IP version 6 that promises significantly more IP address, and built-in Quality of Service (QoS) in a more efficient package. For the purposes of this chapter, we concentrate on TCP/IP version 4.

Address Format

An IP address is made up of four 8-bit binary numbers separated by periods. Each group of 8-bit numbers is called an octet. The following are samples of IP addresses with their binary equivalents:

- 192.168.1.5 11000000.10101000.00000001.00000101
- 10.6.5.1 00001010.00000110.00000101.00000001
- 38.187.83.25 00100110.10111011.01010011.00011001

Valid values for each octet range from 0 to 255; 255 is the largest number an 8-bit binary number can represent (128+64+32+16+8+4+2+1 = 255).

Reserved Addresses

There are a number of reserved IP address schemes used for private networks. If you run Network Address Translation (NAT) on your network, you typically use one of these address schemes to avoid conflicts with IP addresses on the Internet:

- 10.0.0.0 to 10.255.255.255
- 172.16.0.0 to 172.30.255.255
- 192.168.0.0 to 192.168.255.255
- 169.254.0.0 to 169.254.255.255 (Automatic Private IP Addressing)

The last group of IP addresses is called Automatic Private IP Addressing (APIA). These addresses are automatically assigned to a device when a computer is unable to successfully obtain an IP address from a DHCP server. We find that most companies use either a 10.*x.x.x* or a 192.168.x.x. scheme on their network. Usually, when we design the IP scheme for an internal WAN, either we use a 192.168.*x.x* scheme or a 10.*x.x.x* scheme with 24-bit subnet masks. Of the two, we prefer the 10.*x.x.x* schema because it allows you to have more IP addresses and subnets compared to the 192.168.*x.x* scheme. When designing your IP scheme, make sure to plan for growth. Changing the IP scheme on a WAN is difficult, time consuming, and has the potential to cause network outages.

Subnet Mask

The subnet mask is used to determine what part of the IP address is used for packet routing and which part of the IP address is used for the host. The subnet mask determines how many subnets and hosts are possible. A subnet mask works like a Zip or postal code for a snail mail address. The subnet will get you to the correct network segment, just as a Zip code will get you to the general area of a specific address. The host portion of the IP address is like the number and street name of an address. It identifies a unique address for a specific location. For example, if you had a 24-bit subnet mask, you can have 16,777,214 (2^24–2) networks, and 254 (2^8–2) hosts. It helps to think of a subnet mask in terms of the number of bits in the subnet mask when calculating the available hosts. For example, how many hosts are possible with a 29-bit subnet mask? The answer is six. A 29-bit subnet mask only leaves you with a 3-bit binary number for host addresses. 2^3 = 8; however, we have to subtract 2 because the first value of the range is the network number and the last number is reserved for broadcasts. Therefore, we can have six hosts with a subnet mask of 29. How many hosts can you have with a 24-bit subnet mask? The answer is 254 (2^8–2). However, what if you had more than 254 hosts on a network segment? The answer is simple: we would use a 10.*x.x.x* scheme with a 16-bit subnet mask for that network segment. How many hosts can you have with a 16-bit subnet mask? The answer is 65,534 (2^16–2).

Default Gateway

The default gateway is the path that IP packets will take unless a different path is specified by a static route. Think of it as the primary exit out of your network. The default gateway is typically the IP addresses of your firewall or WAN router. However, what if you have both on your network? Which one should you use? In general, we suggest using the WAN router as the default gateway. If you use the firewall as your default gateway, you might run into intermittent routing problems even if you've granted the appropriate routing rules and set up the proper static routes on the firewall. If there is more Internet traffic than WAN traffic, setting the default gateway to the WAN router will generate slightly more traffic, but you will avoid intermittent routing problems if your firewall has difficulty acting as a router.

DNS Servers

Windows 2000/2003 uses DNS for name resolution, refer to the DNS configuration section Chapter 4 for tips on the proper DNS configuration in a Windows 2000/2003 environment. In our experience, DNS is much more stable than the NT method of using Windows Internet Naming Service (WINS) for name resolution on a WAN. If you're still running Win9*x*/Me, you might have to install WINS services for these computers, but if you have Windows 2000/XP clients, you can use DNS exclusively for name resolution. Name resolution is much more important on a WAN because all servers and other critical devices are usually not installed on the same subnet. To find the servers by name, you must have some type of name resolution running on the network.

SELECTING A WAN TOPOLOGY AND CARRIER

If you need to connect up two or more offices, you have a lot of choices for WAN lines. Let your budget, performance and uptime requirements dictate the type of WAN line you select. If you have line-of-sight between your two buildings consider a wireless or a laser connection. These connections offer higher speeds at a lower cost compared to Telco WAN lines.

Types of WAN Connections

Point-to-Point Connection

This is a good solution for companies that need to connect just two offices. Ideally, the offices should be in the same Local Access and Transport Area (LATA). Your local phone company can tell you if the two offices you want to connect are located within the same LATA. Often, point-to-point T1s can be installed for a reasonable charge of $300 to $400 per month. Most point-to-point T1s can be ordered through the local phone company.

Frame Relay

Frame Relay is the traditional method for connecting two or more locations that do not reside in the same LATA. The major advantage of Frame Relay is when the WAN contains more than two sites. For a fully meshed network using point-to-point T1s with four locations, you must install three T1s at each location. With

Frame Relay, you join the Frame relay "cloud" and the Frame Relay carrier handles the connections to the other offices using Data Link Connection Identifiers (DLCIs) to route WAN traffic to the appropriate locations. Frame Relay only requires a single connection at each location. As long as you join the Frame Relay cloud, you are connected to the WAN. Frame Relay connections typically offer a Committed Information Rate (CIR) and a burst rate on each line. Regardless of the Frame Relay traffic, the minimum line speed will not fall below the CIR, and when the bandwidth is available, the WAN traffic can increase up to the maximum burst speed. Frame Relay is a good alternative for Quality of Service QoS applications such as video conferencing because of the CIR. Most video-conferencing units require 384K of dedicated bandwidth to properly function. If your routers are QoS aware and you have a CIR at 384K at each location, you should not have any problems with video conferences due to WAN traffic bottlenecks. The biggest drawback to a Frame Relay network is the cost. They are usually the most expensive (and usually most reliable) method of creating a WAN.

Multiprotocol Label Switching (MPLS)/Hybrid Networks

MPLS networks function similarly to Frame Relay networks, but WAN traffic is converted into MPLS packets, sent across the carrier's internal network, and then converted to its native protocol. It can handle all of the QoS issues that Frame Relay addresses, but the internal network is more efficient because the carrier's network is a switched network versus a routed network with Frame Relay. MPLS networks promised to be the next big item in WAN communications during the boom years of the late 1990s; however, quite a few MPLS companies fell victim to the dot com bust in 2000 and 2001. The biggest selling point for MPLS carriers is they can offer the service level of Frame Relay networks at a reduced monthly cost. Be aware, however, that many of these companies are relatively new to the WAN market, and their service level might not be as good as some of the established Frame Relay carriers.

Virtual Private Networks

If you need WAN connectivity, don't have any QoS issues, and are on a tight budget, consider using a virtual private network (VPN). A VPN uses an encrypting device (usually a firewall) and an Internet connection to scramble data before it is sent across the Internet. A firewall on the other side of the WAN then decrypts the data. A VPN can be established for a fraction of the monthly charges of a Frame Relay or MPLS WAN. For more information on VPNs, refer to Chapter 10 in this book.

Wireless/Laser

If you have line-of-sight between your WAN locations, consider going wireless or laser. These connections are typically implemented as bridges and use either radio waves or laser beams to connect the sites. Radio links can go up to 54 mb/sec with laser connections running at speeds up to 2.5 gb/sec. For the best use of the radio link, place a router in front of the radio bridge, so broadcast packets are not unnecessarily sent over the radio link. We installed a radio link for one of our clients that saves them over $1,000 per month in WAN charges. As long as the units are properly configured and installed, they provide a secure and reliable connection for companies that have line-of-sight between their WAN locations. Laser connections typically run at faster speeds, cost more, and are more secure than radio links because the laser beams are much more focused.

WAN Considerations

When you select a WAN carrier, a number of items will have a significant impact on the performance, reliability, and cost of the WAN. Here are just a few items to consider when selecting a WAN carrier:

- To bring the WAN lines up, are there competent people on both sides of the connection to troubleshoot any problems?
- Once the WAN is up, who will support it?
- Is the WAN mission critical?
- How many users will be affected by a WAN outage?
- What is your cost of downtime?
- How many years has the carrier been in business?
- Does the carrier offer Service Level Agreements (SLAs) in the event of downtime?
- What is their uptime rating on their WAN?
- Will the carrier be in business next year?
- If your WAN will cover a wide geographical area, does the WAN carrier have a national or international presence?
- Does the carrier have strong references?
- How much does the carrier charge per month?
- Does the carrier require a minimum commitment period?
- Do they offer 24x7 support?
- What other services do they offer?
- Does the WAN require Quality of Service (QoS) for time-sensitive applications such as video conferencing?
- How long are the installation lead times for the lines?
- What type of monitoring tools does the WAN carrier have on their lines?

Select your WAN carrier carefully. If the carrier goes out of business after the WAN is installed, expect outages, and many headaches to switch over to a new carrier. In general, try to stay away from longer term (greater than one year) commitments. Often, prices will fall and you might be able to negotiate a better deal when other WAN carriers are competing for your business a year from now. Even if you plan to stay with the same carrier, you can pit carrier against carrier to negotiate the best deal for your company. Monthly recurring WAN charges can have a significant impact on the bottom line, so the carrier's monthly charges are always important.

ACTIVE DIRECTORY

When you run Active Directory (AD) on a WAN, there are very specific configuration requirements to ensure that replication takes place in the most efficient manner. Careful planning and configuration of AD will ensure that your network is stable and makes use of the limited bandwidth available on most WANs.

Global Catalog Servers

If you're planning to use AD to authenticate users, develop the AD model along with the WAN structure. If you have a large number of users who must authenticate on one side of a WAN, consider installing a local domain controller (DC) on that side of the WAN to reduce the amount of authentication traffic on the WAN. If your AD model is running a single domain, make the DC in each location a Global Catalog (GC) server. When a DC is a GC server, it stores a full replica of its domain, along with partial replicas for every other domain in the Active Directory forest. To make a DC a GC server, click on Start, Programs, Administrative Tools, Active Directory Sites and Services. Click on Sites, <*site_name*>, Servers, <*server_name*>, right-click on NTDS Settings, and select Properties. Figure 7.1 will appear.

A DC that is a GC server does not have to query another DC when authenticating users, and will reduce the amount of WAN traffic generated by user authentication.

Active Directory Sites and Services and Site Replication

After you have planned your IP scheme for all of your locations and you're running Windows 2000/2003, you should enter the Site and Subnet information into Active Directory Sites and Services, configure licensing, and set up site links.

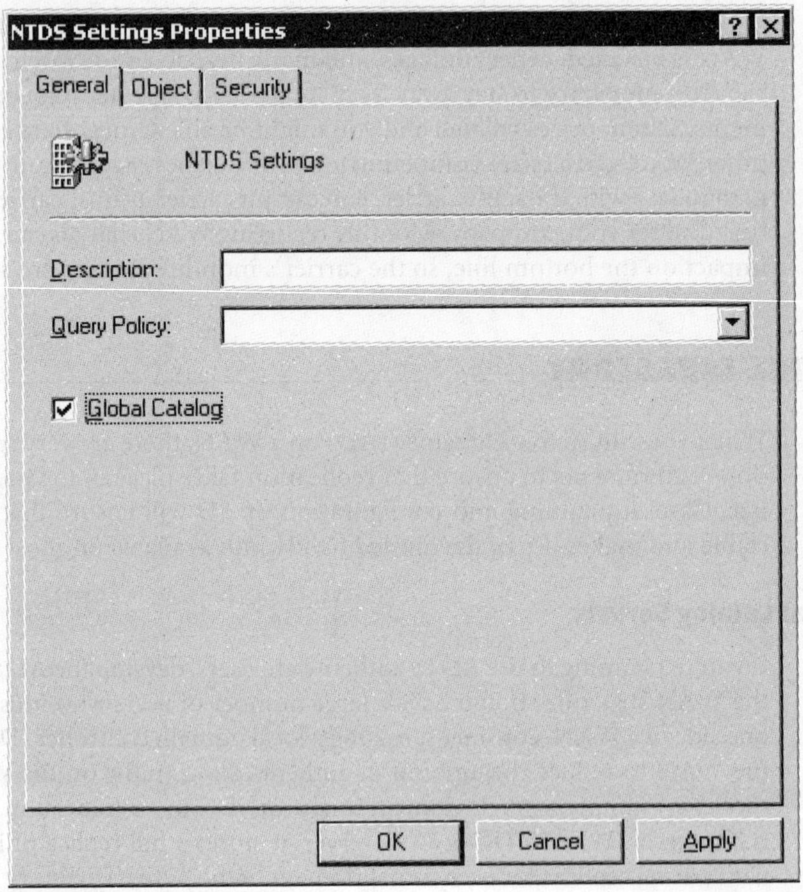

FIGURE 7.1 Making a DC a GC server.

Enter Site and Subnet Information

Start Active Directory Sites and Services by clicking on Start, Programs Administrative Tools, and Active Directory Sites and Services. Right-click on Site and Figure 7.2 will appear.

Enter a name for the site (no spaces) and select the site link. In this case, we're using the DefaultIPSiteLink. You can configure sites to communicate with IP or SMTP. As a rule, use IP to synchronize sites, if you have a WAN link that is 56k or faster. For slower WAN links that are not persistent, or to synchronize an AD domain that has many users and changes, use SMTP. If you must use SMTP for intersite replication, you must install an Enterprise Certificate Authority to ensure the authenticity of the SMTP replication messages. IP uses synchronous communication, and SMTP uses asynchronous communication to replicate AD objects. After

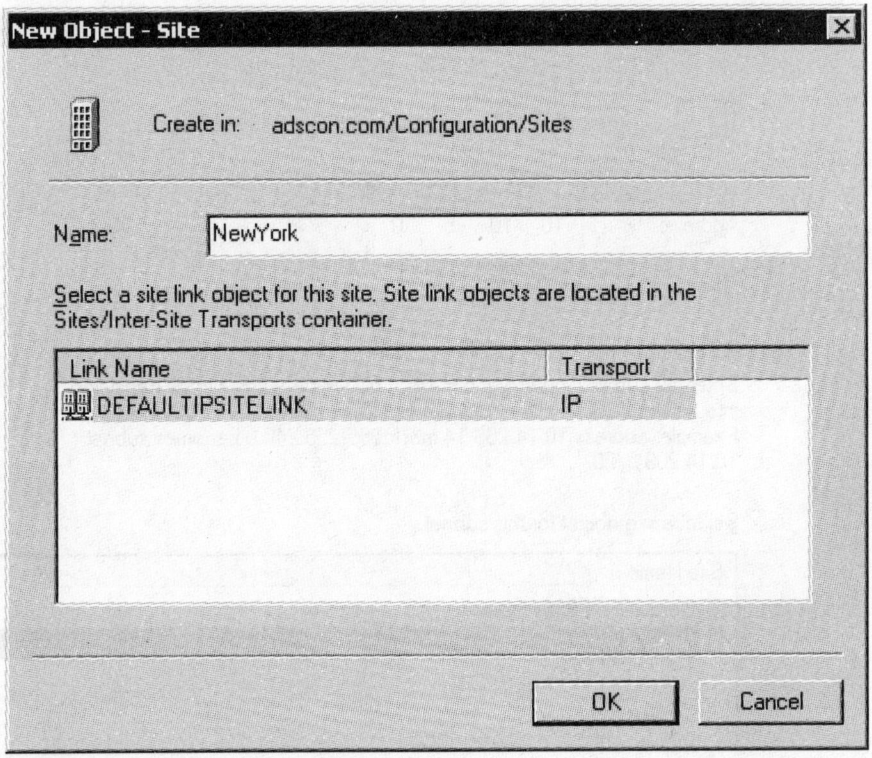

FIGURE 7.2 Create a New Site Object.

you've created the site, you must specify the subnet that is active in that site. Right-click on Subnets and select New Subnet. Figure 7.3 will appear.

Enter the IP address and subnet mask of the site, select the site object that you just created, and click OK. We suggest setting up the sites and subnets before you install a DC in the remote locations. That way, when a DC is installed, it is automatically placed in the correct site based on the IP address of the DC.

Licensing

After you have created the site and subnet, you should designate the licensing computer for the site. This server will store the licensing information for the site. For the best performance, you should designate a local licensing computer for each site.

Change the Replication Schedule

By default, Site Replication is scheduled once per hour. You can change the schedule of Site Replication by clicking on the Site, NTDS Settings. Figure 7.4 will appear.

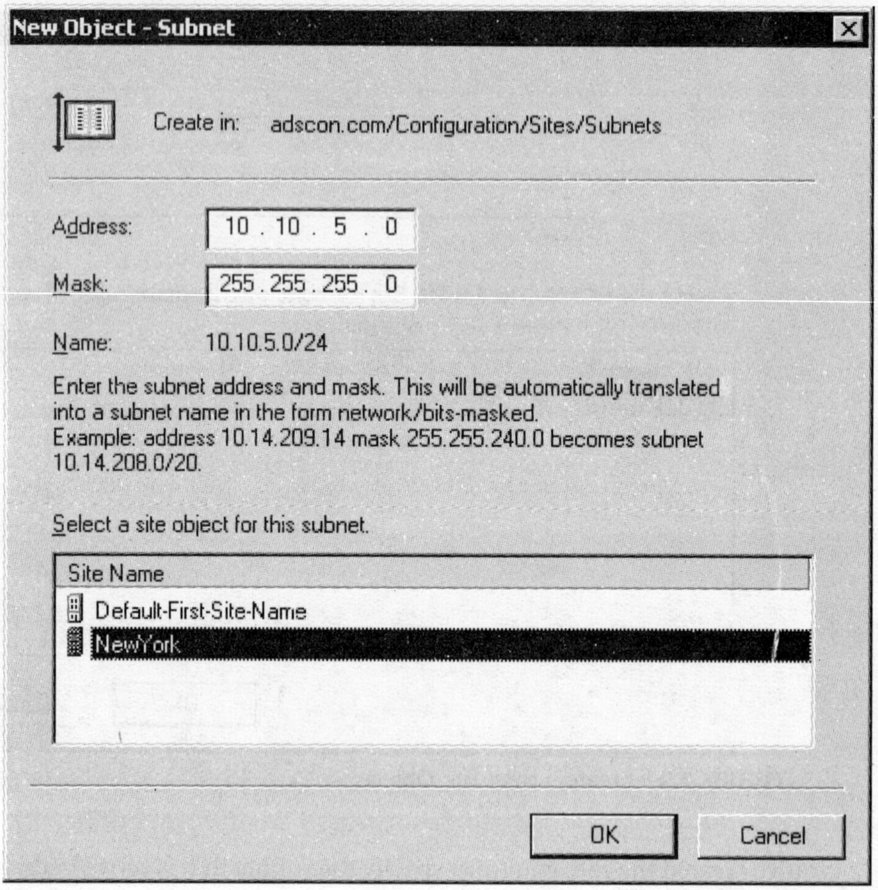

FIGURE 7.3 Adding a new subnet to a site.

Click on Change Schedule to modify the AD replication schedule. You can change the replication frequency from Never to every 15 minutes. Select a replication interval based on the number of changes in AD, and the speed of your WAN links.

Configure Site Links

Your site link configuration is dependant upon the structure of the WAN, speed of the WAN connections, number of users in each site, and cost of the WAN links. If you have a fully meshed WAN (a WAN where every site can communicate directly with every other site), you can configure site links that communicate directly with every site. If you do not have a direct communication with a site, you can have the replication messages relayed through another site by enabling bridging of the site

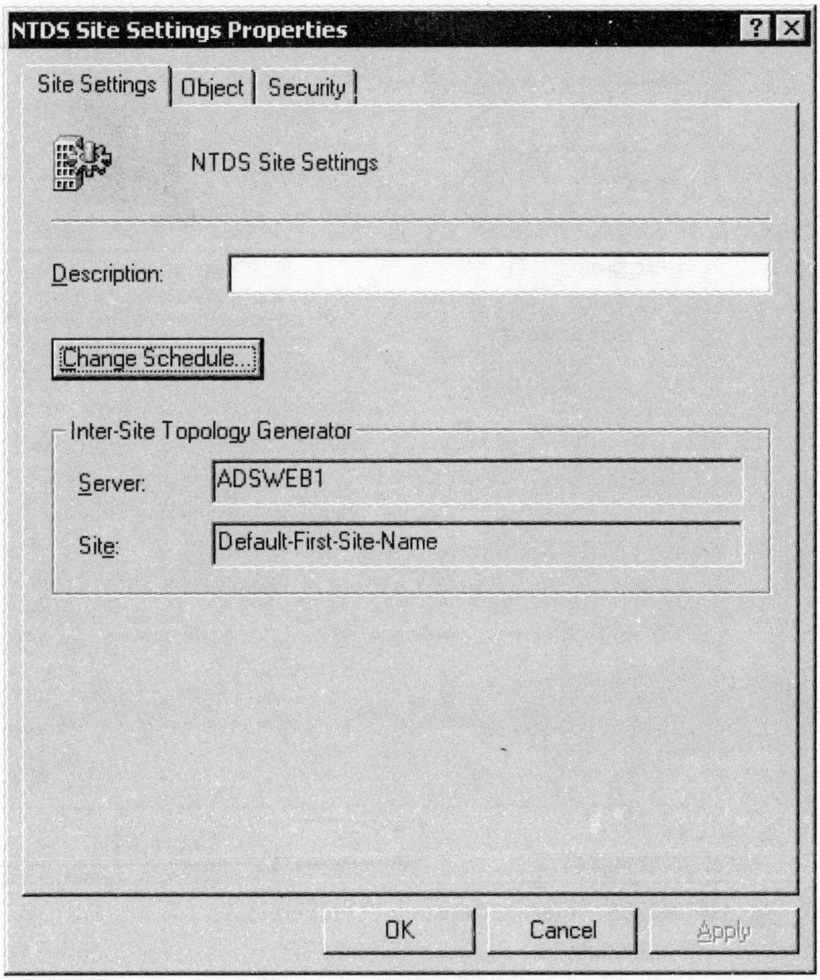

FIGURE 7.4 NTDS Site Settings Properties.

links. This is enabled by default on the IP Intersite transport and disabled by default on the SMTP Intersite transport. To view these settings, right-click on the Intersite-transport protocol (either IP or SMTP) and select Properties. Figure 7.5 will appear.

A fully meshed WAN simplifies the configuration of the site links and adds fault tolerance to the WAN. You should designate one DC in each site to act as a bridgehead between the local site and any remote sites. Then, you can configure the bridgehead server to replicate to any DCs within its local site. Consider the WAN in Figure 7.6.

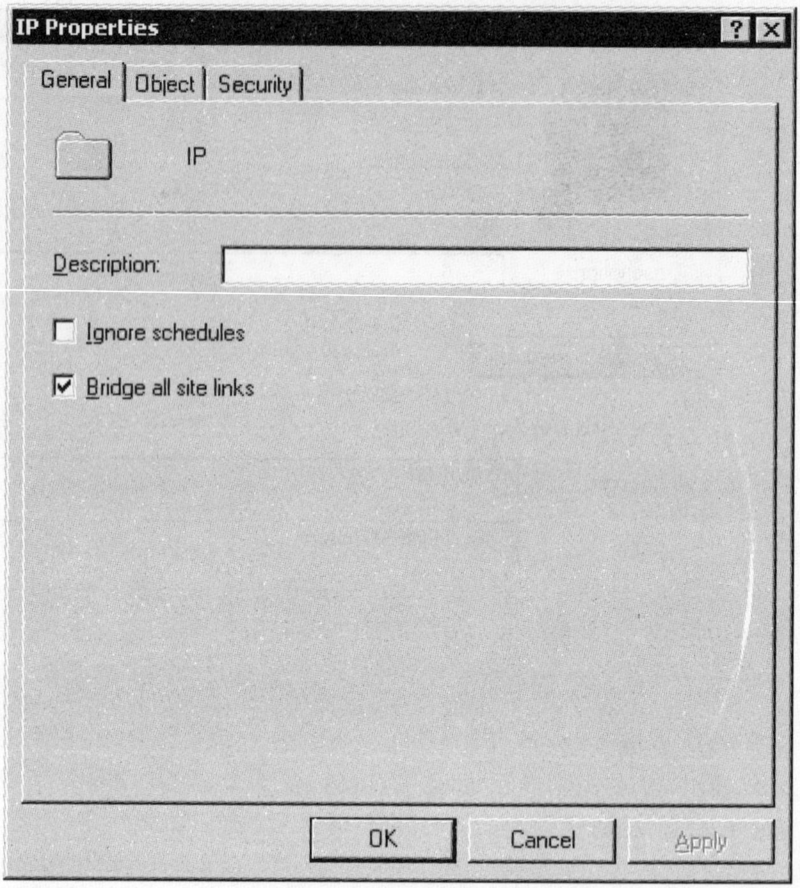

FIGURE 7.5 Intersite Transport IP Properties.

This network has the following attributes:

- Each server is a DC running Windows Server 2003.
- Each location has a local bridgehead server. LA1 is the bridgehead server for Los Angeles, CH1 is the bridgehead server for Chicago, and NY1 is the bridgehead server for New York.
- All of the sites are connected with a Frame Relay network with T1 lines to every site.
- All of the servers are in the same AD domain.
- The bridgehead servers are GC servers.
- The IP protocol is used for AD replication.
- Bridging is enabled on the site connectors.
- The Frame Relay network is a fully meshed network.

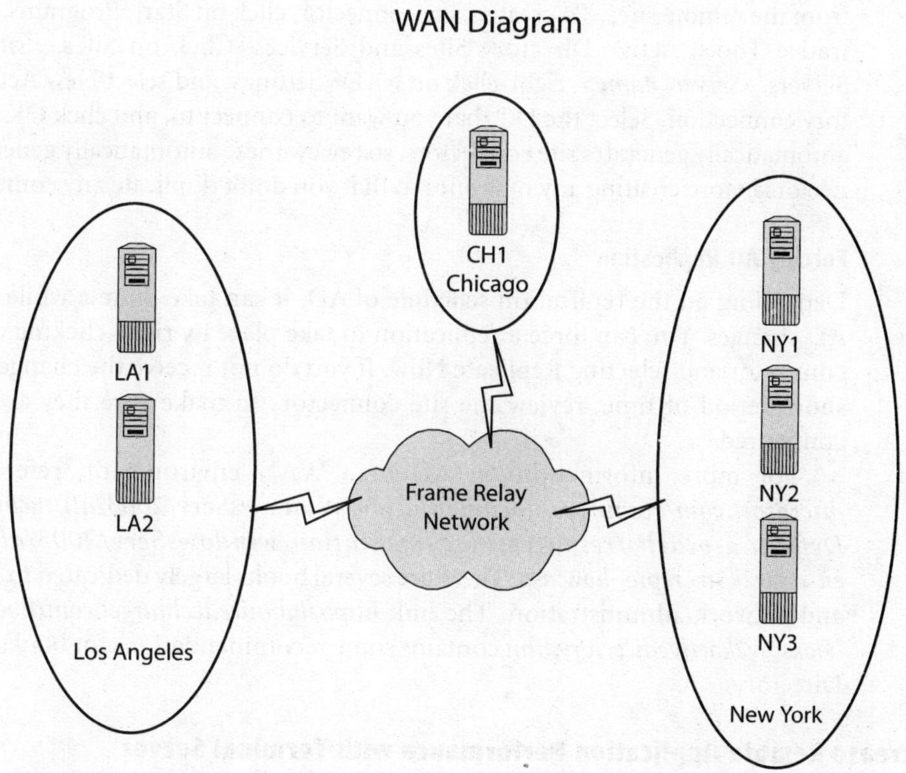

FIGURE 7.6 Active Directory Replication with multiple sites and DCs.

The site connectors for each location should be configured as follows:

- Los Angeles
  - LA1 has a site connector to CH1, NY1, and LA2.
  - LA2 has a site connector to LA1.
- Chicago
  - CH1 has a site connector to LA1 and NY1.
- New York
  - NY1 has a site connector to LA1, CH1, NY2, and NY3.
  - NY2 has a site connector to NY1, and NY3.
  - NY3 has a site connector to NY1 and NY2.

This is a relatively simple WAN, but the concepts remain the same as the complexity increases. The basic strategy is to designate one server as a bridgehead server and have all of the remote sites replicate with the bridgehead server. Then, the bridgehead server replicates with all of the local servers to pass on information obtained from the remote sites. To create a site connector, click on Start, Programs, Administrative Tools, Active Directory Sites and Services. Click on Sites, <*site_name*>, Servers, <*server_name*>, right-click on NTDS Settings, and select New Active Directory connection. Select the DC that you want to connect to, and click OK twice. AD automatically generates site connectors, so review these automatically generated connectors before creating any new ones so that you don't duplicate any connections.

Forcing AD Replication

Depending on the replication schedule of AD, it can take quite a while to receive AD changes. You can force a replication to take place by right-clicking on the site connector and selecting Replicate Now. If you do not receive the changes within a short period of time, review the site connectors to make sure they are properly configured.

For more information on AD in a WAN environment, refer to *www.microsoft.com/resources/documentation/WindowsServ/2003/all/techref/en-us/Default.asp?url=/resources/documentation/windowsServ/2003/all/techref/en-us/w2k3tr_repto_how.asp*. There are several books largely dedicated to AD design and network administration. The link *http://labmice.techtarget.com/BookReviews/books_w2kactivedirectory.htm* contains some recommendations for books on Active Directory.

Increase Remote Application Performance with Terminal Server

If your remote users need access to high-bandwidth applications, consider installing a Terminal server or Citrix server to increase the performance of the applications when running them remotely. A Terminal server allows you to run multiple virtual sessions on one Windows 2000/2003 server. Terminal servers are good solutions when you have more than a few people who need to run applications remotely at the same time. For a lower end solution, Windows XP has a one-user Terminal server license built into the operating system. On Windows 2000/2003, you can install Terminal Server in two modes: Remote Administration mode, and Application Server mode. Remote Administration mode allows you to connect two users to the Terminal server. Application Server mode allows you to connect as many users as you have Terminal Server licenses. If you install Terminal Services on a Windows 2000/2003 server, you must install Terminal Server Licensing Services. To enable Terminal Services on a Windows 2000 server in Remote Administration mode, click on Start, Settings, Control Panel, Add/Remove Programs, Add/Remove Windows Components. Scroll down, select Terminal Services, and click Next. When prompted, make sure to install Terminal Services in Remote Administration mode. To enable Terminal Services on a Windows 2003 server in remote administration mode, right-click on My Computer, Properties, Remote tab, and check "Allow users to connect remotely to this computer." You must install the Terminal Server client on a workstation that needs Terminal Server access. By default, the Terminal Server client setup program is located on the Windows 2003 server in c:\windows\system32\clients\tsclient\win32\setup.exe. Once you install the client, you can connect to a Terminal server by clicking on Start, Programs, Remote Desktop Connection, enter the name of the Terminal server, and click connect.

If you plan to use Terminal Server in Application mode, we strongly recommend that the Terminal server is a stand-alone machine that is not running any other services. Because the Terminal server users will have direct access to local files on the server, a Terminal server user can accidentally delete a critical program or file. If the Terminal server is a stand-alone machine, the Terminal server might crash, but your other servers will stay up. If you run Terminal Server on the same server as Exchange, and files are deleted, you run the risk of taking down both the Terminal server and your Mail server. You can somewhat control access to the local hard drive files through Group Policy; however, it's very difficult to completely lock down the Terminal server.

Some programs like MS Office and others have special installation procedures when installing the software on a Terminal server. Other applications might not even run on a Terminal server. Before you spend the money on a Terminal server, gather a list of all the applications that will run on the Terminal server and check with each software vendor to verify that their application will run on a Terminal server. Check if the software vendor has any special installation procedures prior to installing the application on a Terminal server. It's a bad time to find out that a critical application will not run on the Terminal server after you have completed the Terminal Server application, set up remote users, and established a WAN.

We recently installed a Terminal server on a WAN to increase the performance of an Access database application that used a SQL Server back end. Instead of accessing the Access application directly, the remote users start up a Terminal Server session and run the Access application locally. This has improved the remote response time of the application dramatically. The performance and response times are virtually the same as users locally running the application. Performing an inquiry on a customer takes less than one second, where before it would take 40 to 60 seconds to perform the same query directly over the WAN. Ironically, the client was just about to double their WAN line speeds in an effort to increase the application's performance, when we suggested a Terminal server instead. The Return on Investment (ROI) was roughly six months when you factor in the monthly recurring WAN costs, compared to the cost of the Terminal server. Not only was the Terminal server less expensive in the long run, the performance far exceeds any performance gain by doubling the line speeds of the WAN.

IP ROUTING

When building a WAN, it helps to have a solid understanding of TCP/IP and IP routing. We'll briefly touch on the basics of IP routing and different strategies used to establish IP routes.

Static versus Dynamic Routing

IP routing comes into play when you have multiple WAN segments on your network. Establishing routes notify the router about remote subnets that are not local to the router. What does this mean? Consider this example. Let's assume for a moment that you're a tourist in London, England, lost and driving aimlessly around. You want to get to Liverpool because you're a big Beatles fan, but have absolutely no idea how to get there. You stop someone on the street and ask for directions to Liverpool. He, of course, doesn't know and can barely understand your thick American accent. However, he suggests that you query someone in the local police station just up the road. You enter the police station and ask for directions. Thankfully, you meet a friendly police officer who gives you complete and accurate directions and you're on your way. This in many ways is how a static route works on a router. The first router might not know how to get to your desired destination, but the first router knows another router that *does know* how to get to your desired destination. You can configure your routers with either static or dynamic routes. Static routes must be manually configured on each router. Dynamic routes use a dynamic routing protocol such as Routing Information Protocol (RIP) or Interior Gateway Routing Protocol (IGRP), which must be enabled and supported on the router. These routing protocols advertise their discovered routes to other routers on the network.

In general, we prefer to set up WANs with static routes. Dynamic routing works great if the WAN is constantly changing, but most of the WANs we install remain relatively static. Static routes are initially more difficult to configure, but they are usually easier to troubleshoot than WANs that use dynamic routes. Since dynamic routing protocols discover new routes on the fly, you can run into situations where packets are not routed along the desired/anticipated route. With dynamic routes, you run the risk of taking down a router that you think is no longer in use, only to find out later that an entire WAN segment has gone down because one of the routing protocols was using the router to forward WAN traffic. Because the routers must advertise their routes, they take up some WAN bandwidth, although the newer routing protocols are pretty efficient. The biggest danger of using dynamic routes is setting up a WAN without a complete understanding of how packets are routed on the WAN. When something breaks on the WAN, you have no idea where to start looking and how packets are routed on the WAN. This will leave you in a very uncomfortable position. For this reason alone, we suggest using static routes because it forces you to understand IP routing, and the path that packets take to get to a certain destination. After you feel comfortable with IP routing, you can enable a routing protocol on your routers.

Static Route Example

Consider the WAN diagram in Figure 7.7.

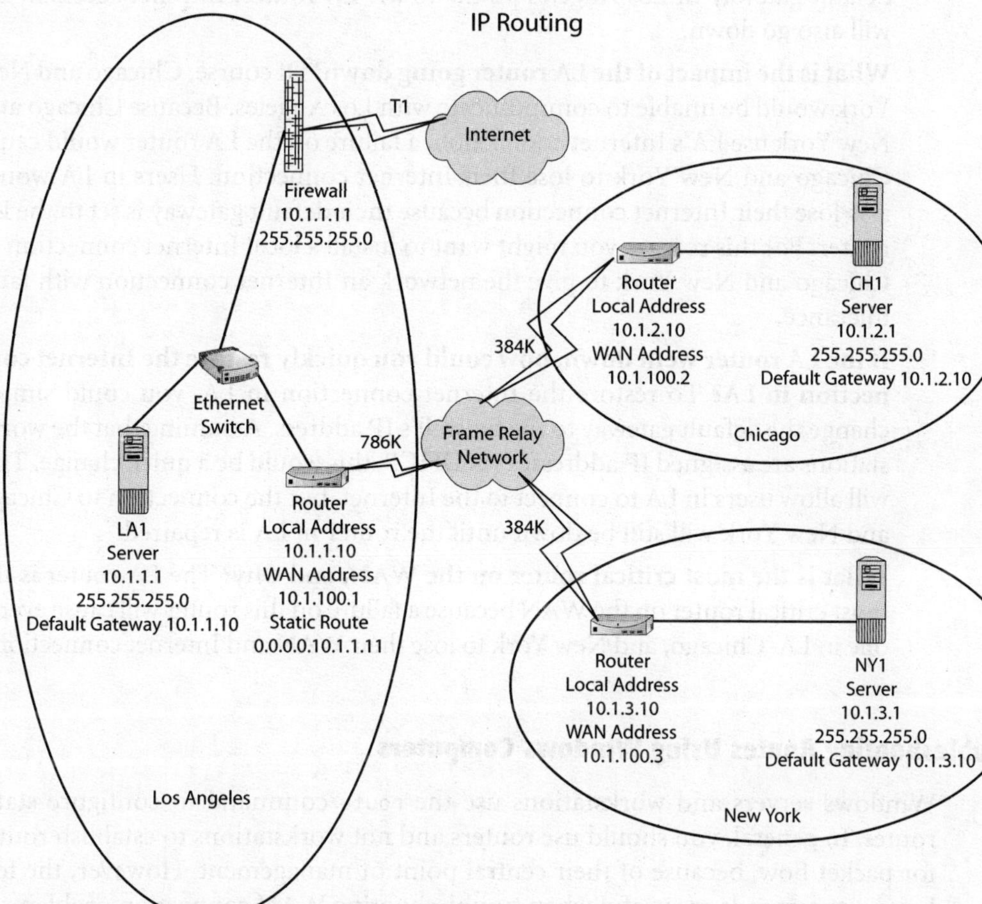

FIGURE 7.7 WAN diagram with static routes.

For this particular WAN to work, a default static route must be placed on the LA router. For LA users, the default gateway is set to the LA router. If the LA router cannot resolve the address (e.g., an Internet address), it uses the static route to forward the request onto the firewall. Chicago and New York users are able to get to the Internet because of the static route. All traffic not destined for the 10.1.1.0 subnet is forwarded to the firewall because of the static route. To test your understanding of IP routing, consider the following questions:

What is the impact of removing the static route on the LA router? If the static route was removed from the router, the remote sites would still be able to access Los Angeles, but they would be unable to access the Internet. Because the default gateway in Los Angeles points to the LA router, Internet access in LA will also go down.

What is the impact of the LA router going down? Of course, Chicago and New York would be unable to communicate with Los Angeles. Because Chicago and New York use LA's Internet connection, a failure on the LA router would cause Chicago and New York to lose their Internet connection. Users in LA would also lose their Internet connection because their default gateway is set to the LA router. For this reason, you might want to install a local Internet connection in Chicago and New York to give the network an Internet connection with fault tolerance.

If the LA router went down, how could you quickly restore the Internet connection in LA? To restore the Internet connection in LA, you could simply change the default gateway to the firewall's IP address. Assuming that the workstations are assigned IP addresses via DHCP, this would be a quick change. This will allow users in LA to connect to the Internet, but the connection to Chicago and New York will still be down until the router in LA is repaired.

What is the most critical router on the WAN, and why? The LA router is the most critical router on the WAN because a failure on this router will cause everyone in LA, Chicago, and New York to lose their WAN and Internet connections.

Troubleshooting Routes Using Windows Computers

Windows servers and workstations use the `route` command to configure static routes. In general, you should use routers and not workstations to establish routes for packet flow, because of their central point of management. However, the following commands are useful when troubleshooting WAN connection problems.

`route print`

When you issue the `route print` command, Figure 7.8 will appear.

The default route is shown with a network destination of 0.0.0.0 and a netmask of 0.0.0.0. The default route on this computer is pointing to 192.168.254.4. You can

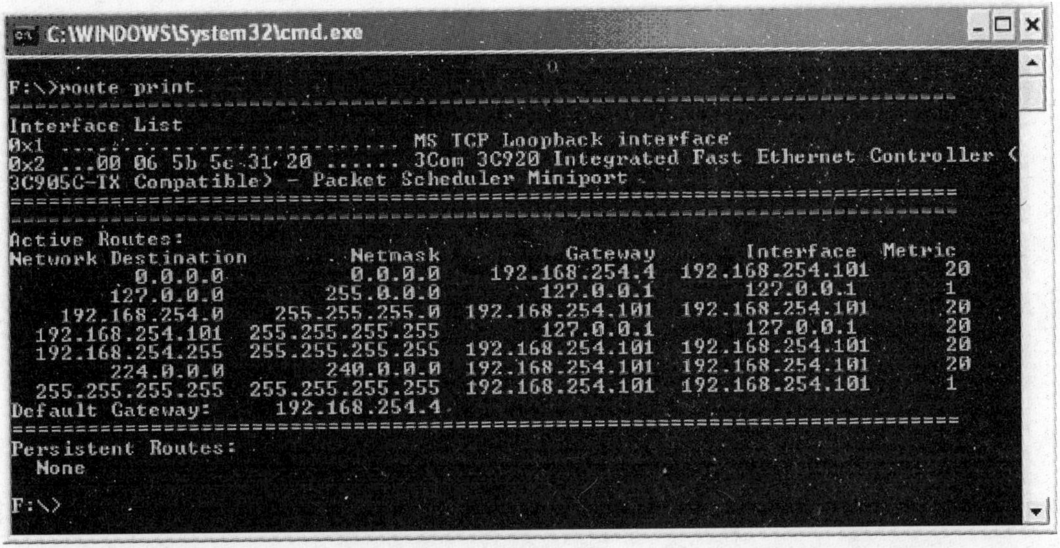

FIGURE 7.8 Output of the `route print` command.

view the route that a packet will take based on its network destination, netmask, and gateway. If you don't explicitly see the network destination using `route print`, you can assume the workstation is using the default route to send packets.

route add

Let's assume that a WAN has just been brought up, the WAN router has an IP address of 192.168.254.11, and a remote subnet has a value of 192.168.253.0 with a 255.255.255.0 subnet mask. If you wanted to configure the workstation with a static route for testing purposes, how would you do this? By using the `route add` command. The syntax is:

```
route add -p 192.168.253.0 mask 255.255.255.0 192. 168.254.11
```

The `-p` flag makes the route persistent. This means the route will remain in place even after the workstation is rebooted. The `-p` flag is not available on Win9*x* and Me computers. This command says if you want to reach the network 192.168.253.0 with a subnet mask of 255.255.255.0, use the router at address 192.168.254.11. Now if you issue the `route print` command Figure 7.9 will appear.

Notice that the `route add -p` command added the Persistent route displayed at the bottom of the screen.

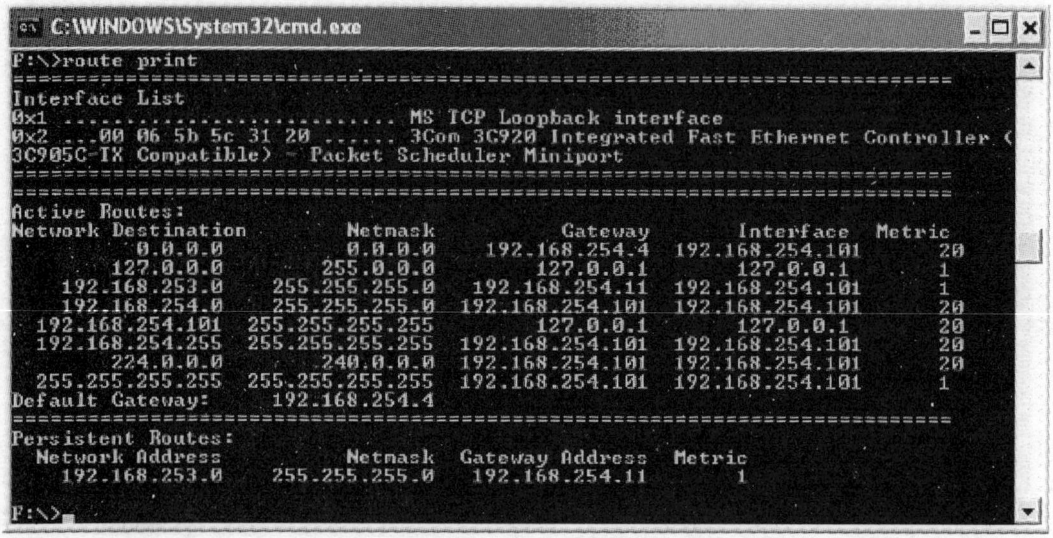

FIGURE 7.9 `route print` with a persistent route.

route delete

You can use the `route delete` command to remove a route. If we issue the command

```
route delete 192.168.253.0
```

it will delete the persistent route we just created in the previous step. You can use the `route print` command to verify that the route has been deleted.

Ping/Pathping Command

Use `ping` to determine if a host is reachable. `Pathping` will give you statistics on packet response times and packet path. The syntax is:

```
Ping <ip_address or host_name>
Pathping <ip_address or host_name>
```

When you use these utilities, try to ping by IP address first, and then by name. If you are able to ping by IP address and not by name, you usually have a DNS problem.

tracert

Use `tracert` <ip_address or host_name> to view the path that packets take to get to a host. Even when you cannot ping a host, you can still use `tracert` to see if the packets take the anticipated route. If the packets take the incorrect route, you can modify the route by using the `route` command to potentially solve the problem.

USING A WINDOWS SERVER AS A ROUTER

You can use a Windows 2000/2003 server as a router on your network instead of purchasing a dedicated hardware router. This typically involves installing two or more network cards in the Windows server. Routing on a Windows 2000/2003 server is configured using the Routing and Remote Access snap-in, which is located in Start, Programs, Administrative Tools, Routing and Remote Access. Here are suggested tips if you plan to use a Windows server as a router:

Install all necessary NICs in the server first. Make sure that all NICs are installed prior to using Routing and Remote Access to configure the router. Assign the NICs network address, subnet mask, default gateway, and DNS configuration.

Use only one default gateway. Make sure to enter a default gateway address on only one NIC. Leave the default gateway address blank on all remaining NICs. If you need to access a remote subnet via a network card with a blank default gateway address, add a static route to inform the server how to reach the remote subnet. If you place a default gateway on two or more NICs, you will run into multiple routing problems. Symptoms include intermittent problems when you attempt to reach remote subnets.

Test the connections. Make sure you can reach all remote subnets on the server before configuring the router with the Routing and Remote Access snap-in. Run a few ping tests from the server to ensure your default gateway and static routes (if any) are properly configured. If you cannot reach a remote subnet use `tracert/pathping` to troubleshoot where the packet dies. Double check your default gateway and static routes to correct the problem.

Use Routing and Remote Access. Use the Routing and Remote Access snap-in to configure the router. Right-click on the Windows server and select Configure and Enable Routing and Remote Access. Use the wizard to select the desired routing configuration for your server.

Workstation default gateway. After you've completed the router configuration, set the default gateway on the workstations to the IP address of the router/server. From the workstation, run a few ping tests to ensure that the workstation can reach all of the desired subnets. Use `tracert/pathping` to troubleshoot any connection problems.

Using a Windows server as a router is a good solution if you have a small network and don't have the budget to purchase a dedicated router like one from Cisco. If you take down your server, be aware that you will also bring down your WAN if you use a Windows Server for your WAN router.

CISCO ROUTERS

If you have a WAN, there's a good chance you are using Cisco routers on your network. The first time you look at an operating system on the router (Cisco IOS) can be a little intimidating. We'll look at some very basic commands to help you perform WAN troubleshooting and router management.

Connecting to the Router

You can either Telnet to the router or use the console port on the router. If the router is already configured with an IP address, you can use the Telnet. If the route has not been configured or you do not know the IP address of the router, use the console cable (flat light-blue cable) that ships with the router. This cable is then plugged into an RJ45 to DB9 serial adapter that then plugs into a computer. Then, use Hyper Terminal to connect to the router if you're using the console port. If you've lost the console cable, you can make one using the information in Table 7.1.

TABLE 7.1 Cisco Console Cable Pinouts

Signal	RJ45	RJ45	DB9
CTS	1	8	7
DTR	2	7	4
TxD	3	6	3
GND	4	5	5
GND	5	4	5
RxD	6	3	2
DSR	7	2	6
RTS	8	1	8

To connect to the router, use a Telnet program. For example, if the router has an IP address of 10.1.1.10, you would issue the following command at a command prompt:

```
telnet 10.1.1.10
```

The router will prompt you for the Telnet password.

Setting Passwords

There are typically three passwords on a Cisco router: enable password, enable secret, and Telnet password. The enable password is used to enter enable mode on the router. To make any changes on the router, you must enter enable mode. The # prompt is displayed on the router when you are in enable mode. To change the enable password, issue the command:

```
Enable password <password>
```

The enable secret password, however, overrides the enable password. It uses stronger encryption than the enable secret password does. We suggest just setting the enable secret password by issuing the command:

```
Enable secret <password>
```

You can set up a Telnet password to protect the router from unauthorized changes. To set the Telnet password, issue the commands:

```
Enable <password> (Enter enable mode)
Configure terminal (Configure the router from telnet)
Line vty 0 (Go the virtual terminal 0)
Password <password> (Change the telnet password on terminal 0)
Ctrl-Z (Exit configure mode)
Write (Save the changes)
```

Recover a Lost Password

What if you lost the password or purchased the router used and don't know the password? Go to *www.cisco.com/en/US/products/hw/routers/ps259/products_password_recovery09186a0080094675.shtml* for instructions on how to reset the Cisco password. To reset the password, you must connect to the router using the console port and serial cable.

Basic Commands

Listed in Table 7.2 are some basic commands that will help you navigate through the Cisco IOS.

Document the Router Configuration

Before making any changes, always back up the router configuration. This will allow you to quickly restore the current configuration. To back up the running configuration, Telnet into the router and go into enable mode. Set a screen capture in

TABLE 7.2 List of Basic Cisco Commands

Command	*Description*
Enable (En)	Enters enable mode that allows you to make changes to the router. The # prompt indicates you are in enable mode.
Show Running (Sh Ru)	Displays the running configuration.
Write (Wr)	Saves the current configuration.
Reload (Rel)	Restarts the router.
No <*command*>	Negates the <*command*>.

Telnet, issue the command `Show Running` to display the router configuration, and save the screen capture to a text file. Whenever you make changes to the router, you should document your changes by capturing the output from `show running`. Keep this file in a safe place for future reference. We suggest entering a meaningful description for all of your router interfaces. This makes it easier to identify the interfaces in the future and will save time in the long run. You can use ! to indicate that the line is a comment to document your router configuration; however, these comments will be lost if you upload the configuration from a text file that contains lines starting with !. After the router configuration is complete, we use a label maker to list the IP address of each router interface.

Making Remote Changes

Sometimes, you will make a change, and are unsure it will work. You can issue the command:

```
reload in <number of minutes>
```

This command will reboot the router in the number of specified minutes, so if you make a mistake on the router configuration, the router will reboot itself and load the original configuration. If the changes that you made are successful, you can cancel the reload of the router by issuing the command:

```
Reload cancel
```

Cisco 2600 Frame Relay Router Configuration

Figure 7.10 shows the WAN diagram for this network. This router uses a point-to-point configuration where each site is set up on its own subnet. This allows the WAN administrator to take down each location individually, rather than the entire WAN.

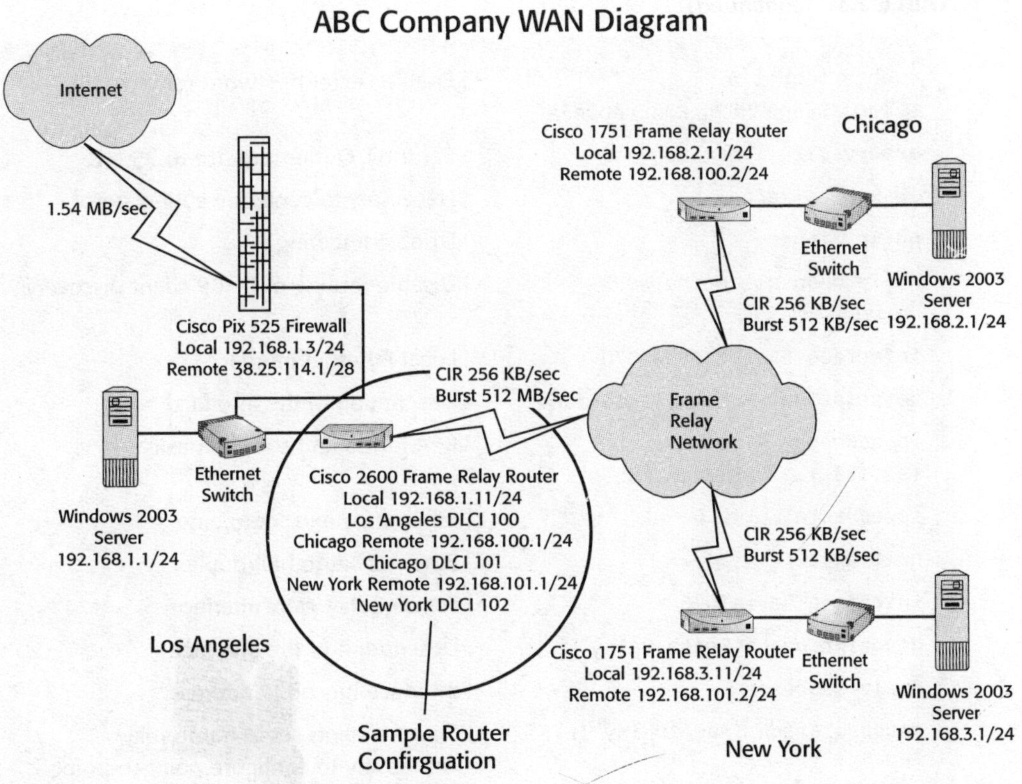

Figure 7.10 WAN diagram for ABC Company.

Listed in Table 7.3 is a sample Cisco 2600 router configuration for ABC Company, and is the result of issuing the command `Show Running` in enable mode on the Cisco 2600 router.

TABLE 7.3 Los Angeles Cisco 2600 Frame-Relay Point-to-Point Configuration

`version 12.1`	! Version of the IOS software
`no service single-slot-reload-enable`	! Disable single line card reloading
`service timestamps debug uptime`	! Enable debug of uptime
`service timestamps log uptime`	! Enable logging of uptime
`hostname LA2600`	! Router Name
`no service password-encryption`	! No service password encryption
`logging rate-limit console 10 except errors`	! Control the logging rate to the console except for errors. Prevent overload of router CPU.

TABLE 7.3 *(continued)*

`enable secret 5 $1$ocJ2$Feg32H62qL8a5ZrabQn5A`	! Enable secret password (encrypted)
`memory-size iomem 25`	! Set the I/O memory size to 25 MB
`ip subnet-zero`	! Necessary to configure subnet zero
`no ip finger`	! Disable fingering
`no ip dhcp-client network-discovery`	! Disable routing of DHCP client discovery
`interface FastEthernet0/0`	! Local Ethernet interface
`description LA Local Interface`	! Description of the interface
`ip address 192.168.1.11 255.255.255.0`	! IP Address and subnet mask
`speed auto`	! Ethernet speed set to auto
`half-duplex`	! Ethernet set to half-duplex
`interface Serial0/0`	! Frame Relay WAN interface
`description LA Frame Relay`	! Description of the interface
`no ip address`	! Interface has no IP address
`encapsulation frame-relay IETF`	! Encapsulation set to frame-relay – necessary to configure point-to-point interfaces
`service-module t1 timeslots 1-8`	! Activate 1 – 8 64K channels for 512K Always set channels for Burst speed, not Committed Information Rate (CIR)
`interface Serial0/0.1 point-to-point`	First point to point interface going to Chicago
`description Frame to Chicago`	! Description of the first point to point interface
`ip address 192.168.100.1 255.255.255.0`	! IP address of the interface
`frame-relay interface-dlci 101`	! DLCI of the interface
`interface Serial0/0.2 point-to-point`	! Second point to point interface going to ! New York
`Description Frame to New York`	! Description of second point to point interface
`frame-relay interface-dlci 102`	! DLCI of the point to point interface
`ip classless`	! Route with the longest prefix match

`ip route 0.0.0.0 0.0.0.0 192.168.1.3`	! Static route pointing to the Firewall for Internet access
`ip route 192.168.2.0 255.255.255.0 192.168.100.2`	! Static route pointing all Chicago traffic to Chicago router
`ip route 192.168.3.0 255.255.255.0 192.168.101.2`	! Static route pointing all New York traffic to New York router
`no ip http server`	! Disable to Cisco HTTP browser interface
`line con 0`	! Console line 0
`transport input none`	! No transport input
`line aux 0`	! Aux interface
`line vty 0 4`	! Telnet interface
`password configme`	! Telnet password
`Login`	! Enable login
`End`	! End of the configuration
`LA2600#`	! Router prompt in enable mode

For your reference, Table 7.4 is an example of the Chicago router configuration.

TABLE 7.4 Chicago Cisco 1751 Frame-Relay Point-to-Point Configuration

`version 12.1`	! Version of the IOS software
`no service single-slot-reload-enable`	! Disable single line card reloading
`service timestamps debug uptime`	! Enable debug of uptime
`service timestamps log uptime`	! Enable logging of uptime
`hostname CH1751`	! Router Name
`no service password-encryption`	! No service password encryption
`logging rate-limit console 10 except errors`	! Control the logging rate to the console except for errors. Prevent overload of router CPU.
`enable secret 5 $1$ocJ2$Feg32H62qL8a5ZrabQn5A`	! Enable secret password (encrypted)
`Memory-size iomem 25`	! Set the I/O memory size to 25 mb

TABLE 7.4 *(continued)*

`ip subnet-zero`	! Necessary to configure subnet zero
`no ip finger`	! Disable fingering
`no ip dhcp-client network-discovery`	! Disable routing of DHCP client discovery
`Interface FastEthernet0/0`	! Local Ethernet interface
`description Chicago Local Interface`	! Description of the interface
`ip address 192.168.2.11 255.255.255.0`	! IP Address and subnet mask
`Speed auto`	! Ethernet speed set to auto
`half-duplex`	! Ethernet set to half-duplex
`interface Serial0/0`	! Frame Relay WAN interface
`description Chicago Frame Relay`	! Description of the interface
`no ip address`	! Interface has no IP address
`encapsulation frame-relay IETF`	! Encapsulation set to frame-relay – necessary to configure point-to-point interfaces
`service-module t1 timeslots 1-8`	! Activate 1 – 8 64K channels for 512K Always set channels for Burst speed, not Committed Information Rate (CIR)
`interface Serial0/0.1 point-to-point`	! First point to point interface going to LA
`description Frame to LA interface`	! Description of the first point to point
`ip address 192.168.100.2 255.255.255.0`	! IP address of the interface
`frame-relay interface-dlci 100`	! DLCI of the interface
`ip classless`	! Route with the longest prefix match
`ip route 0.0.0.0 0.0.0.0 Serial0.0.1`	! Default route for all WAN traffic
`ip route 192.168.3.0 255.255.255.0`	! Static route pointing all New York traffic 192.168.100.1 to LA router
`no ip http server`	! Disable to Cisco HTTP browser interface
`line con 0`	! Console line 0
`transport input none`	! No transport input
`line aux 0`	! Aux interface
`line vty 0 4`	! Telnet interface
`password configme`	! Telnet password
`Login`	! Enable login
`End`	! End of the configuration
`CH1751#`	! Router prompt in enable mode

Troubleshooting Cisco Routers with the Show Command

If you only know one troubleshooting command on the Cisco routers, it should be:

```
Show ip interface brief
```

This command displays a summary and the status of each interface on the router. If the WAN goes down, and we suspect that the WAN line is the problem, we will Telnet into the router and issue this command. If the line status on the WAN link shows "down," we know that we should call the WAN carrier to open a trouble ticket. Some other troubleshooting commands are listed in Table 7.5.

TABLE 7.5 Cisco show Commands

Command	Description
`Show ip arp`	Displays the MAC to IP resolution table
`Show version`	Displays the current IOS version, processor, Interfaces, memory, etc.
`Show ip protocols`	Displays IP protocol information
`Show ip route`	Displays the IP routing table
`Show ip route summary`	Displays the IP routing table in summary form
`Show ip interface`	Displays detailed information about each IP router interface
`Show ip interface brief`	Displays summary status information about router interface
`Show ip traffic`	Displays detailed IP traffic statistics on the router

WAN DOCUMENTATION

As the complexity of your network grows, so does the importance of good network documentation. As the network grows larger, there is a good chance you will work with several IT coworkers in different parts of the country. We suggest creating a detailed WAN diagram that contains the following information:

- **Servers.** Server names, operating systems, IP addresses, subnet masks, and location.
- **Routers.** Router model, IP addresses on all interfaces.
- **WAN link speeds.** Speed of each WAN link. For Frame Relay networks, the CIR, Burst speeds, and DLCI are helpful.

- **Firewalls.** Firewall model, version, and IP addresses and subnet masks for all interfaces.
- **WAN contact information.** Technical support number, circuit IDs, and any contact information.
- **IT department information.** Internal phone numbers and contact people.

It's handy to have this diagram around on a daily basis. It's very helpful to bring new employees or outside consultants up to speed on your network configuration or for planning purposes when you make changes to the WAN. As mentioned before, make sure to document any changes to routers, and store the documentation in a safe place. In our experience, Cisco routers rarely fail, but as long as the router configuration is well documented, you can get a new router, and restore an original router configuration in a matter of minutes.

TROUBLESHOOTING SCENARIOS

Expanding your network from a LAN to WAN raises issues with performance, connectivity, cost, security, and replication. Careful planning and coordination are mandatory for a successful WAN implementation. The following scenarios are some of the issues we have experienced with our client's networks.

Scenario 1 Users In Los Angeles Have Difficulty Accessing Servers In Chicago and New York

Facts

- T1 connection with a Checkpoint Firewall-1 firewall.
- Windows 2003 server with 100 XP workstations.
- Private Frame Relay network with connections in Los Angeles, Chicago, and New York.

The WAN diagram is shown in Figure 7.11.

Symptoms

We received a call from the client that some workstations in Los Angeles were having difficulty accessing the servers in Chicago and New York.

Questions to Ask

Q: Has anything changed? A: No. The WAN has been in place for several months with no problems.

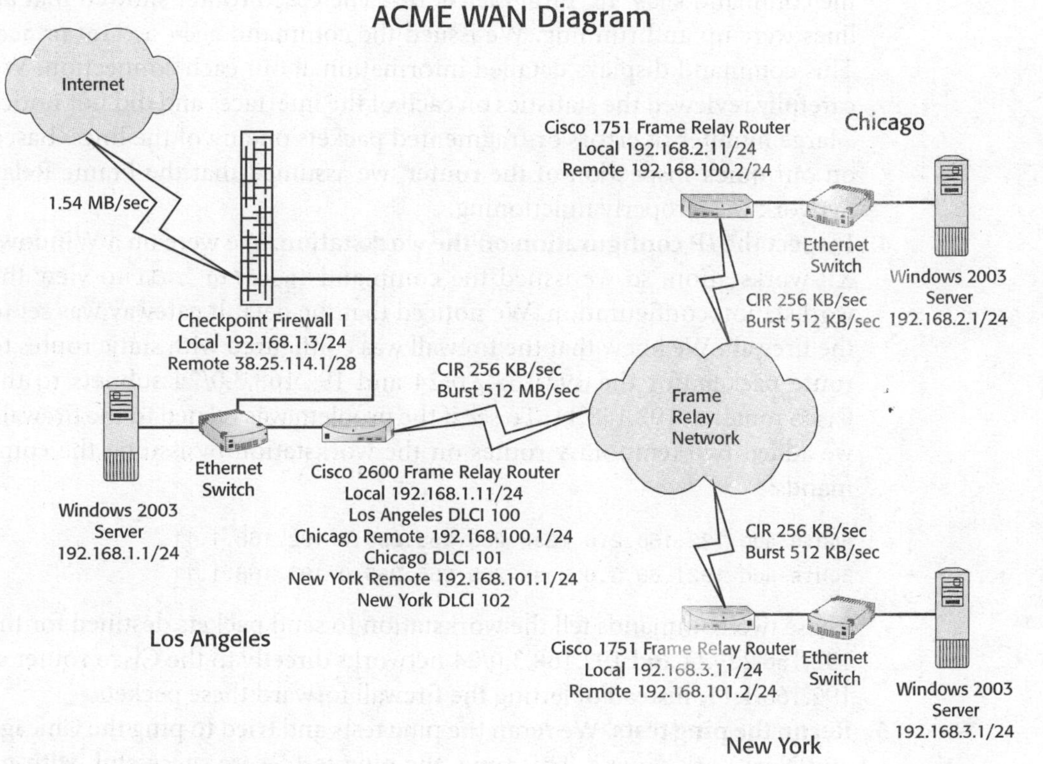

FIGURE 7.11 ACME WAN diagram.

Q: When does the problem occur? A: It appears to happen randomly.

Q: Is the problem related to a specific group of workstations? A: No. We can't relate this specific problem to any group of workstations.

Troubleshooting Steps

1. **Verify the problem.** When we arrived on site, we tried to access the shares on the Chicago server. It did take a while for the share to appear. We also tried New York and received the same slow results.
2. **Run a `ping` test.** We tried a `ping` test to the Chicago and New York servers. Although the initial `ping` test ran fine with response times under 50ms, a repeat of the `ping` test sometimes timed out with no reply. This happened on both the Chicago and New York servers.
3. **Telnet into Cisco Frame Relay router.** Because of the timeout problems on our `ping` test, we suspected that something might be wrong with the Frame Relay network. We started a Telnet session into the Cisco router and issued

the command `show ip interface brief`. The Cisco router showed that all lines were up and running. We issued the command `show ip interface`. This command displays detailed information about each connection. We carefully reviewed the statistics on each of the interfaces and did not notice a large number of errors or fragmented packets on any of the lines. Based on our quick inspection of the router, we assumed that the Frame Relay network was properly functioning.

4. **Inspect the IP configuration on the workstation.** We were on a Windows XP workstation, so we issued the command `ipconfig /all` to view the workstation configuration. We noticed that the default gateway was set to the firewall. We knew that the firewall was configured with static routes to route packets for the 192.168.2.0/24 and 192.168.3.0/24 subnets to the Cisco router at 192.168.11. To see if the problem was related to the firewall, we added two temporary routes on the workstation by issuing the commands:

```
Route add 192.168.2.0 mask 255.255.255.0 192.168.1.11
Route add 1921.68.3.0 mask 255.255.255.0 192.168.1.11
```

These two commands tell the workstation to send packets destined for the 192.168.2.0/24 and 192.168.3.0/24 networks directly to the Cisco router at 192.168.1.11, instead of letting the firewall forward these packets.

5. **Rerun the ping tests.** We reran the ping tests and tried to ping the Chicago and New York servers. This time, the ping tests were successful, with no timeouts and response times very close to 50ms. As a second test, we tried to open shares on both remote servers. We were able to access the shares without any problems. Evidently, the firewall was not correctly forwarding the packets for the 192.168.2.0/24 and 192.168.3.0/24 to the Cisco router on a consistent basis.

6. **Check the firewall configuration.** We examined the static routes on the Checkpoint firewall and the access rules. The static route pointed all traffic destined for 192.168.2.0/24 and 192.168.3.0/24 to the Cisco router at 192.168.1.11. There was also a rule that allowed all traffic to flow between the 192.168.1.0/24, 192.168.2.0/24, and 192.168.3/24 subnets. We couldn't think of anything else on the firewall to configure, so we decided to call Checkpoint technical support.

Resolution

After we called Checkpoint and explained out configuration, Checkpoint suggested not using the firewall as the default gateway for the workstations. They explained that even though the correct rules and static routes were set up on the firewall, we could still run into problems. Based on this information, we reconfigured our DHCP server to use the Cisco router as the default gateway. There was already a static route on the Cisco router configured as

```
Ip route 0.0.0.0 0.0.0.0 192.168.1.3
```

to point to the firewall as the default route. We refreshed the TCP/IP address on one workstation by issuing the command:

```
Ipconfig /release
Ipconfig /renew
```

We verified that the workstation used the Cisco router as the default gateway and tested the configuration. After we verified that this new configuration was properly working, we expired all of the IP addresses leases so the workstations would receive the new default gateway. We removed the static route on the firewall and the access rules for the internal subnets.

Lessons Learned

If you have a WAN with similar issues, check to see if you are using the firewall as a default gateway. Every firewall vendor is different, and some might allow the firewall to be used as a router. If you have intermittent problems, try changing the default gateway to your Frame Relay router and see if the problem goes away. If so, consider reconfiguring your network to use the Frame Relay router as the default gateway instead of the firewall.

Scenario 2 — New User Is Unable to Access Exchange Mailbox

Facts

- WAN running Windows 2000 Active Directory with Exchange 2000.
- Five remote locations on the WAN.
- Single Active Directory domain for all locations.
- Exchange servers running in all locations.
- Each location has a domain controller configured as a Global Catalog server.

Symptoms

We just added a new user to Active Directory, but when we attempt to configure her Outlook profile on the workstation and click the Check name button, her name does not underline.

Questions to Ask

Q: Has anything changed? A: Yes, a new user was added to Active Directory and Exchange, but she is unable to access her mailbox.

Q: Has this happened before? A: Unknown. We don't recall this happening before at this location.

Troubleshooting Steps

1. **Verify the problem.** When we tried to add the new user to the Outlook profile on the workstation and clicked the Check Name button, we were unable to get Outlook to underline the name and validate the user. We were able to log in to the network with the new user's ID and password.
2. **Load Outlook.** Even without the verification, we tried to open Outlook and access the new user's mailbox. Outlook returned an error that it was unable to open the mailbox and prompted if we would like to open the default folders instead.
3. **Delete user and add her back into Active Directory.** We thought that perhaps we made a mistake adding the user the first time, so we decided to delete the user from Active Directory and her mailbox and recreate the account. After we added the user back in, we had the same problem. We could log in to the network with the new user account, but we couldn't access the Exchange mailbox. We had performed this task many times before, and the inability to complete such a simple task was very frustrating!
4. **Service pack the server.** We noticed that the Server and Exchange were behind one service pack, so we decided to upgrade the system to the latest service pack.
5. **Check the user again.** After the service packs were installed, we decided to access the new user's mailbox again. This time it worked! Was it the service pack that fixed the problem? To test this theory, we added a new test user with a mailbox and tried to access it. We had the same problem as before—the user could log in to the network, but was unable to access his Exchange mailbox. Most likely, the service pack did not fix the problem, but why was the previous problem user now working, but the test user was not?

Resolution

We thought about the steps that had taken place over the last hour. The only difference we could see was that more time had elapsed since we tried to access the new user's mailbox. We decided to review the site connectors in Active Directory Sites and Services. This was a fully meshed WAN, so each site could directly see the other sites. A review of the site connectors revealed that they were improperly configured. We reconfigured the site connectors so that each site communicated to the designated bridgehead server at each remote site. All sites only had one server in each location, so we didn't have to worry about intrasite replication. We also modified the replication schedule to take place every 15 minutes, not once an hour, which is the default.

Lessons Learned

Using Active Directory Sites and Services, you can right-click on a site connector and select Replicate Now to force a replication with a remote site. As a rule, you might have to wait at least 15 minutes for Active Directory changes to replicate, or even longer depending on your AD replication schedule and speed on your WAN links. Proper site link configuration is critical for efficient replication of AD objects. For more information on WANs and Active Directory, refer to *www.microsoft.com/resources/documentation/WindowsServ/2003/all/techref/en-us/Default.asp?url=/resources/documentation/windowsServ/2003/all/techref/en-us/w2k3tr_repto_how.asp*.

Scenario 3 USERS ARE UNABLE TO ACCESS REMOTE SERVERS

Facts

- WAN running Windows 2003 Active Directory with Exchange 2003.
- Four remote locations on the WAN, with 50 users at each location.
- Frame Relay network is used for their WAN.
- Single Active Directory domain for all locations.
- Cisco routers used for Frame Relay network.

Symptoms

Users are suddenly unable to access resources on any remote server.

Questions to Ask

Q: Has anything changed? A: No, but users are not able to access remote servers.

Q: Was it working before? A: Yes, the WAN has been stable over the past few months.

Troubleshooting Steps

1. **Verify the problem.** When we arrived on site, we tried to ping the server in the remote locations. Attempts to ping any remote server timed out. Attempts to ping local servers were successful.

2. **Telnet into the router.** We connected to the Frame Relay router via Telnet and went into enable mode. We issued the command:

```
show ip interface brief
```

The results of this command indicated that the line and protocol were down on the Frame Relay connection.

Resolution

We called the Frame Relay provider and they verified that the line was down. We opened a trouble ticket with the provider and asked for an estimated time when they thought the server would be restored. After two hours, the line was repaired and users were able to connect to the remote servers.

Lessons Learned

When you select a WAN carrier, find out what type of monitoring they use for notification when a problem occurs. The most responsive carriers can notify you of an outage, even before the users are aware of it. If they give you notification that the line is down, it reduces your troubleshooting time, because you know that the line is the cause of the WAN outage. Ask if the carrier has a Service Level Agreement (SLA) that provides refunds on the monthly line charges if the line stays down for an extended period of time. For mission-critical WANs, consider installing a backup ISDN line that is configured for auto dial-up in case the primary WAN connect goes down.

Scenario 4 USERS ARE UNABLE TO ACCESS COMPANY WEB SITE

Facts

- WAN connects four sites.
- Each location has a SonicWALL Pro 2040 configured as a fully meshed VPN that connects all four locations.
- Windows 2003 and Exchange 2003 server are installed at each location.
- Company Web site is hosted at the Los Angeles location in the DMZ.
- Single Active Directory domain for all locations.
- Users in Denver and New York are unable to access the Web server at 192.168.10.1 in the DMZ. Their VPN diagram is shown in Figure 7.12.

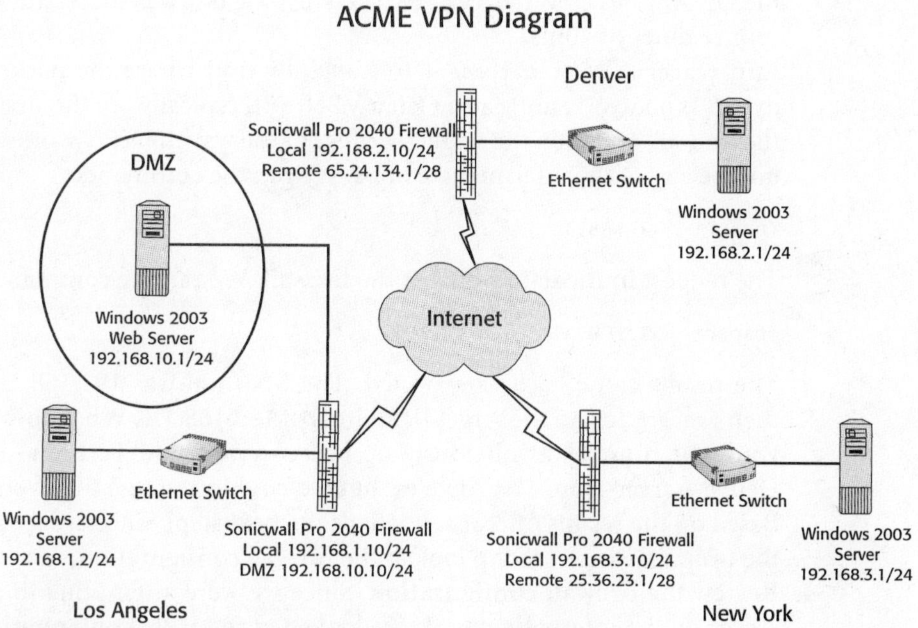

FIGURE 7.12 ACME VPN diagram with four locations.

Symptoms

The company's Web site was recently moved from a hosting facility to their internal network. Users in Los Angeles can reach the Web server at 192.168.10.1 with no problems. Users in Denver and New York are unable to access the Web server.

Questions to Ask

Q: Has anything changed? A: Yes, the company's Web site was moved to the internal network from a hosting location.

Q: Was it ever working? A: Only users from Los Angeles are able to access the site. Users in Denver and New York are unable to access the site.

Troubleshooting Steps

1. **Verify the problem.** We used the Terminal Server client to connect to the remote server in Denver and tried to access the company Web site. Internet Explorer timed out with an error that the page could not be displayed.
2. **Ping test.** Using the Denver server, we tried to ping the Web server at 192.168.10.1, but the request timed out. However, we knew that the tunnel was up because we were able to connect to the Denver server from Los Angeles with the Terminal Server client. Just as a sanity check, we tried to ping

the Los Angeles server at 192.168.1.1. The ping test was successful with response times of 40ms.

3. **Run `tracert`.** We ran `tracert` to hopefully find where the packets were dying. When you run `tracert` on a VPN, you typically see the first hop as the firewall, and then the target. Because of the way the VPN works, you do not see any of the intermediate hops. We ran the command:

   ```
   Tracert 192.168.10.1
   ```

   The request immediately died at the firewall. We ran the command:

   ```
   Tracert 192.168.1.1
   ```

   The results came back as expected. The first hop was 192.168.2.10, and then `tracert` found the target IP address of 192.168.1.1. What does this tell you? The tunnel was obviously up because we could Terminal into the Denver server from Los Angeles, but we couldn't access the Web server. Based on the results of `tracert`, what's the next step? Since `tracert` died at the firewall, we decided to look at the firewall configuration.

4. **Review the firewall configuration**. Since we were attempting to access a server on the internal network, we looked at the VPN configuration. The SonicWALL indicated that the tunnel between Los Angeles and Denver was up and running. We tried to ping the Web server again and reviewed the firewall log. It revealed an access denied on the 192.168.10.1 address.

Resolution

Why were we getting an access denied error on the 192.168.10.1 address? This one had us stumped for a while. We went back and reviewed our configuration on the firewall. Then it hit us. The firewall was in the DMZ on a different subnet! When you set up a VPN, you must specify all of the remote subnets to which the VPN will connect. We added a subnet of 192.168.10.0/24 on both the Denver and New York firewalls. After we saved the configuration and reestablished the tunnels, the users could access the Web server in the DMZ.

Lessons Learned

When you create a VPN tunnel, make sure to include *all* of the remote subnets to which this tunnel will connect.

CHAPTER SUMMARY

Migration from a LAN to a WAN raises some unique challenges with design, replication, remote user performance, coordination, and support. A properly designed, configured, and maintained WAN will be stable and will increase employee productivity. A poorly designed WAN will be unstable, difficult to maintain, and employees will never benefit from the potential of the network. Plan carefully when implementing a WAN from your TCP/IP scheme, bandwidth requirements, carrier selection, Active Directory design, and remote access requirements.

REVIEW QUESTIONS

1. How many hosts can you have with a 28-bit subnet mask?
   a. 16.
   b. 14.
   c. 6
   d. 8
   e. 254.
2. What's the best solution for companies that need to connect two or more buildings where all of the buildings have line-of-sight?
   a. Point-to-point T1s
   b. Frame Relay
   c. Wireless
   d. VPN
   e. MPLS
3. How can you force Active Directory Replication to take place immediately?
   a. Modify the replication schedule to take place once a minute.
   b. Modify the replication schedule to take place once every 15 minutes.
   c. Create a site connector to the location where you want immediate replication.
   d. Set the replication protocol to SMTP instead of IP.
   e. Using Active Directory Sites and Services, right-click on the appropriate site connector and select Replicate Now.
4. Which of the following is true about static routes?
   a. They must be manually configured on the router.
   b. They use RIP.
   c. They use IGRP.
   d. They are only supported by Cisco routers.
   e. They cannot be made permanent on Windows XP workstations.

5. What command should you use on a Cisco router to view the status of a Frame Relay connection?
   a. `Show ip interface brief`
   b. `Show ip route`
   c. `Show running`
   d. `Show ip route summary`
   e. `Show me the money`

8 Wireless Networking

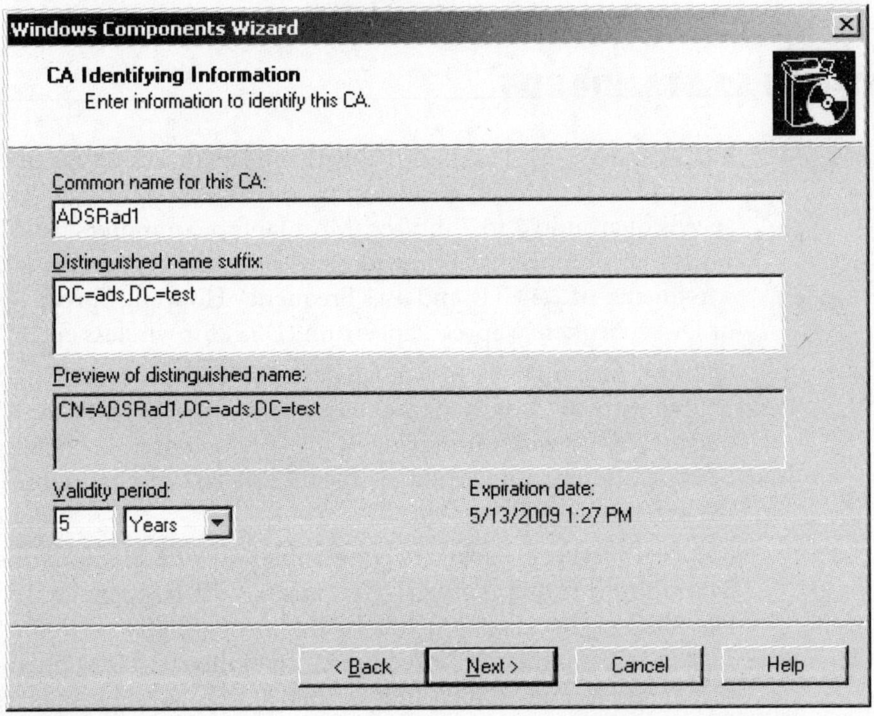

CHAPTER PREVIEW

Wireless networking presents some interesting challenges for the network administrator, especially from a security standpoint. Wireless networks offer tremendous flexibility and are an ideal solution for areas where the seating arrangements are not fixed, where it is difficult or impossible to run cable, or when a network must be quickly installed. Most of the wireless problems arise not from the wireless units themselves, but because of their lack of security. This leads to a variety of other problems with hackers and bandwidth hijackers. Because of this, we decided to give some very detailed instructions on how to secure a wireless access point (AP) in the enterprise in the first part of this chapter. Properly securing wireless AP is not simple, which is probably why many people decide not to bother with it. However, if your network is compromised because you failed to take the time to secure your wireless APs, you will spend a lot more time fixing the damage, and you still have to secure the APs! In this chapter, we use Windows Server 2003, Windows XP wireless clients, and the Cisco AP1200 as the foundation for securing a wireless network.

WIRELESS STANDARDS

802.11b or Wi-Fi. This is arguably the most common type of wireless connection today. It runs at speeds up to 11 mb/sec, although you'll typically see speeds of around 5 to 7 mb/sec. Most laptop computers have built-in wireless cards that support 802.11b, with newer laptops supporting 802.11g. It runs at a frequency of 2.4 GHz and uses Frequency Hopping Spread Spectrum (FHSS) or Direct Sequence Spread Spectrum (DSS) for wireless encoding.

802.11a. Although it can run at speeds up to 54 mb/sec, 802.11a is not compatible with 802.11b. It runs at a frequency of 5 GHz. It uses Orthogonal Frequency Division Multiplexing (OFDM) for wireless encoding. Most likely because of its incompatibility with 802.11b, 802.11a has not really caught on in the wireless world.

802.11g. 802.11g is backward compatible with 802.11b and runs at speeds up to 54 mb/sec. It runs at both 2.4-GHz and 5-GHz frequencies. It uses OFDM just like 802.11a. Because of its backward compatibility with 802.11b and higher speeds, this standard is more popular than the 802.11a standard. Because of its higher speeds and compatibility with 802.11b, 802.11g is emerging as the next wireless standard.

802.11i/Wi-Fi Protected Access (WPA). This is a security supplement for 802.11a, 802.11b, and 802.11g for increased security on wireless networks. This security standard is far more secure than the old Wired Equivalency Protocol (WEP), which has already been cracked at AT&T Labs using the Fluhrer, Mantin, and Shamir attack. For more information on this attack, refer to *www.isoc.org/isoc/conferences/ndss/02/proceedings/papers/stubbl.pdf.*

802.11n. This is an emerging standard that will probably be finalized at the end of 2005. It has speeds of at least 100mb/sec, most likely operating in the 5-GHz range. It promises increased range compared to earlier standards.

Most likely, you'll encounter APs using the 802.11b and 802.11g standards.

WIRELESS AUTHENTICATION METHODS

Before you can use an AP, you must connect or authenticate to it. Most APs support the following methods of AP authentication, ranging from least to most secure.

No Authentication

Unfortunately, this is the default for most APs. No authentication is necessary, so any user can connect to the AP if you are in range of the AP and have a compatible wireless card. Worse yet, most APs by default broadcast their Service Set Identifier (SSID), making it even easier to find them. Most APs can turn off the broadcast of their SSID, but don't get a false sense of security just because you disabled SSID broadcasts on your AP. All a user has to do is wait until someone connects to the AP and sniff out the SSID using one of the wireless sniffers such as Airsnort or WEPCrack. Still, it's a good idea to disable SSID broadcasts, but don't think you're going to keep out any serious hacker from connecting to your AP. Make sure to change the SSID of the AP to something other than the default SSID.

Media Access Control Address

Some APs allow you to enter the Media Access Control (MAC) address of the client's wireless cards and only allow those clients with specific MAC addresses to connect to the AP. This is better than no authentication, but it is easily bypassed. All a hacker has to do is use a wireless sniffer, capture the MAC address of the clients connected to the AP, and then spoof the MAC address of an authenticated client to gain access.

Wired Equivalent Privacy (WEP) Key Authentication

If you enable WEP with the four encryption keys, you can transmit one of the WEP keys (usually WEP key one) as a way of authenticating to the AP. If you are implementing WEP, it is a good idea to use one of the WEP keys as a means to authenticate to the AP. However, WEP has already been cracked using the Fluhrer, Mantin, and Shamir attack, so it's still subject to security breach. A hacker can obtain the WEP keys by performing a passive, or man-in-the-middle attack, and still gain access to the AP. A man-in-the-middle attack spoofs a legitimate AP with a rogue AP and then captures information from unsuspecting wireless users. Utilities like Ettercap can configure the rogue AP as a pass through device to the legitimate AP and gather all of the packet information that passes through the AP. A hacker can also obtain the WEP keys with other methods such as social engineering. Once a hacker has the WEP keys, your network is completely vulnerable.

Remote Authentication Dial-In User Service (RADIUS) Authentication

Some of the newer APs have RADIUS servers built into the AP. Typically, these APs support the new Wi-Fi Protected Alliance (WPA) wireless security standard. Using a RADIUS server, a user must supply a valid user ID and password before connecting to the AP. This user ID and password is validated against the RADIUS server, during the process of authenticating to the AP. Using this authentication method requires the additional step of configuring a RADIUS server. Windows 2000/2003 has a built-in RADIUS server (called IAS), and there are many Linux-based RADIUS solutions for little or no cost. Because the username and password are controlled centrally on the RADIUS server, you can quickly change or delete a suspected compromised user.

RADIUS Authentication with Certificates or Smart Cards

This is one of the most secure ways to authenticate to an AP. In addition to providing a valid user ID and password for the RADIUS server, the computer and user must have a valid certificate issued from a Certificate server. Windows 2000/2003 servers have the capability to issue certificates by installing and configuring Certificate Services.Smart card authentication requires a physical device along with a PIN or password to authenticate users on the network.

WIRELESS ENCRYPTION

On APs that support encryption, data are scrambled before it's sent across the radio signal. If someone happens to trap some of the wireless packets, the data contained inside the packets will look like a bunch of garbage, protecting the data that is transmitted across the wireless link. You have the following encryption options, ranging from least to most secure.

No Encryption

By default, most WAPs do not have encryption enabled. All of the data is sent via the radio signal in clear text. Someone with a wireless sniffer can trap the wireless packets and review the information contained in the packets.

WEP

WEP was the first attempt at securing wireless networks. Unfortunately, WEP has been cracked by the Fluhrer, Mantin, and Shamir attack. The main weakness of WEP is its 24-bit initialization vector that guarantees the reuse of the same key stream. On a busy AP, the key stream can repeat in as little as five hours. Another major weakness of WEP is the use of static encryption keys. Unlike traditional VPNs, which use dynamic encryption keys, WEP encryption keys remain static.

Once a key is discovered, an unauthorized user can access the AP, or decrypt data using the static encryption key. Although WEP is better than no encryption, we suggest using a stronger encryption method to secure your wireless networks. If you use an AP at home, at least turn on WEP if your AP does not support WPA. Even though WEP's been cracked, it's better than nothing.

Wireless Virtual Private Network

Prior to WPA support on APs, some vendors such as Netmotion and SonicWALL used a combination of a traditional virtual private network (VPN) with their wireless connection. During the process of establishing the wireless connection, a VPN tunnel is set up between the AP and the wireless client. Because a VPN uses dynamic encryption keys, it addresses most of the security shortcomings of WEP. However, many of these solutions are propriety and require the use of additional hardware or software to establish the VPN tunnel.

Cisco's Lightweight Extensible Authentication Protocol (LEAP) or Extensible Authentication Protocol-Transport Layer Security (EAP-TLS)

This was a stop-gap measure to address the weaknesses of WEP and to provide enhanced security over WEP until the WPA standard was finalized. It allows for authentication via a RADIUS server and uses dynamic encryption keys to secure wireless data. Today, most of these security features have been incorporated into WPA. It uses 802.1*x* authentication with dynamic encryption keys for security.

Wi-Fi Protected Access

WPA was developed to address WEP's weaknesses. It uses dynamic encryption keys and 801.*x* authentication. Many vendors now support WPA on their APs. When purchasing an AP, look for an AP that supports this improved wireless security standard. Some AP vendors such as Cisco also have a built-in RADIUS server to authenticate users to the AP. For enhanced security, use certificates or smart cards as an AP authentication method.

PURCHASING AP EQUIPMENT

We have some basic suggestions when purchasing AP and wireless cards. We strongly suggest purchasing an AP that supports the new WPA security standard, or one that supports 802.1*x* authentication and LEAP/EAP-TLS. WPA is much more secure than WEP. However, WPA and LEAP/EAP-TLS are great solutions for securing wireless networks. If you decide to purchase a WPA-compliant AP, be prepared to purchase that vendor's wireless network card, or make sure that your wireless cards support WPA. Earlier wireless cards built into laptops probably do not support WPA, although you might be able to download firmware/software to upgrade your wireless card to work with WPA.

If you're running Windows XP with Service Pack 1, you can download OS support for WPA that is built into Windows XP from *www.microsoft.com/downloads/details.aspx?FamilyId=009D8425-CE2B-47A4-ABEC-274845DC9E91&displaylang=en*. Note that you need both a wireless card that supports WPA and the Windows XP WPA add-in, or a wireless card that supports WPA and the wireless vendor's client software that supports WPA to authenticate to an AP running WPA. Although not absolutely necessary, you'll run into fewer problems if you use the wireless AP and network cards from the same wireless vendor.

PREPARING THE WIRELESS NETWORK INFRASTRUCTURE

Before rolling out your wireless LAN (WLAN), there are a number of tasks you must complete. Although some of these wireless components are available to secure a WLAN and are supported on platforms as early as Windows NT 4.0 Server, we strongly suggest using Windows Server 2003 and Windows XP clients. These operating systems have the best support for wireless communications. Setting a secure wireless environment is no small undertaking; it involves many components and configuration steps. Using the latest version OS on the servers and clients will help ease the pain of implementing this potentially complex infrastructure. If you plan to use auto-enrollment of user certificates through Group Policy, the Certificate server must run the Enterprise or Datacenter versions of Windows Server 2003.

Perform a Site Survey

Many wireless vendors supply site survey utilities to determine AP coverage. After you determine the areas where you need wireless coverage, use a site survey utility to determine the optimum location and number of APs you will need. 802.11b uses 11 channels, but many of the channels overlap, leaving only channels 1, 6, and 11 that can be used without conflicting with other channels. Make sure to position adjacent APs so their signals just overlap each other, but are on different channels.

Plan Your Public Key Infrastructure

Adequately plan your Public Key Infrastructure (PKI) before rolling out Certification Authority (CA) certificates to the IAS/RADIUS server and wireless clients. Take into account the number of users who will be issued certificates, the authentication method, location of the users when authenticating, Active Directory structure, physical location of the users, current load of Windows 2000/2003 domain controllers, and location and load of the IAS servers.

Decide on the Authentication Method for Your Wireless Clients

For enhanced security on a wireless network, we suggest using Extensible Authentication Protocol-Transport Layer Security (EAP-TLS) for wireless client authentication with computer and user certificates. This is one of the most secure methods of authentication when it is correctly implemented. EAP-TLS with certificates or smart cards and 802.1*x* authentication is one of the best ways to secure a wireless network.

WLAN Diagram

An enterprise network running a WLAN with EAP-TLS authentication with certificates might involve up to three or more servers. A typical Enterprise WLAN will look something like Figure 8.1.

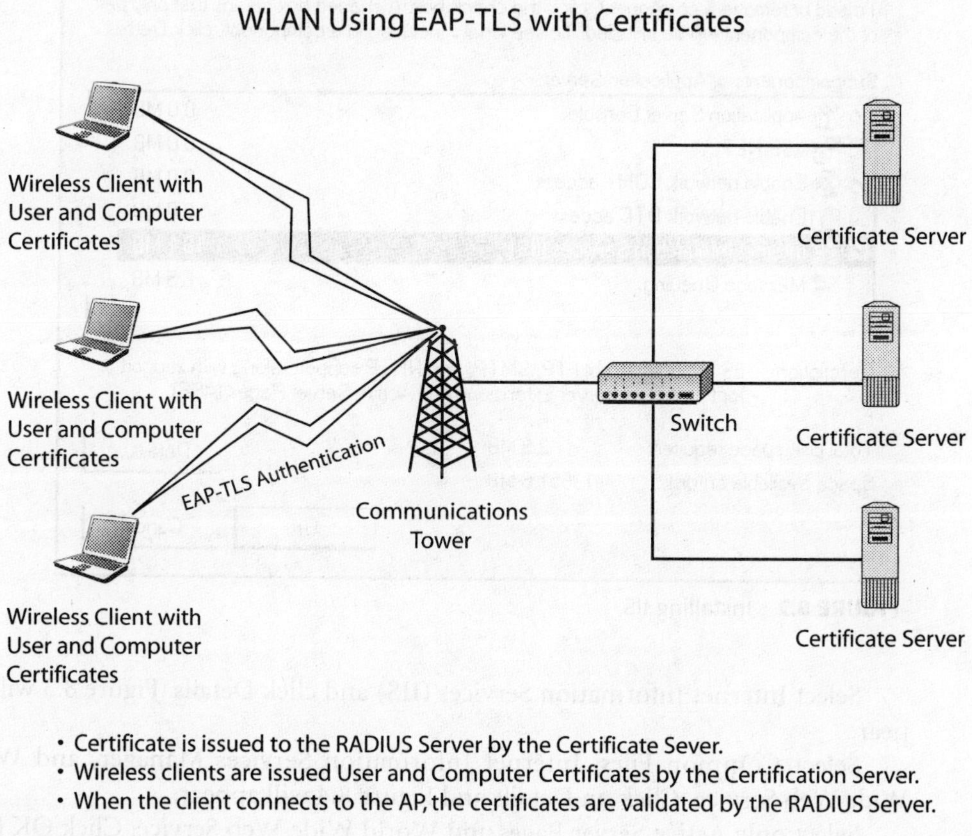

FIGURE 8.1 Enterprise WLAN.

Set Up the Certificate Server

To use authentication with certificates, you must install and configure at least one Certificate server. The Certificate server is used to distribute computer and user certificates during the authentication process.

Install IIS on the Windows 2003 Certificate Server

Install Windows Server 2003 on a computer with any critical updates and the latest service packs. To install IIS, click on Start, Settings, Control Panel, Add/Remove programs. Click on Add/Remove Windows Components. Select Application Server and click Details. Select Application Server Console and Internet Information Services (see Figure 8.2).

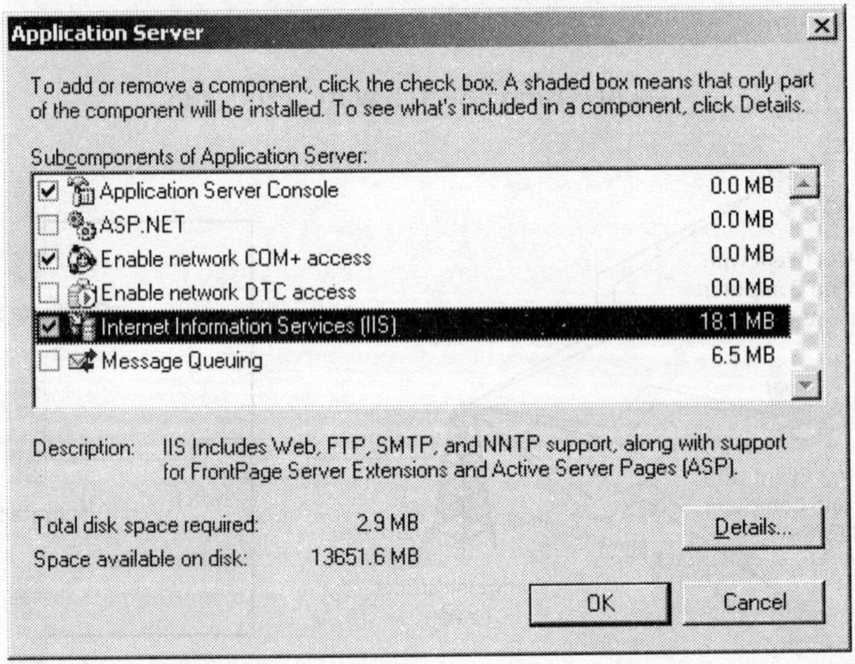

FIGURE 8.2 Installing IIS.

Select Internet Information Services (IIS) and click Details. Figure 8.3 will appear.

Select Common Files, Internet Information Services Manager, and World Wide Web Service. Click on Details and Figure 8.4 will appear.

Select only Active Server Pages and World Wide Web Service. Click OK three times, click Next, and then click Finish.

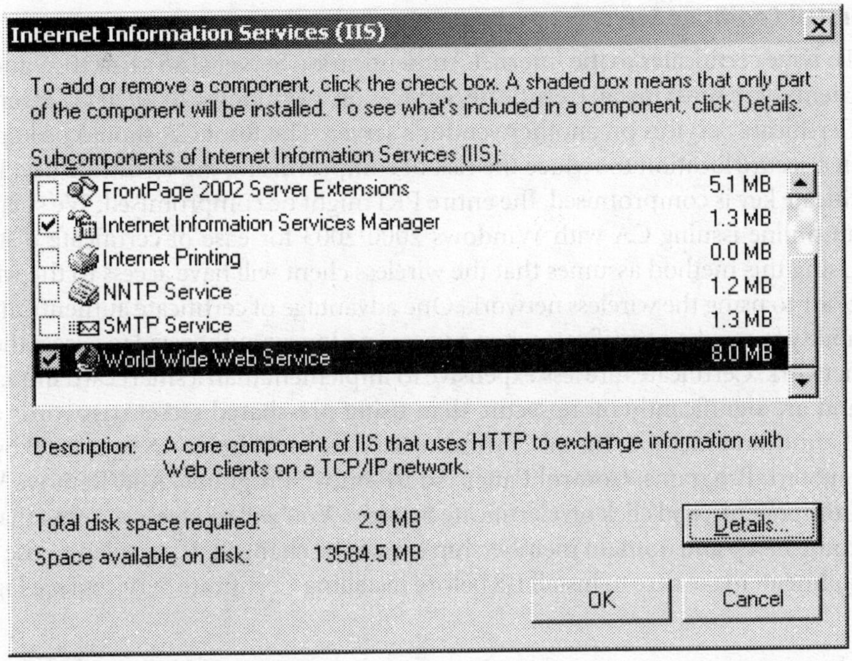

FIGURE 8.3 IIS Details settings.

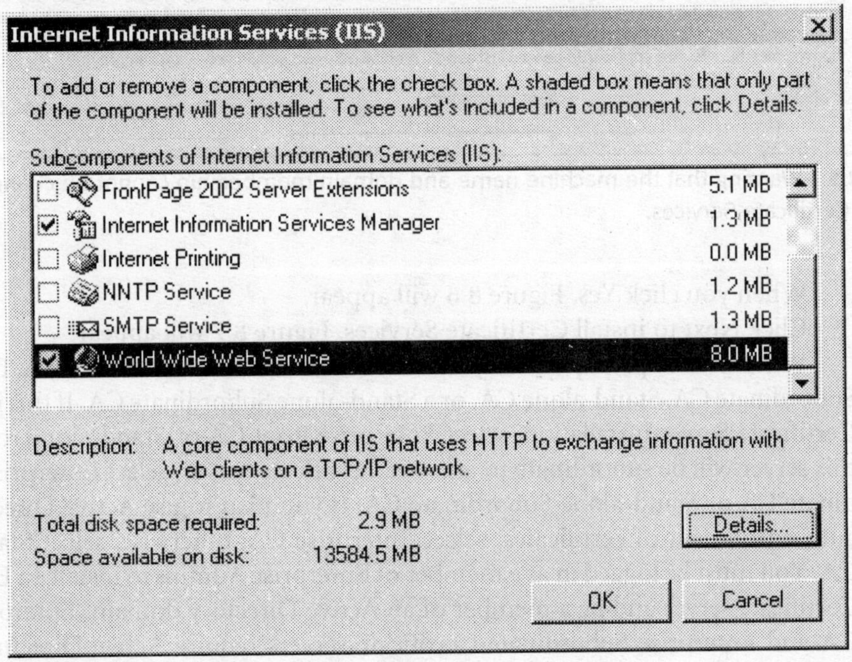

FIGURE 8.4 Detailed settings for World Wide Web Service.

Install Certificate Server

To issue certificates to the Internet Authentication Server (IAS)/RADIUS and wireless clients, you must install Certificate Services on a Windows 2000/2003 server or set up Certificate Services on another vendor's server. The Root CA should be kept off-line in a secure location to reduce the risk of compromising the certificate key. If the certificate key is compromised, the entire PKI might be compromised. We suggest using an online issuing CA with Windows 2000/2003 for ease of certificate distribution. Using this method assumes that the wireless client will have access to the wired LAN prior to using the wireless network. One advantage of certificate authentication is the ability to revoke a certificate when a user is no longer authorized to access the wireless network. Certificates are less expensive to implement than a smart card infrastructure, and are significantly more secure than using pre-shared secret passwords as an authentication method. Install Certificate Services on Windows Server 2003 by clicking on Start, Programs, Control Panel, Add/Remove Programs, Add/Remove Windows Components, and click on Certificate Services. You will receive a warning that the machine name and domain membership cannot be changed. If you plan to use Web Enrollment, make sure to install IIS before installing Certificate Services (see Figure 8.5).

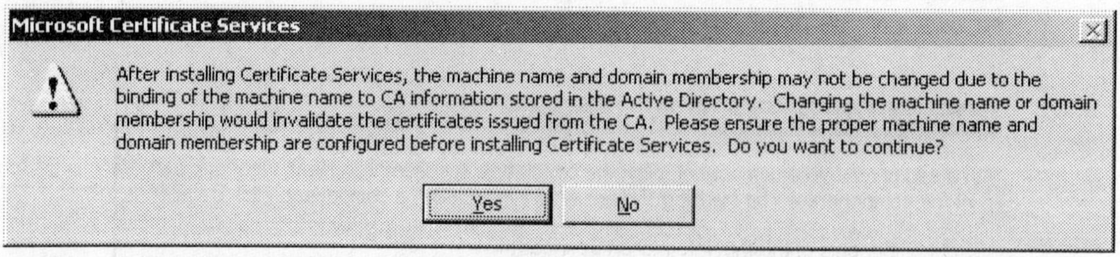

FIGURE 8.5 Warning that the machine name and domain membership cannot be changed after installing Certificate Services.

When you click Yes, Figure 8.6 will appear.

Click Next to install Certificate Services. Figure 8.7 will appear.

Windows will prompt you if you want to install an Enterprise root CA, Enterprise Subordinate CA, Stand-alone CA, or a Stand-alone Subordinate CA. If this is the first Certificate Server installation, select Enterprise Root CA or Stand-alone root CA. If this server will be subordinate to another Certificate Server, select Enterprise Subordinate CA or Stand-alone Subordinate CA. If you plan to use Active Directory and auto-enrollment of certificates, select Enterprise CA; otherwise, select Stand-alone CA. You must be logged in as a member of Enterprise Admins to install an Enterprise Certificate server and be a member of an Active Directory domain. Enterprise Root CA and Enterprise Subordinate Certificate servers require Active Directory, while Stand-alone Root CA and Subordinates do not. For this example, we wanted to integrate Certificate Services with Active Directory, and this is the first Certificate server,

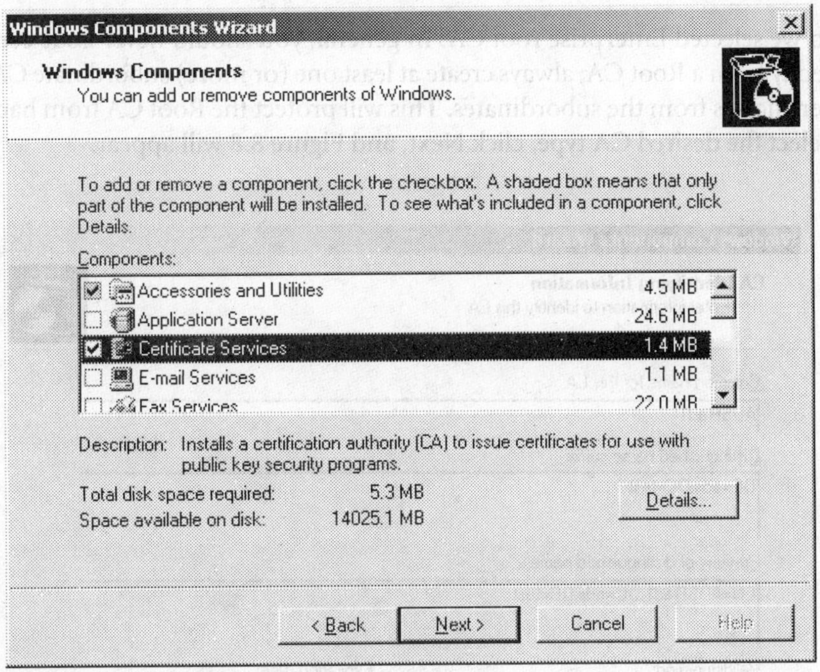

FIGURE 8.6 Installing Certificate Services.

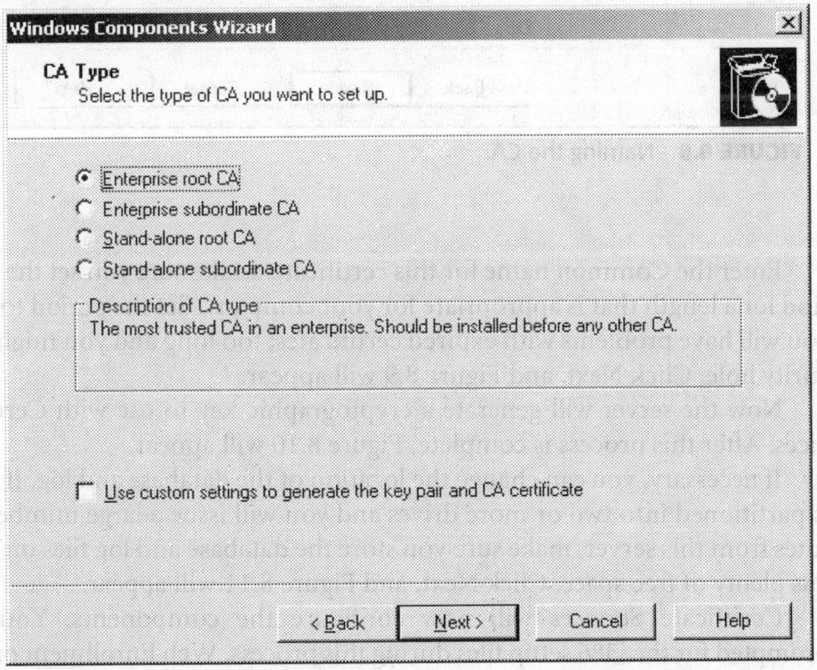

FIGURE 8.7 Selecting the CA type.

so we selected Enterprise root CA. In general, you should never issue certificates directly from a Root CA; always create at least one (or more) subordinate CAs and issue certificates from the subordinates. This will protect the Root CA from hack attempts. Select the desired CA type, click Next, and Figure 8.8 will appear.

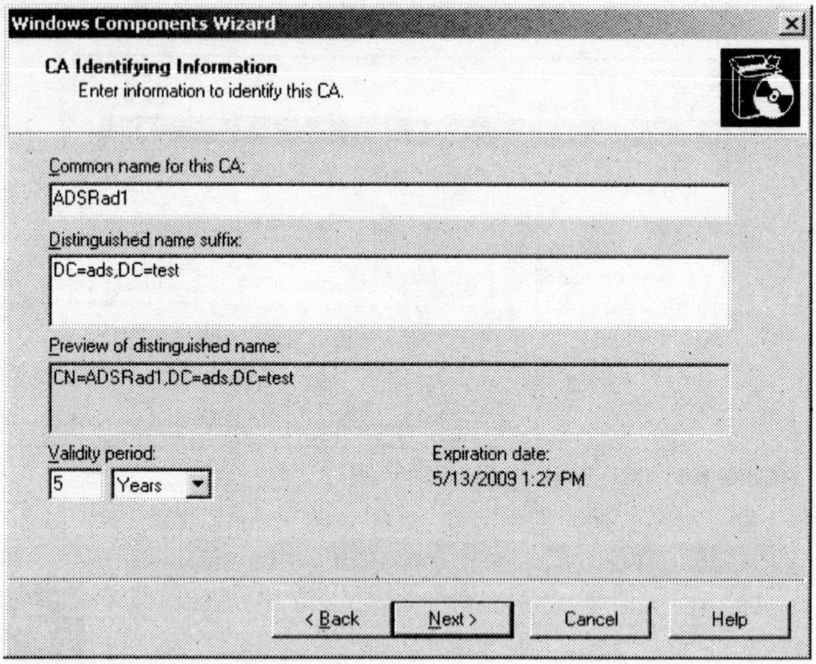

FIGURE 8.8 Naming the CA.

Enter the Common name for this certificate. Make sure you set the validity period for a length that is appropriate for your company. Set the period too short and you will have problems with expired certificates; too long and you might have a security hole. Click Next, and Figure 8.9 will appear.

Now the server will generate a cryptographic key to use with Certificate Services. After this process is complete, Figure 8.10 will appear.

If necessary, you can change the location of the database and log. If your server is partitioned into two or more drives and you will issue a large number of certificates from this server, make sure you store the database and log files on a drive that has plenty of free space. Click Next, and Figure 8.11 will appear.

Certificate Services will now configure the components. You might be prompted for the i386 setup files during this process. Web Enrollment of Certificate Services requires Internet Information Server (IIS) with Active Server Pages (ASP).

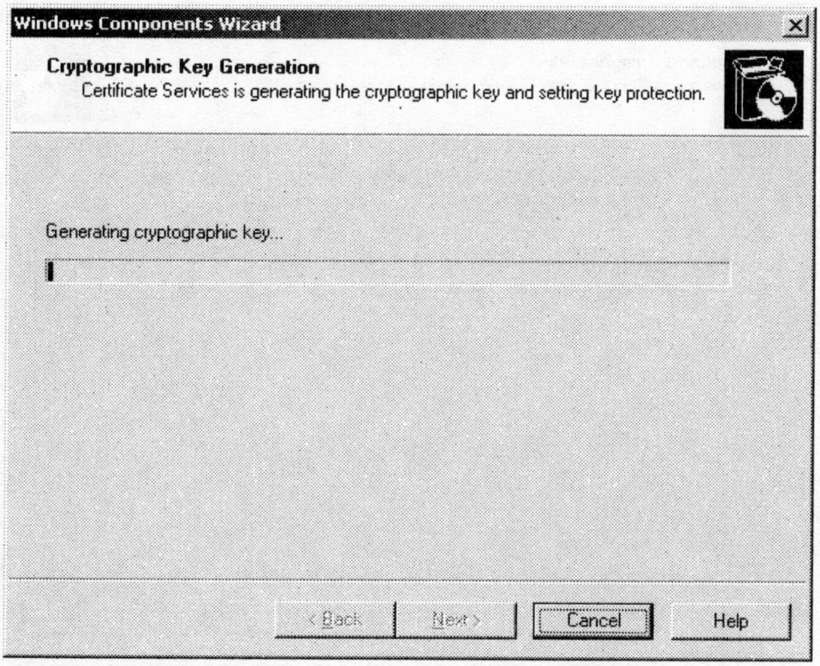

FIGURE 8.9 Generating the cryptographic key for Certificate Services.

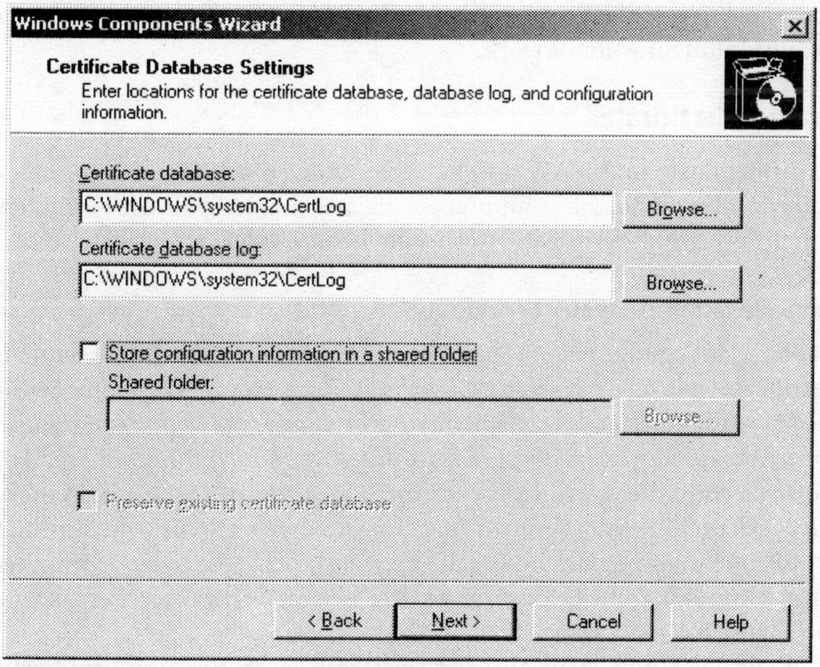

FIGURE 8.10 Certificate database settings.

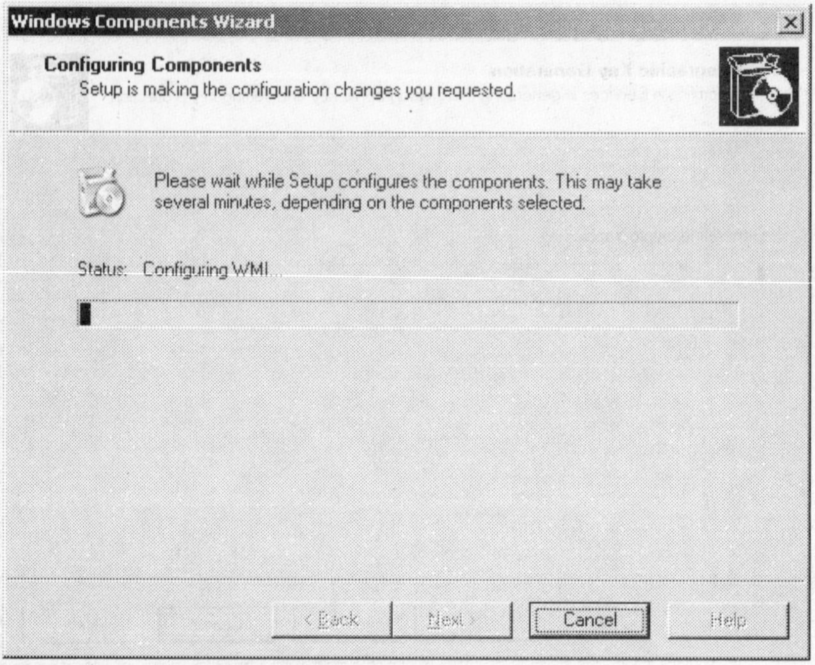

FIGURE 8.11 Configuring Certificate Services components.

Make sure to install IIS and ASP before installing Certificate Services; otherwise, the Web Enrollment will not work.

Issue Computer Certificates

To authenticate to the AP, the client computer must have a computer certificate. You can either issue the computer certificates manually or use Group Policy to automatically install certificates to specified computers.

Manually Install Computer Certificates

If you do not configure auto-enrollment of computer certificates, you must use the Certificate snap-in or execute a Capicom script to install computer certificates. For more information on Capicom scripts refer to *http://msdn.microsoft.com/library/default.asp?url=/library/en-us/dnsecure/html/intcapicom.asp*. To manually request a computer certificate, click on Start, Run, and type `mmc`. In the MMC console, click on File, Add/Remove Snap-in, and then click the Add button. In the Add Standalone snap-in, click on Certificates, and click Add. Select Computer Account, Local computer, Finish, Close, and OK. Click on Certificates, Personal Certificates, and Figure 8.12 will appear.

Right-click on Certificates and select All Tasks, Request New Certificate. The Certificate Request Wizard will start. Click Next, select the appropriate Certificate

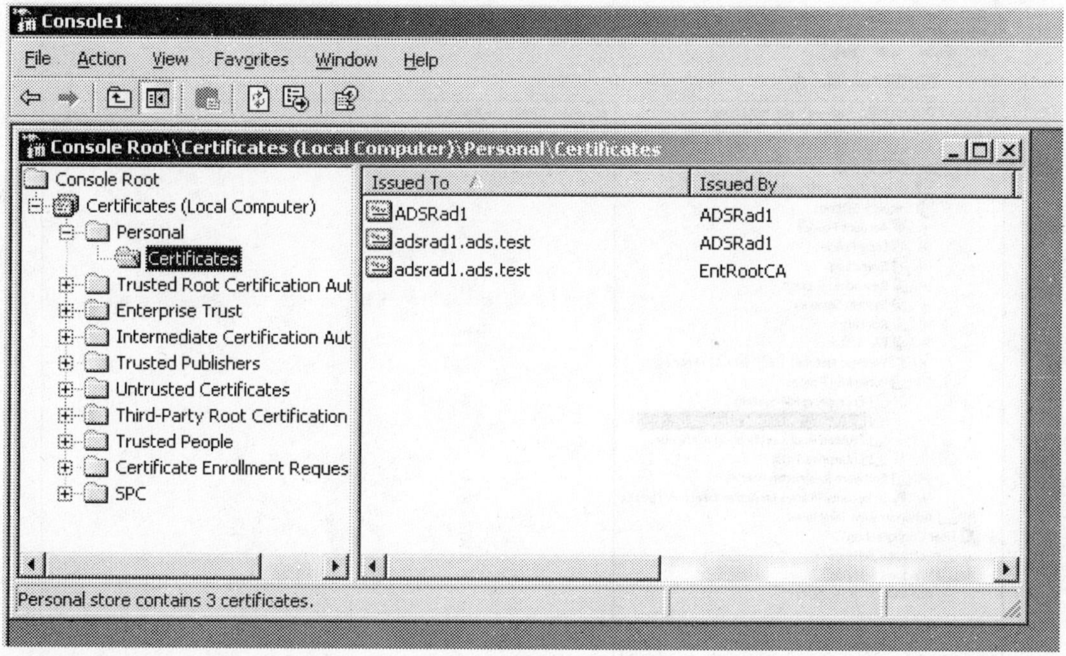

FIGURE 8.12 A list of installed computer certificates.

Type, and click Next. Enter a Friendly name and Description for the Certificate, click, Next, and then click Finish. The certificate issued by the CA should appear in the right window.

Auto-Enrollment of Computer Certificates with Group Policy

Alternately, you can configure a group policy for auto-enrollment of computers that are members of the Windows 2000/2003 Active Directory domain. To set up auto-enrollment of Computer Certificates:

1. **Open the default domain policy.** Click on Start, Programs, Administrative Tools, Active Directory Users and Computers. Right-click on the domain that you want to configure for auto-enrollment and select Properties. Click on the Group Policy tab, select the Default Domain Policy, and click Edit. Click on Computer Configuration, Windows Settings, Security Settings, Public Key Policies, and Automatic Certificate Request Settings. The screen in Figure 8.13 will appear.
2. **Right-click on Automatic Certificate Request Settings and select New.** The Automatic Certificate Request Wizard will start. Click Next, and Figure 8.14 will appear.

   Select Computer, click Next, and click Finish.

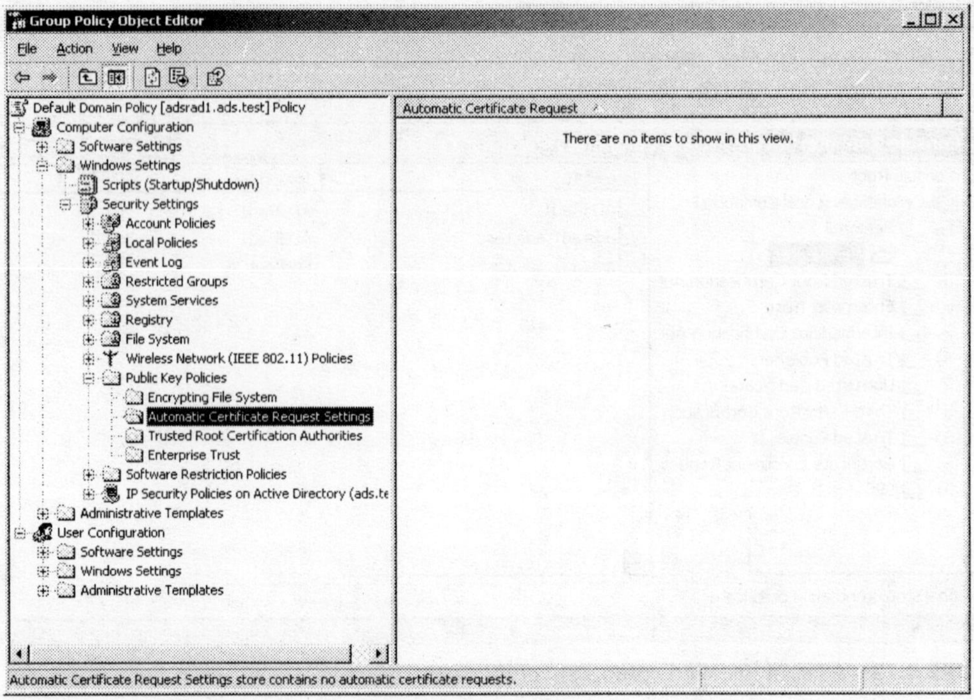

FIGURE 8.13 Setting up Automatic Certificate requests.

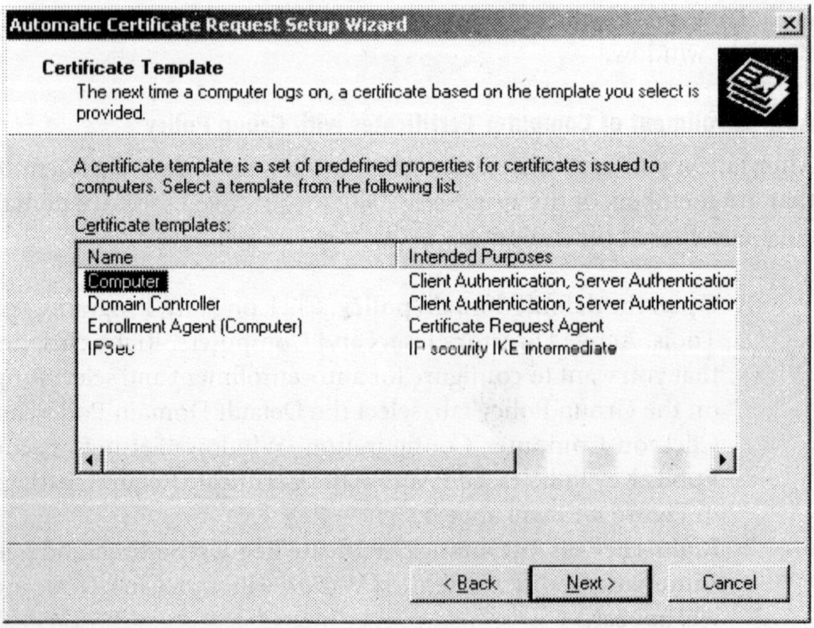

FIGURE 8.14 Selecting the Computer Certificate Template.

Install User Certificates

Both computer and user certificates are necessary to authenticate to the IAS server and network. You can manually request a user certificate or use Group Policy to automatically distribute user certificates to authenticated domain users.

Manually Request User Certificates

You can manually request a user certificate using Internet Explorer and the issuing CA's Web interface. To manually request a user certificate, open Internet Explorer and enter `<certificate_server_name>/certsrv` in the Address field. You will be prompted for a valid user and password. When you successfully log in, Figure 8.15 will appear.

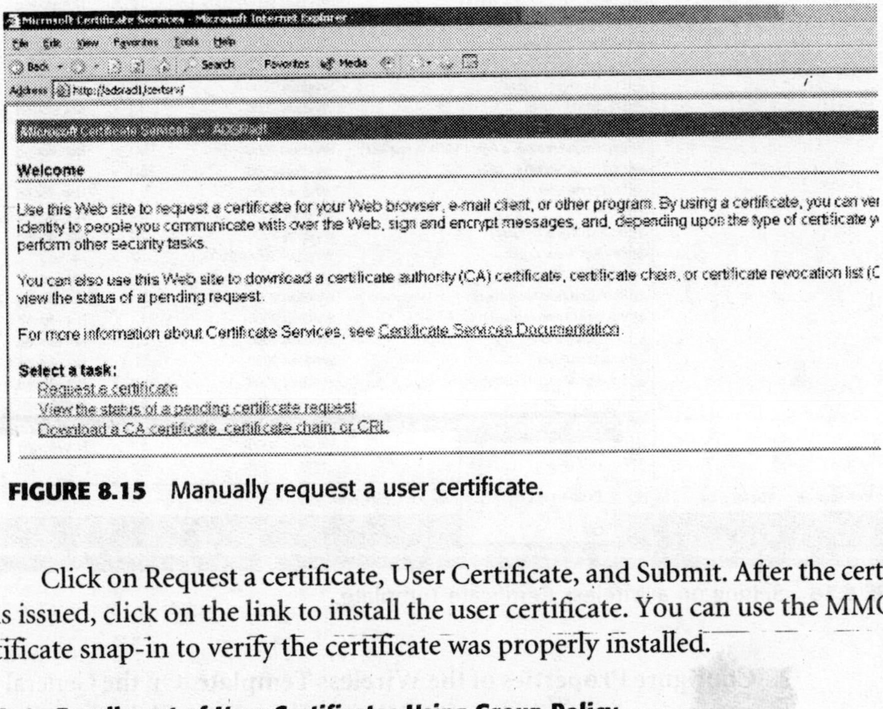

FIGURE 8.15 Manually request a user certificate.

Click on Request a certificate, User Certificate, and Submit. After the certificate is issued, click on the link to install the user certificate. You can use the MMC Certificate snap-in to verify the certificate was properly installed.

Auto-Enrollment of User Certificates Using Group Policy

Alternately, you can configure Group Policy for auto-enrollment of user certificates.

You can configure a group policy for auto-enrollment of user certificates, only if your issuing Certificate server is running Windows 2003 Enterprise or Datacenter Server. If you use the standard version of Windows Server 2003 for your Certificate server, users must manually request a user certificate. To set up auto-enrollment of user certificates on a Windows Server 2003 Enterprise server or higher:

1. **Set up Wireless Certificate Template.** To set up auto-enrollment for user certificates, click on Start, Programs, Administrative Tools, and Certification Authority. Right-click on Certificate Templates and select Manage. The Certificate Templates Manager will start. Click on Certificate Templates, right-click on User, and select Duplicate Template (see Figure 8.16). When you select Duplicate Template, Figure 8.17 will appear.

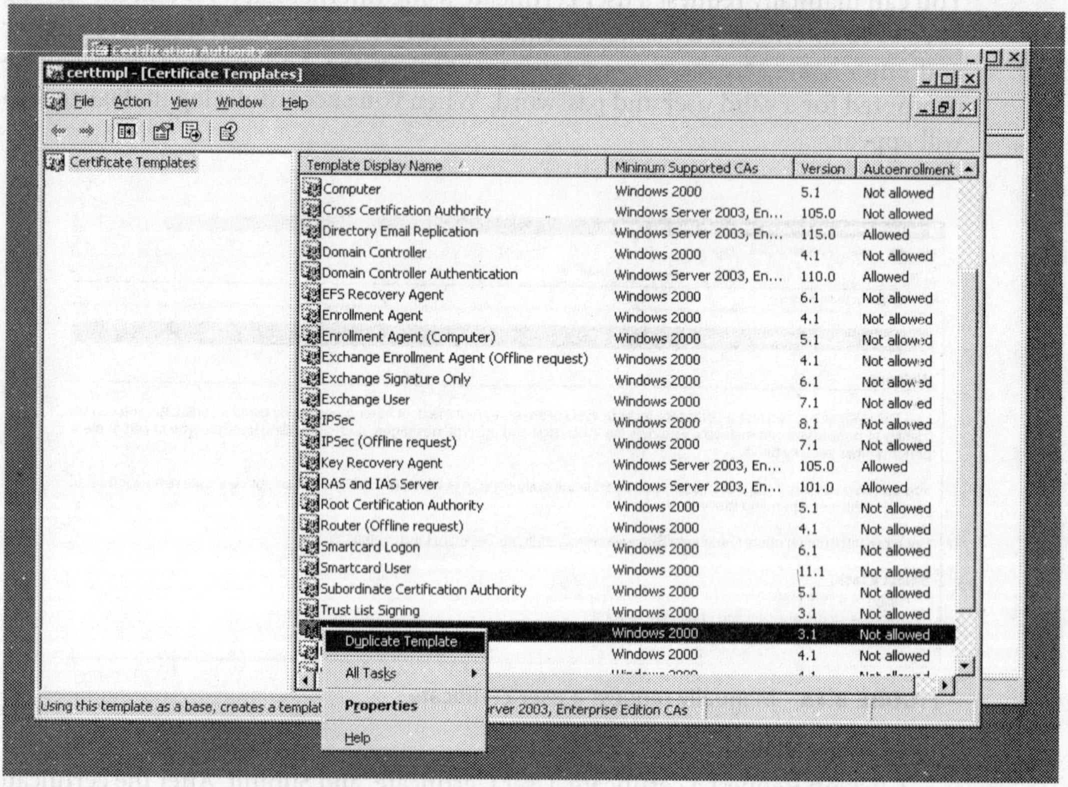

FIGURE 8.16 Setting up a Wireless Certificate Template.

2. **Configure Properties of the Wireless Template.** On the General tab, enter a name such as Wireless for the template name. Make sure "Publish certificate in Active Directory" is checked. Click on the Security tab, and Figure 8.18 will appear.

   Select Domain Users and check Autoenroll. Click OK. Start the CA by clicking on Start, Programs, Administrative Tools, Certification Authority. Click on the *<Server_Name>*, right-click on Certificate Templates, Certificate Template to issue (see Figure 8.19).

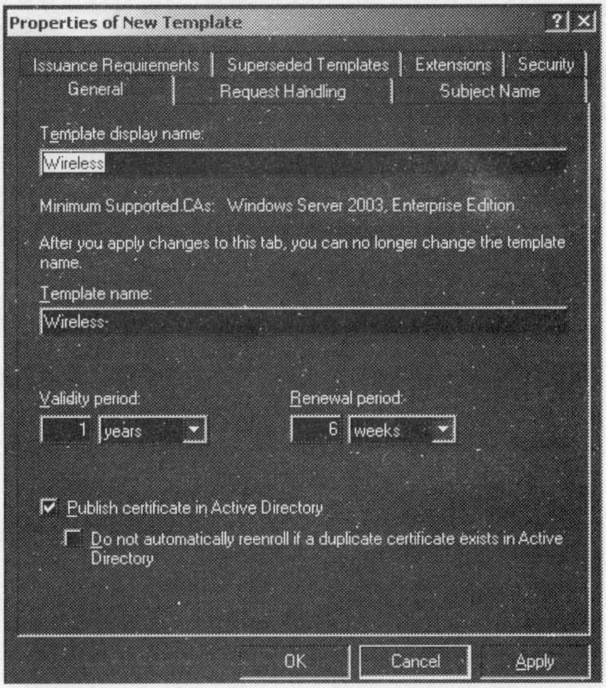

FIGURE 8.17 Properties of Wireless Certificate Template.

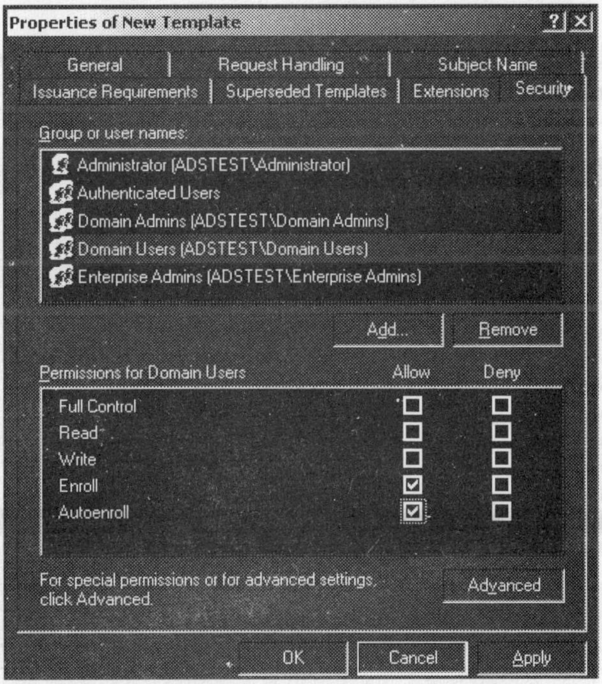

FIGURE 8.18 Security Properties of the Wireless Certificate Template.

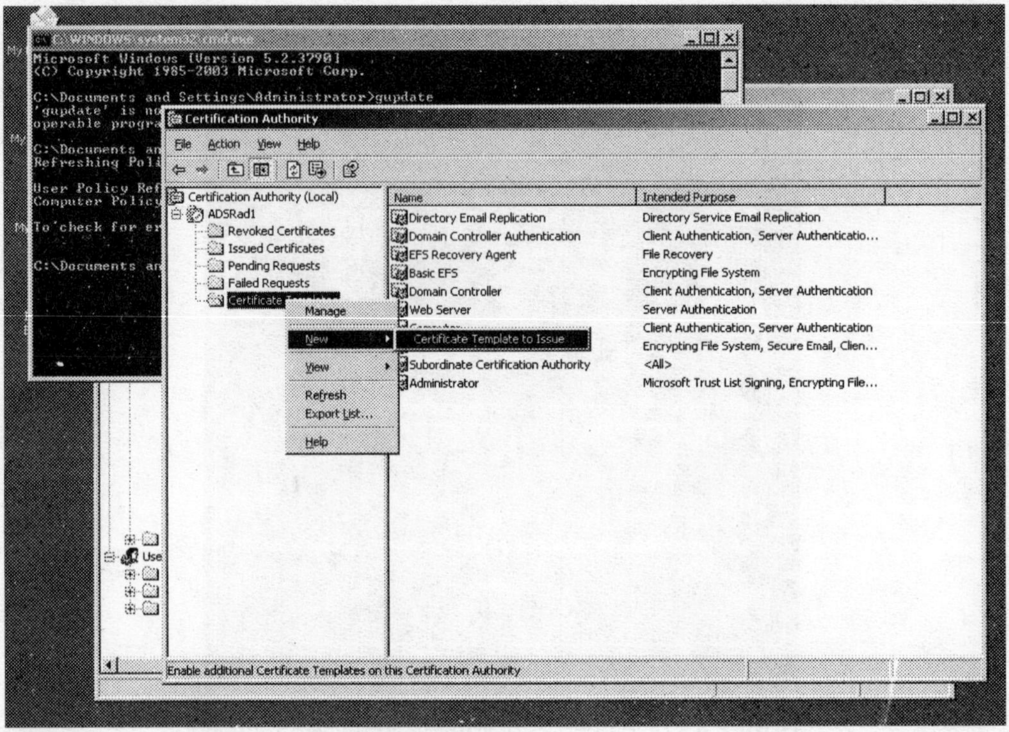

FIGURE 8.19 Issuing a New Certificate Template.

3. **Select Wireless Certificate Template.** A window will display the available templates (see Figure 8.20).

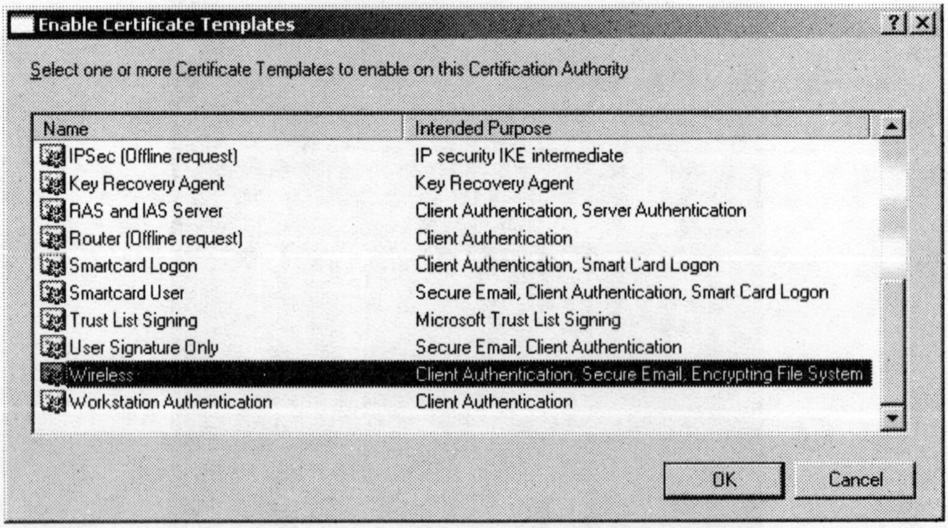

FIGURE 8.20 Selecting a New Certificate Template.

Select the Wireless certificate created in the previous step and click OK. If the Wireless template does not appear, you are probably running the standard version of Windows 2003. *To configure auto-enrollment from a Windows 2003 server, you must run the Enterprise or Datacenter version.*

4. **Set up auto-enrollment for user certificates.** Open Active Directory Users and Computers, right-click on the Domain, Properties, Group Policy tab, highlight the Default Domain Policy, and click Edit (see Figure 8.21). When you click Edit, Figure 8.22 will appear.

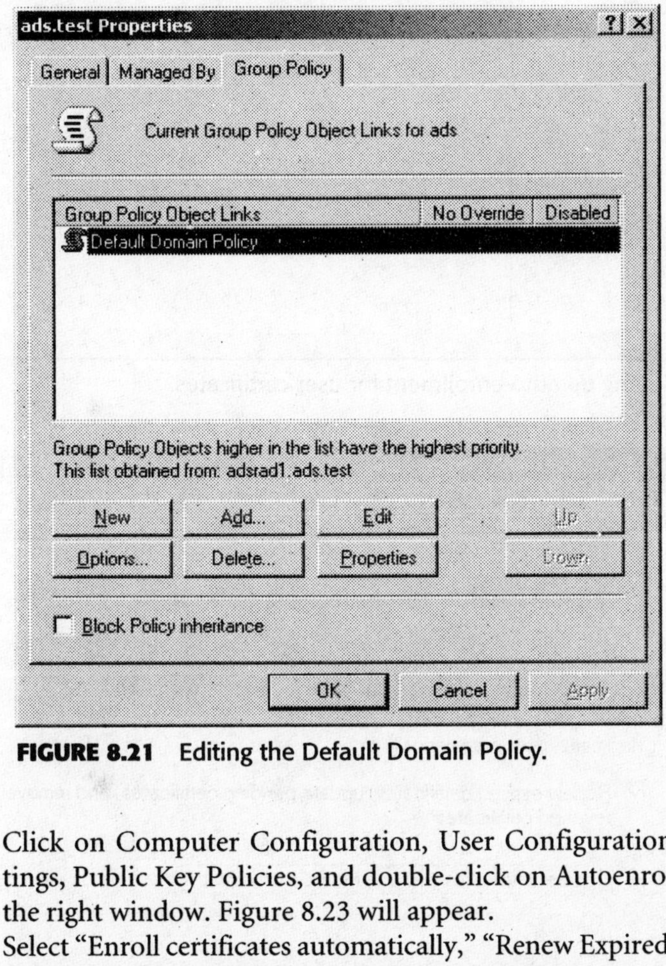

FIGURE 8.21 Editing the Default Domain Policy.

Click on Computer Configuration, User Configuration, Windows, Settings, Public Key Policies, and double-click on Autoenrollment settings in the right window. Figure 8.23 will appear.
Select "Enroll certificates automatically," "Renew Expired certificates," and "Update certificates that use certificate templates," and click OK.

5. **Set up a wireless group and enable dial-in access**. Using Active Directory Users and Computers, select the Dial-in tab and "Allow access" or "Control Access through Remote Access Policy" for every user who requires

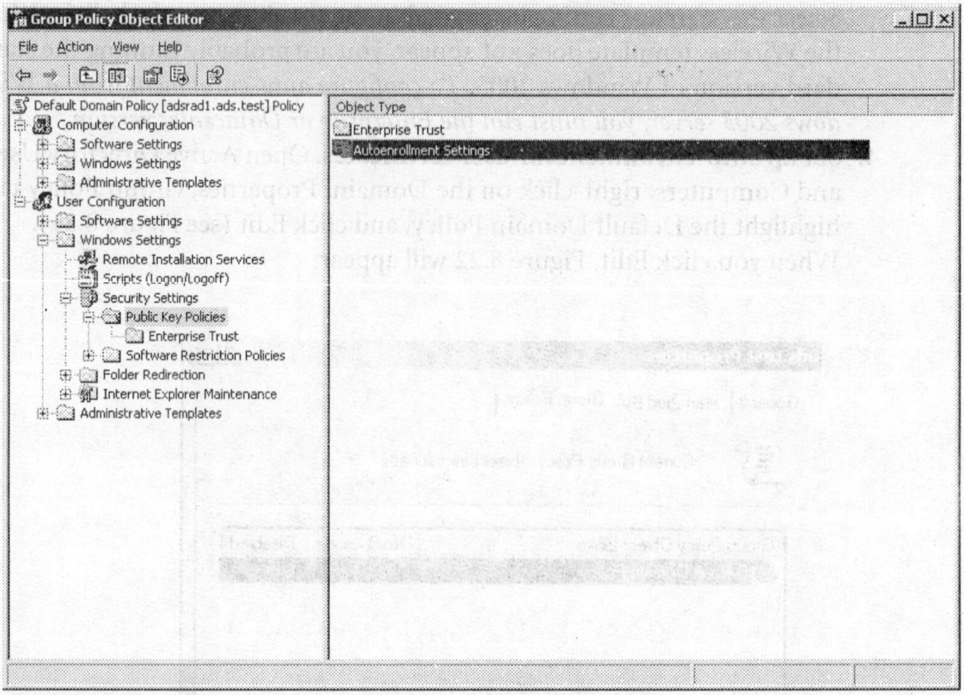

FIGURE 8.22 Setting up auto-enrollment for user certificates.

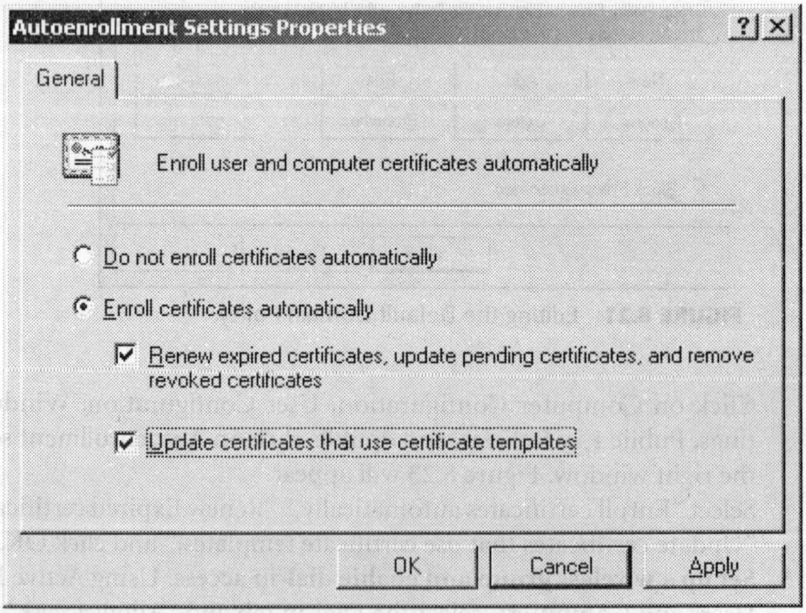

FIGURE 8.23 Configuring auto-enrollment of user certificates.

wireless access. Consider controlling remote access through Group Policy, which gives you more control and is easier to maintain. If your domain is in native mode, we suggest creating a Universal Security Group that includes all of your wireless users. This will make it easier to assign wireless access rights going forward.

Install and Configure IAS (RADIUS)

Some APs have RADIUS servers built into the AP itself, so the installation of the separate IAS/RADIUS server is not necessary. Make sure that any AP that you select has either a built-in RADIUS server or the capability to use an external RADIUS server for AP authentication. Wireless vendors Cisco and Orinoco both support RADIUS with their APs. Although Cisco's 1100 and 1200 AP support a built-in RADIUS server, it has a limitation of 50 users in the RADIUS database. If you need to support more than 50 authenticated users, consider using an external RADIUS server for enhanced scalability/manageability. Windows 2000/2003 has built-in support for RADIUS. On the Windows 2000/2003 platform, the RADIUS server is called the Internet Authentication Service (IAS). If you plan to use Windows 2000 Server and IAS, make sure to install Service Pack 4 or later, which includes wireless support with IAS. Ideally, the IAS server should be installed on a dedicated Windows 2003 server. Consider making the IAS server a domain controller to reduce the amount of authentication traffic and simplify the configuration of the IAS server. The IAS server requires a computer certificate to properly function. If you've already configured auto-enrollment of the computer certificates, the IAS server will automatically receive a certificate if the IAS server is a member or domain controller of the Active Directory domain. If you have not configured auto-enrollment, you must manually install the computer certificate on the IAS server. To protect the traffic between the APs and the RADIUS server, use an IPSec tunnel between the two devices. To configure an IPSec tunnel, the AP must support this feature.

Install IAS

To install and configure IAS:

1. **Install IAS.** Click on Start, Control Panel, Add or Remove Programs, and Add/Remove Windows Components. Scroll down and select Network Services, Details, and select Internet Authentication Service (see Figure 8.24).

   Click OK and Next to install IAS. In an enterprise environment, consider setting up at least two IAS servers for fault tolerance. The IAS server should be separate from the Certificate server, although smaller installations can use the same server.

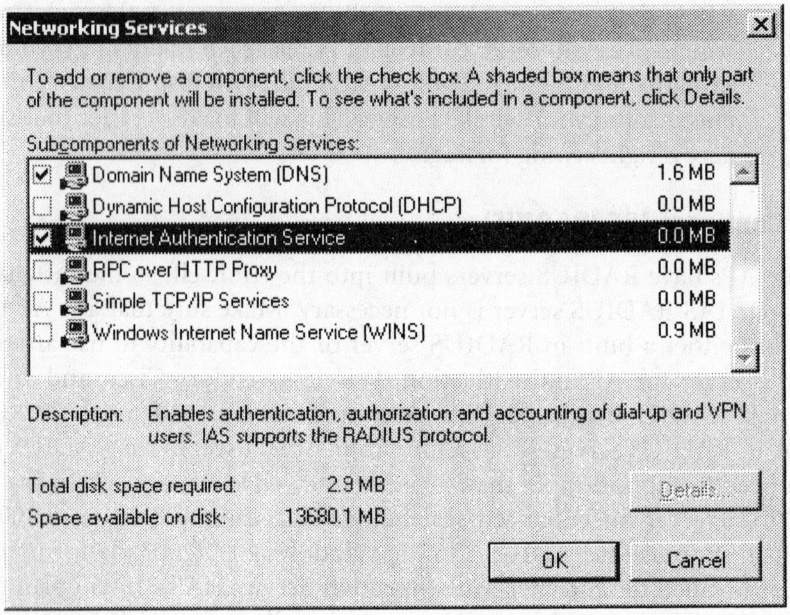

FIGURE 8.24 Installing IAS.

2. **Register IAS in Active Directory to read Active Directory accounts.** After IAS is installed, open the IAS Manager and register the IAS server in Active Directory by opening the IAS Manager, right-clicking on the IAS server, and selecting "Register IAS server in Active Directory."
3. **Add AP clients to the IAS server.** When you configure the APs on the network, assign the AP static IP addresses, and then label the IP address on the outside of the AP itself. The APs are clients to the IAS server, and should have a static address to prevent problems if their IP address changes with dynamic addresses. Add the AP as clients to the IAS server by opening the IAS snap-in and right-clicking Clients, New Client. Select RADIUS for the protocol, and enter the IP address of the AP (see Figure 8.25).

   Optionally, configure the AP and the IAS server to communicate via an IPSec tunnel. You can use a shared secret to establish the tunnel, but ideally, you should use certificates on both the AP and IAS server to establish the tunnel. Of course, the AP must support an IPSec tunnel between the AP and the IAS server and support the use of certificates to establish the tunnel. Make sure to use at least 3DES or AES as an encryption method for the IPSec tunnel. Avoid DES because it can be cracked. If you must use shared secrets, use a random number of letters and numbers for each shared secret and use a unique shared secret for each AP. For this example, we will use a shared secret. When you click Next, Figure 8.26 will appear.

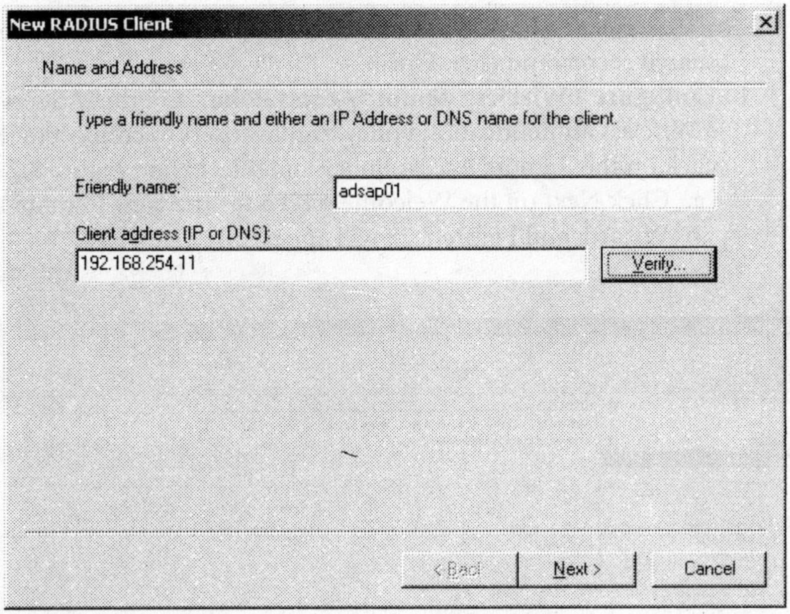

FIGURE 8.25 Setting up the AP as a RADIUS client.

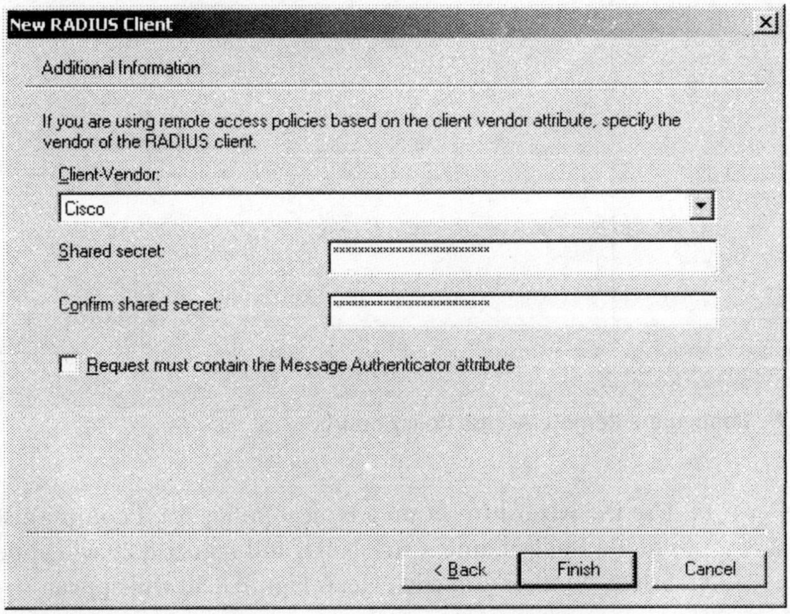

FIGURE 8.26 Setting up a shared secret for the Cisco AP.

Select the Client-Vendor of your AP (in this case, Cisco), enter a shared secret, and click Finish.

4. **Configure a Wireless Remote Access Policy.** On the IAS server, configure a Wireless authentication policy to allow users to connect to the AP. Right-click on the Remote Access Policy and select New. Figure 8.27 will appear.
   a. Click Next on the Welcome screen for the New Remote Access Policy Wizard, and Figure 8.28 will appear.

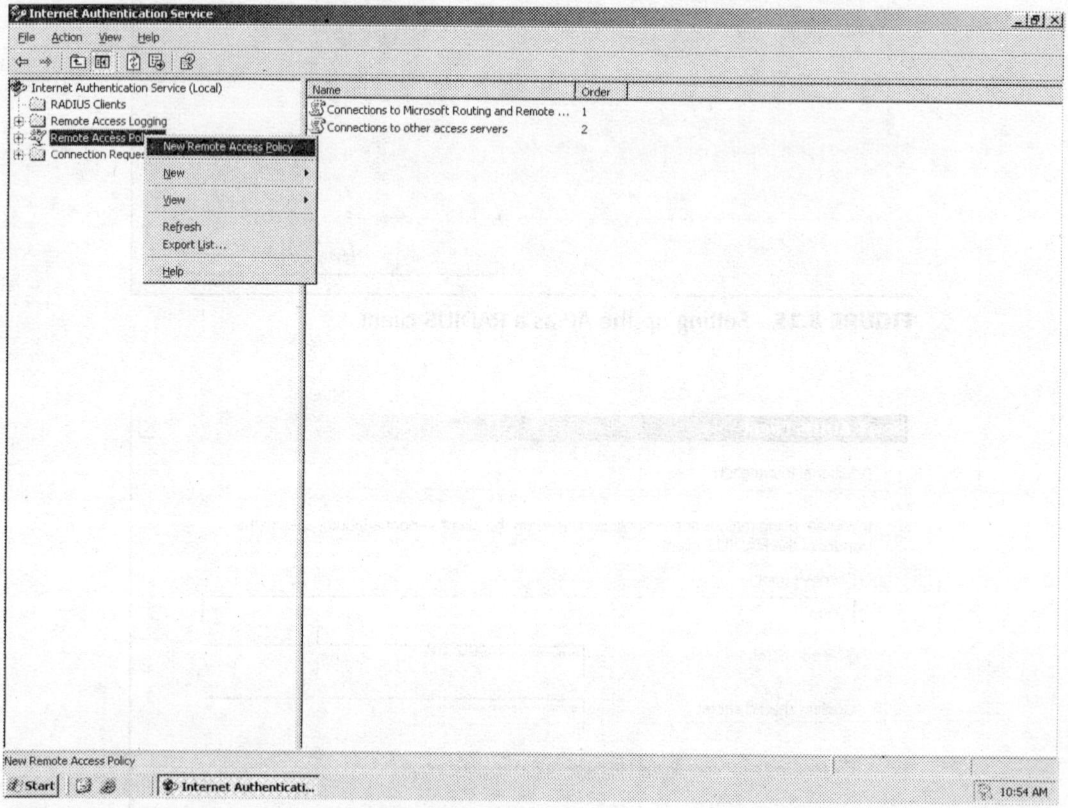

FIGURE 8.27 Configure a Remote Access Policy on IAS.

   b. Use the wizard to set up a typical policy for a common scenario, and enter a Policy name. Click Next, and Figure 8.29 will appear.
   c. Select Wireless and click Next. Figure 8.30 will appear.

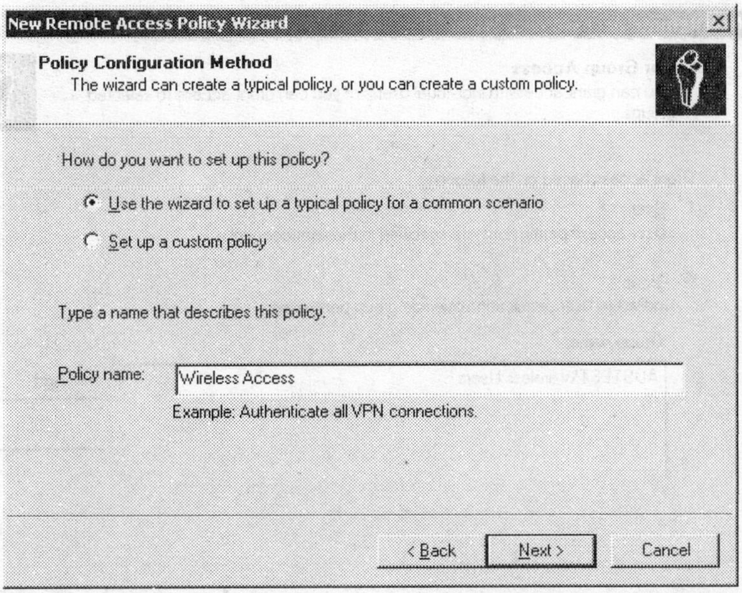

FIGURE 8.28 Using the Policy Wizard for Wireless Access Method.

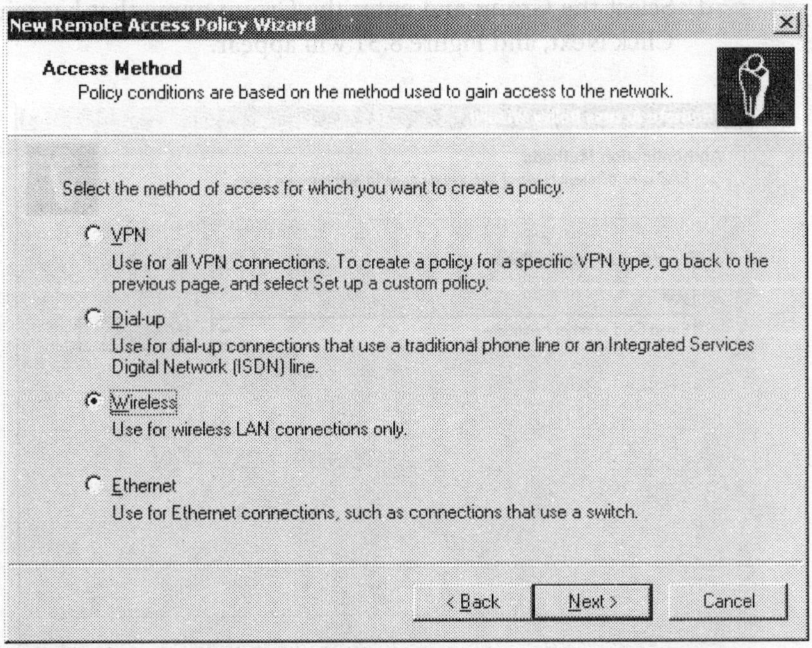

FIGURE 8.29 Selecting Wireless for the Remote Access Method.

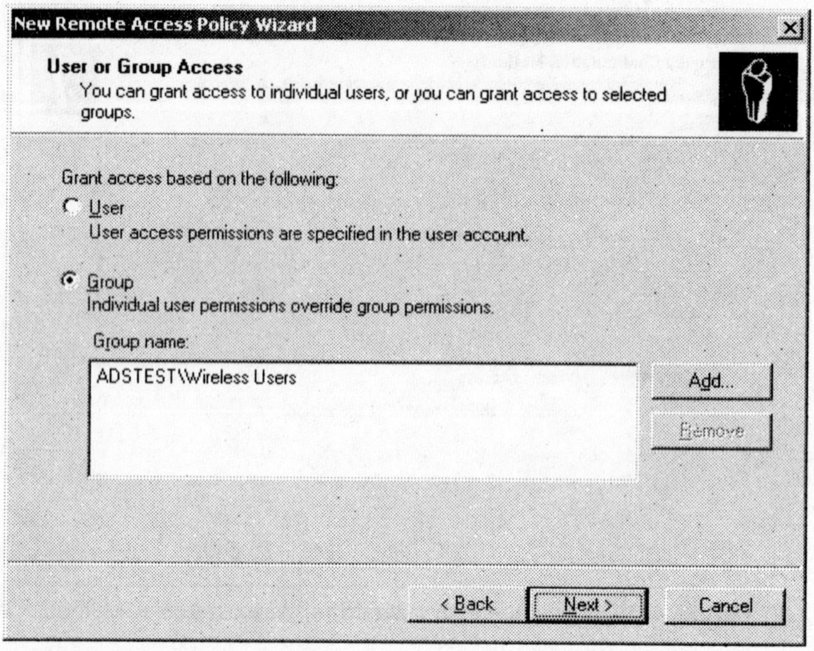

FIGURE 8.30 Assigning wireless access to the Group Wireless Users.

d. Select the Group and enter the Group name that has wireless access. Click Next, and Figure 8.31 will appear.

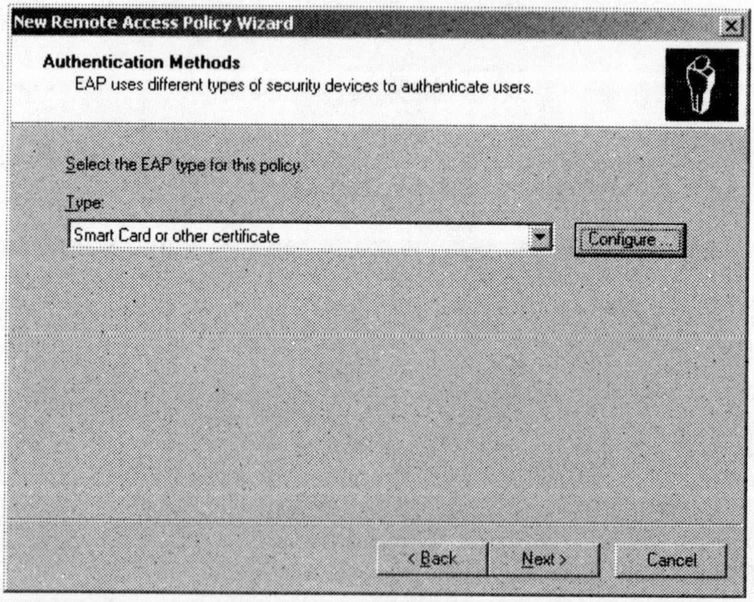

FIGURE 8.31 Select EAP with Certificates for the Authentication Method.

e. Select Smart Card or other certificate for EAP-TLS authentication. Click Finish to complete the wizard.

5. **Optionally configure a secondary IAS server.** If you must authenticate a large number of users, or the wireless network is mission critical, consider configuring a second IAS server for fault tolerance. To configure a second IAS server, install Windows Server 2003 and IAS on a second machine and complete the following steps to configure the secondary IAS server.
   a. Open a command prompt on the primary IAS server.
   b. Issue the command `netsh aaaa show config > <configuration_file_name>`. This command stores the IAS configuration to the specified file. Copy the configuration file to the secondary IAS server.
   c. Issue the command `netsh exec <configuration_file_name>`. This will import the configuration of the primary IAS server to the secondary server.

Configure Wireless Access with Group Policy

Using Group Policy, you can set up a list of preferred networks to automatically configure the wireless settings for clients running Windows XP or Windows Server 2003. To configure wireless access, open the Default Domain Policy. Click on Start, Programs, Administrative Tools, Active Directory Users and Computers. Right-click on the domain that has the certificates and select Properties. Click on the Group Policy tab, select the Default Domain Policy, and click Edit. Figure 8.32 will appear.

Click on Computer Configuration, Windows Settings, Security Settings, right-click on Wireless Network (IEEE 802.11) Policies, and select Create Wireless Network Policy. Click Next on the Welcome screen, and Figure 8.33 will appear.

Enter in a name and description for wireless access. Click Next and Finish. The properties of the wireless policy should appear (see Figure 8.34).

Make any necessary changes, click on the Preferred Networks tab, and click the Add button (see Figure 8.35).

Enter the SSID of the AP and a description. As of this writing, Group Policy in Windows Server 2003 does not support WPA authentication and encryption settings. Most likely, WPA will be supported in Windows 2003 Service Pack 2 and will be available in late 2004. However, since we're using 802.1*x* authentication, it addresses the major weakness of WEP—static encryption keys. Click on the IEEE 802.1*x* tab and Figure 8.36 will appear.

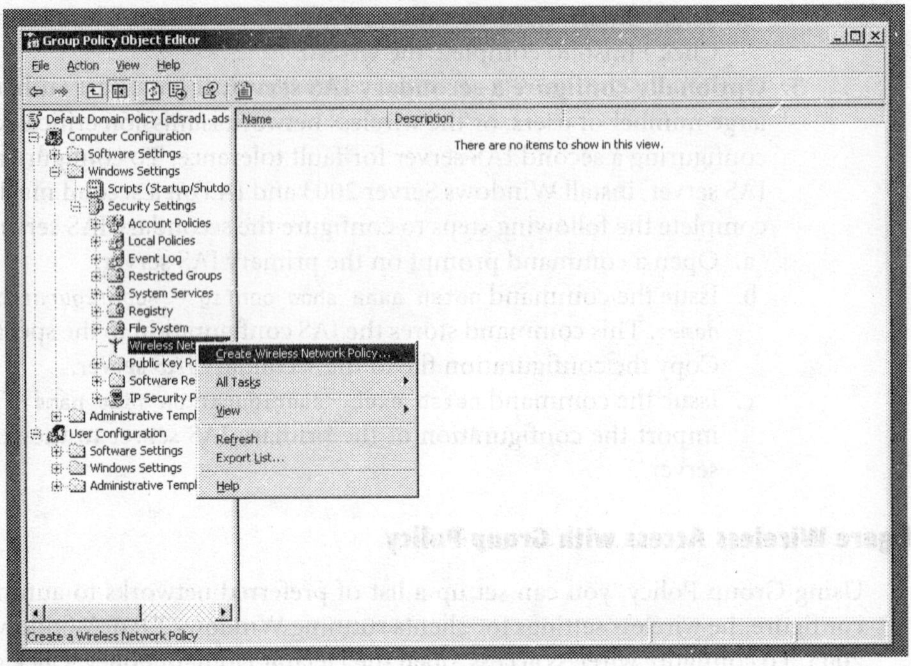

FIGURE 8.32 Create a wireless network policy.

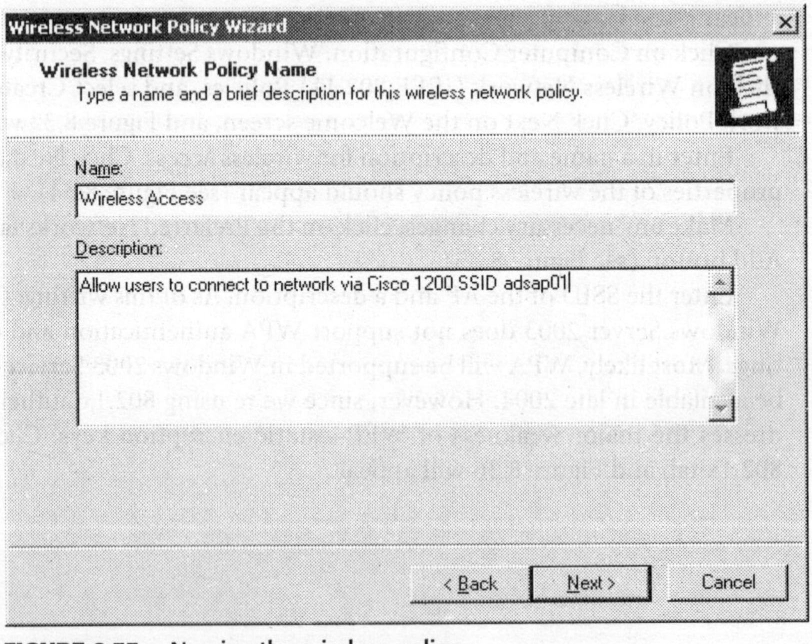

FIGURE 8.33 Naming the wireless policy.

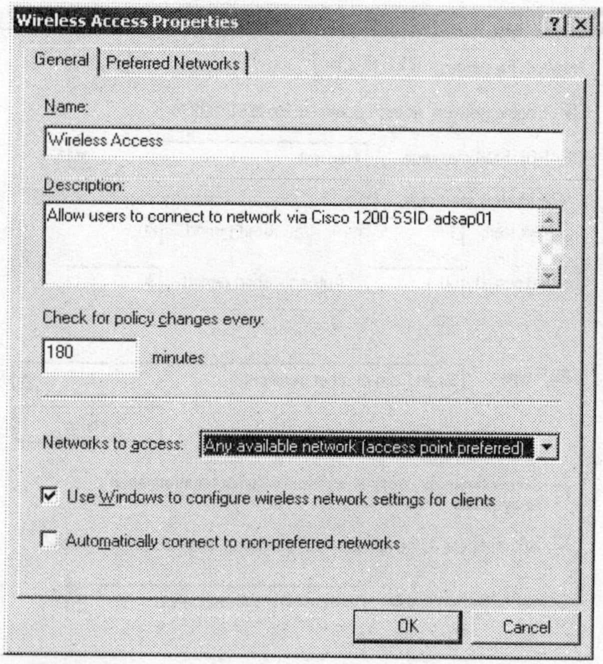

FIGURE 8.34 Editing the Wireless Access Properties.

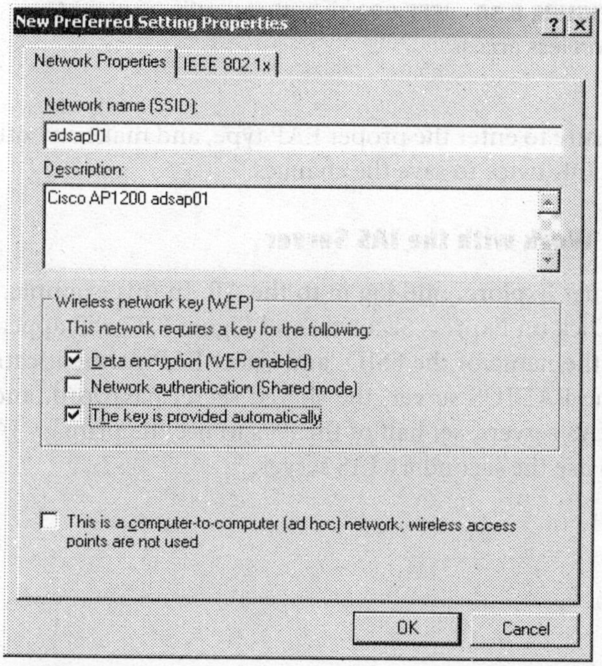

FIGURE 8.35 Adding the SSID to the preferred networks.

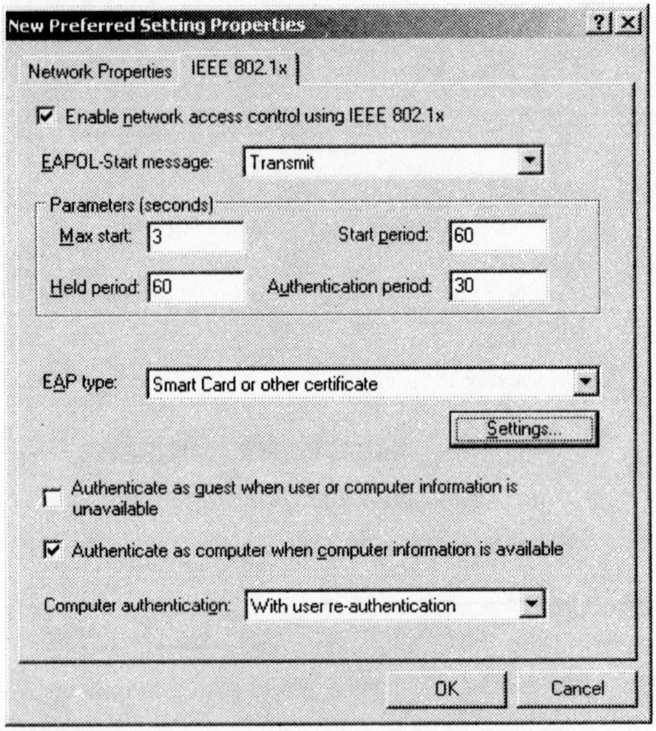

FIGURE 8.36 IEEE 802.1x Authentication settings for wireless access.

Make sure to enter the proper EAP type, and make any other changes as necessary. Click OK twice to save the changes.

Configure APs to Work with the IAS Server

Start Internet Explorer and log in to the AP. In this example, we are using Cisco's AP1200. Click on Express Security, and Figure 8.37 will appear.

Enter the name of the SSID, and select EAP Authentication. Enter the IP address of the RADIUS server, the shared secret password, and click Apply. If you have two IAS servers, set half of the APs to use the primary IAS server, and half of the APs to use the secondary IAS server.

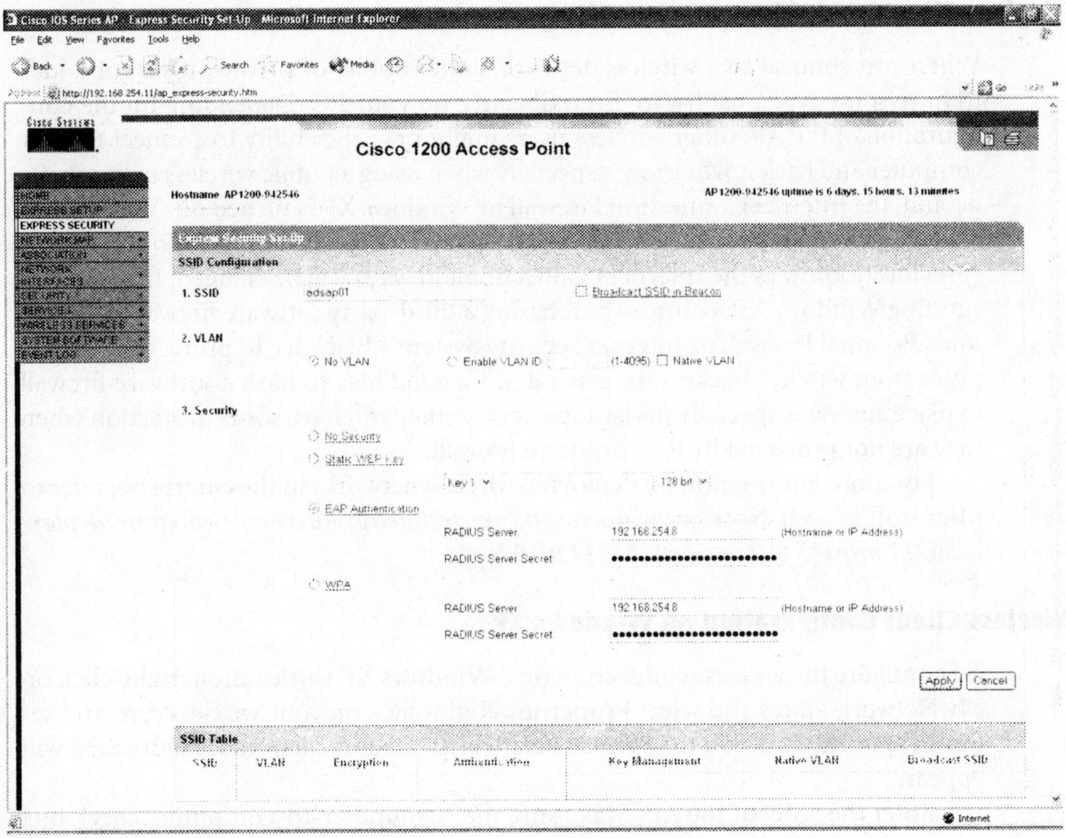

FIGURE 8.37 Configuring the Cisco AP1200 to use EAP Authentication.

CLIENT-SIDE SETUP

Windows XP has native support for wireless connections using enhanced security. If you plan to use WPA on Windows XP, download WPA support for Windows XP at *www.microsoft.com/downloads/details.aspx?FamilyId=009D8425-CE2B-47A4-ABEC-274845DC9E91&displaylang=en*. Optionally, you can install the vendor-supplied client software that supports WPA. For Windows 2000, you can download 802.1*x* client as long as you have Service Pack 3 installed on your system. Service Pack 4 for Windows 2000 includes the 802.1*x* client features. This will allow you to authenticate using a RADIUS server with a certificate on your mobile computer. For earlier versions of Windows, you must rely on the vendor's wireless support for your operating system. If you have to support wireless clients that are running earlier OS versions, check with the wireless vendor to make sure that your OS is supported by the wireless vendor.

Wireless Clients and Windows Firewall

When you connect to a wireless network, either public or private, it's a good idea to have some type of software firewall active on your PC. Depending on the configuration of the AP, other wireless users might have the ability to connect to your computer and hack it wirelessly, especially when using a public wireless network. By default, the Internet Connection Firewall in Windows XP is turned off. With the release of Windows XP Service Pack 2 due out in late 2004, the Windows Firewall (previously know as the Internet Connection Firewall) will be enabled. If you're not running Windows XP, consider purchasing a third-party software firewall like Norton's Personal Firewall or Internet Security System's Black Ice to protect your computer from wireless hackers. In general, it's a good idea to have a software firewall in place anyway, especially for laptop users, so they will have some protection when they are not protected by the corporate firewall.

For more information on deploying wireless networks in the enterprise, refer to Microsoft's Tech Note *www.microsoft.com/technet/prodtechnol/winxppro/deploy/ed80211.mspx#XSLTsection124121120120s.*

Wireless Client Configuration on Windows XP

To configure the wireless connection on a Windows XP workstation, right-click on My Network Places and select Properties. Right-click on your wireless card and select Properties. Click on the Wireless Networks tab and click Add. Figure 8.38 will appear.

Enter the SSID of the AP. Make sure the "Computer-to-computer" check box is unchecked. Click on the Authentication tab, and Figure 8.39 will appear.

Enable 802.1*x* client authentication and set the EAP type to Smart Card or other Certificate. Click OK to finish the client configuration. If you have the proper computer and user certificates installed through either auto-enrollment or a manual request with Internet Explorer, you should be able to authenticate to the network.

UPGRADING THE FIRMWARE ON A CISCO AP1200

As a general rule, it's always a good idea to verify you have the latest version of the firmware for your AP, even if you just purchased the AP. You should also check for new AP firmware updates on a regular basis. Firmware updates often include new and enhanced features as well as bug fixes. To upgrade the firmware on a Cisco AP1200 running VxWorks:

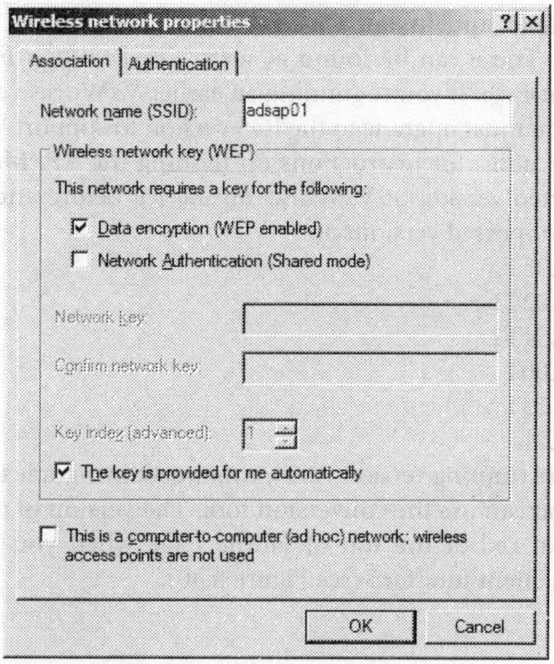

FIGURE 8.38 Wireless network association.

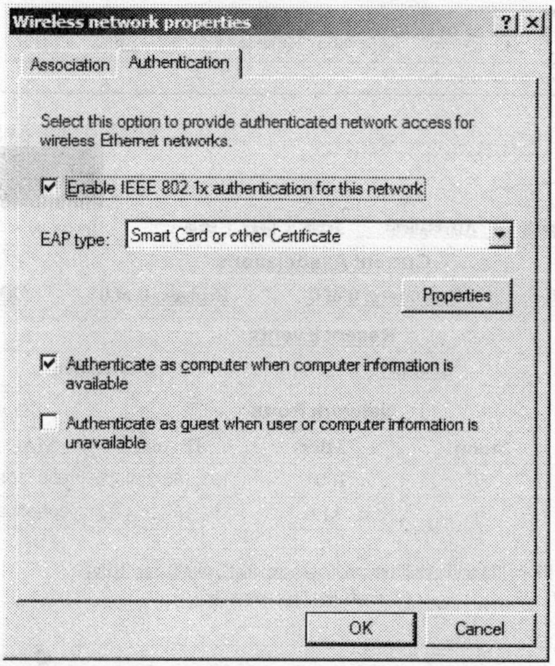

FIGURE 8.39 Setting up 802.1*x* authentication for the wireless network.

1. **Download and install Cisco Aironet Conversion Tool and Upgrade Image**. These can be found at *www.cisco.com/pcgi-bin/Software/WLAN/wlplanner.cgi*. If you're running an earlier VxWorks version of the Aironet IOS, you must upgrade to the IOS version to support WPA. Download the Release notes for instructions on flashing the AP. Make sure you have a supported version of VxWorks on the AP before attempting to flash the unit. Supported versions are:
   a. 12.03T
   b. 12.02T1
   c. 12.01T1
   d. 12.00T
   e. 11.23T
   f. 11.21

   If you're running version 12.04, you must downgrade to version 12.03T before you can use the conversion tool. The version of the VxWorks OS appears in red at the top of Home Page when you use the Web-based management interface (see Figure 8.40).

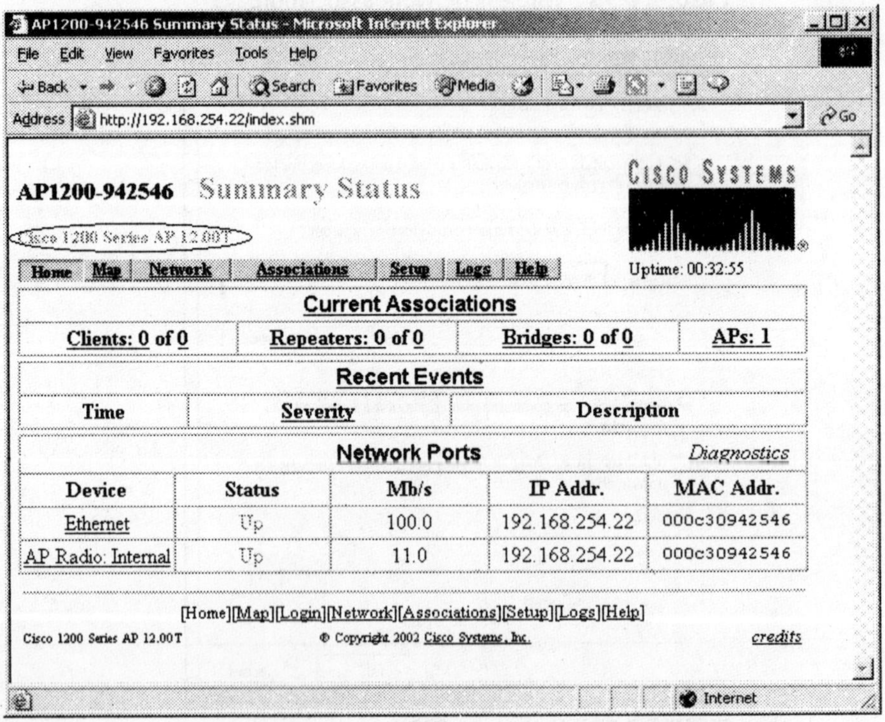

FIGURE 8.40 Display the version of VxWorks software on Cisco AP1200.

In this case, the VxWorks version is 12.00T. Using the conversion tool will retain your current AP configuration. You can also install IOS without the conversion tool, but the AP configuration will return to its factory defaults.

2. **Save the AP configuration.** Install Cisco's Aironet conversion tool and start it. You will use the conversion tools to save the AP configuration to the Cfg file. Then, this file along with the Upgrade image will be used to flash any AP that you want to upgrade. To create the Cfg file, click Add Task (see Figure 8.41).

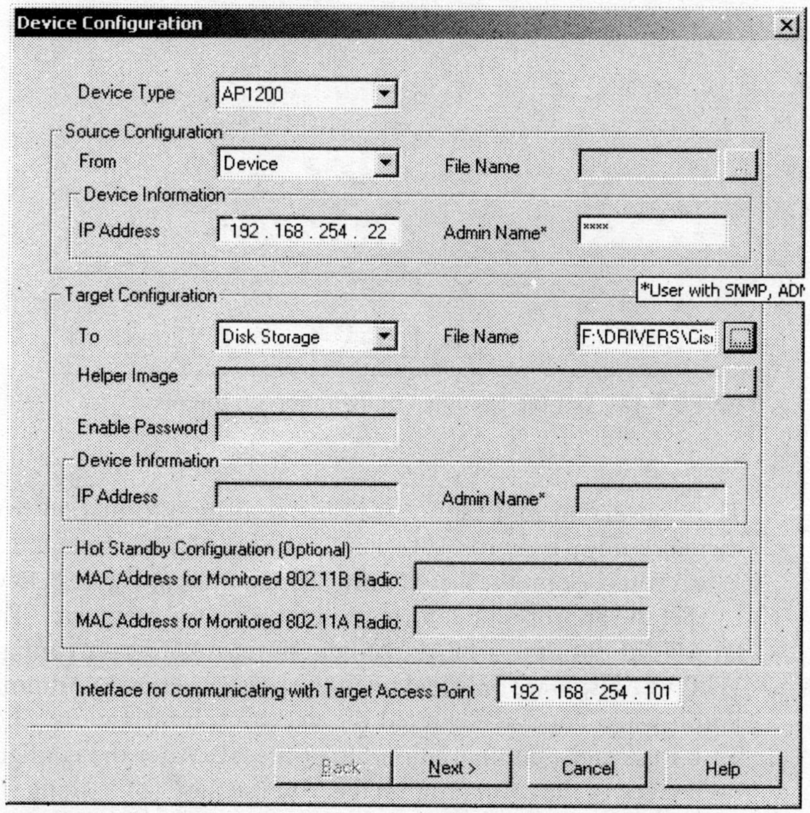

FIGURE 8.41 Filling out the Device Configuration information.

Since we want to save the AP configuration, we select the device and specify the IP address and Admin name in the Source Configuration. We select Disk Storage and specify a filename to save the AP configuration. Click Next. Figure 8.42 will appear.

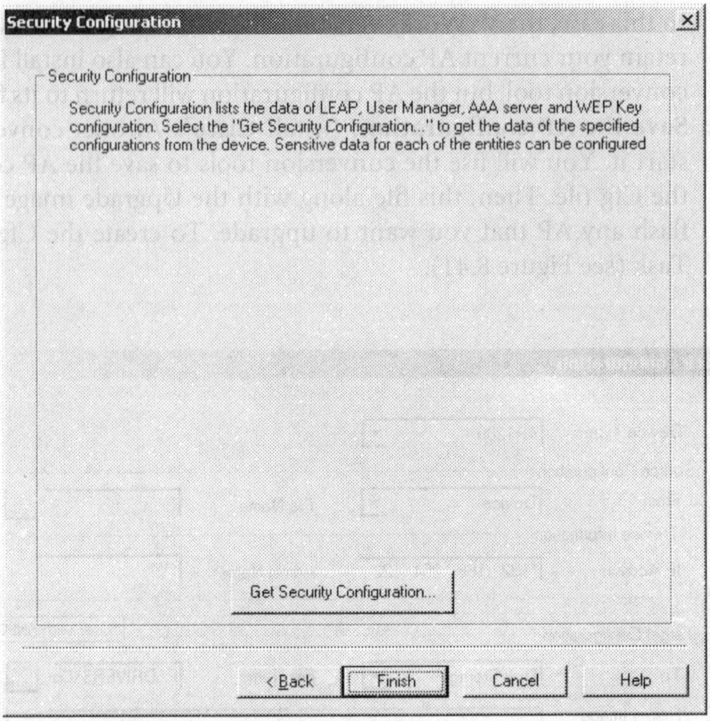

FIGURE 8.42 Get the Security Configuration on the AP.

The Conversion tool cannot read the security information from the AP; therefore, any passwords, WEP keys, and so forth must be manually entered. When you click on the Get Security Configuration, Figure 8.43 will appear.

Set the appropriate information for each the categories. This particular AP did not have a LEAP configuration, AAA Server configuration, or WEP VLANs, so we only had to set the password for the Admin user. Click Finish when you have entered the necessary information. Click on Start Task to save the configuration file of the AP. After the configuration has been saved to the configuration file, you use the Cfg file along with the Img file to update the AP. Click on Add Task and enter the information shown in Figure 8.44.

3. **Upgrade the firmware on the AP1200.** Now that we've saved the configuration, we can use the Cfg file along with the firmware Img file to upgrade the AP. In the Source Configuration, specify Disk Storage and enter the filename of the Cfg file saved in the previous step. In the Target Configuration, select Device, and in the helper image field, specify the firmware image for the AP. Specify the enable password, IP addresses of the AP and Admin name, and click Finish. After this information is entered, you will

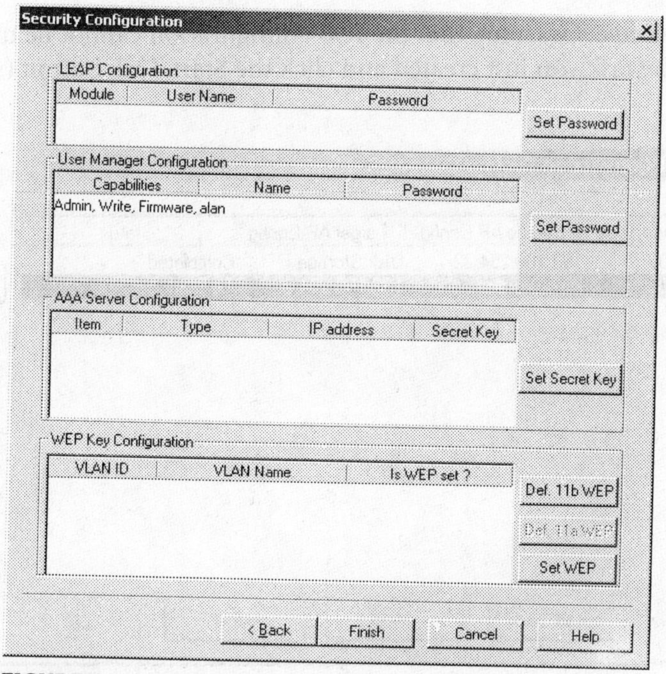

FIGURE 8.43 Entering the Security Configuration on the AP.

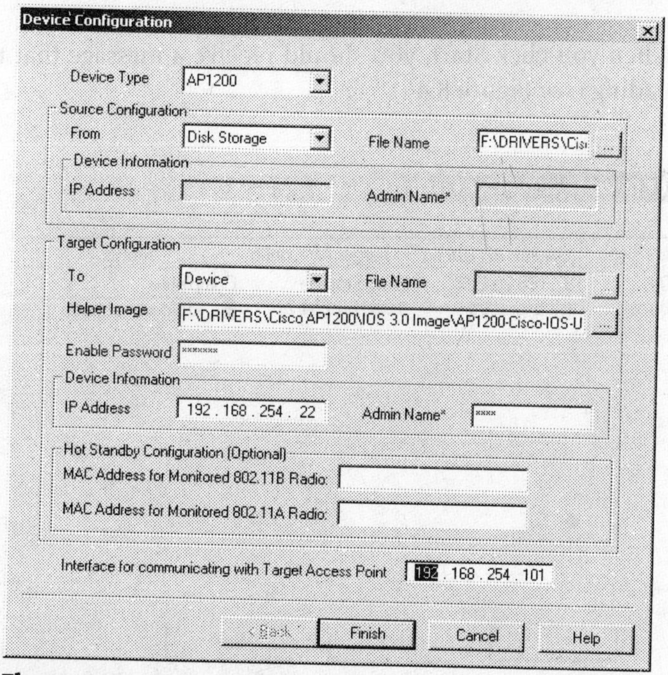

Figure 8.44 Using the AP configuration file and firmware image to upgrade the AP.

receive a warning that the IOS configuration cannot be undone. Click on the task you just created and click the Start Task button (see Figure 8.45).

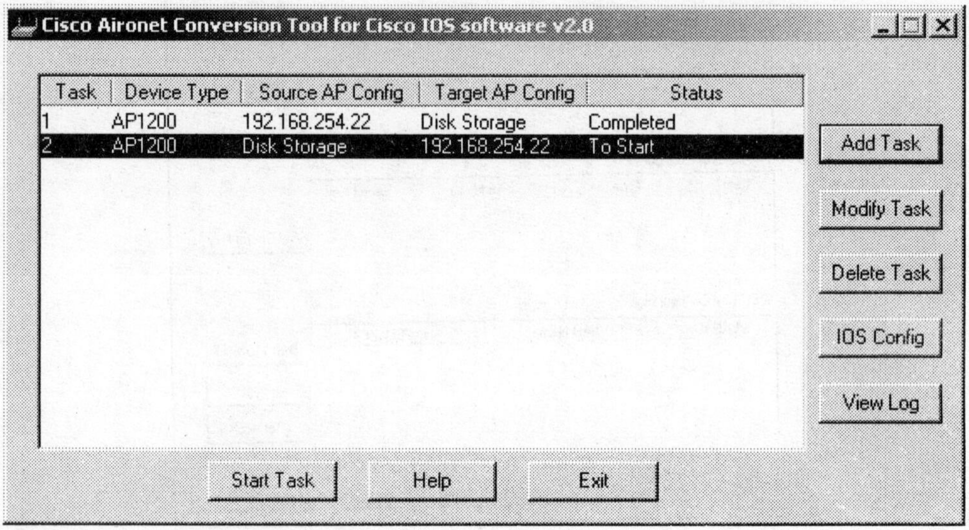

FIGURE 8.45 Viewing the configured tasks for the AP.

When you click Start, you should receive a message that the image is uploading (see Figure 8.46).

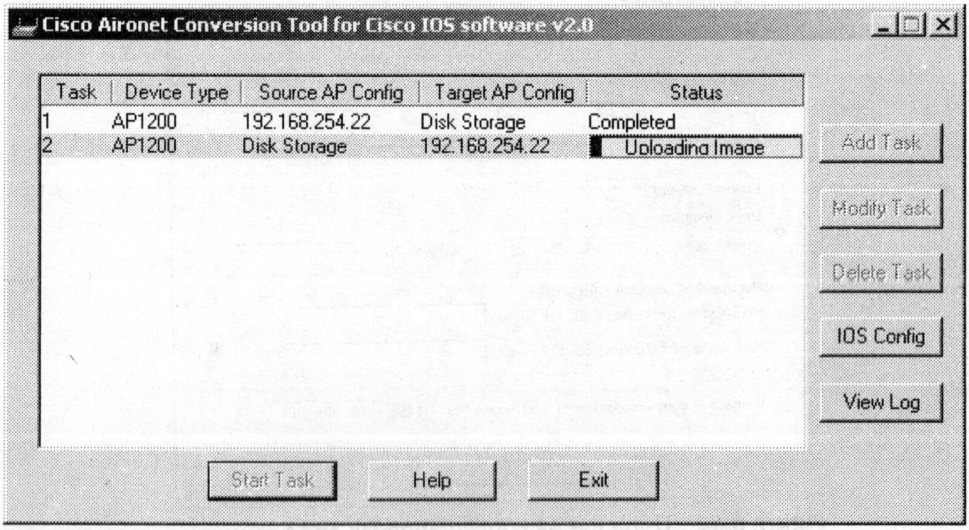

FIGURE 8.46 Running the firmware upgrade.

4. **Upgrade the IOS image on the AP.** After you upgrade from the VxWorks OS to the IOS, check Cisco's Web site for updated IOS software. Although the VxWorks-to-IOS upgrade upgrades the AP to IOS, it does not upgrade the AP to the latest version of the IOS firmware. As of this writing, the most current version is 12.2(15). Go to *www.cisco.com/pcgi-bin/Software/WLAN/wlplanner.cgi* and download the latest version of the firmware to your computer. Then, log in to the AP and select System Software, Software Upgrade from the menu on the left. You must use the Trivial File Transfer Protocol (TFTP) Upgrade because the image file 12.2(15) is larger than 4 MB. Attempting to load an image over 4 MB using the HTTP upgrade method will fail. If you don't have TFTP software, you can download a version from the Internet. It's handy to have a TFTP program anyway, because many hardware vendors such as 3Com and Cisco require a TFTP server in order to perform firmware upgrades on their hardware. One of our favorite TFTP programs is 3Com's. You can download it from *http://support.3com.com/software/utilities_for_windows_32_bit.htm*. If you have difficulty installing the TFTP program, because the install program cannot locate one of the installation components, try copying the TFTP setup files to the local hard drive and try the installation again. After you start the TFTP program and point it to the folder where the AP firmware is, you can flash the AP. Log in to the AP using a Web browser and click on System Software, Software Upgrade. Figure 8.47 will appear.

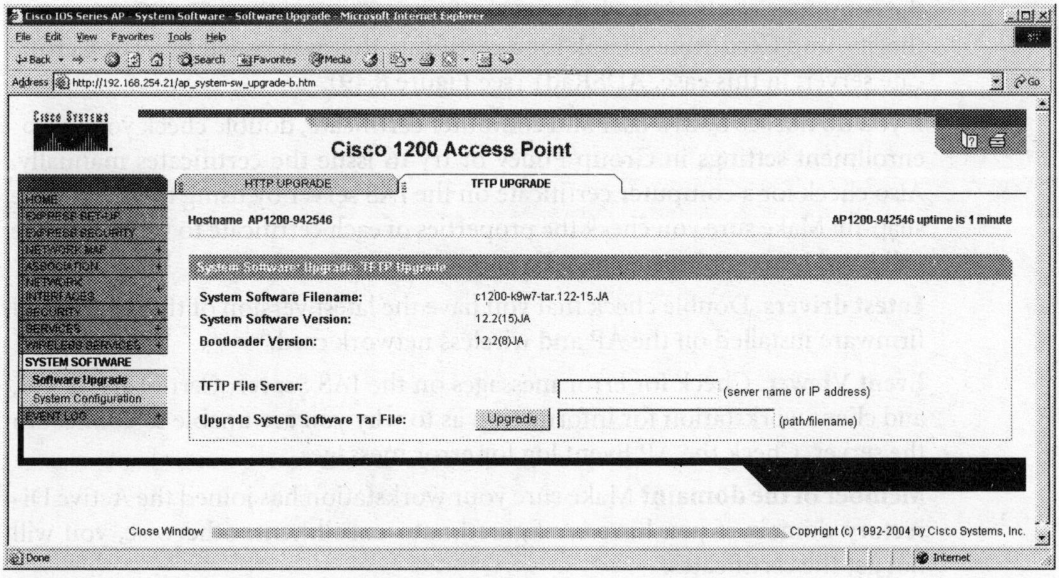

FIGURE 8.47 Upgrading the firmware on the AP.

Specify the IP address of the TFTP server, the firmware image name, and click Upgrade. This process takes 5 to 15 minutes to complete depending on the speed of your network.

TROUBLESHOOTING STEPS FOR WIRELESS CLIENTS

If you have difficulty getting your wireless clients to connect to an AP here are some suggestions to help you solve the problem:

Verify each step. There are many components and installation steps necessary to complete this installation. Carefully review each of the steps outlined earlier in this chapter and verify that all the steps were properly completed. It's very easy to miss one important step that can cause the AP connectivity to fail.

Check certificates. Make sure that the certificates are properly installed on the IAS and the client workstations. For the wireless clients, you need both a computer and user certificate to authenticate to the AP and network. To verify the certificates are installed on a client computer, click on Start, Run, type `mmc` in the Open field, and click OK. Click on File, Add/Remove Snap In, Add, click on Certificates in the Available Standalone Snap-In window, Add, My User Account Finish, and OK. Click on Certificates-Current User, Personal, Certificates, and Figure 8.48 will appear.

In this example, we have two certificates issued to Alan by ADSRad1. To view the computer certificates, click on Certificates, Trusted Root Certification Authority, and Certificates. Look for a certificate that was issued by your Certificate server; in this case, ADSRad1 (see Figure 8.49).

If you do not see both a user and computer certificate, double check your auto-enrollment settings in Group Policy or try to issue the certificates manually. Also check for a computer certificate on the IAS server by using the Certificate snap-in. Make sure you check the properties of each certificate to verify they are valid and have not been revoked.

Latest drivers. Double check that you have the latest version of the drivers and firmware installed on the AP and wireless network card.

Event Viewer. Check for error messages on the IAS Server, Certificate Server, and client workstation for information as to why you are unable to connect to the server. Check the AP Event log for error messages.

Member of the domain? Make sure your workstation has joined the Active Directory domain if you have configured auto-enrollment; otherwise, you will not get the certificates.

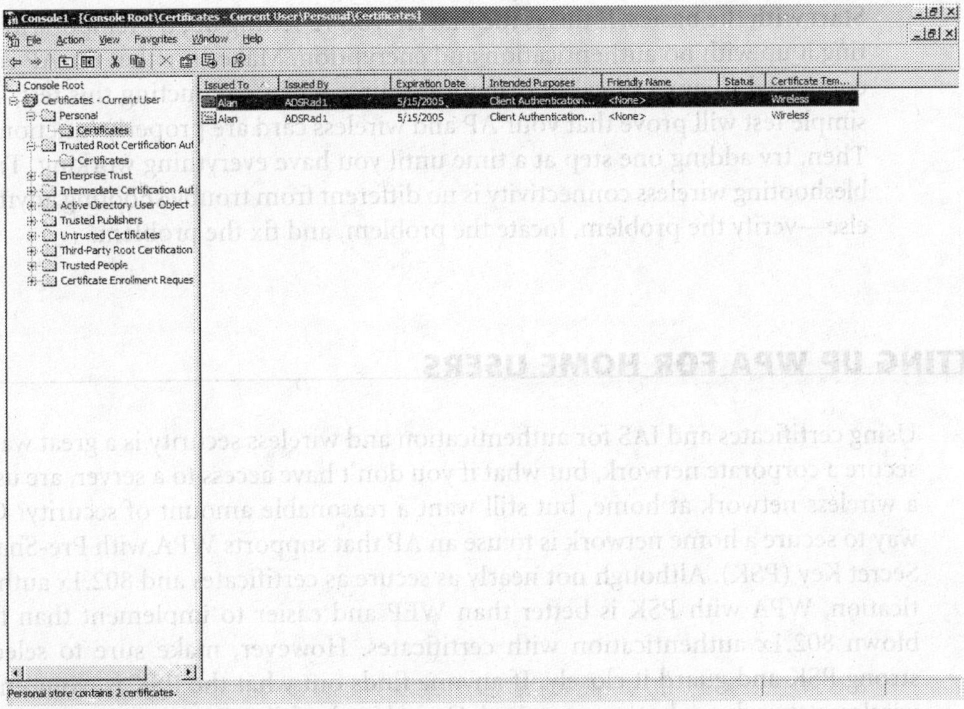

FIGURE 8.48 View user certificates using the Certificates snap-in.

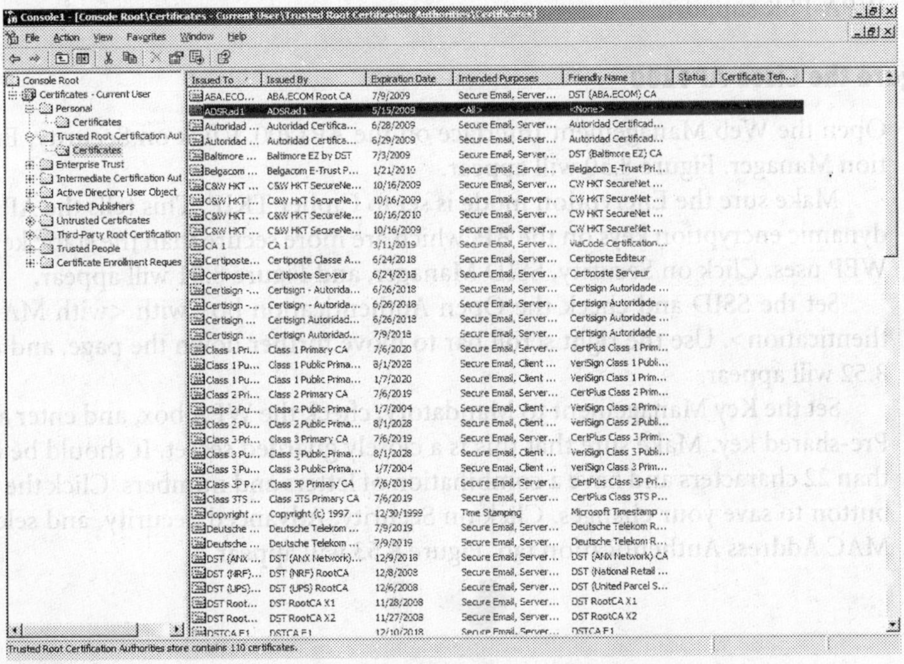

FIGURE 8.49 Viewing computer certificates using the Certificates snap-in.

Start with the basics. If this is the first AP you're setting up, try temporarily setting it up with no authentication and encryption. Make sure that the AP is not connected to any critical information source when conducting this test. This simple test will prove that your AP and wireless card are properly functioning. Then, try adding one step at a time until you have everything working. Troubleshooting wireless connectivity is no different from troubleshooting anything else—verify the problem, locate the problem, and fix the problem.

SETTING UP WPA FOR HOME USERS

Using certificates and IAS for authentication and wireless security is a great way to secure a corporate network, but what if you don't have access to a server, are using a wireless network at home, but still want a reasonable amount of security? One way to secure a home network is to use an AP that supports WPA with Pre-Shared Secret Key (PSK). Although not nearly as secure as certificates and 802.1*x* authentication, WPA with PSK is better than WEP and easier to implement than full-blown 802.1*x* authentication with certificates. However, make sure to select a strong PSK and guard it closely. If anyone finds out what the PSK is, your entire wireless network can be compromised. Complete the following steps to set up WPA with PSK on a Cisco AP1200 and a Windows XP Professional workstation with WPA-PSK support.

Configure the Cisco AP1200

Open the Web Management Interface on the AP1200. Click on Security, Encryption Manager. Figure 8.50 will appear.

Make sure the Encryption mode is set to Cipher TKIP. This tells the AP to use dynamic encryption keys on the AP, which are more secure than the static keys that WEP uses. Click on Security, SSID Manager, and Figure 8.51 will appear.

Set the SSID and check the Open Authentication box with <with MAC Authentication>. Use the right scroll bar to move further down the page, and Figure 8.52 will appear.

Set the Key Management to Mandatory, check the WPA box, and enter a WPA Pre-shared key. Make sure that this is a closely guarded secret. It should be longer than 22 characters and have a combination of letters and numbers. Click the Apply button to save your changes. Click on Security, Advanced Security, and select the MAC Address Authentication tab. Figure 8.53 will appear.

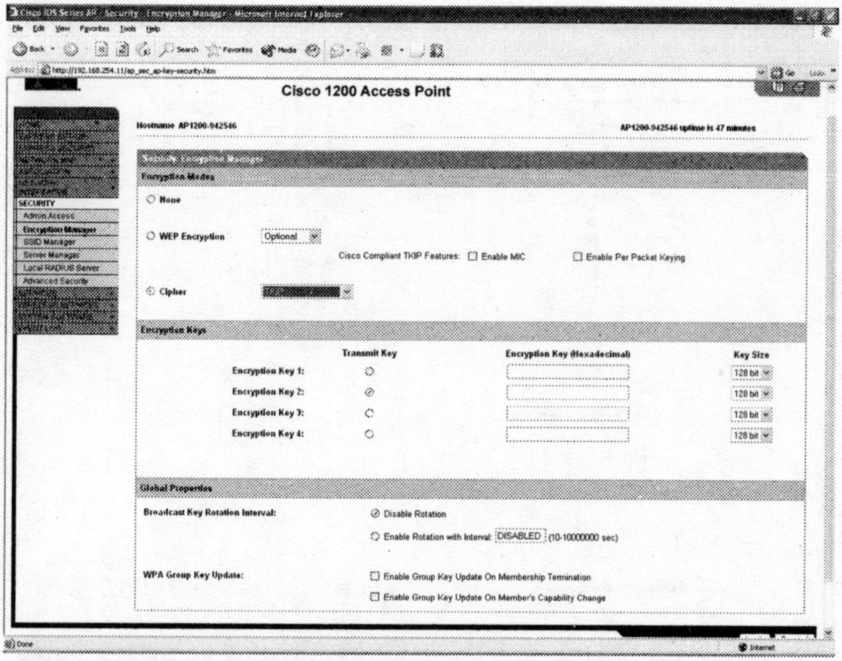

FIGURE 8.50 Encryption Manager settings on Cisco 1200.

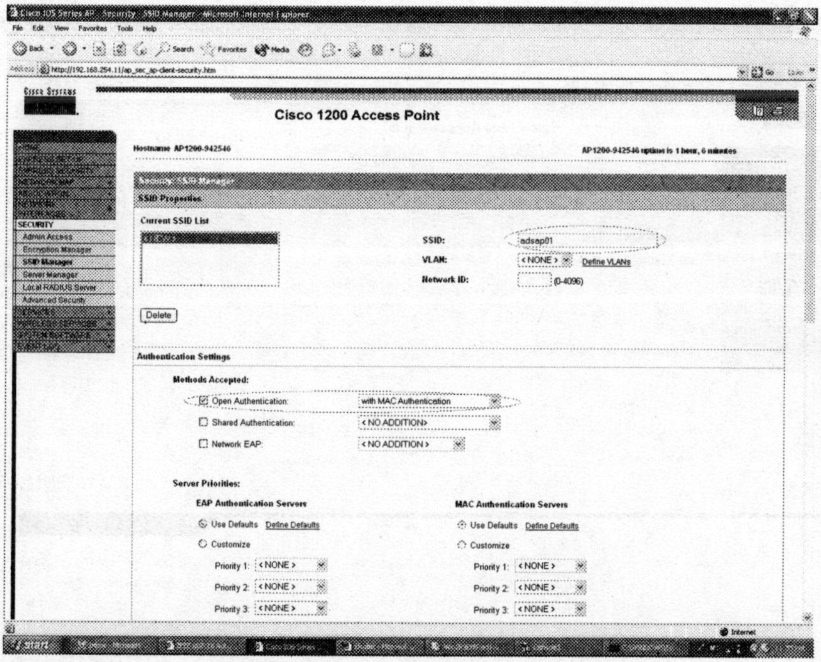

FIGURE 8.51 Setting the SSID and authentication method.

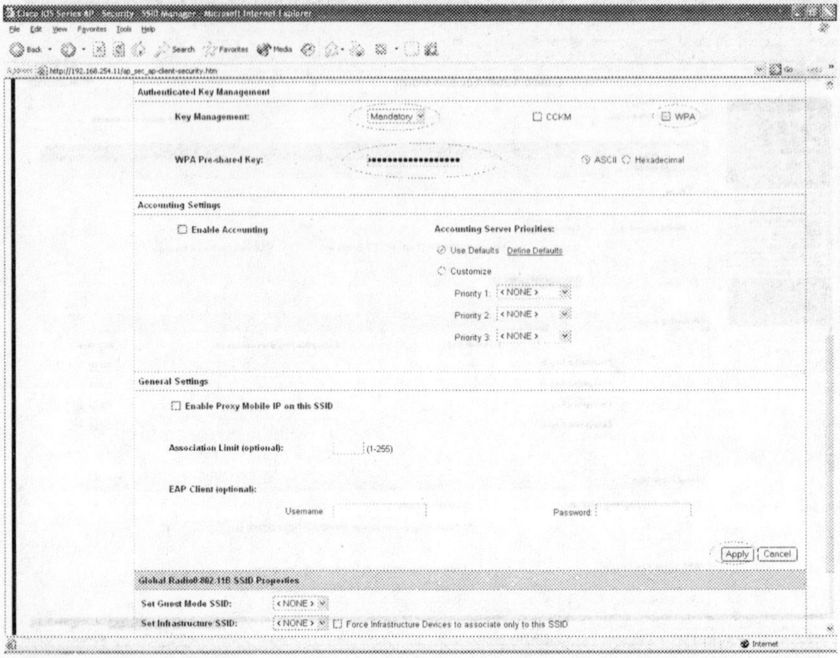

FIGURE 8.52 Setting the Key Management Type, WPA Pre-shared secret.

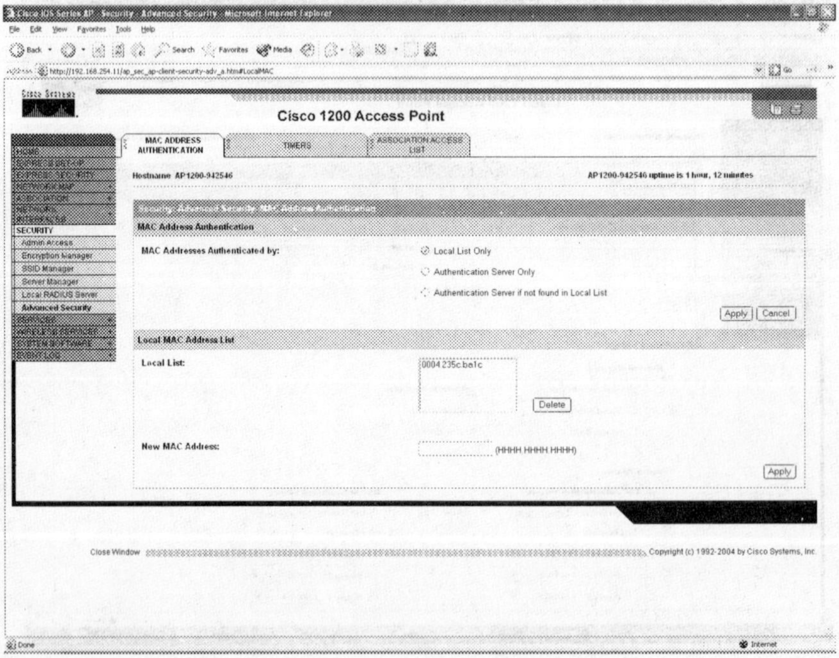

FIGURE 8.53 Adding the MAC address of the wireless client.

You can determine the MAC address of your wireless card by clicking on Start, Run, type `cmd` in the open window, and click OK. In the command prompt, type `ipconfig /all` and look for the physical address of your wireless card. It should be a Hex number in the form of xx-xx-xx-xx-xx-xx. Record this number, enter it in the New MAC Address field, and click Apply. To authenticate to this AP, you need the WPA Pre-shared Key and the MAC address of the wireless card entered into the AP. Of course, this is not even close to the security with 802.1*x* authentication with certificates, but it's better than nothing and better than plain WEP.

Configure the Windows XP Workstation

Check the wireless vendor's Web site for an updated driver for your wireless card. Unless you have a very new laptop, there's a good chance that the wireless card driver does not support WPA. For most wireless cards, you need the latest driver to use WPA. Even if your card already supports WPA, it's still a good idea to install the latest driver. After you've installed the latest driver for your wireless network card, make sure that Windows XP Service Pack 1 is installed before installing WPA support on the workstation. Click on Start, Run, type `winver`, and click OK to see if you have Windows XP Service Pack 1 installed on your computer. You can download WPA support for Windows XP from *www.microsoft.com/downloads/details.aspx?FamilyId=009D8425-CE2B-47A4-ABEC-274845DC9E91&displaylang=en*. Right-click on My Network Places, click Properties, right-click on your wireless connection, and select the Wireless Network tab. Figure 8.54 will appear.

Make sure that the "Use Windows to configure my wireless network settings" is checked. Click on the Add button, and Figure 8.55 will appear.

Enter the SSID of the AP in the Network name field. Select WPA-PSK (Pre-shared Key) for the Network Authentication, and set the data encryption to TKIP (Temporal Key Integrity Protocol). Enter in the pre-shared key in the Network key and Confirm network key fields. This is the same key that was entered in the WPA Pre-Shared key on the AP. Make sure that the key matches *exactly*. Keys are case sensitive. Click OK to save your settings. It might take a few minutes for the workstation to authenticate to the AP. If you authenticate to the AP, but cannot get an IP address assigned to the workstation via DHCP, try assigning a static IP address to the wireless client and then try connecting.

This configuration is easier to set up than the full-blown 802.1*x* configuration, but it is not as secure. However, for home use it's a good compromise. When you're not using the AP at home, power off the unit so no one can connect to it to protect your network.

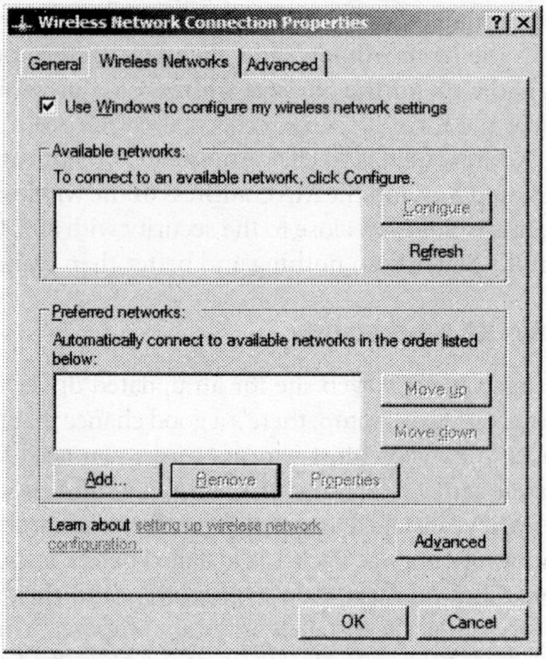

FIGURE 8.54 Wireless network connection properties.

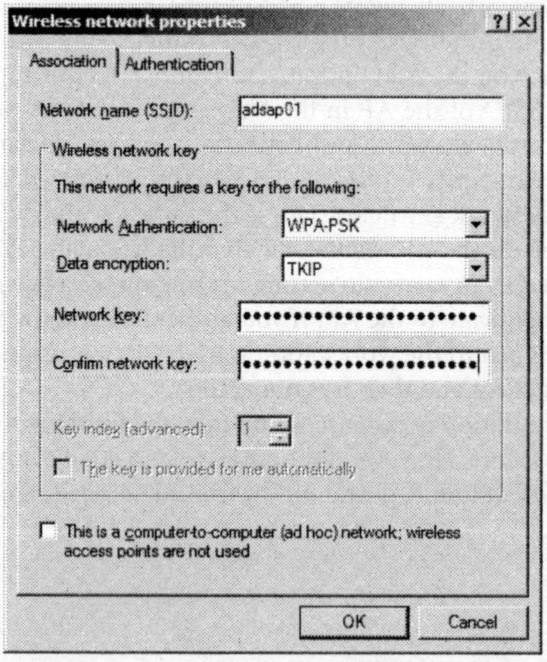

FIGURE 8.55 Configuring the wireless connection.

WIRELESS TOOLS

There are quite a few wireless tools that can help sniff out rogue APs and perform site surveys. Most of the tools are shareware, and some have limited hardware support.

NetStumbler

NetStumbler can be downloaded at *www.netstumbler.com/download.php?op=viewdownload&cid=1&orderby=hitsD*. This utility works on the Windows 2000 and XP platforms. This is a wireless utility that can help you find poor coverage areas on your wireless network, detect other networks that might cause interference with your network, and detect rogue APs on your network.

WEPCracking Tools

Two tools to capture WEP keys are WepCrack *http://sourceforge.net/projects/wepcrack/* and Airsnort *http://airsnort.shmoo.com/*. Both these utilities run under Linux and can recover lost WEP keys.

TROUBLESHOOTING SCENARIOS

As we mentioned in the chapter preview, most of the wireless problems come not from the wireless APs themselves, but because of problems that occur if the wireless units are not properly secured. Of course, there is no way to make a network 100-percent secure, but if you follow the previous instructions, it should keep out all but the most motivated hackers. Secure your wireless AP properly, keep out unauthorized users, and prevent problems from happening in the first place. The following troubleshooting scenarios are our experiences with WLAN and their unique challenges.

Scenario 1 Internet Connection Running Very Slow

Facts

- DSL connection running at 384K/1.5 ADSL with a SonicWALL SOHO3 Firewall.
- Windows 2000 server with five workstations.
- Linksys WAP54AG access point.

Symptoms

We received a call from the client complaining that their Internet connection was very slow and sometimes timed out.

Questions to Ask

Q: Has anything changed? A: Nothing, they noticed that lately, the Internet connection is running very slow.

Troubleshooting Steps

1. **Verify the problem.** When we arrived on site, we opened up an MSN Web page, and it did load very slowly.
2. **Run DSL speed test.** We went to DSL Reports and tried to run the speed test at *www.dslreports.com/stest*. You must have the Java runtime module installed on your computer to run this test. This can be downloaded from *www.java.com/en/download/windows_automatic.jsp*. We had difficulty even bringing up the Web page and eventually got the test to run. The results were 12 KB/sec upload and 32 KB/sec download speeds. Obviously, these test speeds are nowhere near the performance they should get on their DSL line.
3. **Observe the firewall and DSL router.** We took a quick look at the traffic lights on the firewall and DSL router. Both devices were blinking quite rapidly, indicating a high volume of traffic. Most likely, the performance problems on the DSL were caused by some internal network problem or denial-of-service (DoS) attack, and most likely, the DSL line was properly functioning. What could it be? A beaconing card, bad Ethernet switch, or other cause?
4. **Check the AP.** We noticed that the client had installed an AP that was located next to the firewall. We started the management interface on the AP (using the default password for access) and noticed that 24 users were connected to the AP.

Resolution

Obviously, the unauthorized users were causing the DSL performance problems. The AP configuration was entirely open, so that anyone within range could connect to the AP. It turns out that there was a Starbucks located on the bottom floor of their office building, and most of the connections were coming from this location. We changed the password to the AP, turned on WEP, and reconfigured the workstations to connect with the WEP shared secret key. Unfortunately, this AP does not support WPA. We suggested that they upgrade the AP to one that supports WPA. Because of their small size, they could not afford to implement WPA and 802.1*x* authentication.

We warned them that WEP can be cracked, and they should upgrade to an AP that supports WPA as soon as possible.

Lessons Learned

Wireless is one of these neat technologies that is easy to set up and use, and has the power not only to shoot yourself in the foot, but to blow off the lower part of your body. Fortunately, the unauthorized users just wanted Internet access, but if someone was serious, he could have caused significant damage on their network. If you plan to use wireless, secure it before it goes into production.

Scenario 2 HACKER ATTACKS WEB SITE

Facts

- Client was internally hosting their Web site in the DMZ.
- SonicWALL Pro 200 Firewall with a T1 to the Internet.
- Web site runs on IIS 5.0 with Windows 2000 Server with Service Pack 3.
- Network has a mix of Windows 2000 and 2003 servers.
- 200 workstations running a mix of Windows 2000 and Windows XP.

Symptoms

The client's Web site was recently defamed.

Questions to Ask

Q: Has anything changed? A: No. Someone informed the IT department that there was inappropriate content on the company's Web site.

Troubleshooting Steps

1. **Verify the problem.** When the site was reviewed, there was inappropriate material on the site. Reviewing the time and date stamps of the changed files indicated that the changes took place a few days ago.
2. **Apply patches.** We patched the Web server with Service Pack 4 and installed all of the critical updates. All other servers on the network were patched with the latest service pack and critical updates.
3. **Run IIS lockdown tool.** We downloaded the IIS lockdown tool from *www.microsoft.com/downloads/details.aspx?displaylang=en&FamilyID=DDE9EFC0-BB30-47EB-9A61-FD755D23CDEC*. We disabled any unnecessary services on the Web server.

4. **Replace firewall with SonicWALL Pro 4060.** We replaced the older SonicWALL Pro 200 with a newer SonicWALL Pro 4060 and placed the IIS server in the DMZ. This was already scheduled to take place before the hack occurred, but because of the hack, the firewall was upgraded sooner. We configured the firewall to only allow HTTP traffic to the Web server in the DMZ. The old SonicWALL Pro 200 was configured to allow any traffic out of the firewall. On the new 4060, we changed the outbound rule to only allow on HTTP, HTTPS, FTP, SMTP (internal mail server only), and DNS traffic. The logging level was turned up and configured to forward the logs to the system administrator on a daily basis.
5. **Change passwords.** All of the passwords were changed for every user in Active Directory. Any old user accounts were deleted.
6. **Web page hacked again.** A few weeks later, the Web site was hacked again. The date and time stamps on the modified files indicated they were changed overnight.
7. **Evaluate log files.** We reviewed the log files and Event Viewer on the IIS server for clues. We paid especially close attention to the firewall logs shortly before the time of the modified files on the Web server. The firewall logs did not turn up anything unusual. The Event Viewer did not reveal anything unusual. This particular network only had a connection to the Internet, and no other WAN connections to remote sites. Although a hack through the Internet was still possible, this was looking more like an inside job. If the hack did happen from the Internet, the firewall log files should have revealed *something*, like an FTP transfer when the Web site was changed.
8. **Any recent changes?** We asked the client if there were any recent changes to the network or to any employees. The system administrator did mention that one of the help desk people was fired about a month ago.
9. **Run NetStumbler.** On a hunch, we decided to run a wireless sweep to see if we could find any wireless AP. This particular client did not use any wireless APs. NetStumbler can be downloaded from *www.netstumbler.com/download.php?op=viewdownload&cid=1&orderby=hitsD*.

Resolution

After roaming the building with the laptop and wireless card, we discovered an AP connected to the network in an unused office. Evidently, someone had plugged in the AP and was performing the hack from outside the building. The AP was removed, the Web site was repaired, and the network has had no known hacking activity since the AP was removed.

Lessons Learned

We could have waited until the hacker connected to the rogue AP and try to catch him in the act, but it was decided by the client just to remove the AP to prevent further hacking. As part of any security audit, we now recommend full wireless sweeps of a client's premises. You can use utilities like NetStumbler to find rogue APs, but you must roam the entire office for any unauthorized APs. If you already have WLAN in place, you can leverage your existing APs to find a rogue AP by using tools similar to Airware (*www.airwave.com/*). Since most APs are managed with a Web Interface, you can use a port scanner such as NetScan Tools Pro (*www.netscantools.com/*) or SuperScan (*www.foundstone.com/index.htm?subnav=resources/navigation.htm&subcontent=/resources/proddesc/superscan.htm*) to identify devices that answer on port 80 and then investigate any device that looks suspicious.

Scenario 3 Wireless Users Cannot Connect to the Network

Facts

- 802.11b wireless network.
- Three APs connecting 30 wireless users.
- Windows Server 2003.
- SonicWALL Pro 4060 Firewall with T1 to the Internet.
- Wireless users running laptops with Windows 2000 and XP.

Symptoms

Wireless users lose their connection to the wireless network.

Questions to Ask

Q: Has anything changed? A: No. The wireless network was working fine, but now wireless users lose their connection to the network.

Troubleshooting Steps

1. **Verify the problem.** We asked one of the wireless users to demonstrate when the connection was lost to the AP.
2. **Try a different AP.** Since this network had three APs, we tried connecting to an AP in a different part of the building. We were able to connect to the other two APs on the WLAN.
3. **Test AP.** At this point, we suspected that something was wrong with this particular AP. We swapped out the AP with one of the working APs from a different location and changed the configuration to match the original

AP, but the problem continued. We also swapped the suspected bad AP and put it in the location of the other AP. The suspected bad AP worked fine in that location. It could be a bad cable run connecting the AP to the network, but in our earlier test, something was preventing the wireless clients from authenticating to the AP itself, so the drop was probably okay. It seemed as though the problem was specific to that location.

4. **Perform site survey.** When this site was first installed, we performed a site survey to determine the location and number of APs the client would need to provide connectivity in the desired locations. Although 802.11b has 11 channels, most of these channels overlap each other. Because of the overlapping signals, only channels 1, 6, and 11 can be used simultaneously with no chance of overlapping the signal. We placed the APs so they just overlapped their signals, but we configured the APs so the adjacent APs were always on different channels. A new tenant had just moved into the office space on the floor above, and we suspected that one of their APs might be interfering with our AP. We turned off our AP and used the Cisco's Site Survey Utility to pick up any other AP signals in the area.

Resolution

Sure enough, the Cisco Site Survey picked up an AP on the next floor. Of course, it was set up on the same channel as our AP. Since the client had two other APs in their office, we decided to change the channel on the AP that was having problems. The other AP was far enough away that the signal from the new tenant's AP did not interfere with the AP on the same channel. After the channel change, the wireless worked flawlessly.

Lessons Learned

When performing a site survey, you not only have to worry about your own APs, but often the signals from beside, below, and above you, especially in an office building. The 2.4-GHz airspace is getting crowded. If you can't resolve an AP conflict with a neighbor, consider upgrading to a unit that operates on a different less-used frequency such as 802.1a/g, which runs at 5 GHz. If your WLAN has been stable in the past and suddenly stops working, run a site survey first to determine if another AP was recently turned on in the area.

Scenario 4 — Unable to Flash the Cisco AP1200 Using HTTP

Facts

- Cisco AP1200 running IOS.
- Attempting to flash unit with IOS version 12.2(15)JA.
- Attempting to flash the AP using HTTP is unsuccessful.

Symptoms

This AP1200 was just upgraded from VxWorks to IOS. However, there was a later version, 12.2(15)JA, available that we wanted to install on the AP1200.

Questions to Ask

Q: What happened? A: We just upgraded the AP1200 from VxWorks to IOS.

Q: What happens when you attempt the IOS upgrade with HTTP? A: Nothing. The upgrade appears to happen, but even waiting up to 30 minutes, the AP is not upgraded.

Troubleshooting Steps

1. **Verify the problem.** We attempted to upgrade the AP1200 by logging in to the AP Web interface and selecting System Software, Software Upgrade, HTTP Upgrade tab, selected the correct firmware image file using the Browse button, and then clicked the Upgrade button. After 30 minutes of waiting, the firmware upgrade had not completed. When we rebooted the AP, the firmware still remained at the previous version. We verified that we were attempting to upload the correct firmware file.
2. **Search Cisco's Web site.** We found references to upgrades of the firmware, but nothing related to the specific problem we had with firmware upgrade.
3. **Review Release Notes for 12.2.(15)JA.** On page two of the release notes is a notice that if you attempt to upgrade the AP1200 using the HTTP interface, the upgrade will fail. This is because the 12.2(15)JA firmware image file is larger than 4 MB. To upgrade the firmware on the AP, we had to use the TFTP interface.

Resolution

We downloaded 3Com's TFTP program from *http://support.3com.com/software/utilities_for_windows_32_bit.htm* and installed it on a workstation. We started the TFTP program, clicked the Configure TFTP Server button, and changed the upload/download directory to the location of the AP1200 flash image. We logged in to the Web Interface of the AP1200 and selected System Software, Software Upgrade, TFTP Upgrade, specified the IP address of the TFTP server, filename of the flash image, and clicked Upgrade. This time, the upgrade was successful and took roughly five minutes to complete.

Lessons Learned

Remember to read the directions! It's especially tricky to upgrade the AP1200 from VxWorks to IOS. For more information on upgrading the AP firmware, refer to the *Upgrading the Firmware on a Cisco AP1200* section earlier in this chapter.

Scenario 5 — Unable to Authenticate to Cisco AP1200 Using WPA With Pre-shared Key (PSK)

Facts

- Just purchased one AP1200 for home use.
- Wireless client is a Toshiba Satellite Pro M10 with integrated wireless card.
- SonicWALL TELE3 Firewall connected to a DSL modem.

Symptoms

After configuring the AP1200 for WPA with PSK, the notebook is unable to authenticate to the AP.

Questions to Ask

Q: What has changed? A: Just purchased a AP1200 for home use, and the user is unable to connect to the AP.

Q: Was it working before? A: No, this the first attempt at this installation, and so far, it has been unsuccessful.

Troubleshooting Steps

1. **Verify the problem.** When we attempted to authenticate to the AP using the Toshiba laptop, we were unsuccessful.
2. **Verify connections on the AP.** We examined the configuration of the AP1200. It was set to receive a dynamic IP address from the DHCP server on the SonicWALL. We changed the IP address on the AP to the static IP address with the correct subnet mask and default gateway. Since the AP1200 was previously able to obtain an IP address from the SonicWALL, we knew that the connection to the network was properly working.
3. **Turn off encryption.** Because this was a brand new installation, we wanted to verify that the AP and wireless card in the laptop were properly working.

We temporarily disabled encryption and configured the AP to allow completely open authentication. After these settings were changed, we were able to connect to the AP and surf the Internet. What does this tell you? That the AP and wireless card work okay, and the connection issue with WPA is most likely a configuration error.

4. **Require MAC authentication.** We recorded the MAC address of the wireless card by issuing the command `ipconfig /all` at a command prompt. We then entered this MAC address into the AP1200 and enabled open authentication with MAC authentication. We tested the connection with this setting and verified we were still able to connect to the AP.
5. **Download WPA support on the wireless laptop.** We downloaded the WPA support for Windows XP at *www.microsoft.com/downloads/details.aspx?FamilyId=009D8425-CE2B-47A4-ABEC-274845DC9E91&displaylang=en*. The WPA update requires Windows XP with Service Pack 1. Before we installed the update, we verified that the laptop was running Windows XP with Service Pack 1 by clicking on Start, Run, typed in `winver` in the open field, and clicked OK. After installing the wireless card, the WPA-PSK settings did not appear in the Wireless Properties, Network Authentication field. We thought that perhaps the WPA update did not properly install, so we removed the WPA update, rebooted the computer, and reinstalled the WPA. After the reinstallation, the WPA-PSK option was still missing.
6. **Update network card driver.** We reviewed the driver date of the wireless network using the Device Manager and noticed that the driver was almost two years old. We went to *www.toshiba.com* and downloaded and installed the latest driver for the wireless card. After the driver was updated, the WPA-PSK option appeared in the Network authentication field.

Resolution

After the drivers were updated, we entered a 22-character PSK on the AP and on the wireless card. We enabled WPA with PSK on the AP1200 as mandatory to authenticate to the AP. We configured the wireless card to use WPA-PSK and entered the Pre-shared key on the laptop wireless card properties. After these changes were complete, we were able to authenticate to the AP using WPA with PSK. For more information on this WPA-PSK, refer to the section *Setting up WPA for Home Users* earlier in this chapter.

Lessons Learned

Whenever you set up an AP for the first time, it's a good idea to change one item at a time. First, try to connect to the AP without any authentication or encryption settings. Then, add *one* item at a time until you reach the desired configuration. If you try to completely configure the AP all at once, and it doesn't work, you might have a difficult time identifying where the problem resides. Resist the temptation to get the AP quickly up and running, and configure the AP in steps. Although this approach might initially take more time, you will save time and a lot of frustration.

CHAPTER SUMMARY

Congratulations, you made it! As you've seen, securing WLANs in the enterprise is no small feat. By now, you're well on your way to building a secure enterprise wireless network, or reasonably secure wireless home network. Remember, most of the problems on a wireless network come from an improperly configured AP, or APs that do not have any security. For enterprise networks, budget enough time to correctly configure your wireless network in the first place. In the long run, you'll save time and money, and will significantly reduce the risk of a wireless hacker attacking your network.

REVIEW QUESTIONS

1. Which of the following methods offers the greatest wireless security?
   a. WEP with 56-bit encryption.
   b. WEP with 128-bit encryption.
   c. WPA with 802.1*x* authentication using certificates.
   d. WPA with a Pre-shared key.
   e. WPA with MAC authentication.
2. Which of the following wireless standards are compatible? (Choose two.)
   a. 802.11a
   b. 802.11b
   c. 802.11i
   d. 802.11g
   e. 802.11n
3. When an AP is configured to use EAP-TLS authentication with certificates in a Windows 2003 environment, which of the following are true? (Choose three.)
   a. Both computer and user certificates are required to authenticate.
   b. Smart cards are required.
   c. An IAS/RADIUS server must perform user authentication.
   d. The AP must support EAP-TLS authentication.
   e. The AP does not have to support EAP-TLS authentication.

4. Which of the following methods can be used to sniff out rogue APs?
   a. Laptop with NetStumbler.
   b. Use existing APs with third-party software to identify rogue APs.
   c. Review the Server Event viewer.
   d. L0phtcrack.
   e. Run a port scan on all IP devices with port 80 open.
5. A majority of wireless problems come from?
   a. Missing smart cards.
   b. Hardware failure on the RADIUS server.
   c. Wi-Fi channel conflicts with neighbors.
   d. Improperly secured APs.
   e. Hardware failure in APs.

9 Firewall Troubleshooting

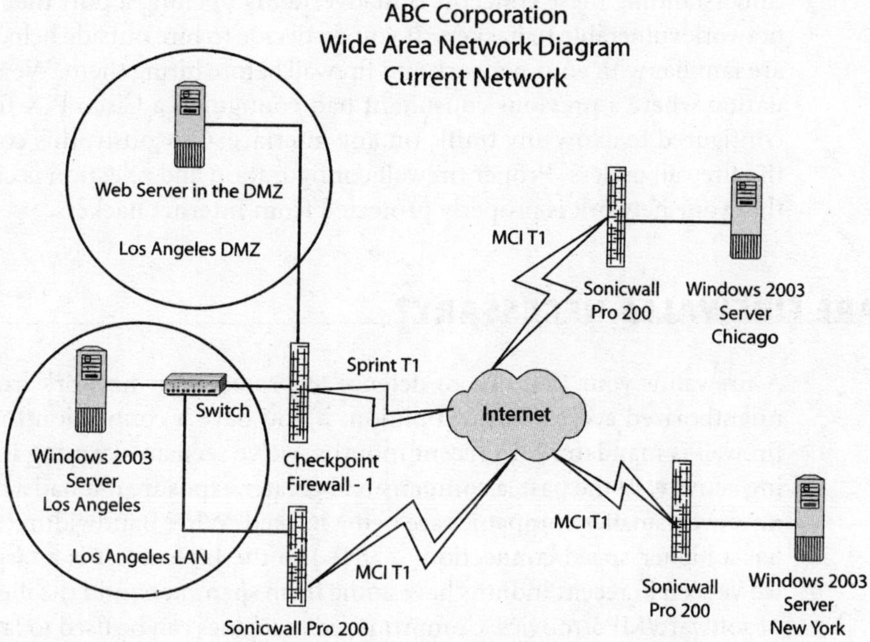

CHAPTER PREVIEW

The first part of this chapter examines proper firewall topology, selection, configuration, maintenance, and developing a hacking recovery plan. Proper firewall selection and maintenance can prevent many firewall-related problems from occurring. We placed this chapter near the end of the book because you must have a good understanding of the following concepts:

- IP routing
- TCP ports
- Network Address Translation (NAT)
- Wide area network (WAN) connectivity (T1, Frame Relay, DSL, cable modems)

A good understanding of these topics will make it easier to troubleshoot firewall problems. If you don't feel comfortable with the preceding list, we suggest obtaining outside help from a consultant or other source. One danger of not understanding these concepts is inadvertently opening a port that will make your network vulnerable to hackers. If you do decide to hire outside help, make sure they are familiar with your network and firewall before hiring them. We ran into one situation where a previous consultant had configured a Cisco PIX firewall that was configured to allow any traffic on any interface. Obviously, this configuration left the firewall useless. Proper firewall configuration and selection is critical to ensure that your network is properly protected from Internet hackers.

ARE FIREWALLS NECESSARY?

A firewall is your first line of defense to protect your network from hackers and unauthorized access. In our opinion, if you have a connection to the Internet, a firewall is mandatory. In recent months, we've seen an alarming increase in hacking activity. In the past, a company had greater exposure if it had a high profile, but now even smaller companies are being hacked. Why? Bandwidth. If your company has a higher-speed connection (>384K) to the Internet, it is a target. Most hacks we've seen in recent months have come from spammers, and the illegal distribution of software/MP3/movies. Compromised machines can be used to launch denial-of-service (DoS) attacks against other computers. If a hacker can obtain access to your network, he can add a rogue user and:

- Use the rogue user to authenticate to your internal mail server to relay spam.
- Use the rogue user to install an unauthorized FTP server and distribute illegal software.
- Compromise the machine to launch a DoS attack against another machine.
- Add a user to the Administrators group.
- Completely compromise the security of your network.
- Install "root kits" to compromise other machines on your network.

This is the case where an ounce of prevention is definitely worth a pound (or metric ton!) of cure. It's much easier to keep hackers out of your network, rather than trying to repair the damage once they're in. If a hacker does manage to compromise a machine, the only way to ensure that the machine is clean is to reformat the hard drives and reload everything from scratch. Some hacking tools can even damage a computer's Basic Input/Output System (BIOS). Of course, you can always try to repair the damage manually, but if you miss a vulnerability, chances are the hacker will get in again.

Firewall Topology

For companies that connect to the Internet, we suggest a dedicated firewall appliance or stand-alone firewall. We do not recommend workstation software firewalls or firewalls that are installed on the server (with the exception of laptop users with direct Internet/wireless connections when they cannot be protected with a corporate firewall). Why? The firewall should be configured to be the "sacrificial lamb" on your network. If a hacker can compromise the firewall and that firewall is installed on your internal server, guess what? Not only has the hacker broken through your firewall, but your server as well. With the server used as a firewall, the "honey pot" (target computer with valuable information) is included with the hack on the firewall. The hacker's work is done. The machine is his and no longer yours. Figure 9.1 shows a Windows 2003 server with two network interface cards (NICs). One NIC is set up as the "public" interface, and the other is used as the "LAN" interface.

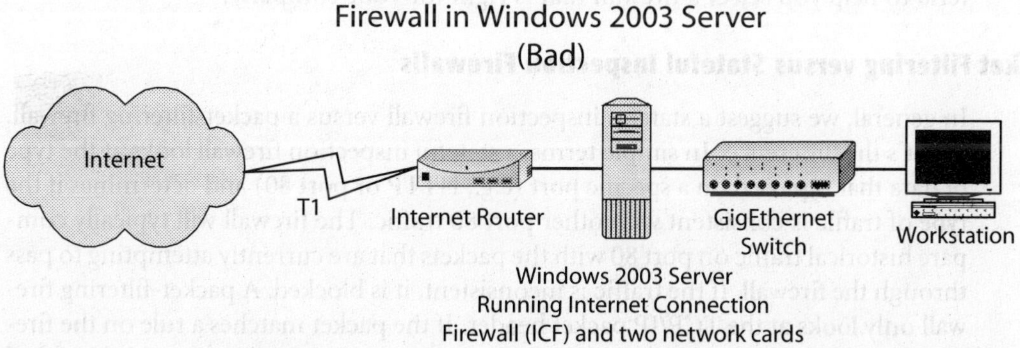

FIGURE 9.1 A firewall installed on a Windows 2003 server that is also used as a file and print server.

The firewall topology in Figure 9.2 is more secure, because only firewall services run on it. If the firewall is hacked, the last thing you want to do is give more information to the hacker about your network configuration. If the hacker manages to compromise the firewall in Figure 9.1, most likely this server will have Active Directory, DNS, and DHCP, not to mention the valuable data residing on the server.

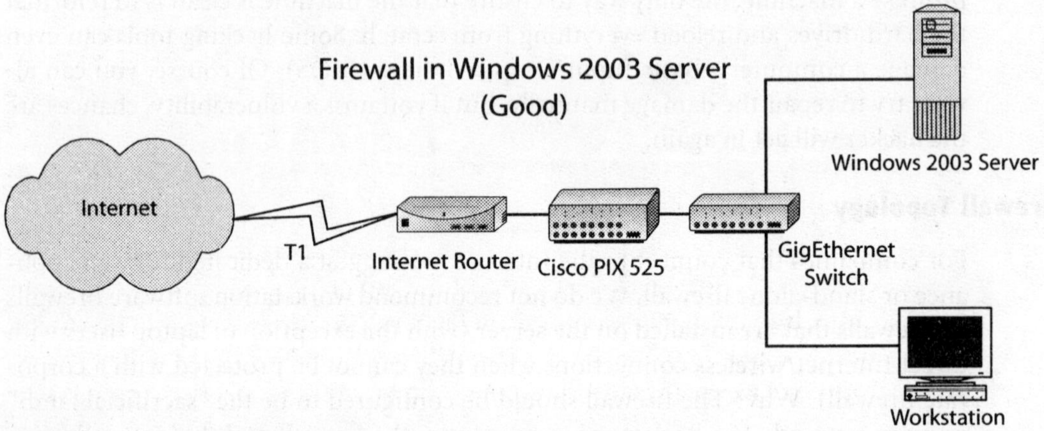

FIGURE 9.2 A dedicated firewall with no other services running on it.

SELECTING THE PROPER FIREWALL

There is a wide range of firewalls from which to choose. They range from low-end software-based home firewalls ($39) to stand-alone dedicated high-speed firewall appliances ($30,000+). Which one is right for your company? Use the following criteria to help you select a firewall that is right for your company.

Packet Filtering versus Stateful Inspection Firewalls

In general, we suggest a stateful inspection firewall versus a packet-filtering firewall. What's the difference? In simple terms, a stateful inspection firewall looks at the type of data that is passed on a specific port (e.g., HTTP or port 80) and determines if the type of traffic is consistent with other port 80 traffic. The firewall will typically compare historical traffic on port 80 with the packets that are currently attempting to pass through the firewall. If the traffic is inconsistent, it is blocked. A packet-filtering firewall only looks at the TCP/IP packet header. If the packet matches a rule on the firewall, it is allowed to pass regardless of whether or not it is consistent with historical traffic on the same port. Some low-end, and almost all mid- and upper-range firewalls perform some type of stateful inspection. Stateful inspection requires more computing power on the firewall, because it does a "deeper" inspection of each packet that passes through. Packet-filtering firewalls are more vulnerable to hacking programs that spoof the IP header information because they only look at the header of the packet, not the information contained therein. IP header spoofing simply replaces the port number in the TCP/IP header with a different (and usually less dangerous) port number. For example, you want to access a Windows server on port TCP 139 (a very dangerous port) to establish a null session with a server, but this port might be closed on a firewall. A hacker can establish a null session on your server with a null (blank) user and password, and list share names and other information on your server. A hacker can use port-spoofing software to change port TCP 139 to TCP 80 (HTTP) to gain access to your network by using a vulnerability in Windows NT/2000/2003 by using a null session to dump the share names on your server.

Packet Filtering versus Stateful Inspection—An Analogy

Let's assume that it is pre 9/11/01 and we're traveling via airplane. We check in a plain brown box that contains contraband. If the inspection process represents the firewall and our checked luggage represents a TCP/IP packet, there is a good chance we will get our checked luggage through the screening process. This rather lax screening process represents a packet-filtering firewall. Based on the outside appearance of the package, it would make it through the screening process. Similarly, the packet-filtering firewall just looks at the TCP/IP header information to determine if the packet is allowed to pass through the firewall or not, regardless of the actual contents of the packet. Now let's move to 9/11/02. By now, all checked baggage must be x-rayed as part of the screening process. This is very similar to a stateful inspection firewall. A stateful inspection firewall reviews the TCP/IP header information, and inspects the information contained in the packet to ensure it is consistent with other packets of a similar type.

Remember, the stateful inspection firewall does a much more thorough investigation of the packets before they are allowed to pass through.

Number of Ports

One of the selection criteria is the number of anticipated firewall ports your company will need. Answer the following questions to help you decide what's best for your company:

- Do you host your own Web servers or other public servers?
- How many connections do you have to the Internet?
- What are your fault tolerance requirements?
- What are your anticipated growth requirements?
- Do you have any WAN connections with other companies?
- Do any of your internal departments (Human Resources) require segregation?

Of course, at a minimum you will need two ports, one for the public side and one for the LAN side. Software-based firewalls like the Symantec Enterprise Firewall and Checkpoint's Firewall-1 and some hardware appliances like Cisco's PIX have the flexibility of adding additional network cards to expand the number of ports running on the firewall. If it's difficult to predict how your company will grow, consider one of these firewalls to ensure that you have the capacity for future growth. Your network and firewall will be easier to manage if you have all of your connections running through a single firewall. However, be aware that if the firewall is compromised, all of your connections are at risk, and you have a single point of failure. We strongly recommend that any external connection from a separate entity be run through a firewall. This protects your company in case the separate entity is hacked, and provides protection for the separate entity in case your company is hacked.

Number of Users

How many users does your firewall have to protect? In general, the greater the number of users, the greater the load on the firewall. If you are running multiple public servers that experience heavy traffic, ensure that you account for this traffic when sizing your firewall. Make sure to purchase a firewall that has the capability for future growth.

Traffic Load

What are the bandwidth requirements for the firewall? In most cases, the bottleneck will be the speed of your Internet connection. If you are running a T3 (45 mb/sec) or higher, a slow firewall can prevent your company from using the entire bandwidth of your expensive Internet connection.

Virtual Private Network (VPN) Traffic

VPN traffic can place an extremely heavy load on your firewall; running multiple VPNs to different locations can bring a firewall to its knees. Make sure your firewall has enough processing power to encrypt/decrypt traffic from all of your VPNs. Note that running higher levels of encryption (3DES) will place a heavier load on the firewall. Most firewall manufacturers have VPN throughput statistics that are one-fourth the throughput of non-VPN traffic. Make sure you consider this if your firewall will run multiple VPNs.

Fault Tolerance

Does your company have 100-percent uptime requirements for your Internet connection? If so, consider a redundant Internet connection with redundant firewalls. If you decide to purchase a redundant connection to the Internet, consider purchasing each line from separate ISPs that use different backbones. We have run into situations where a client thought that they were purchasing redundant connections on different backbones, only to find out that both connections shared a common backbone. If you purchase a redundant firewall, make sure it has an auto-rollover feature in case of an Internet connection failure. If you're running VPNs and have a redundant connection, consider a firewall that has automatic rollover to a secondary firewall in case of an Internet connection failure.

PROPER CONFIGURATION

Of course, any firewall is only as good as its configuration. A low-end properly configured and maintained firewall is arguably more secure than a high-end firewall that is poorly configured. Some firewalls are shipped by default with all ports open, requiring you to close the ports you don't need. Other firewalls are shipped with all ports closed, requiring you to selectively open ports as necessary. In general, a firewall that has all of the ports closed by default will be more secure. Although this firewall might be more difficult to initially configure, it will be more secure because each port must be selectively opened, rather than attempting to shut down unnecessary ports. Some firewalls allow all outbound traffic by default. We suggest only allowing necessary outbound traffic. This will make it more difficult for a hacker to compromise your network if dangerous ports are closed. The golden rule for firewall configuration is to close everything, and open ports as necessary. This method of firewall configuration is much more secure than having all ports open, and then attempting a selective shutdown of ports.

DANGEROUS PORTS FOR WINDOWS

Make sure the ports listed in Table 9.1 are not open on your firewall.

TABLE 9.1 Particularly Dangerous Ports

Port	*Service*
TCP and UDP 135–139	NetBIOS
TCP 389	LDAP
TCP 445	SNMP
TCP 3268	AD Global Catalog
TCP 3389	Terminal Server
6667 and 6668	Internet Relay Chat (IRC)

These ports are particularly dangerous because they can reveal sensitive information about your network. One of the best books we've seen on hackers is *Hacking Exposed Network Security Secrets & Solutions* by Stuart McClure, Joel Scambray, and George Kurtz. This is a must-have book if you want to defend your network against hackers. Do not allow Terminal Server access from the Internet. Terminal Server is a service that runs on the Windows Server platform that allows a remote session to the server, similar to pcAnywhere™ or WinVNC™. We see this port open time and time again. Some administrators feel that it's all right to allow Terminal Server access if you restrict access to a certain IP or range of IP addresses. Although this is better than allowing any user to attempt to connect with a Terminal server, it is relatively easy for a hacker to spoof the IP address and connect to a Terminal server session. If you need remote access to a Terminal server or similar session, we suggest creating a VPN session first, and then use the VPN tunnel to connect to the Terminal Server session. By using the VPN, all of the traffic is encrypted and is much more difficult to hack compared to allowing a Terminal Server session without encryption.

Some firewalls (SonicWALL) allow all outbound traffic by default. We strongly recommend closing this hole and only enabling the necessary outbound ports like the ones listed in Table 9.2.

TABLE 9.2 Necessary Outbound Ports for Most Companies

Port	*Service*
20 and 21	File Transfer Protocol (FTP)
25	Simple Mail Transfer Protocol (SMTP)
80	Web HTTP
443	Web Encrypted HTTPS

Of course, your company might require additional outbound ports. You might think it is unnecessary to close down outbound ports, but if a hacker ever compromises one of your internal systems, he often will initiate an outbound connection from the compromised system on a lesser-known port. At the very least, if you have logging turned on on the outbound ports, you will have a better chance of catching the hacking activity sooner. Be warned that if you attempt to close down outbound ports on an existing firewall, be prepared for some "tuning" time, and possibly upset users until you get the necessary outbound ports open on the firewall.

FIREWALL MAINTENANCE

It's vital to stay current with firewall software/firmware updates—new vulnerabilities are discovered all the time. When a new version of the firewall is released, consider upgrading the latest version after it's been proven stable. The longer a firewall is out in the public, the longer hackers have a chance to crack it. Your firewall is only as good as the last patch. Make sure to review the logs on a regular basis to get a good feel for what type of traffic on the firewall is "normal" and "abnormal."

Stay Current with Patches/Firmware

After the firewall is properly configured, there is a tendency to set it and forget it. Do not make this mistake! Like any other piece of network equipment, the firewall should be properly backed up and maintained. New vulnerabilities/bugs are discovered every day on firewalls. When a new vulnerability is discovered, you might have only a few weeks to patch the firewall before someone develops a program that can exploit this vulnerability. Vendors release patches to correct these issues, but they obviously have to be installed to be effective. Some firewalls such as SonicWALL have the capability to notify you when a new firmware release is available. Unfortunately, firewall patches are becoming like virus patterns—a firewall is only as good as its latest patch.

Review the Logs on a Regular Basis

It is important to review the firewall logs on a regular basis. Some firewalls store the logs on a local hard disk, and the firewall can e-mail logs to a specified user. Some firewalls like the PIX require a Syslog server, if you want to save any historical logs. There are analysis tools on the market that can import log files from different firewalls and generate reports and graphs that display traffic patterns, utilization, and traffic type. For example:

www.stonylakesolutions.com/
http://eiqnetworks.com/products/products.shtml

It's important to get a good "feeling" of the type of traffic that your firewall is subject to on a daily basis. This will make it much easier to determine if any questionable traffic is "normal" or "abnormal." Consider the following questions:

- Does heavy traffic on the firewall indicate that you are under a DoS attack?
- Does a drop in outbound mail traffic indicate a problem with your internal mail server?
- Does a drop in inbound traffic indicate a problem with your MX record?

- Should I be concerned with a Sub Seven attack on the firewall?
- Should I worry about particularly heavy mail traffic from a specific range of IP addresses?

These types of questions will be easier to answer if you are familiar with the type of traffic that your firewall encounters. When troubleshooting any firewall problem, the firewall logs are your best friend. Most firewalls log a wealth of information about the type of traffic that flows through the firewall. Any firewall troubleshooting session should begin with a review of the firewall logs.

Firewall Backup

Anytime you make changes to the firewall, make sure to back up the configuration. We also suggest making a "manual" backup; that is, a Word document or other notes that document the firewall configuration. Some firewalls have the capability to save their configurations in encrypted form, but for one reason or another, you might not be able to restore the configuration when you need it most. This seems especially true when you are attempting to restore a firewall configuration saved with an earlier version of the software or firmware. One of the most frustrating tasks an IT manager will face is rebuilding a firewall configuration from scratch. It's a time-consuming process that usually is never done correctly on the first attempt, unless the firewall configuration is extremely simple. It's difficult enough rebuilding the firewall with good notes, but it can be a nightmare if you have to rebuild the firewall configuration from scratch. We suggest labeling each interface with an IP address and name of the connection. This will make it easier to identify the connections in case they are accidentally disconnected. This is even more important if the firewall has multiple interfaces.

Run Port Scans on a Regular Basis

Whenever you make a change to the firewall, it's a good idea to run a port scan on the firewall to ensure you haven't accidentally opened a critical port. The port scan will help you determine how your firewall "appears" from the outside.

HAVE A HACKING RECOVERY PLAN IN PLACE

You've been hacked! Now what? Probably, the first emotion to set in is panic, closely followed by anger. We suggest having a hacking recovery plan in place before a hack occurs. That way, you can follow the plan with a cool head, and your next step will be dictated by logic, not emotion. A hacking recovery plan, like a disaster recovery plan, should be a part of any IT documentation,. Developing a hacking recovery plan is outside the scope of this book, but here are a few suggestions:

Perform regular security audits. Just like an external CPA firm, consider hiring an outside source to perform an IT audit. This audit should be performed at least annually. Work with the outside company to implement their suggestions to improve your network security.

Implement firewall monitoring. Some firewalls either maintain their own logs or have the capability to send the log information to a Syslog server or other external logging server. Of course, it's a double-edged sword to turn up the logging level, because it places a heavier load on the firewall and requires more storage space. Consider implementing logging access to sensitive information and critical files.

Assess the damage. You've been hacked. How do you know you've been hacked? How did the hacker get in? What has changed? What was he after? Where's your latest backup? Once a hack has occurred, it's a good idea to isolate your network from any outside connections to prevent further damage. This is the point where it's most critical to document what has happened. This will help you close the holes, repair the damage, and prevent the hacker from gaining access to your network again.

The following are some symptoms that can tip you off to a hack:

Review the firewall logs. Review the firewall logs on a regular basis. Look for port scans, Sub Seven attacks, and other hacking tools that hackers use on a regular basis. Although port scans and other attacks are common, make note of the IP addresses to see if they come from a consistent location. Of course, a hacker will probably spoof his IP address to hide his identity, but it's a good place to start. Refer to the Internet Assigned Numbers Authority at *www.iana.org/ipaddress/ip-addresses.htm* for links to determine the ISP that was assigned a block of IP addresses.

Check the Run and Run Once keys. Check the registry keys in the following locations:

HKEY_LOCAL_MACHINE\SOFTWARE\Microsoft\Windows\Current Version\RunHKEY_CURRENT_USER\Software\Microsoft\Windows\CurrentVersion\Run

HKEY_LOCAL_MACHINE\SOFTWARE\Microsoft\Windows\CurrentVersion\Policies\Explorer\Run

Check these areas for any unauthorized programs loading from these locations. Often, a compromised machine will load a number of hacker tools from these locations when the computer starts up. You can download the Autoruns utility from *www.sysinternals.com/ntw2k/freeware/autoruns.shtml* that will display every program or process that is set to start automatically on your computer.

Check for root kits. Root kits are used by hackers to run a remote command shell and other hacking tools. Look for batch files in the root directory, winnt or winnt\system32 directory.

Check for hidden files off the Recycle Bin directory. Often, a hacker will hide his tools in hidden files and folders off the Recycle Bin directory. Review this location on a regular basis to verify that unauthorized programs are not loading from this location.

Unusually heavy loads on a server. If your server suddenly responds slowly and appears sluggish, you might be under a hack attack. The server might be used as a spam relay or as a zombie to launch a DoS attack against another machine.

Rogue users. Check your user list on a regular basis. Make sure you delete users when they leave the company. When you add a new user, we suggest entering a description of his or her title and other related information. This will make it easier to spot a rogue user on your network, because he or she usually will have a missing description.

Check the Administrators group. Check the Administrators group and other privileged groups on your network, and verify that only authorized members belong to the group.

Patch the holes. Determine how the hacker gained access to your network in the first place, and patch the hole(s). If necessary, get outside help. If you do not patch the hole, the hacker will get in again and you'll have to start from scratch. During the initial phase of any attack, we suggest turning off all external communication to your network until you can determine the point of entry. Don't forget to check for any rogue wireless access points (WAPs).

Repair the damage. Once the hacker has compromised a machine, it's no longer yours. The only way to ensure that all of the hacker programs are removed is to format the drives and reload the operating system from scratch. If you try to remove the programs manually, and you miss one program, the hacker will get in again. Instead of formatting the hard drives, consider replacing the drives, so you (and the authorities) can examine the compromised machine after the crisis is over. A lot of valuable forensic data are lost because a company will reformat a drive rather than replacing it with a new drive. Preserving this information will help you prevent future attacks, by examining the programs loaded onto the machine. It might help authorities catch the hacker.

Additional monitoring. If you suspect a hack, consider turning up the log settings on your firewall, internal server, and any other network device that's capable of logging information. Note that hackers sometimes use utilities to clear any Event logs to cover their tracks. Consider backing up the logs to a different location in case the hacker uses a log-clearing utility.

Notify authorities. No one wants to admit he or she has been hacked, but it's a good idea to notify authorities if you suspect a break-in. The more information you can provide authorities, the better. At the very least, you might prevent another unsuspecting user or company from getting attacked by the same hacker.

Review the plan on a regular basis. Just like a disaster recovery plan, make sure the hacking recovery plan is reviewed on a regular basis. Changes in technology, infrastructure, operating system, and business model will have a significant impact on any recovery plan. We suggest reviewing your recovery plan at least annually or more often if your computing infrastructure changes on a regular basis.

BASIC FIREWALL TROUBLESHOOTING TOOLS

Whenever you have to troubleshoot a firewall issue, consider these tools to resolve the problem. The firewall logs can provide detailed information about the traffic passing through your firewall.

Firewall Log Files

Anytime you have a connectivity issue with a firewall—trying to pass traffic through it, attempting a VPN connection, setting up a public server, or tracing down a suspected hack attack—check the firewall logs. The logs are your best friend when it comes to troubleshooting a firewall problem. For example, you might need a new application to connect through the firewall, but you don't have any idea about the port(s) that must be open on the firewall. One of the ways we overcome this difficulty is to complete the following steps to get the application working:

1. Attempt to run the application.
2. Review the firewall logs.
3. Determine the port(s) that the application is attempting to use.
4. Create a rule on the firewall to allow traffic to pass on the specified ports.
5. Test the application.

You might have to repeat these steps a couple of times before the application works. Sometimes, you have to open multiple ports on the firewall to get the application to work. The logs can provide help when creating a VPN to remote locations.

Syslog Servers

Some firewalls (PIX) hold a limited amount of logging information, but can forward log information onto a Syslog server. If you want historical tracking of firewall activity, make sure that you set up a Syslog server when you install the firewall. This Syslog server can provide valuable troubleshooting information and record past hacking activity.

TROUBLESHOOTING SCENARIOS

With proper maintenance and monitoring, you can avoid most firewall and hack attacks. Make sure you review your rules and firewall log files on a regular basis.

Scenario 1 UNABLE TO ACCESS ONLINE BANKING SITE

Facts

- New Windows Server 2003 network with XP workstations.
- Symantec Enterprise Firewall version 7.04.
- 768 SDSL connection to the Internet.

Symptoms

When a user tries to access an online banking site, she eventually receives an error from Internet Explorer (IE) that the page cannot be displayed.

Questions to Ask

Q: Can other pages be displayed? A: Yes, other Web sites work fine.

Q: Has anything changed? A: Yes, this is a brand-new network.

Troubleshooting Steps

1. **Verify the problem.** We received the same error when we tried to access an online banking site.
2. **Try other sites.** We were able to get to other Web sites.
3. **Try to access the online banking site from another workstation.** To narrow down the problem, we tried accessing the online banking site from an-

other workstation. The site timed out on this workstation as well. What does this tell you? Most likely, this problem is not workstation specific, and is more of a global or networkwide problem. If the site worked properly from the second workstation, we would look more closely at the IE settings on both machines.

4. **Check the firewall logs.** At this point, we suspect a networkwide problem, so we check the firewall logs. We had the user attempt to connect to the online banking site and then refreshed the firewall logs. The firewall logs indicated that the user was attempting an HTTPS session that was denied by the firewall.

Resolution

We modified the rule that allowed HTTP. To configure HTTPS on the Symantec Enterprise Firewall, select the http* protocol, and click on the Configure button (see Figure 9.3). HTTPS is the secure sockets layer for HTTP. When you establish an HTTPS session, you get the lock icon on the lower right of IE.

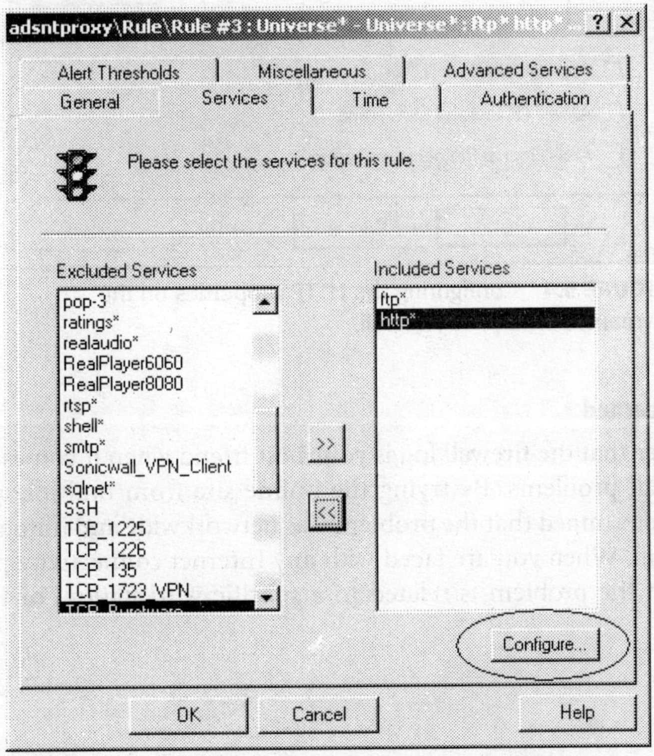

FIGURE 9.3 Configuring HTTP on the Symantec Enterprise Firewall.

When you click on the Configure button the screen in Figure 9.4 will appear. Check the "Allow HTTP over valid SSL on the following ports," and select the appropriate ports for SSL. In this example, we have selected SSL on the standard ports 443 and 563.

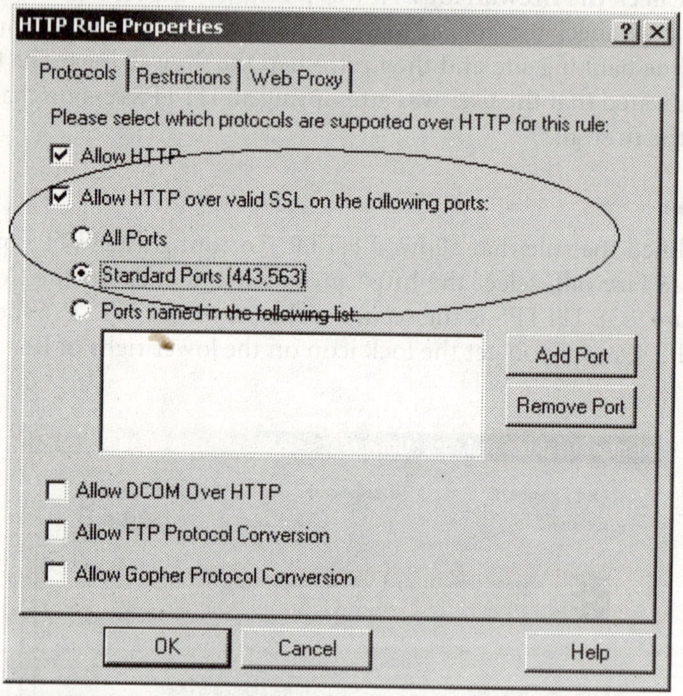

FIGURE 9.4 Configuring the HTTP properties on the Symantec Enterprise Firewall.

Lessons Learned

Remember that the firewall log is your best friend when it comes to troubleshooting firewall problems. By trying the online site from multiple workstations, we quickly determined that the problem was networkwide and immediately suspected the firewall. When you are faced with any Internet connectivity problem, first determine if the problem is related to a specific workstation, or is a networkwide problem.

Scenario 2 UNABLE TO ACCESS THE INTERNET

Facts

- Existing SonicWALL SOHO3. It has been in place for one year.
- Windows 2003 network with 20 XP workstations.
- The company has a 384K SDSL connection to the Internet.

Symptoms

When anyone tries to access the Internet, IE times out and displays an error message that the page could not be displayed.

Questions to Ask

Q: Has anything changed? A: No.

Q: Was the Internet working before? A: Yes, yesterday it was working fine.

Troubleshooting Steps

1. **Verify the problem from multiple workstations.** Verify that this is a networkwide problem. Attempts to get to the Internet from multiple workstations fail.
2. **Check the firewall.** SonicWALL uses a Web-based management interface. We opened a browser and pointed it to the SonicWALL, but there was no response. IE timed out with an error message that the page could not be displayed.
3. **Verify that the line is up.** At this point, we suspected the firewall, but just in case, it's a good idea to make sure the line is functioning properly. We disconnected the firewall from the DSL router and connected it to our laptop. When setting up any firewall, we strongly recommend labeling the firewall with all of the IP addresses. This makes it very easy to identify the IP addresses of the firewall. This also saves time because you don't have to search for the paperwork on the DSL configuration. Fortunately, the firewall interfaces were labeled, so we simply changed the IP address, subnet mask, and default gateway of our laptop to match the firewall. After we verified we had link integrity on the laptop, we were able to get out to the Internet with no problems. While we were on the Internet, we went to *www.dslreports.com* and used their bandwidth meter to check their line speed. Both upload and download speeds tested very close to the 384K speed, so we knew the line was properly working. Anytime we install a new Internet line, we use *www.dslreports.com* to check the speed of the line and verify it is running at the correct speed.

4. **Troubleshoot the SonicWALL.** At this point, we knew that the DSL line was fine, and the SonicWALL was most likely the problem. However, the SonicWALL was unreachable on its configured IP address. On a hunch, we connected our laptop to the SonicWALL LAN port, and then reconfigured our laptop to use the following IP address parameters:

IP Address	Subnet Mask	Default Gateway
192.168.168.100	255.255.255.0	192.168.168.168

This IP address was selected because the SonicWALL ships from the factory with a default address of 192.168.168.168.

Resolution

After we configured the IP address of the laptop, we were able to reach the SonicWALL on 192.168.168.168. After reviewing the SonicWALL configuration, it looked like the SonicWALL was reset to the factory defaults. After reconfiguring the SonicWALL with the proper configuration, users could access the Internet again. A new firmware release was available for this firewall, which we installed and tested.

Lessons Learned

Occasionally, we see this type of problem with SonicWALLs, where they are magically reset to their factory default settings. It seems more common with the lower-end TELE3 and SOHO3 and less common with the higher-end Pro200, Pro230, Pro3060, and Pro4060 models. If you have difficulty connecting to a SonicWALL, try the factory default IP address first. If that doesn't work, try resetting the firewall to the factory defaults by pressing the Reset button for 10 seconds. If your firewall does not have a Reset button, refer to the product documentation for the procedure to reset the firewall. On rare occasions, the firmware on the firewall might be corrupted. This is usually indicated by the test light remaining on after the firewall reboots. You can replace corrupted firmware on a SonicWALL by completing the following steps:

1. Disconnect the power cable on the SonicWALL .
2. Wait 30 seconds.
3. Press and hold the Reset button, and plug in the power cable at the same time.
4. Hold the Reset button until the test light stops blinking and remains lit.
5. Open a Web browser to 192.168.168.168.
6. You should receive a "Firmware appears to be corrupted." error message.
7. Click Browse to a File Open dialog box.

8. Browse to the location of the firmware file. A rescue version of the firmware should be included on the CD-ROM that ships with the SonicWALL .
9. After restoring the firmware, update the SonicWALL with the latest firmware.

Note that these steps are for the SOHO TZW. The procedure for your model might vary.

Scenario 3 USERS ARE UNABLE TO CONNECT TO THE INTERNET

Facts

- Recently installed Symantec Enterprise Firewall 7.04.
- Windows Server 2003 network with a mix of Windows 2000 and Windows XP workstations.
- T1 connection to the Internet, using a Cisco 2620 router.

Symptoms

When a user tries to connect to the Internet, he receives an error from his browser that the page could not be displayed.

Questions to Ask

Q: What has changed? A: A new firewall was installed, but now we can't connect to the Internet.

Q: Was it working before? A: Yes, the Internet was working fine before the new firewall was installed.

Troubleshooting Steps

1. **Verify the obvious.** A check of two workstations returned the same error that the page could not be displayed.
2. **Review the lights on the router.** It's not a bad idea to at least double check the lights on the WIC T1 card on the Cisco router. In this case, the AL(arm) light was off on the WIC T1 card.
3. **Check the firewall rules.** A quick review of the firewall indicated that a rule was correctly entered to allow Internet access.
4. **Check the firewall log.** The firewall log was checked. Every time someone tried to access the Internet, a series of error messages like the one in Figure 9.5 was displayed.

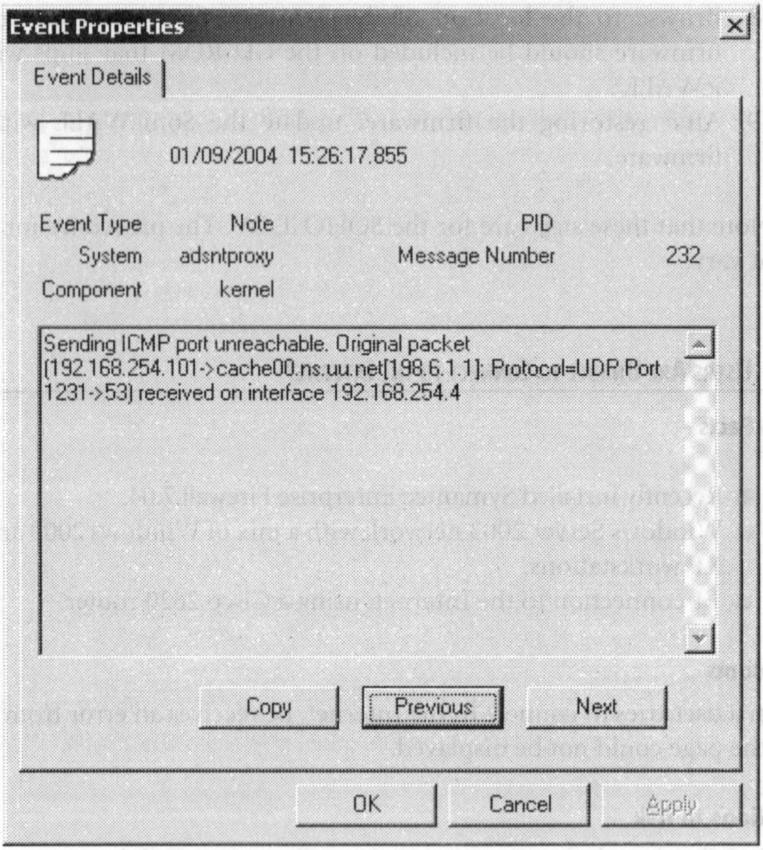

FIGURE 9.5 Error message displayed in the log file while attempting to connect to the Internet.

Firewall logs can be quite cryptic the first time you look at them. The error text "Sending ICMP port unreachable" indicated that a Internet Control Message Protocol (ICMP or ping) port was unreachable. The second part of the error message displays the source (192.168.254.101) and the destination (198.6.1.1) of the packet. The last portion of the error message lists the protocol that was attempted; in this case, the source port was UDP 1231, and the destination port was UDP 53. In general, when troubleshooting a firewall problem, you usually look at the destination port (in this case, UDP 53).

5. **What's UDP 53?** Let's assume for a moment that you didn't know what type of traffic resides on UDP 53. How could you find this out? You could perform a search on *www.google.com* for UDP 53 or refer to *www.iana.org/assignments/port-numbers* for port numbers. Hint: We suggest printing the port assignments from *www.iana.org/assignments/port-numbers* just to have it handy. It's an excellent reference to determine port numbers. It

turns out the UDP 53 is the port for Domain Name Server (DNS). This port is used for resolving IP addresses to names.

6. **Verify DNS at the workstation.** At this point, it looks like we have a problem with name resolution. How could we test this? From a workstation, you can perform the following tests:
   a. **Ping a known IP address on the Internet.** Assuming that the firewall does not block ping packets, ping an IP address on the Internet. It's a good idea to memorize a few valid, reliable, and pingable IP addresses on the Internet for testing purposes. We typically use 198.6.1.1 and 198.6.1.2, which are UUNet's DNS servers. The syntax for ping is:

      ```
      ping 198.6.1.1
      ```

      Replies to ping requests indicate they are alive and responding. What does this tell us? The T1 is up and running. The router is most likely properly configured. A rule exists on the firewall to allow ping packets. There is good connectivity between the workstation, switch, and firewall. When performing a simple ping test, always ping by IP address first, and then by name.
   b. **Ping that same IP address by name.** If you refer back to Figure 9.5, the IP address 198.6.1.1 resolves to cache00.ns.uu.net. The next step is to try to ping by name instead of IP address:

      ```
      ping cache00.ns.uu.net
      ```

      Normally, the name cache00.ns.uu.net should resolve to an IP address, and the DNS server should respond. In this case, ping replies with a "host unreachable" error message. Since we are able to ping by IP address and not by name, we most likely have a name resolution problem.

Resolution

The Symantec Enterprise Firewall uses a DNS proxy for DNS requests, so you have to configure your IP address settings to point to the internal IP address of the firewall for DNS requests. The firewall proxies the DNS request and then passes this request to the Internet. It's important to remember this fact if you ever replace this firewall with another vendor's firewall, because you must change the DNS address on your network to get Internet access working.

Lessons Learned

Don't forget ping. It's a simple yet valuable tool to help you solve complex problems. Even without any knowledge of this particular firewall, you can determine you have a name resolution problem simply by using the `ping` utility.

Scenario 4 PROBLEMS WITH A SONICWALL PRO 4060

Facts

- New SonicWALL Pro 4060 replacing Checkpoint Firewall-1.
- Relatively new firewall on the market.
- SonicWALL Pro 4060 will also replace existing SonicWALL Pro 200 that is currently used for VPN traffic.
- The Pro 4060 firmware version is 2.0.0.1E.
- This installation was attempted in early 10/2003.
- Current network diagram (see Figure 9.6).
- Proposed network diagram (see Figure 9.7).

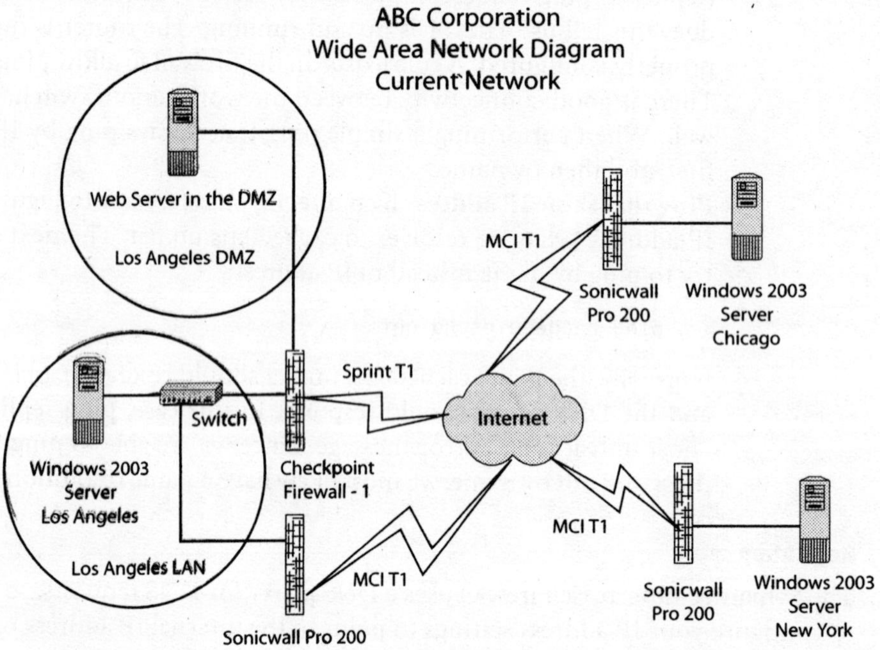

FIGURE 9.6 ABC's current network diagram.

The plan is to consolidate both the existing Checkpoint Firewall-1 and SonicWALL Pro 200 in Los Angeles using the SonicWALL Pro 4060. ABC Corporation uses the Firewall-1 firewall to handle its Web server and inbound/outbound mail traffic. The SonicWALL Pro 200 in Los Angeles is used for VPN traffic to Chicago and New York. The SonicWALL Pro 4060 was selected because it has six ports, hardware failover, and the capability to load balance two WAN connections. ABC Corporation also plans to open a new office in San Francisco, so after the Pro 4060

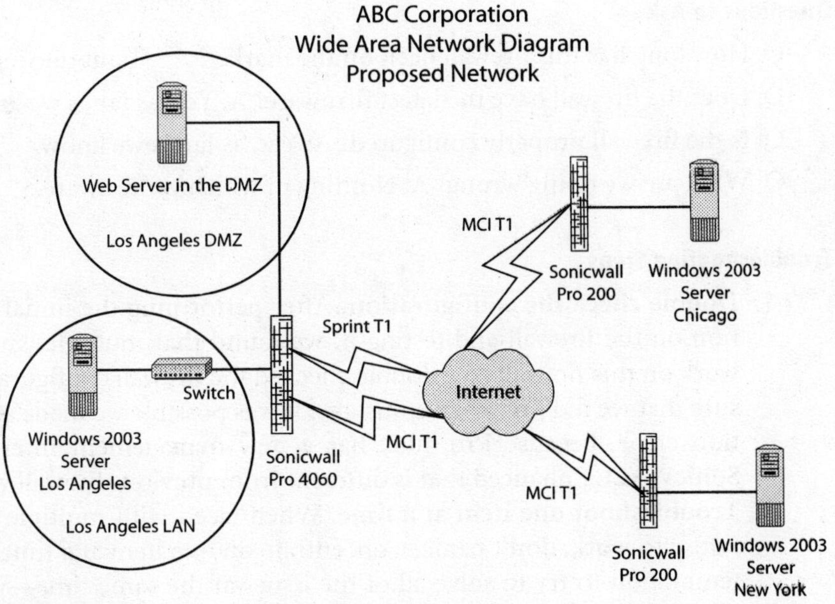

FIGURE 9.7 ABC's proposed network diagram.

is installed in Los Angeles, the old Pro 200 will be moved to the new San Francisco office. The Pro 4060 is around $4,300 and represents great value for its feature set. To get this functionality, you typically are in PIX territory that starts at $8,000 and goes up from there.

Symptoms

Unfortunately, during the installation of the SonicWALL Pro 4060, a number of issues have arisen.

- **WAN failover/load balancing.** When load balancing or failover is activated, users cannot access the Internet.
- **VPN does not work on secondary WAN port.** The Pro 4060 has the option of designating one of the WAN ports for VPN traffic. If the designated WAN port is not the primary port, the firewall does not establish the VPN tunnels.
- **Outbound DMZ access to the Internet.** A rule exists to allow the Web server access to the Internet, but the Web server cannot connect. The Web server must access the Internet to download the latest virus patterns. A rule was also set up to allow public access to the Web server. This is working.

Questions to Ask

Q: How long has this firewall been on the market? A: About one month.

Q: Does the firewall have the latest firmware? A: Yes, as far as we know.

Q: Is the firewall properly configured? A: Yes, as far as we know.

Q: What are we doing wrong? A: Nothing of which we're aware.

Troubleshooting Steps

1. **Double check the configuration.** After performing the initial configuration on the firewall and testing it, we found that multiple issues did not work on this firewall. We double checked the firewall configuration to ensure that we did not make a mistake. It was possible we made a configuration error, because Pro 4060 has a new management interface called SonicWALL Enhanced that is different from previous firewall versions.
2. **Troubleshoot one item at a time.** When faced with multiple issues that refuse to work, don't panic. Concentrate on one item at a time. Resist the temptation to try to solve all of the issues at the same time—you'll most likely end up more confused. When troubleshooting complex problems, take good notes. Write down what works and what doesn't. That way, you won't get stuck in a troubleshooting loop. Your notes will help tech support solve your problem (hopefully) faster.
3. **If you become stuck, move on.** As important as it is to concentrate on one problem at a time, if you become stuck and have tried everything you can think of, move on to the next problem. Alternately, sometimes it helps to take a break, get some food, or get some sleep. Many times, we've solved problems 10 minutes after leaving the office, because we could think with a clear head. Sometimes, a solution to a current problem will help you fix another previously unsolvable problem. Remember, take good notes so you don't become stuck in a loop!
4. **Replace the Checkpoint firewall.** The client's Checkpoint firewall really needed replacing, because the hardware was needed in a different department. The problems we were experiencing with the Pro 4060 mostly prevented us from consolidating the Pro 200 and Checkpoint firewalls. As a temporary solution, we decided to replace the Pro 4060 as a straight swap with the Checkpoint firewall. Even if the firewall was working correctly, we still recommend this phased approach, because it gives you a fallback plan in case things don't go smoothly.
5. **Testing load balancing.** Our first indication of trouble is when we tried to activate the load-balancing feature of the firewall. It's relatively simple to activate load balancing on the Pro 4060. You designate a port on the Pro 4060 as a secondary WAN port, enter the correct IP address, and then de-

fine how you want to use the port. With the Pro 4060, you can use the secondary WAN port as a failover port, or as a load-balancing port. If you select load balancing, you can load balance traffic by the following methods:

a. **Round-robin based.** Outbound requests are alternated between the two WAN ports.
b. **Spillover based.** When the primary connection exceeds a user-defined traffic in kbits/sec, a secondary interface is used.
c. **Percentage based.** You can determine the percentage that each WAN interface will be used.

When we disconnected the WAN connection from the old SonicWALL Pro 200, connected to the secondary port on the Pro 4060, and activated load balancing, users suddenly could not access the Internet. We knew the secondary line was working properly, because all of the VPN traffic using the SonicWALL 200 was working. We double checked the IP settings (IP address, subnet mask, DNS, and default gateway) on the secondary WAN port on the Pro 4060, and everything was correct. At this point, we suspected a bug with the Pro 4060.

6. **Testing the VPN.** We decided to move on to the VPN connection to see if we could get it running. We duplicated the VPN settings from the Pro 200 and entered them into the Pro 4060. The Pro 4060 allows you to designate which WAN port the firewall will use for VPN traffic. We selected the secondary WAN interface for VPN traffic. Unfortunately, the tunnels did not come up. We first suspected that some of the VPN information was entered incorrectly. We double-checked our settings and none of the tunnels could be established. As a troubleshooting step, we reconfigured the firewall and set up the VPN on the primary WAN interface and tunnels came up! At this point, it looks like we had some serious problems using the secondary WAN port.
7. **Web server testing.** ABC Corporation hosts their Web server. We created a NAT translation and rules to allow Internet users access to the Web server. This was working, however the Web server itself could not access to Internet. The Web server needed Internet access to update its virus pattern.
8. **Call technical support.** With multiple items not working, we called tech support. We explained our experiences with the three outstanding issues. We configured the firewall to allow tech support to access the firewall using HTTPS. They reviewed our configuration, and indicated that our configuration looked good, but all three issues remained. They indicated that they were about to release a new firmware version. We decided to wait until this firmware version was released to see if it solved our problems.
9. **Upgrade to Firmware 2.0.0.3E release date 11/12/03.** Installing the firmware on the Pro 4060 fixed the load balancing problem, but the other

two issues remained. We called back into Technical Support and had our case escalated. We were promised a call back, but never received one. After a week, we decided to call our SonicWALL sales representative to see if they could assist. The sales representative connected us with technical support.

10. **Troubleshoot with technical support.** We connected the secondary WAN interface to the Pro 4060 for testing. We enabled HTTPS management from both primary and secondary WAN interfaces. From this test, it was learned that even tech support was unable to manage the Pro 4060 on the secondary WAN port, even though we enabled management on the secondary port. (They could access the SonicWALL on the primary WAN port). This was consistent with the problems we had with the VPN connection. We theorized that the Pro 4060 was not respecting the origin of the packets coming in from the secondary WAN port. Most likely, the SonicWALL would "answer" on the Primary port regardless if the request came in from the primary or secondary port.
11. **Upgrade to Firmware 2.0.1.3E release date 12/23/03.** Technical support notified us that a new release of their firmware was available, which we installed.

Resolution

After upgrading the firmware to 2.0.1.3E, the VPN problem was fixed. We were able to fix the Web server Internet access in the DMZ by creating a rule to allow DNS requests to pass through the firewall.

Lessons Learned

Unfortunately, it took over three months to resolve this problem, but persistence pays off. Usually, we do not recommend any product that was recently released, but the Pro 4060 was such a good fit for this client that we decided to take a chance. Of course, when possible, stay away from new products and let others find out the bugs. If you do become stuck in this unfortunate situation, don't be afraid to become the "squeaky wheel" with tech support; otherwise, you might get lost in the shuffle. For more complex installations, try to implement the project in phases, and always have a fallback plan in case things don't go smoothly.

Scenario 5 PIX Firewall Scrambles Rules

Facts

- Brand-new Cisco PIX 525 with one four-port Ethernet card.
- Cisco IOS 6.3(1) unrestricted version.
- This firewall will replace an existing Symantec Enterprise Firewall (SEF).

- When the firewall is fully functional, it will have eight active ports, which will require the addition of another four-port Ethernet card.
- All of the rules on the old firewall were printed, so they can be duplicated on the PIX firewall.
- Primary management of the firewall will be through Cisco's PIX Device Manager (PDM), a Web-based management utility that allows the PIX to be configured using a GUI interface. It was decided to install the PDM to make it easier for the client to make any future modifications on the firewall. As you probably know, the PIX can also be managed using the traditional text-based "telnet" interface. Most PIX administrators prefer the telnet interface. The syntax is similar to the Cisco IOS for routers, but the differences are significant enough to drive a novice user crazy. To reduce the learning curve for the client, the decision was made to use the PDM. In theory, both the PDM and the telnet interface can be used interchangeably.

Symptoms

Corresponding rules were added to the PIX using the PDM. After entering the configuration, the firewall refused to work. One particularly troublesome symptom was the descriptions for each rule. Using the PDM, you can document each rule by entering a description for each rule. However, when the configuration was saved to the firewall, the description for a rule appeared on the following rule.

Questions to Ask

Q: Why is this happening? A: Unsure.

Q: Are the rules correctly entered? A: As far as we know, the rules are correctly entered.

Troubleshooting Steps

1. **Verify the obvious.** After entering the configuration, the firewall refused to work correctly. Access to the Internet was intermittent at best, and access through the firewall was very unstable. We carefully double-checked our rules to ensure they were an equivalent match for the rules on the old firewall.
2. **Start with one simple rule.** We tried deleting all of the rules and entered two simple rules. The firewall still scrambled the descriptions of the two rules we entered every time the configuration was saved to the firewall.
3. **Contact Cisco technical support.** At this point, we suspected that something was very wrong with the firewall, either software or hardware. We contacted Cisco tech support for help. We strongly suggest keeping any Cisco equipment on a maintenance contract. This contract entitles you to

technical support and free upgrades of any new software releases. It also provides for quick replacement should the problem turn out to be hardware related. Before you call Cisco tech support, it's a good idea to get the following:

a. Serial number of the unit.
b. Issue the `show version` command. This will display the version number of the software you are running on the Cisco hardware.
c. Issue the `show running` command. This will dump the current running configuration of the unit.
d. If you already have a login to Cisco's Web site, you can open the case by going to *www.cisco.com/tac/*. You can usually open a technical support case faster on the Web than by placing a phone call.

4. **Technical support will usually ask for these items.** After explaining the situation to the tech support person, we were asked to e-mail the configuration to technical support. We explained our concern with rules descriptions jumping to the next rule, and that we were using the PDM to configure the PIX. This particular technical support person did not know the PDM that well and preferred to configure the PIX using the telnet interface rather than the PDM. At first it was thought that the PDM version required an update, but it was later determined that the version of the IOS we were running IOS 6.3(1) had problems if the PDM was used to configure the PIX. The tech support person e-mailed us a new copy of the IOS 6.3.3.100 for us to upload to the PIX.
5. **Upload IOS 6.3.3.100 to the PIX.** To update the IOS on the PIX, you have to obtain a Trivial File Transfer Program (TFTP) in order to upload the new IOS software to the PIX. You can obtain a TFTP program at *http://tftpd32.jounin.net*. Cisco recommends this TFTP program. The syntax for updating the PDM software is:

```
copy tftp://<Your_TFTP_Server_IP_Address>/<Your_pdmfile_name>
flash:pdm
```

The syntax for updating the IOS software on the PIX is:

```
copy tftp://<Your_TFTP_Server_IP_Address>/<Your_pdmfile_name>
flash:ios
```

If your PIX has difficulty connecting to the TFTP server running on your workstation, try rebooting the workstation and then reload the TFTP program. In this particular case, we only had to update the IOS software and not the PDM. Be careful when updating either of these programs. The version of the PDM software and the version of the IOS software must be compatible. In this particular case, we verified that the PDM software was compatible with the IOS upgrade.

6. **Test the firewall.** After flashing the IOS software, we were able to save the configuration to the PIX without it rearranging the rule descriptions, but the firewall still didn't work. At this point, we were a little frustrated after jumping through this many hoops without having a working firewall. What's the next step?
7. **Reinstall the old firewall?** At this point, we were seriously considering reinstalling the old firewall. Fortunately, we attempted this installation on a Friday night and had the weekend to fix the firewall in case anything went wrong. We decided to try one last thing before reinstalling the old firewall: resetting the PIX to the factory defaults and entering the rules from scratch. This sounds like a radical idea, and frankly, the client wasn't too keen on it either. We took a step back and mentally reviewed all of the steps we had taken so far. We theorized that somehow the configuration using the defective IOS could have caused a corruption in the current configuration that wasn't fixed by the new IOS. Moreover, we knew that we could reenter all of the rules onto the PIX in about 40 minutes. We figured it was worth a try, and if it worked, the relatively small time investment was worth it.

Resolution

Use the `write erase` command to return the PIX to the factory defaults. After resetting the configuration and reentering it from scratch, the firewall worked. Evidently, something in the old configuration was preventing the PIX from working properly.

Lessons Learned

Persistence pays off. One of the most frustrating things about this business is going over a configuration, but for one reason or another, it still doesn't work. Don't be shy about calling technical support, especially if the item already has a maintenance contract. We strongly recommend placing any Cisco equipment on a maintenance agreement. It can get a little expensive, but it will pay for itself the first time you need it. This is especially important for mission-critical equipment like firewalls and core routers. Try to schedule any type of major installation over a weekend to give you time to recover in case things don't go smoothly.

CHAPTER SUMMARY

Firewall troubleshooting can be an extremely complex task. It requires expertise in WAN connectivity, IP routing, proper IP address configuration, DNS, TCP/IP/UDP ports, and network security. If you feel you're in over your head, get some outside help. Remember to carefully plan any firewall implementation and always have a fall-back plan. Give yourself a buffer to recover if things don't go smoothly. When troubleshooting existing firewall problems, the firewall log is your best friend. This should be one of the first places you check when troubleshooting any firewall problem.

REVIEW QUESTIONS

1. What is the best firewall topology?
   a. Software firewall installed on a workstation.
   b. Firewall software running on a Windows 2003 server and SQL server.
   c. Stand-alone firewall with no additional services.
   d. Firewall software running on a Linux server used as a file and print server.
2. Which firewall is the most secure?
   a. Setting up an access-list on a Cisco router that performs packet filtering.
   b. Installing a stateful packet inspection firewall on a Windows 2003 server also running Exchange 2003.
   c. Running a dedicated firewall appliance with packet filtering.
   d. Installing stateful packet inspection firewall software on each workstation.
   e. Running a dedicated firewall appliance that performs stateful packet inspection.
3. What utility can you use to determine if DNS is working properly?
   a. `ping`
   b. `nslookup`
   c. `tracert`
   d. `dir`
   e. `nbtstat`
4. Which of the following is *not* a great source that you can use to troubleshoot a firewall problem?
   a. Windows Event Viewer.
   b. Firewall vendor's knowledgebase.
   c. Firewall log files.
   d. ping.
   e. Outside consultants.

5. If you suspect that a computer running Windows has been hacked, where should you look first?
   a. See if the workstation has poor performance.
   b. Look for excessive Internet traffic.
   c. The run keys in
      HKEY_LOCAL_MACHINE\SOFTWARE\Microsoft\Windows\CurrentVersion\Run
      HKEY_CURRENT_USER\Software\Microsoft\Windows\CurrentVersion\Run
      HKEY_LOCAL_MACHINE\SOFTWARE\Microsoft\Windows\CurrentVersion\Policies\Explorer\Run
   d. The firewall logs.
   e. See if there is a heavy load on the mail server.

10 Virtual Private Network Troubleshooting

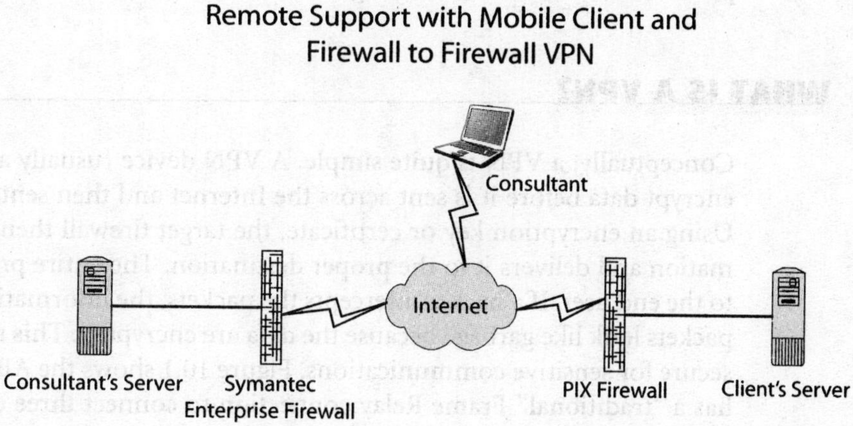

CHAPTER PREVIEW

Over the past few years, virtual private networks (VPNs) have increased in popularity as a cost-effective means to connect remote offices via the Internet. Companies that do not have strict bandwidth requirements can use a VPN to replace an existing private Frame Relay connection. The Return on Investment (ROI) can be as little as six months to a year, depending on the availability and cost of an Internet connection and VPN device (usually the firewall). Careful planning before the VPN is established will ensure a successful implementation. Most of the problems we've seen with VPNs are caused by poor planning. The good news is that once the VPN is established, it requires little maintenance to keep it running. Occasionally, you'll have to reboot the firewalls to reestablish the tunnels. In this chapter, we'll look at different VPN configurations, VPN limitations, implementation steps, cross-vendor VPNs, VPNs with a dynamic IP address, and troubleshooting tools. The last part of the chapter describes some real-world VPN troubleshooting scenarios that we've experienced in our troubleshooting adventures.

WHAT IS A VPN?

Conceptually, a VPN is quite simple. A VPN device (usually a firewall) is used to encrypt data before it is sent across the Internet and then sent to a target firewall. Using an encryption key or certificate, the target firewall then decrypts the information and delivers it to the proper destination. The entire process is transparent to the end user. If a hacker intercepts the packets, the information contained in the packets look like garbage because the data are encrypted. This makes the VPN very secure for sensitive communications. Figure 10.1 shows the ABC Corporation that has a "traditional" Frame Relay connection to connect three offices: Los Angeles, Chicago, and New York.

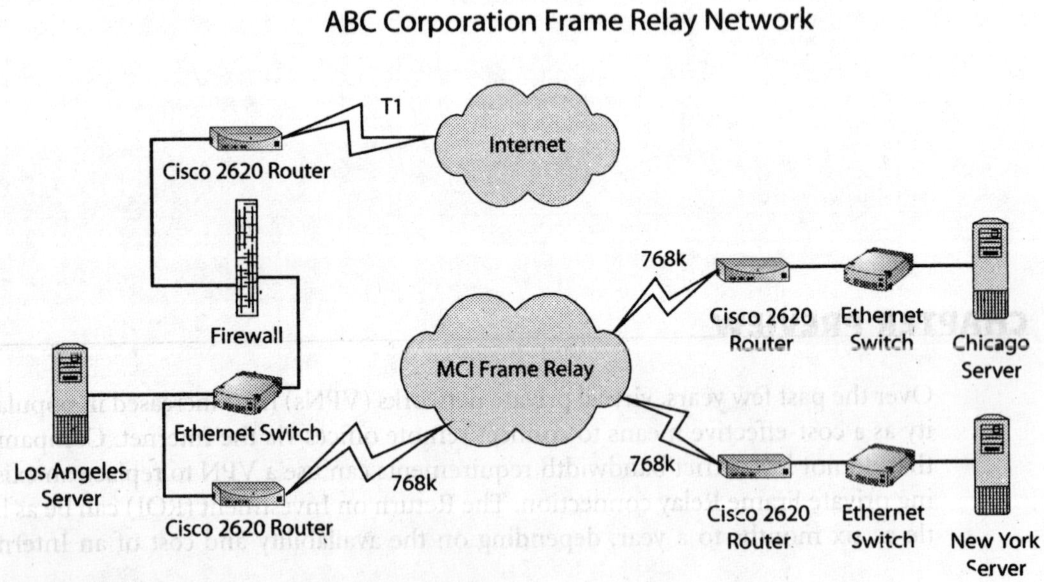

FIGURE 10.1 Traditional Frame Relay network.

If the company decides to replace its existing Frame Relay network with a VPN, the network diagram might look like Figure 10.2.

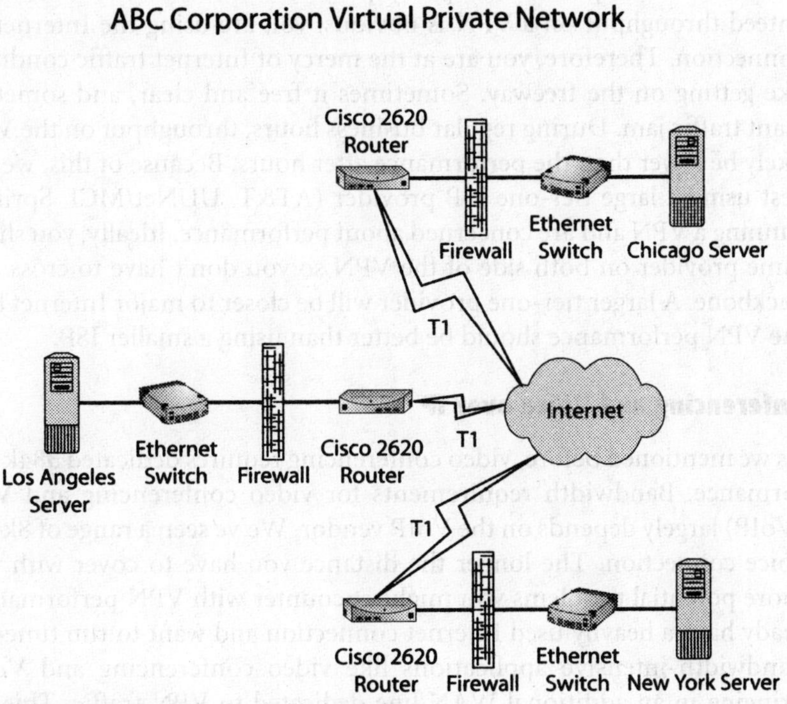

FIGURE 10.2 Virtual private network.

Most likely, the company would benefit from greater throughput because the VPN would run T1s at all locations compared to 768K with the Frame Relay network. Their monthly WAN charges should go down because they can eliminate the Frame Relay network. New York and Chicago should experience better Internet performance, because they will access the Internet directly, rather than routing their Internet request through Los Angeles. From that perspective, Internet access is more fault tolerant, because each location has its own connection to the Internet.

VPN LIMITATIONS

Of course, there are some drawbacks when using a VPN. Probably the greatest limitation is the lack of guaranteed throughput. Most Frame Relay providers guarantee a baseline speed and a burst speed on their Frame Relay lines. For example, a

384k/768k Frame Relay line would guarantee a minimum of 384k throughput and a maximum of 768k throughput when it's available. Time-sensitive and bandwidth-intensive applications such as videoconferencing typically require dedicated speeds of 384k to provide acceptable performance. The reason for the lack of guaranteed throughput on a VPN is obvious: you are using the Internet to make the connection. Therefore, you are at the mercy of Internet traffic conditions. It's just like getting on the freeway. Sometimes it free and clear, and sometimes it's one giant traffic jam. During regular business hours, throughput on the VPN will most likely be lower than the performance after hours. Because of this, we strongly suggest using a large tier-one ISP provider (AT&T, UUNet/MCI, Sprint) if you are running a VPN and are concerned about performance. Ideally, you should have the same provider on both side of the VPN so you don't have to cross another ISP's backbone. A larger tier-one provider will be closer to major Internet backbones, so the VPN performance should be better than using a smaller ISP.

Video Conferencing and Voice over IP

As we mentioned before, video conferencing requires dedicated 384k for good performance. Bandwidth requirements for video conferencing and Voice over IP (VoIP) largely depends on the VoIP vendor. We've seen a range of 8k up to 64k per voice connection. The longer the distance you have to cover with the VPN, the more potential problems you might encounter with VPN performance. If you already have a heavily used Internet connection and want to run time-sensitive and bandwidth-intensive applications like video conferencing and VoIP, consider bringing in an additional WAN line dedicated to VPN traffic. This will give you some fault tolerance if the other Internet connection goes down. If you cannot afford a second WAN line, consider a firewall vendor (Lucent VPN Firebrick) that supports Quality of Service (QoS) with their VPN support. This ensures that your large FTP transfer to a branch office will not interfere with a video conference between the CEO and Regional Manager.

If you do run a VPN with video conferencing, most vendors suggest doubling (768 kb/sec) the company's connections to the Internet. We have established VPNs for clients that run video conferencing between Los Angeles, New York, and Asia using T1s (1.54 mb/sec) on all sides of the VPN with a tier-one ISP. Even with this increased bandwidth, they occasionally get breakups in the video conference. However, compared to the cost of running a Frame Relay network, the client considers it a good compromise. Based on this experience, we suggest a minimum speed of a T1 at 1.54 mb/sec if the company plans to do any video conferencing. It usually makes sense to run a T1 anyway, because the monthly cost differential between a 768k line and a full T1 is usually very small.

IMPLEMENTING A VPN

Implementing a VPN requires careful planning. The firewall, authentication method, encryption type, and WAN line speeds must be decided upon before the VPN is brought up. Ideally, the VPN should have fixed IP addresses on both sides of the tunnel, but some firewall vendors support a dynamic IP address on one side of the tunnel.

What's Required for a VPN?

To establish the VPN, a device must perform the encryption and decryption for the VPN. Typically, this device is a firewall. Assuming you will use the same firewall for your Internet access and VPN connectivity, make sure you have sufficient licenses and VPN tunnel capacity before making your purchase decision. Make sure that the firewall has the processing capacity to handle all of your VPN traffic, and allow some room for growth. Don't forget telecommuters when determining your licensing requirements.

Expected Throughput

In general, expect the throughput on the VPN to be roughly one-half to one-third of a dedicated connection. This can vary widely depending on the ISP, load on the Internet connection, number of users, number of VPN tunnels, and VPN distance. When determining your VPN bandwidth requirements, always plan for the peak usage. We've never had any complaints about the network being too fast, but we guarantee that users will complain if they feel the network is too slow. If your application bandwidth requirements are high, consider installing a Terminal server or other remote control software to increase the performance of the system.

Fully Meshed Network

If you decide to create a "fully meshed" network—one where each site can directly communicate with the other sites—you must establish a tunnel for each location. If you're running Exchange 2000/2003, consider configuring the VPN as a "fully meshed" network, because by default, Exchange servers want to communicate directly with a server in a given site. Windows 2000 and 2003 have the capability to perform encryption built into their operating system; however, we feel it's more secure to have a dedicated device performing the VPN responsibilities. For more information on dedicated firewall devices, refer to Chapter 9. Referring back to Figure 10.2, each location must establish two tunnels if they want a "fully meshed" network. Don't forget, for a fully meshed network you need <number of sites> – 1 VPN tunnels to create the network. For example, if your company has five locations, each firewall must create four (5–1) tunnels to directly communicate with each other. Of course, you can configure the VPN to route packets through a central or hub site, but considering the encryption/decryption overhead, it is usually more efficient to create a fully meshed network. It you create a VPN that routes packets through a central site, you will make the network less fault tolerant because if the central site goes down, you will break the VPN in all locations.

VPN Topology for Remote Users

Telecommuting has become a popular trend over the past several years. It allows users to spend more time with their families and less time commuting to and from work. With today's technology and the right IT infrastructure, you can provide a computing environment that is nearly identical to the nontelecommuting worker. However, telecommuting is not without its risks (see Figure 10.3).

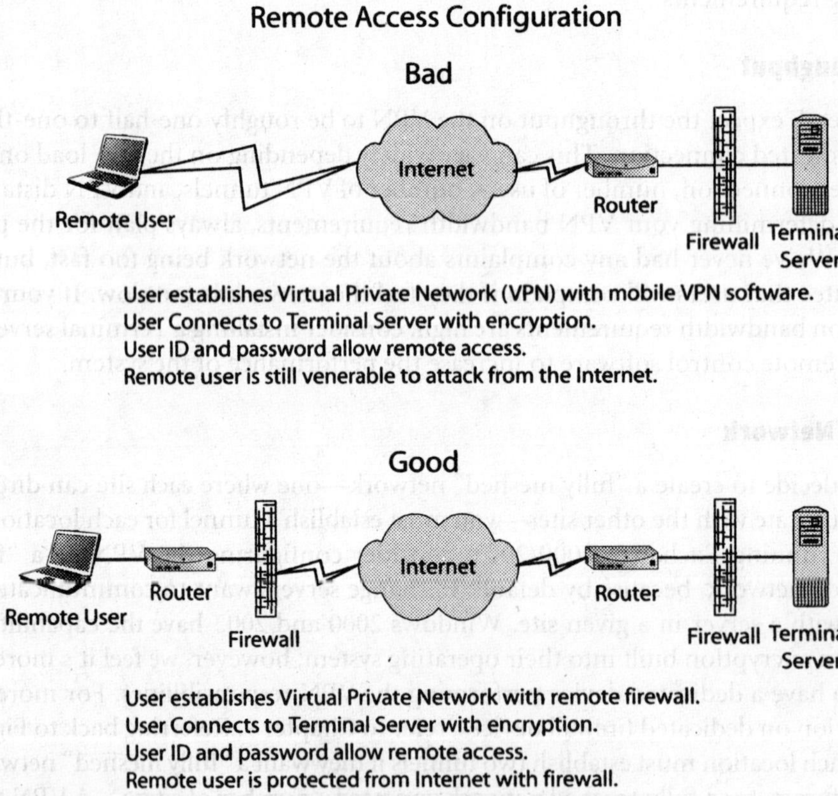

FIGURE 10.3 A comparison of VPN remote connectivity.

In the first example, a remote user connects to the corporate network using mobile client software installed on his home computer. The mobile client software is used to establish the VPN connection. Although the VPN itself is very secure, the remote user is left unprotected, because he is not behind a firewall. This leaves him vulnerable to an attack by a hacker. In the second example, the remote user sits behind a firewall. This firewall creates the VPN tunnel and protects the remote user. If you have any remote users who use a broadband connection (cable modem or DSL), we strongly suggest purchasing a "baby" firewall to protect the user. This, of course, becomes less practical if the remote user is on a dial-up connection, but he still has some type of software firewall installed on his home computer. Don't forget to install anti-virus software on any remote computers! Remember, with this increased connectivity, you must manage the potential threats to your network. With VPNs, your network is only as secure as its weakest point.

Ordering Internet Service–Get Static IP Addresses

When placing the order for your Internet connection, make sure to consider your bandwidth requirements at each location and order the appropriate line. Consider the upload and download requirements based on the communication requirements of the users at each location. Whenever possible, try to order an Internet connection with static IP addresses. Most broadband business services offer fixed IP addresses. We suggest ordering the line with a few extra IP addresses to allow some room for growth. VPNs with static IP addresses are easier to configure, and are typically more stable than VPNs with dynamic IP addresses.

ISP Blocking VPNs?

If you're ordering new service, make sure that the ISP does not block VPN traffic. Usually, with business service, this is not an issue, but some cable companies and DSL home service providers prohibit VPN traffic on their network. Make sure to do your homework first to ensure that your ISP does not block VPN traffic.

Cross-Vendor Firewall VPNs?

When firewall vendors first released support for VPNs, the probability of getting a VPN established with another vendor's firewall was very small. It seems like no one could agree on the VPN "standards." Fortunately, this has changed. We have many clients running VPNs with different vendors' firewalls with great success. If you plan to establish a cross-vendor VPN, check the vendor's Web site to see if they already have instructions on how to establish a VPN with the firewall to which you want to connect. If you have to establish a VPN with another vendor's firewall, and you haven't purchased your firewall yet, try to purchase the same vendor's firewall.

Doing so will make it easier to bring the VPN connection up. If you must establish a VPN using two different firewalls, do some research ahead of time to verify they are compatible. A little homework ahead of time will make the VPN implementation go much smoother.

Fixed versus Dynamic IP Addresses

If it's not possible to order service with a fixed IP address, are you out of luck? Sometimes yes, sometimes no. Some firewall vendors such as Watchguard and SonicWALL support VPN connections with dynamic IP addresses on one side of the tunnel as long as the VPN uses the same manufacturer's firewall on both sides of the tunnel.

Mobile Client Software

As shown in Figure 10.3, the preferred way to make the VPN connection is through a firewall, not the mobile client software. Most firewall vendors provide mobile client software that is used to create the VPN tunnel using the processor on the remote user's laptop. Sometimes, this is the only practical solution, especially if a user is constantly on the road. In general, we have found that different vendors' VPN client software are not compatible. For example, you cannot use the Symantec Enterprise Firewall Mobile Client to establish a VPN connection on a SonicWALL—you must use SonicWALL's mobile client to create the tunnel on the SonicWALL. In addition, we have found that you can only have one VPN client software loaded on your laptop at the same time. If you attempt to install another vendor's VPN client software, your computer will usually crash, and force you to reinstall all of the networking components, and sometimes reinstall the operating system. This is because the VPN client software wants to "take charge" of the entire TCP/IP configuration on the computer. Whatever you do, don't attempt to install two mobile VPN clients on the same machine at the same time. By avoiding this situation, you will save yourself a lot of grief and misery and possibly a broken computer. We have to support many different clients with different firewalls. If a client requires mobile support and we're out of the office, we use our mobile client to establish a connection to our network, and then bring up a tunnel between our firewall and client's firewall. This allows us to support clients on a secure connection from any location where we have Internet access. Of course, once the support issue is addressed, we break the tunnel connection. We only bring up the tunnel connection when a client requires remote support, and then disable the tunnel when we're finished.

DEFINING THE VPN CONNECTION ON THE FIREWALL

Defining a VPN connection on any firewall requires the following steps:

1. **IP address of the remote firewall.** If the remote firewall uses a dynamic IP address, you typically need a firewall serial number or some other way to uniquely identify the remote firewall.
2. **Remote subnet.** The remote subnet of the VPN. Some firewall vendors such as Symantec Enterprise Firewall support a VPN configuration that has the same subnet addresses on both sides of the VPN, but most firewall vendors require unique subnets.
3. **Data integrity algorithm.** This specifies the type of Authentication Header (AH) that is added to a beginning of the packet sent through the tunnel. Typical selections are Message Digest 5 (MD5) and Secure Hash Algorithm 1 (SHA1). You can think of MD5 and SHA1 as an industrial-strength hash total to ensure that the data sent and received on either side of the VPN tunnel is consistent. If you use a data integrity algorithm, it can be applied to just the data portion of the packet (Encapsulated Security Payload—ESP) or the entire IP datagram packet (Authentication Header—AH).
4. **Data encryption method.** This is the method used to encrypt/decrypt the data. Typical selections include the Data Encryption Standard (DES), 3DES, and Advanced Encryption Standard (AES). The encryption bit length for each encryption type is listed in Table 10.1.

TABLE 10.1 Encryption Bit Length for Each Encryption Type

Encryption Method	*Encryption Bit Length*
Data Encryption Standard (DES)	56 bit
Triple Data Encryption Standard (3DES)	168 bit
Advanced Encryption Standard (AES)	128 bit
Strong Advanced Encryption Standard (AES)	192 bit
Very Strong Advanced Encryption Standard (AES)	256 bit

AES is a newer encryption standard and is more secure than DES. However, be aware that higher levels of encryption create a greater load on the firewall.

5. **Shared secret key or certificate.** This is an agreed-upon key by both firewalls that is used to establish the tunnel. A certificate is more secure, but requires more administrative work, because you must establish a Certificate server and issue the certificate to both firewalls. A shared secret key is a text or hex string that is used in the initial establishment of the tunnel. The shared key should be a closely guarded secret. If the key is compromised, it will be possible for a hacker to establish a VPN with your firewall. The shared secret key should be a nontrivial key (i.e., *not* 111111111111), and a combination of numbers and letters that do not contain words. Shared secrets keys are fine for a testing environment, but if you plan to roll out an enterprisewide VPN, use a certificate for VPN authentication.

The following parameters are optional for most firewalls:

Data volume timeout. This is the amount of data that passes through the tunnel before the encryption keys are set to a different value. This option might not be available on all firewalls.

Lifetime volume timeout. This is the amount of time that is allowed to pass before the tunnel is rekeyed. This option might not be available on all firewalls.

Inactivity timeout. This is the amount of inactivity time, usually in seconds, before the tunnel is closed. For example, if the inactivity timeout is 600 seconds, the tunnel will be closed after 10 minutes of inactivity. This option might not be available on all firewalls.

Perfect forward secrecy. This allows you to specify parameters for key generation. This makes it more difficult for hackers to guess successive encryption keys. If you specify perfect forward secrecy, you usually must specify a Deffie-Hellman preference. Deffie-Hellman is an IKE standard for establishing shared keys. Group 1 is 768 bits long, and Group 2 is 1024 bits long. Group 2 is more secure, but requires more CPU power for the encryption.

One of the most critical steps to establishing the VPN is that everything must match exactly. If you make a mistake and enter the wrong value for any of the required VPN parameters, the tunnel will fail to come up. If a tunnel fails to come up, double check the IP address of the remote firewall, shared secret key (remember, this is case sensitive), data integrity, data encryption method, and remote subnet. Most likely, a correction in one or more of these values will fix the tunnel.

SETTING UP A VPN WITH A DYNAMIC IP ADDRESS ON ONE SIDE

Although not ideal, most firewall vendors do support one end of a VPN tunnel that has a dynamic IP address. When possible, try to obtain Internet service that offers a static IP address. VPNs with static addresses are generally more stable than a VPN with one dynamic IP address. If you have to order Internet service with a dynamic IP address, make sure you have addressed the following issues:

Verify that the firewall vendor supports a dynamic IP address on one side of the VPN. Make sure that the firewalls you want to use support a dynamic IP address on one side of the tunnel.

Use the same firewall vendor for both sides of the VPN. It's usually possible to establish a VPN between two different vendors' firewalls if you have static IP addresses on both sides. However, if one side has a dynamic IP address, most firewall vendors require that both firewalls come from the same vendor.

A VPN with a dynamic IP address is less secure. Because one side of the firewall can have a dynamic IP address, the VPN will not be as secure as a VPN with static IP addresses on both sides of the VPN. The dynamic IP address makes is slightly easier for a hacker to spoof the dynamic end of the VPN tunnel.

VPN setup with a dynamic IP address. The procedure for establishing a VPN with a static IP address is usually different from establishing a VPN with a dynamic IP address on one side. Make sure to download the firewall vendor's documentation and read the instructions carefully before attempting to establish the VPN. Usually, a VPN with a dynamic IP addresses requires some type of firewall ID (SonicWALL uses the firewall serial number by default) to establish the VPN.

A VPN with a dynamic IP address is less stable. In our experience, VPNs with dynamic IP addresses are less stable than VPNs with static addresses. This seems especially true when the ISP constantly resets their network, causing the dynamic IP address to change frequently. Often, the firewall fails to recognize that a network reset has occurred, especially if the firewall receives its IP address from DHCP. This causes the tunnel and Internet access to fail. Sometimes, a manual refresh of an IP address will fix the problem, and sometimes, a complete reboot of the Internet router and firewall is necessary.

VPN TROUBLESHOOTING TOOLS

If you have difficult establishing a VPN tunnel, or passing data through the tunnel, use these tools to narrow down the problem. Often, VPN turnnels do not come up because of errors in the VPN tunnel definition. Check your VPN settings carefully.

Firewall Log

Just like firewall troubleshooting, the firewall log is an excellent source for troubleshooting connection problems. Use the following guidelines when a VPN will not come up:

The firewall log reports that the remote firewall is not reachable. Double check the IP address of the remote gateway. From the firewall, see if you can ping the IP address of the remote gateway. Note that some firewalls by default will not respond to a ping request. If this is the case, enable ping requests on the firewall to help with the troubleshooting process. If the firewalls cannot ping each other after ping is enabled, you might have a routing issue with the ISP. If you cannot ping, try using the `trace route` utility to determine where the packet dies.

Peer negotiation/IKE negotiation fails. Double check the shared secret key/certificate, data integrity algorithm, and data encryption method on both sides on the VPN. They must match exactly. Most shared secret keys are case sensitive. If the VPN still fails to come up, your ISP might be blocking VPN traffic on their network.

Reset the firewalls. From time to time, the VPN might go down. Usually, it's caused by a temporary disruption in service to the Internet, and the VPN tunnel does not get reestablished. If the VPN goes down and both sides can still get to the Internet, try resetting both firewalls at the same time. If one side cannot get to the Internet, your ISP might be down. Often, a reset of the firewall will bring the tunnel back up.

TROUBLESHOOTING SCENARIOS

When possible, order your Internet connection with static IP addresses on both sides of the VPN. It makes it easier to establish the VPN and gives you more flexibility if you have to create a VPN with two different firewalls. The next section includes some of the problems we've run across with VPNs.

Scenario 1 VPN GOING UP AND DOWN

Facts

- Watchguard SOHO6 TC with dynamic IP address at the remote location. Cable modem to the Internet. This remote side has one user using a Windows XP workstation. The workstation uses the IP address of the remote Windows 2003 server for DNS, so when the VPN connection is broken, it also breaks Internet access. The workstation is using the Windows 2003 server for DNS, because Windows 2003 uses DNS for name resolution. If the workstation used the ISP's DNS server, they would be unable to resolve any internal Windows 2000/2003 resources on the remote side of the VPN. The firewall is assigned an IP address via DHCP by the cable modem provider.
- Watchguard II with a static IP address at the main location. T1 connection to the Internet. The main location has a Windows 2003 server network.
- This VPN has been in place for three months.

Symptoms

Every one to two weeks, the VPN connection goes down. Sometimes, a reset of the cable modem and firewall will fix the problem; sometimes it will not.

Questions to Ask

Q: What has changed? A: Nothing.

Q: Can you correlate the VPN failing to anything you're doing on the network? A: No, it seems to go down randomly.

Troubleshooting Steps

1. **Verify the problem.** When the user tries to connect to the Internet, the browser displays an error that the page cannot be displayed.
2. **Verify the line is working.** To verify the problem is not the line, we disconnected the cable modem from the firewall and connected it directly to the laptop. The laptop was able to obtain an IP address from the cable modem. In this configuration, the user can get out to the Internet without any problems.
3. **Check the firewall.** The Watchguard 500 is configured with a Web browser. The firewall was plugged back into the cable modem. When we looked at the WAN interface on the router, the firewall reported 0.0.0.0. An IP address of 0.0.0.0 indicates that the firewall was unable to obtain an IP address from the cable modem.

4. **Reset the cable modem and the firewall.** Both the cable modem and the firewall were powered down and reset, but the user could still not connect to the Internet.
5. **Check the firewall.** A look at the WAN interface on the firewall still displayed an IP address of 0.0.0.0. With the Watchguard 500, there is a Reset button that attempts to refresh the IP address.

Resolution

When a Reset button was clicked, the firewall was finally able to obtain an IP address. Once the firewall obtained an IP address, the user was able to connect to the Windows 2003 server, and surf the Internet. This particular ISP resets their IP addresses on a regular basis. This causes the user's VPN and Internet connection to go down, because the firewall is unable to recognize that it needs to refresh its IP address.

Lessons Learned

As a short-term solution, we suggested that the user first reset her cable modem, wait three minutes, and then reset the firewall. By resetting the cable modem first, and then the firewall, there is a better chance that the firewall will be able to obtain an IP address from the cable modem. We trained the user to click the Reset button and try to refresh the IP address on the firewall if it displayed 0.0.0.0 as the WAN address, or if the user had trouble getting out to the Internet. In the future, the user will try to order Internet service with a fixed IP address. In general, we have found that VPNs with fixed IP addresses are more stable than are VPNs with dynamic IP addresses.

Scenario 2 VPN TUNNEL GOES DOWN

Facts

- Symantec Enterprise Firewall 7.0 in Los Angeles. They have a T1 connection to the Internet.
- SonicWALL SOHO3 in Chicago. They have a T1 connection to the Internet.
- VPN is running between Los Angeles and Chicago using the Symantec Enterprise Firewall and SonicWALL SOHO3.
- Windows 2003 network running Exchange 2000, SQL Server 2000, and Terminal Server in Los Angeles.
- Chicago users run a database application on the Los Angeles Terminal server.
- VPN has been up for four months.

Symptoms

We received a call that the users in Chicago were unable to access the database application on the Terminal server.

Questions to Ask

Q: What has changed? A: No recent changes to the network.

Q: Can users get out to the Internet? A: Yes, both Los Angeles and Chicago can get out to the Internet.

Troubleshooting Steps

1. **Verify the problem.** An attempt to access the database application in Los Angeles fails.
2. **Ping the Terminal server.** When Chicago attempts to ping the Los Angeles Terminal server by IP address, it times out.
3. **Test Internet access.** When both Los Angeles and Chicago start Internet Explorer, they are able to get out to the Internet. Running a speed test at *www.dslreports.com/stest* reveals that both lines test very close to T1 (1.54 mb/sec) speeds. Since both sides are able to get out to the Internet, we suspect a problem with the tunnel.

Resolution

We had Los Angeles and Chicago reset their firewalls. When the firewalls were reset, Chicago was able to ping the Los Angeles Terminal server and get into the database application.

Lessons Learned

If a VPN goes down after it's been up and running for a while, try resetting both firewalls. This will fix the problem roughly 70 percent of the time. On the SonicWALL , if you go to the VPN Summary page and look under VPN Policies/Currently Active VPN Tunnels, it will display all of the VPN policies and active tunnels (see Table 10.2).

In the VPN Policies section, look for the "green ball" next to the VPN policy. This indicates that the VPN policy is active. Verify that the tunnel shows up under the Currently Active VPN Tunnels. This indicates that the tunnel is up and active. If the VPN Definition does not appear in the Currently Active VPN Tunnels section, the tunnel is not up, and you probably have some VPN troubleshooting to perform. This tunnel was for testing purposes only. For production VPNs, use either 3DES or AES encryption. Regular DES is cryptographically weak and can be cracked.

TABLE 10.2 SonicWALL VPN Policies and Active Tunnels

VPN Policies

Disabled	*Name*	*Gateway*	*Destinations*	*Phase 2 Encryption/ Authentication*
*	GroupVPN			ESP DES HMAC MD5 (IKE)
	Chicago VPN	65.111.1.24	10.1.2.1 – 10.1.2.254	ESP DES HMAC MD5 (IKE)

SAs enabled: 1

SAs defined: 2

SAs Allowed: 501

Currently Active VPN Tunnels

Name	Local	Remote	Gateway
Chicago VPN	10.1.1.1 – 10.1.1.255	10.1.2.1 – 10.1.2.254	65.111.1.24

Scenario 3 Two Mobile Clients on Same Laptop

Facts

- Windows XP workstation with Symantec Enterprise VPN Client 7.0.
- SonicWALL VPN Client 8.0 recently installed.

Symptoms

After the SonicWALL client was installed and the workstation was rebooted, the workstation blue screens and freezes.

Questions to Ask

Q: What has changed? A: The SonicWALL VPN client was installed.

Q: Why was this done? A: This was one of our workstations. We have clients who have different firewalls that require remote support.

Troubleshooting Steps

1. **Verify the problem.** The workstation blue screens during the booting process.
2. **Boot machine in safe mode.** We were able to boot the machine in safe mode by pressing F8 when XP first boots and selecting Safe Mode from the menu. In safe mode, we successfully ran the uninstall program to remove the SonicWALL client.
3. **Boot the machine normally.** When the machine was rebooted, it did not blue screen, but it was generally unstable. All of the networking components were uninstalled and reinstalled.

Resolution

After the workstation's networking components were removed and reinstalled, the workstation worked again. If the uninstall of the SonicWALL client was unsuccessful, another alternative to try is the Windows XP system restore.

Lessons Learned

Because of the nature of the VPN client software, it is not possible to install more than one mobile client on the same computer. Essentially, the VPN client software wants to "monopolize" the TCP/IP stack. Installing more than one mobile client will create major problems on your computer. To get around this limitation, you can use virtual machine software like Virtual PC to create a virtual machine on the computer and load the second VPN client software. Another option is to establish a firewall-to-firewall VPN, use the mobile client software to connect to one side of the VPN, and then use the firewall-to-firewall VPN to connect to the remote site (see Figure 10.4).

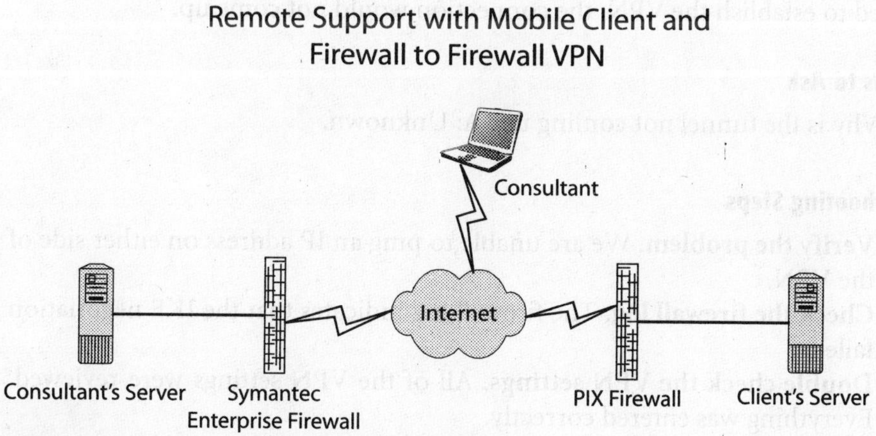

FIGURE 10.4 Remote support with mobile client.

Let's assume that the client's server is running low on disk space, so some files must be moved/deleted. The following steps are required to provide the client with remote support:

1. Consultant connects to the Internet.
2. Consultant establishes a tunnel with the Symantec Enterprise Firewall.
3. Consultant establishes a tunnel with the client's PIX firewall and the Symantec Enterprise Firewall.
4. Consultant uses Terminal Server on the client's server to move/delete files.

By establishing a firewall-to-firewall VPN, the consultant can support any client as long as the client's firewall can establish a VPN with the Symantec Enterprise Firewall.

Scenario 4 CANNOT ESTABLISH A VPN WITH A DYNAMIC IP ADDRESS

Facts

- SonicWALL Pro 200 with a dynamic IP address using DSL in the Atlanta branch office. This firewall has the 6.5.0.4 firmware installed on it. The SonicWALL uses PPPoE to authenticate to the ISP's network. There are 100 remote users behind the Pro 200.
- SonicWALL Pro 4060 with a static IP address using DSL in the New York corporate office. This firewall has the SonicWALL 2.0 enhanced firmware on it. This network is running Windows Server 2003 with 300 users.

Symptoms

We were attempting to establish a VPN between Atlanta and New York. When we attempted to establish the VPN, the connection would not come up.

Questions to Ask

Q: Why is the tunnel not coming up? A: Unknown.

Troubleshooting Steps

1. **Verify the problem.** We are unable to ping an IP address on either side of the VPN.
2. **Check the firewall log.** The firewall log indicates that the IKE negotiation failed.
3. **Double check the VPN settings.** All of the VPN settings were reviewed. Everything was entered correctly.

4. **Search the Web for answers.** We performed a search on SonicWALL's knowledge portal site for VPN, and found the article "Creating IKE IPSec VPN Tunnels between SonicWALL Firmware 6.5.*x.x* and SonicOS 2.0.0.0 Enhanced." On pages 9 and 10 are instructions on how to establish a VPN when one side of the firewall has a dynamic IP address.

Resolution

The steps to establish a VPN with one dynamically assigned IP address are slightly different from setting up a VPN that has static IP addresses on both sides. There are also differences in the VPN setup between the 6.5.*x.x* version and SonicOS 2.0 enhanced software.

Figure 10.5 shows the VPN parameters on the SonicWALL 4060. This screen is accessed from the VPN, Settings menu.

FIGURE 10.5 VPN>Settings on the SonicWALL 4060.

VPN configuration steps for the firewall that has the fixed IP address:

1. **Note the unique firewall identifier** on the SonicWALL 4060 and Tele3. This value defaults to the serial number of the firewall.
2. **Add a new VPN policy.** Click on VPN, Settings, and the Add button under VPN Policies to get to the screen shown in Figure 10.6.
3. **Name the VPN tunnel.** Enter the unique firewall ID of the remote firewall for the name of the VPN tunnel.
4. **IPSec primary/secondary address.** Enter 0.0.0.0 in both fields, because the IP address on the remote firewall is dynamically assigned.
5. **Shared secret.** Make sure the shared secret matches on both sides of the firewall.
6. **Local IKE ID.** Select SonicWALL identifier from the drop-down list box, and enter the unique firewall ID shown in Figure 10.6.

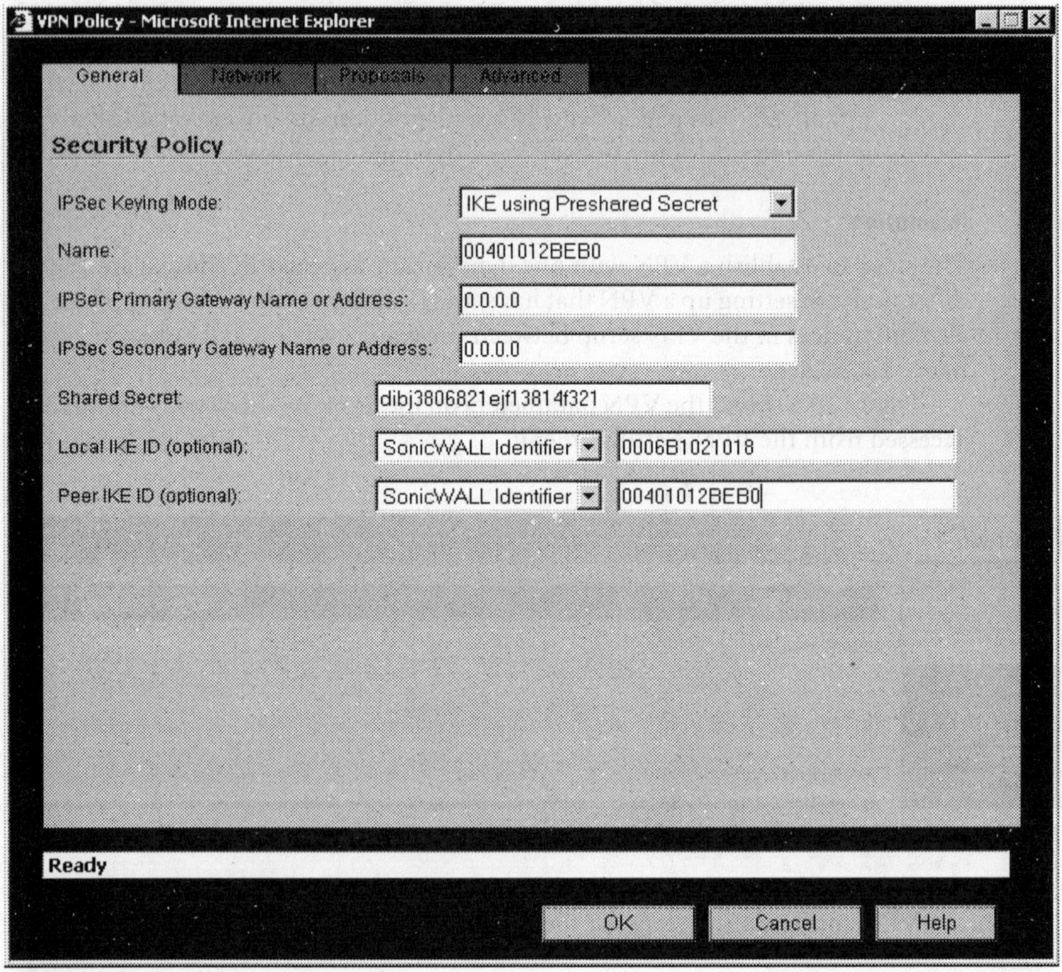

FIGURE 10.6 General VPN settings.

7. **Peer IKE ID.** Select SonicWALL identifier from the drop-down list box, and enter the unique firewall ID (usually the serial number) of the remote firewall shown in Figure 10.7.

VPN configuration steps for the firewall that has the dynamic IP address.

1. **Note the firewall serial number.** Make sure this matches the Peer IKE ID value on the remote firewall described in step 7. Make sure to name the Tunnel the same as the Firewall Serial number. This is shown in Figure 10.8.
2. **Add a New SA.** Select Add New SA from the Security Association drop-down list box.

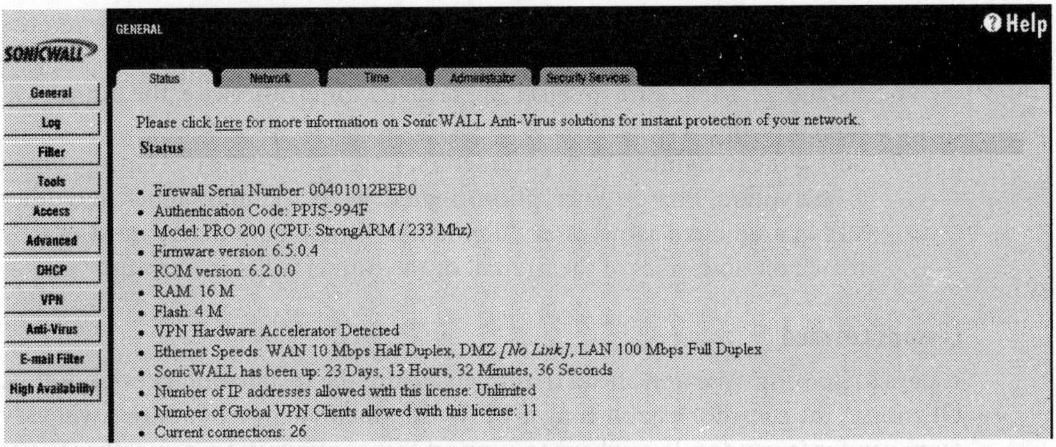

FIGURE 10.7 The General, Status screen on a SonicWALL Pro 200.

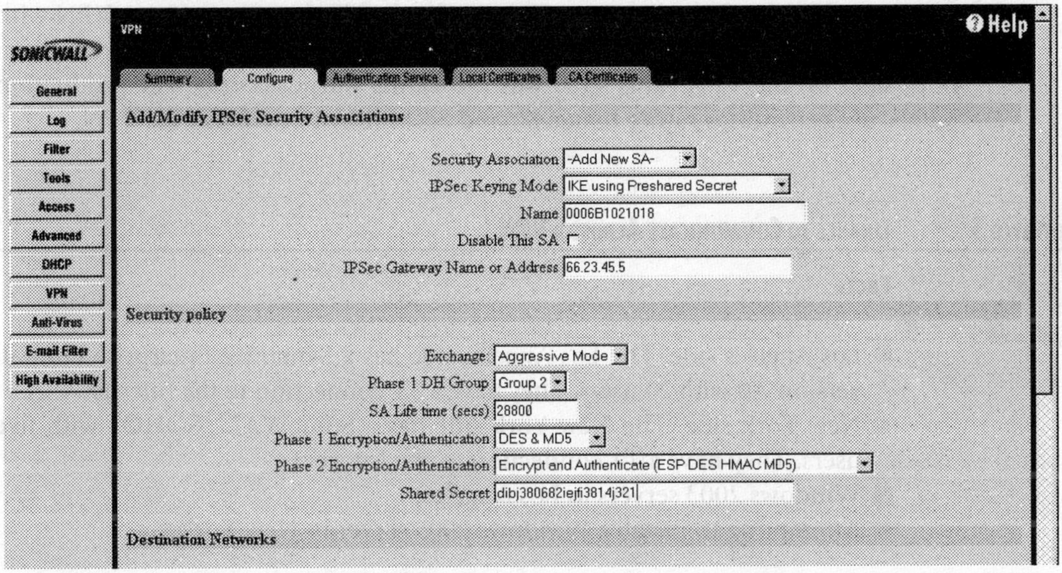

FIGURE 10.8 Setting up the VPN configuration on a SonicWALL Pro 200.

3. **Select IKE using Pre-shared Secret from the IPSec Keying Mode.**
4. **Name the tunnel the same as the remote firewall unique identifier**. The name of the VPN tunnel must match the remote firewall SonicWALL identifier exactly. If you do not enter this SonicWALL identifier, the VPN will not come up.

5. **IPSec gateway name or address.** Enter the WAN IP address of the remote firewall.
6. **Exchange.** Make sure to select Aggressive Mode; otherwise, the tunnel will not come up.
7. **Set up the remaining VPN parameters.** This includes the DH Group, Phase 1 Encryption, Phase 2 Encryption, Shared Secret, remote subnet, and other VPN parameters as necessary. Remember, these parameters must exactly match on both sides of the firewall or the tunnel will not come up.

Lessons Learned

It pays to do some research ahead of time to ensure the installation goes smoothly. Of course, the steps for establishing a VPN with one dynamic IP address will vary from vendor to vendor. If you have to support this configuration, remember to use the same firewalls from the same vendor on both sides of the VPN. Most firewall vendors that support this type of VPN require you to enter some type of additional parameter like the firewall unique ID to make the VPN more secure. A VPN with one dynamic IP address is usually only supported with the same vendor firewalls on both sides on the VPN. This VPN was for testing purposes only. For production VPNs, use certificates rather than a Shared Secret Key to establish the VPN.

Scenario 5 Unable to Communicate Across a VPN

Facts

- Los Angeles side. The Los Angeles side has a Symantec Enterprise Firewall version 7.0 with 20 users. They have a T1 connection to the Internet.
- New York side. The New York side has a SonicWALL SOHO3 with five users. They have a T1 connection to the Internet.
- Windows 2003 servers in Los Angeles.
- Attempting to install a Windows 2003 server in New York.

Symptoms

Both firewalls indicate that the VPN tunnel was up and running. Both Los Angeles and New York can ping addresses on the remote side of the VPN. We were in the process of installing a new Windows 2003 server in New York. We wanted the New York server in the same Windows 2003 domain as the Los Angeles server. When we attempted to join the Los Angeles domain, we received an error that the domain controller was unreachable.

Questions to Ask

Q: Is the VPN up? A: Yes, logs on both firewalls indicate that the VPN is up and running.

Troubleshooting Steps

1. **Ping the remote server.** Both servers were able to ping each other with no packet loss.
2. **Isolate the problem.** We were unable to join the domain. When faced with a problem, always verify the basics first. At this point, we knew we could ping the remote server, but could we use any resources on it? When we were prompted for credentials to join the domain, we used the Administrator user and password, so we knew that we had enough rights to join the domain. If we didn't use the Administrator user, what group must you belong to in order to join the domain? You must be a member of the Domain Admins Group in order to join a Windows 2000/2003 domain.
3. **Try `net use \\<server_ip_address>\c$ /u:adminstrator`.** We tried the `net use` command in a command window to see if we could attach to the remote server. Note that we attempted to contact the remote server using the IP address, not the name of the server. When troubleshooting problems like this, always use the IP address first. If you are successful, then use the name of the target. By using the IP address first, you eliminate the variable of name resolution. This command returned the message "System error 53, the network patch was not found." At this point, we suspected something was wrong with the VPN because the `net use` command was unsuccessful.
4. **Review the firewall log.** The Symantec Enterprise Firewall generates more detailed logs by default, so we looked at this firewall first. We attempted the `net use` command and reviewed the firewall logs. They indicated that VPN packets were being dropped when we issued the `net use` command.

Resolution

We double checked the settings on both firewalls to ensure our VPN settings were correct. Since packets were being dropped, we tried enabling Fragmented Packet Handling on the SonicWALL (see Figure 10.9).

This screen is accessed from the VPN, Summary menu. After we enable fragmented packet handling, we were able to successfully issue the `net use` command and join the domain.

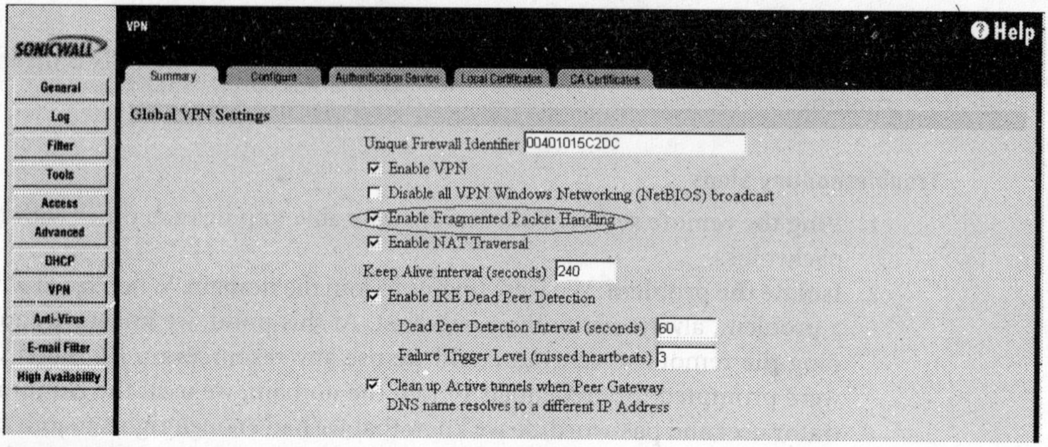

FIGURE 10.9 SonicWALL fragmented packet support.

Lessons Learned

When creating a VPN between different firewalls, budget extra time to work out any issues that might arise when creating a tunnel. Do research ahead of time to see if the firewall vendor offers any instructions on to create a cross-vendor VPN. SonicWALL, Cisco, Watchguard, and others all have instructions on how to establish a VPN from their firewall to a different vendor's firewall. Make sure to pre-read and follow the instructions carefully. They will save you time and frustration.

Scenario 6 UNABLE TO COMMUNICATE ACROSS A VPN

Facts

- Los Angeles side. The Los Angeles side has a SonicWALL Pro 200 with firmware 6.3.1.0. They have a T1 connection to the Internet with one Windows 2000 server.
- Boston remote user. The Boston remote user has a SonicWALL SOHO3 with 25 users and 6.4.0.1 firmware. They have a cable modem connection to the Internet with a dynamic IP address.

Symptoms

A remote VPN tunnel was set up for the Boston user. This VPN has a dynamic IP address on the remote side. The VPN was working for a few days, and then the remote user went on vacation. Two weeks later when the user returned, the VPN would not come up.

Questions to Ask

Q: Is the VPN up? A: No. The remote user cannot access the Los Angeles server.

Q: Was it working? A: Yes, the tunnel was working for a few days. The user went on vacation for two weeks. When the remote user returned, the tunnel was broken.

Q: What has changed? A: Nothing.

Troubleshooting Steps

1. **Review the firewall logs.** A review of the SonicWALL Pro 200 indicated an IKE responder timeout from the remote site.
2. **Ping the firewall.** We attempted to ping the remote firewall, but it did not respond. We could ping the default gateway of the remote firewall from the LA location. Most likely, ping packets were blocked on the remote firewall. Because the firewall logs received a packet from the remote firewall during IKE negotiation, we assumed that the firewalls could at least "see" each other.
3. **Recreate the tunnel.** Since the tunnel was working two weeks ago, we thought that possibly, the tunnel definitions were corrupted. The remote side did have a power outage while the user was on vacation. We saved the settings on both firewalls, and recorded the VPN tunnel settings. We deleted the VPN definitions on both firewalls and recreated the tunnel. After rebuilding the tunnel, the firewall logs still had the IKE responder timeout message, and the tunnel did not come up.
4. **Contact cable modem provider.** Some cable modem providers block encrypted traffic on their networks. We thought that possibly the cable modem provider started blocking VPN traffic while the user was on vacation. We contacted the cable modem provider's technical support. They indicated that they were not blocking any VPN traffic.
5. **Upgrade the firmware on the SonicWALL.** We noticed that the firmware on the SonicWALL Pro 200 was out of date. We downloaded the latest firmware (6.5.0.4) from *mysonicwall.com* and installed it on the Pro 200.

Resolution

After the Pro 200 was rebooted with the new firmware, the tunnel came up. We were able to ping computers on the remote site and access the management interface on the SOHO3. The firmware on the SOHO3 was also outdated. Just to be safe, we updated the firmware on the SOHO3 to 6.5.0.4.

Lessons Learned

Whenever you create a VPN with any firewall, make sure to upgrade the firewall to the latest firmware. This can reduce future firewall/VPN problems. Unfortunately, firewall firmware versions are becoming like virus patterns; they're only as good as their latest version. Make sure to regularly check for new firmware upgrades for your firewall and update them if necessary.

CHAPTER SUMMARY

The easiest way to avoid problems with VPNs is through careful planning. When possible, try to implement the VPN in phases, and have a fallback plan in case the implementation does not go smoothly. VPNs can save a significant amount of money in WAN charges compared to a traditional Frame Relay network. Be aware, however, that the performance might not be as good as the Frame Relay network the VPN replaces. When possible, we suggest establishing a VPN with static IP addresses on both sides of the tunnel. The tunnel is easier to create, and will be more stable in the long run. Static tunnels give you more flexibility with the types of firewalls you can use to establish the VPN.

Just like firewall troubleshooting, the firewall log is an excellent troubleshooting source. We suggest reviewing the logs on a regular basis, so you can become familiar with your firewall logs. Don't wait until you have a problem to review your firewall logs; you'll be fighting the learning curve of decoding the firewall logs, as well as trying to solve the VPN problem. After the VPNs are created, we suggest creating a WAN diagram that documents all of your VPN settings. This will make it easier to reestablish lost connections in the event of a catastrophic failure.

REVIEW QUESTIONS

1. What parameters are necessary to establish an IKE pre-shared secret VPN? (Choose four.)
   a. Remote subnet.
   b. Shared secret key.
   c. Encryption method.
   d. Firewall software running on a Linux server used as a file and print server.
   e. Perfect forward secrecy.

2. Which of the following is not a valid encryption method?
   a. DES
   b. AES—128 bit
   c. 3DES
   d. MD5
   e. AES—256 bit
3. Which of the following is a great resource when troubleshooting VPN problems?
   a. `ping`
   b. Firewall logs
   c. `tracert`
   d. `net use`
   e. `nbtstat`
4. Which of the following configuration(s) is/are not supported by most firewall vendors? (Choose two.)
   a. A VPN with static IP addresses on both firewalls.
   b. A VPN with dynamic IP addresses on both firewalls.
   c. A VPN with one static and one dynamic IP address using two different vendors' firewalls.
   d. A VPN with one static and one dynamic IP address using the same vendor's firewalls.
   e. A VPN with mobile client software using a dynamic IP address connecting to a firewall with a static IP address.
5. Assume that the VPN you just established supports Quality of Service (QoS). Assume that each side of the VPN only has one firewall and QoS is active. For the VPN, QoS will not have any effect on what following conditions during a video conference between VPN sites? (Choose two.)
   a. A large file transfer between the remote sites.
   b. Heavy Internet traffic.
   c. A mass e-mail sent out from both sites.
   d. The speed on the Internet links on both sites.
   e. Speed of downloading files from an FTP site on the Internet.

A Answers to Review Questions

Chapter 1

1. b, c, and d
2. a
3. , b, c, d, and e
4. e
5. c

Chapter 2

1. c
2. a, b, c, and d
3. a
4. d
5. a and d

Chapter 3

1. c
2. d
3. b
4. a, c, and e
5. b and c

Chapter 4

1. e
2. b and c
3. a, b, and d
4. e
5. d

Chapter 5

1. b
2. d
3. b, c, and d
4. b
5. b and d

Chapter 6

1. a
2. c and d
3. d
4. b
5. a, b, c, d, and e

Chapter 7

1. b
2. c
3. e
4. a
5. a

Chapter 8

1. c
2. b and d
3. a, c, and d
4. a, b, and e
5. d

Chapter 9

1. c
2. e
3. a
4. a
5. c

Chapter 10

1. a, b, c, and d
2. d
3. b
4. b and c
5. b and d

B About the CD-ROM

A CD-ROM is included with *The Real-World Network Troubleshooting Manual: Tools, Techniques, and Scenarios* book.

CD-ROM FOLDERS

Open up index.htm with Internet Explorer. The CD-ROM contains the following information:

- **Web Links by Chapter.** This link contains all of the Web links referenced in the book sorted by chapter.
- **Sysinternals troubleshooting tools.** This link contains some troubleshooting tools that we use from Sysinternals. This link includes a brief description of the tools: Autoruns, Filemon, Regmon and TCPview, and how we use them.
- **Troubleshooting Resources.** Links to software/hardware vendor's technical support sites, search engines, other troubleshooting web sites. This link includes tips for researching problems on the Internet.
- **About the CD-ROM.** This page.
- **Readme.** Legal disclaimer for the CD-ROM.

OVERALL SYSTEM REQUIREMENTS

- Windows NT/2000/XP
- Internet Explorer 5.0 or higher
- Internet Connection
- Pentium II Processor or greater
- CD-ROM drive
- 128 MBs of RAM, minimum 256 recommended

Index

A

access points (APs), wireless
- *see also* wireless networking
- authentication methods, 267–68
- configuring, to work with IAS server, 296–97
- equipment purchasing, 269–70
- installation and configuration of IAS, 287–93
- setting up, for home users, 308–12
- upgrading firmware on, 298–306
- wireless encryption, 268–69

Active Directory (AD), 231–39
- forcing replication, 238
- Global Catalog (GC) servers, 231
- new user added to, 257–59
- site and subnet information, 232–33
- site link configuration, 234–38
- Site Replication, 233–34
- Sites and Services, 231–33

Airsnort, 313

anti-spam filtering software, 191–92

APs. *see* access points

Authentication Header (AH), 365

authoritative name servers, 190

B

backups
- differential vs. transaction log, 167–68
- of Exchange servers, 188
- firewall, 334
- importance of, 10, 93–94
- incremental, 106–8
- restoring server from, 133
- SCSI bus timeout errors, 155–57
- server, 106–8
- of SQL Servers, 166–68
- strategies for, 167–68
- types of, 166

Bayesian filtering, 191

Best Practices Analyzer, 169

binary searches, 3–4

blacklists, 191

booting problems, 142–45

C

cabling problems, 8

cache, 118

Certificate servers, 272–78

Certificate Services, 268, 274–78

Cisco AP1200
- configuring, for home users, 308–11
- unable to authenticate, 320–22
- unable to flash, 319–20
- upgrading firmware on, 298–306

Cisco console cable pinouts, 246

Cisco routers, 246–53
- basic commands, 248
- connecting to, 246
- Frame Relay configuration, 248–52
- recovering lost passwords in, 247
- remote changes to, 248
- setting passwords in, 247
- show command, 253

commands
- Cisco, 248, 253
- IP routing, 242–45
- Recovery Console, 125–33

computer certificates, 278–80

cookies, 48

critical mass, of knowledge, 15–16

critical updates, 169

cross-vendor firewalls, 363–64, 378–80

D

daisy-chained hubs, 63–65

data encryption methods, 365

data integrity algorithm, 365

database administrators (DBAs), 171
database maintenance plans, for SQL Servers, 168–69
DCs (domain controllers), 102
default gateway, 6, 227–28
DHCP servers
  examining, 72–73
  IP addresses and, 105
differential backups, 167–68
disk configuration, 95–98, 118
disk partitions, 100
disk performance, 116–19
DNS
  configuration, 102–5, 150–51
  incorrect settings on, 7
  verify workings of, 6
DNS records, reverse, 204–7
DNS servers, 228
domain controllers (DCs), 102
domains
  Mail Exchange (MX) records for, 189–90
  registering, 189
downtime costs, 12
drivers
  printer, 29–30
  updating, 12, 21, 47
DSL routers
  corrupted settings, 9–10
  visual inspection of, 7
dynamic IP addresses, 364, 365, 367, 374–78

E

EAP-TLS, 169, 271
EDB files, 184
802.11a, 266
802.11b, 266
802.11g, 266
802.11i, 266
802.11n, 266
email problems
  see also Exchange servers
  in Outlook, 86–88, 212–16
  spam, 191–93, 202
encryption methods, 365
error messages
  event 9582, 208–9
  inaccessible boot device error, 142–45
  SCSI bus timeout errors, 155–57
event 9582, 208–9
Event Viewer, 109
  error messages in, 72–73
  event 9582, 208–9
Exchange databases, 184–87
  EDB files, 184
  log files, 184–85
  mail storage limitations, 185–86
  Standard vs. Enterprise editions, 185–86
  STM files, 184
Exchange servers, 183–223
  backing up, 188
  clustering, 187
  databases, 184–87
  disk space on, 219–21
  event 9582, 208–9
  Internet mail and, 189–90
  mail access problems, 204–7, 210–12, 218–19
  mail storage limitations, 216–17
  monitoring disk space on, 186–87
  open relay, 192–93, 200
  OSs for, 188
  Outlook Web Access (OWA), 193–98
  performance issues, 186
  problems opening messages in, 212–16
  proper placement of, 187
  public folder replication problems, 221–22
  running slow, 199–204
  spam and, 191–93
  troubleshooting scenarios, 199–22
  unable to send scheduling information on, 216–17
  unavailable, 219–21
  versions, 188
  virus protection of, 188–89
extensible authentication protocol-transport layer security (EAP-TLS), 269, 271

F

fault tolerance, 330–31
files
  firewall log, 333–34, 337–40, 368
  unable to access, 136–41
firewall logs, 333–34, 337–38, 339–40, 368
firewalls
  access problems and, 338–45
  backing up, 334
  configuration of, 190, 196, 331
  cross-vendor, 363–64, 378–80
  dangerous ports and, 331–32
  defining VPN connections on, 365–66
  examination of, 6–7
  fault tolerance, 330–31
  hacking recovery plan for, 334–37
  maintenance of, 333–34
  necessity of, 326–28
  number of ports and, 329–30

number of users and, 330
packet-filtering, 328–29
ping tests from, 7
PIX, 350–53
problems with SonicWall and, 342–43, 346–50
selecting proper, 328–31
stateful inspection firewalls, 328–29
topology, 327–28
traffic load and, 330
troubleshooting, 325–54
troubleshooting scenarios, 338–53
troubleshooting tools for, 337–38
VPNs and, 330, 363–64, 378–80
WebDAV and, 198
wireless clients and, 298

firmware
corrupted, 9
updating, 12–13, 21, 47, 380–82
upgrading, on Cisco AP1200, 298–306

Frame Relay, 228–29, 248–52, 358
fully meshed networks, 361–62

G

GFI Mail Essentials, 191
Global Catalog (GC) servers, 102, 231
Group Policy, configuring wireless access with, 293–96

H

hacker problems
see also security issues
on Exchange servers, 199–204
firewalls and, 326–27
on Windows servers, 137–41
on wireless networks, 315–17

hacking recovery plans, 139–41, 334–37
hard drives, duplexing, 117–18
hardware
disk configuration, 95–98
memory, 98–99
problems, 108
processors, 98–99
server, 94–99
for SQL Servers, 161–62
standardizing, 94
uninterruptible power supply (UPS), 99
using quality, 20

HTTPS, 339–40
hubs
daisy-chained, 63–65
network problems and, 108–9

I

i386 setup files, 100–1
IAS servers
configuring APs to work with, 296–97
installation and configuration of, 287–93

IDSs. *see* intrusion detection systems
inaccessible boot device error, 142–45
incremental backups, 106–8
Internet
access problems, 341–45
problems surfing, 81–82
slow connections to, 313–15

Internet Explorer (IE), 48
Internet Information Services (IIS), 272–73
Internet mail
Exchange servers and, 189–90
problems receiving, 210–12

Internet Mail Connector, 190
intrusion detection systems (IDSs), 139–40
IP addresses
default gateway, 227–28
DHCP servers and, 105
dynamic, 364, 365, 367, 374–78
fixed vs. dynamic, 364
format of, 226
inability to obtain, 8
incorrect settings on, 7
ordering static, 363
pinging, 6, 345
problems with, 369–70, 374–78
reserved, 226–27
subnet mask, 227
verify settings of, 6

IP configurations, changing, 79–80
IP routing, 240–45
static vs. dynamic, 240–42
troubleshooting, 242–45

`ipconfig`, 52–54
ISPs (Internet Service Providers)
blocking of VPNs by, 363
calling, 7

K

keyword searches, 191

L

laser WANs, 230
Last Known Good Configuration (LKGC), 124
lightweight extensible authentication protocol (LEAP), 269
log files, 184–85, 333–34, 337–40, 368
login problems, 77–81, 166

M

mail access problems, 204–7, 210–12, 218–19
Mail Exchange (MX) records, 189–90, 204–5
mail storage limitations, 216–17
Media Access Control (MAC) address, 267
memory, 98–99, 114–16
mobile client software, 364
mobile clients, multiple, 372–74
multiprotocol label switching (MPLS)/hybrid networks, 229
My Network Places, 149–51

N

name resolution, 228
name servers, authoritative, 190
NAV Corporate Edition, 88–89
NetBIOS problems, 146–49
NetStumbler, 313
network bottlenecks, 122
network connections, troubleshooting tools, 48–54
network printing, 25–42
  see also printing/printers; wireless networking
  dedicated print servers for, 28
  garbled printing, 32–34
  printer drivers, 29–30
  purchasing decisions, 26–28
  queue configuration, 28–32
  troubleshooting scenarios, 34–41
  unable to add, to workstation, 84–86
  Web-based, 30–32
networks
  see also Internet; virtual private networks (VPNs); wireless networking
  connection problems, 71–77
  multiprotocol label switching (MPLS)/hybrid networks, 229
  problems with, and servers, 108–9
  SANs, 119
  workstations dropping off, 61–66
newsgroups, 21
NIC, bad, 8
`nslookup` utility, 211

O

online banking site, unable to access, 338–40
open-relay databases, 191, 193
open-relay servers, 192–93, 200
operating systems (OSs)
  Exchange server, 188
  problems, 108
  server, 100
  upgrades over existing, 13
  Windows, 47–48
Outlook
  address book problems, 86–88
  problems opening messages in, 212–16
Outlook Web Access (OWA), 193–98
  architecture, 194–96
  firewall configuration, 196
  installing Secure Socket Layer (SSL) certificate on, 194
  mail access problems in, 218–19
  with SSL Proxy server, 196–98

P

packet-filtering firewalls, 328–29
panicking, 16
`pathping`, 48–51, 244
Performance Monitor, 109, 110–22
  how to use, 111–14
  what to monitor with, 114–22
  when to use, 110–11
persistence, 14–15
`ping/pathping` command, 48–51, 244
ping tests
  of default gateway, 6
  from firewall, 7
  of known IP addresses, 6, 345
  of workstation, 6
PIX firewalls, 350–53
PKI (Public Key Infrastructure), 270
point-to-point connections, 228
port scans, 334
ports, dangerous, 331–32
power supplies, 134–36
Pre-Shared Secret Key (PSK), 308, 320–22
print servers, dedicated, 28
printer drivers, installation of additional, 29–30
printing/printers
  garbled, 32–34
  IP addresses of, 105
  network, 25–42
  purchasing decisions, 26–28
  queue configuration, 28–32
  troubleshooting scenarios for, 34–41
  unable to add network, 35–36
  unable to add, to workstation, 84–86
  unable to install, 40–41
  unable to print to, 36–40
  Web-based, 30–32
problem isolation, 2–10, 12
  binary searches for, 3–4
  steps in, 5–10
problems
  locating, 6
  verifying existence of, 5–6
  walking away from, 16

processors, 98–99, 119–22
public folders, 221–22
Public Key Infrastructure (PKI), 270
public perimeter servers, 138

R

RADIUS servers, 287–93
RAID 0, 95
RAID 1, 95–96
RAID 1+0, 97–98, 118–19, 175
RAID 5, 96–97, 175
RAID configurations, 95–98, 186
RAID controllers, 118
Recovery Console, 124–33, 143–44
recovery tools
  Last Known Good Configuration (LKGC), 124
  Recovery Console, 124–33, 143–44
  safe mode, 123–24
  for servers, 122–33
  startup disks, 122–23
remote authentication dial-in user service (RADIUS) authentication, 268
remote servers, 259–60
remote sites, 202–3
remote subnets, 365
`route add` command, 243
`route delete` command, 244
`route print` command, 242–43
routers
  Cisco, 246–53
  documenting configuration of, 247–48
  DSL, 7, 9–10
  using Windows servers as, 245–46

S

safe mode, 123–24
SANs (storage area networks), 119
scandisk, 48
SCSI bus timeout errors, 155–57
SCSI controllers, 143
Secure Socket Layer (SSL) certificates, 194
security issues
  see also firewalls; hacker problems
  security breaches, 137–41
  SQL Server, 169–71
  wireless encryption, 268–69
serial numbers, 21
servers
  access difficulties in WANs, 254–57
  authoritative name, 190
  backing up, 106–8
  Certificate, 272–78
  DHCP, 72–73, 105
  disk configuration, 95–98
  disk partitions, 100
  DNS, 102–5, 228
  domain controllers (DCs), 102
  Exchange, 183–223
  Global Catalog (GC), 102, 231
  hardware, 94–99
  IAS/RADIUS, 287–93, 296–97
  inaccessible boot device error, 142–45
  My Network Places and, 149–51
  network, 71–77
  print, 28
  problem categories for, 108–9
  problems connecting to, 151–54
  problems logging in to, 77–81
  public perimeter, 138
  rebuilding, 138–39
  recovery tools for, 122–33
  restoring, from tape, 133
  SCSI bus timeout errors, 155–57
  slow performance of, 154–55
  software, 100–8
  SQL Server, 159–82
  SSL Proxy, 196–98
  Syslog, 338
  system restore problems on, 146–49
  troubleshooting scenarios, 134–57
  troubleshooting tools for, 109–22
  unable to access files from, 136–41
  virus protection of, 106
  Windows, 54–61, 93–158
  won't boot, 134–36
  workstations unable to use resources on, 66–70
service packs, 21
  integration of, 100–1
  SQL Server, 169
  Windows, 47
`show` command, 253
site surveys, 270, 317–18
smart card authentication, 268
software
  anti-spam filtering, 191–92
  disk partitions, 100
  DNS configuration, 102–5
  domain controllers (DCs), 102
  mirroring, 145
  mobile client, 364
  OS, 100
  server, 100–8
  service packs, 100–1
  Terminal Server, 101–2
  virus protection, 106, 188–89

solutions
  asking for help finding, 18
  attempts at, 14–15
  being conservative with, 11–12
  documenting, 20
  i386 setup files, 100–1
  last-resort, 18–19
  obvious, 14
SonicWALLs
  corrupted settings, 9
  problems with, 342–43, 346–50, 372–74
spam, 191–93, 202
SQL Profiler, 180
SQL Server, 159–82
  backup/maintenance of, 166–69
  basics, 160–66
  Best Practices Analyzer, 169
  cannot update records on, 179–81
  connecting to, 164–66
  database administrators (DBAs), 171
  hardware selection, 161–62
  performance issues, 176–79
  physical file location, 163–64
  security, 169–71
  structure, 162–63
  troubleshooting scenarios, 171–81
  users cannot access, 171–75
  versions, 161
SSL Proxy servers, 196–98
startup disks, 122–23
stateful inspection firewalls, 328–29
static IP addresses, 363
steps, retracing your, 14
STM files, 184
storage area networks (SANs), 119
subnet mask, 227
switches, 108–9
Syslog servers, 338

T

Task Manager, 109–10, 214
TCP/IP
  address format, 226
  basics, 226–28
  default gateway, 227–28
  DNS servers, 228
  properties, 79–81
  reserved addresses, 226–27
  subnet mask, 227
technical support
  contacting, 20–21, 153–54
Telnet, using to test Internet mail, 190, 210–11
temporary files, 47–48, 49, 83
Terminal Server, 101–2
Terminal servers, 238–39
tools
  Best Practices Analyzer, 169
  Event Viewer, 109
  firewall, 337–38
  `pathping`, 48–51
  Performance Monitor, 109, 110–22
  `ping`, 48–51
  recovery, for servers, 122–33
  Task Manager, 109–10
  troubleshooting, for servers, 109–22
  VPN, 368
  wireless, 313
tracert command, 244–45, 262
transaction log backups, 167–68
troubleshooting
  firewalls, 325–54
  general rules for, 10–20
  IP routing, 242–45
  scariness of, 17
  taking notes about, 17–18
  VPNs, 357–82
  WANs, 254–62
  Windows OS, 47–48
  Windows servers, 93–158
  wireless clients, 306–8
  workstations, 45–91
troubleshooting scenarios
  Exchange servers, 199–22
  firewalls, 338–53
  network printing, 34–41
  SQL Server, 171–81
  VPNs, 368–82
  Windows servers, 134–57
  wireless networking, 313–22
  workstation, 54–89
troubleshooting skills, practicing, 19–20

U

UDP 53, 344–45
uninterruptible power supply (UPS), 99
upgrades
  of drivers, 12, 21, 47
  of firmware, 12–13, 21, 47, 298–306, 380–82
  over existing OS, 13
user certificates, 281–87
utilities
  `ipconfig`, 52–54
  `ping/pathping`, 48–51
  `winipcfg`, 52

V

video conferencing, 360
virtual private networks (VPNs), 229, 260–62
  blocking of, by ISPs, 363
  communication problems with, 378–82
  connection problems, 369–72
  cross-vendor firewalls and, 363–64, 378–80
  defined, 358–59
  defining connection, on firewall, 365–66
  dynamic IP addresses and, 364, 365, 367, 374–78
  expected throughput on, 361
  firewalls and, 330, 363–64, 378–80
  fully meshed networks, 361–62
  implementing, 361–64
  IP address problems on, 369–70
  limitations of, 359–60
  mobile client software, 364
  optional parameters for, 366
  requirements for, 361
  topology, for remote users, 362–63
  troubleshooting, 357–82
  troubleshooting scenarios, 368–82
  troubleshooting tools for, 368
  wireless, 269
virus protection, 106, 170
  on Exchange servers, 188–89
  public folders and, 221–22
Voice over IP (VoIP), 360

W

WANs. *see* wide area networks
Web-based printing, 30–32
Web sites
  hacker problems on, 315–17
  unable to access, 260–62
WebDAV, 198
WEP, 268–69
WEPCracking tools, 313
whitelists, 191
Wi-Fi, 266
Wi-Fi Protected Access (WPA), 266, 269
wide area networks (WANs)
  access problems, 260–62
  Active Directory (AD), 231–39
  carriers for, 230–31, 259–60
  Cisco routers, 246–53
  connections, 228–30
  documentation for, 253–54
  Exchange server placement on, 187
  increasing performance of, 238–39
  IP routing, 240–45
  laser, 230
  server access difficulties, 254–57
  Terminal servers and, 238–39
  topology, 228–30
  troubleshooting scenarios, 254–62
  unable to access remote servers, 259–60
Windows OS, troubleshooting, 47–48
Windows servers
  hardware, 94–99
  inaccessible boot device error, 142–45
  licensing modes, 67–70
  My Network Places, 149–51
  problem categories for, 108–9
  problems connecting to, 151–54
  recovery tools for, 122–33
  restoring, from tape, 133
  SCSI bus timeout errors, 155–57
  slow performance of, 154–55
  software, 100–8
  startup disks, 122–23
  system restore problems on, 146–49
  troubleshooting scenarios, 134–57
  troubleshooting tools for, 109–22
  unable to access files from, 136–41
  using, as routers, 245–46
  won't boot, 134–36
  workstation unable to connect to, 54–61
  workstations unable to use resources on, 66–70
Windows XP
  configuring, for home users, 311–12
  wireless clients on, 298
`winipcfg`, 52
Wired Equivalent Privacy (WEP) key authentication, 267
wireless access, configuring, 293–96
wireless cards, 269–70
Wireless Certificate Templates, 282–85
wireless clients
  firewalls and, 298
  troubleshooting steps for, 306–8
  on Windows XP, 298
wireless encryption, 268–69
wireless networking, 265–322
  authentication methods, 267–68
  client-side setup, 297–98
  connection problems, 313–15, 317–18
  equipment purchasing for, 269–70
  hacker problems, 315–17
  infrastructure preparation, 270–97
  setting up, for home users, 308–12
  standards, 266
  tools, 313
  troubleshooting scenarios, 313–22
  upgrading firmware, 298–306

wireless WANs, 230
WLANs (wireless LANs)
  see also wireless networking
  diagram of, 271
workstations
  bad NIC in, 8
  categories of problems, 46
  drop off network, 61–66
  guidelines for troubleshooting, 47–48
  pinging, 6
  problems logging in to servers, 77–81
  troubleshooting, 45–91, 45–91
  troubleshooting scenarios, 54–89
  troubleshooting tools, 48–54
  unable to add printer to, 84–86
  unable to connect to network server, 71–77
  unable to connect to Windows server, 54–61
  unable to install NAV Corporate Edition on, 88–89
  unable to surf Internet, 81–82
  unable to use resources on server, 66–70
  unstable, 82–83
WPA
  setting up, for home users, 308–12
  unable to authenticate Cisco AP1200 using, 320–22

Z

Zone Transfers, 104